Sheila Carapico's book on civic participation in modern Yemen makes an authoritative, pathbreaking contribution to the study of political culture in the Arabian Peninsula. Relying on in-depth documentary and field research, the author traces the political dynamics of the last fifty years that culminated in Yemeni unification, focusing on efforts to develop the political, economic, and social structures of a modern, democratic government. Her wide-ranging analysis of the legal, institutional, and financial aspects of state building and of popular dimensions of political liberalization, protest, and participation challenge the stereotypical view of conservative Arab Muslim society. The political economy approach to the study of a surprising degree of "activism in Arabia" helps to interpret the nature of civil society from a broader theoretical perspective. This is an important book which promises to become the definitive statement on twentieth-century Yemen.

Cambridge Middle East Studies

Civil society in Yemen

Cambridge Middle East Studies 9

Cambridge Middle East Studies has been established to publish books on the nineteenth- and twentieth-century Middle East and North Africa. The aim of the series is to provide new and original interpretations of aspects of Middle Eastern societies and their histories. To achieve disciplinary diversity, books will be solicited from authors writing in a wide range of fields including history, sociology, anthropology, political science and political economy. The emphasis will be on producing books offering an original approach along theoretical and empirical lines. The series is intended for students and academics, but the more accessible and wide-ranging studies will also appeal to the interested general reader.

1 Parvid Paidar, *Women and the political process in twentieth-century Iran*
2 Israel Gershoni and James Jankowski, *Redefining the Egyptian nation, 1930–1945*
3 Annelies Moors, *Women, property and Islam: Palestinian experiences, 1920–1990*
4 Paul Kingston, *Britain and the politics of modernization in the Middle East, 1945–1958*
5 Daniel Brown, *Rethinking tradition in modern Islamic thought*
6 Nathan J. Brown, *The rule of law in the Arab world: courts in Egypt and the Gulf*
7 Richard Tapper, *Frontier nomads of Iran: the political and social history of the Shahsevan*
8 Khaled Fahmy, *All the Pasha's men: Mehmed Ali, his army and the making of modern Egypt*

Civil society in Yemen

The political economy of activism in modern Arabia

Sheila Carapico
University of Richmond

CAMBRIDGE
UNIVERSITY PRESS

CAMBRIDGE UNIVERSITY PRESS
Cambridge, New York, Melbourne, Madrid, Cape Town, Singapore, São Paulo

Cambridge University Press
The Edinburgh Building, Cambridge CB2 8RU, UK

Published in the United States of America by Cambridge University Press, New York

www.cambridge.org
Information on this title: www.cambridge.org/9780521590983

First published 1998
First paperback version 2006

A catalogue record for this publication is available from the British Library

Library of Congress Cataloguing in Publication data

Carapico, Sheila.
Civil society in Yemen: the political economy of activism in
modern Arabia / Sheila Carapico
p. cm. – (Cambridge Middle East studies: 9)
Includes bibliographical references (p. 236) and index.
ISBN 0-521-59098-1 (hardcover)
1. Civil society – Yemen. 2. Political participation – Yemen.
3. Yemen – Politics and government. I. Title. II. Series.
JQ1842.A91C37 1998 97-23259 CIP
306.2–dc21

ISBN 978-0-521-59098-3 hardback
ISBN 978-0-521-03482-1 paperback

Transferred to digital printing 2007

Contents

List of tables viii
Preface and acknowledgments ix
Note on transliteration and terminology xii
List of abbreviations xiii
Map xv

1 Civil society in comparative perspective 1
2 Twentieth-century states and economies 19
3 Islam, tribes, and social services 60
4 Colonialism, activism, and resistance 84
5 Self-help, social capital, and state power 107
6 Unity, pluralism, and political participation 135
7 Civic responses to political crisis 170
8 Political movements, cultural trends, and civic potential 201

Endnotes 212
Glossary 234
Bibliography 236
Index 254

Tables

1.1 A snapshot of three political openings in Yemen 16
2.1 States and economic conditions, three historical periods 20
2.2 Regime changes in the YAR and PDRY 37
2.3 Basic economic indicators, YAR and PDRY, 1987 40
2.4 Central government expenditures, YAR and PDRY, 1977 42
2.5 Proportional value of production by ownership and sector, PDRY, 1982 45
2.6 Investments by ownership and sector, YAR, 1974–1986 47
5.1 Government and independent roads, schools, and water projects, North Yemen, 1961–1986 111
5.2 Project funds from citizens, LDAs, and government, YAR, 1973–1981 128
5.3 Sources of LDA revenues, 1976–1981 128
6.1 Major parties and party newspapers, 1990–1994 141
6.2 Results of parliamentary elections, 1993 and 1997 149
6.3 Percentage votes by party and governorate, 1993 elections 150
7.1 Major cabinet changes, Republic of Yemen, 1990–1997 190

Preface and acknowledgments

I hope my colleagues find this work worthy, for it is the product of many years' research, and a great many people provided information and insights. My interest in Yemen began with my first visit to Sana'a, Hodeida, Taiz, and Aden in 1972, as part of a larger tour of the region made possible by my undergraduate year at the American University in Cairo in 1971–72; it has continued ever since.

Research on which this book was based has been supported, directly or indirectly, from a range of sources. I returned to Sana'a in January 1977, with a grant for PhD dissertation research from the State University of New York at Binghamton. During the next four years of continuous residence in North Yemen, I worked as a "freelance" social scientist, conducting baseline surveys for several international development agencies and contractors, including the US Agency for International Development and the World Bank. These included an urban planning survey of workplaces in the five cities of the YAR; a short study of women's economic activities in three rural locations; "rural economic recognizance" in Ḥajja and Hodeida governorates; a comparative study of agricultural production in Ibb and 'Amrān, conducted in conjunction with the American Institute for Yemeni Studies; and a nationwide survey conducted in twenty-two communities for the national rural electrification project. Between expeditions for these studies, I worked from my home in Sana'a with what was then called the Confederation of Yemeni Development Associations, preparing a dissertation on the "cooperative movement."

During the 1980s and 1990s, I returned to North Yemen on several occasions: in 1982 on behalf of Cornell University's rural development research project; in 1986 with a research grant from the University of Richmond; in 1987 as a consultant for the International Fund for Agricultural Development; in 1989 and 1990 in my capacity as then president of the American Institute for Yemeni Studies (AIYS); and in 1991 as a consultant for the United Nations Development Programme on management development problems after unification. In 1993, while on sabbatical from the University of Richmond, and after several months in Egypt under a grant from the American Research Center in Egypt, I went back to Yemen as a Fulbright fellow. The Fulbright offered the luxury of full-time research, which in that period meant reading newspapers, conducting interviews, and attendance at public events such as seminars, conferences, and sessions of parliament. Again I extended my stay past the grant period, supported by the Netherlands embassy through the Women's Studies and Social Research program at Sana'a University. I had packed my papers and books for a planned departure in early May 1994. In the event, however, I evacuated on a US military aircraft, only to return in July 1994 to help with a Human Rights Watch report on the war. Finally, the University of Richmond generously paid for a short trip in the summer of 1996 to update the narrative in this book beyond the war.

During a total of about six years in the country, I have visited every governorate except distant al-Mahra, taken notes on over 2,000 interviews, and collected shelves full of materials. This necessitates a certain selectivity in content, citations, and acknowledgments in this book.

First, while striving to provide a clear historical perspective, I have avoided recapitulating historical details already published in English. Thus many important figures are not named, some political events and policies are not explained, there is no military information, and foreign policy is not addressed systematically.

Secondly, I have not cited interviews, which are far too numerous to document, although this is the convention among political scientists. Instead I have adopted an ethnographic voice in describing many of the events and processes I observed firsthand, while citing published sources for factual information and individual interpretations.

Thirdly, the list of persons who have helped me is too long to publish. My interpretations are deeply influenced and informed by the work of my friends the Yemen research community, including the "old-timers" from the 1970s and the new generation in the 1990s, with whom I have shared adventures, interviews, stories, notes, panels, and critiques and from whom I have benefited immeasurably. Without the political historians who explained regime changes, the ethnographers who recorded village life, and the consultants who compiled statistics, this work could not have been done. Among the foreigners, therefore, I single out only two whose colleagueship I value still but who will not read this, Ron Hart and Leigh Douglas.

Among Yemenis, moreover, the responsiveness, cooperation, and hospitality toward a Western woman with no government or family sponsors and an insatiable appetite for information has been incredible.

There is a true lady, an extended family, and a whole neighborhood in old Sana'a who opened to me a feminine network to which I still retreat for emotional sustenance. I suspect that the manners and idioms they taught me stood me in good stead elsewhere. In any case, I enjoyed unmitigated, unrelenting hospitality virtually wherever I went: ministries, businesses, provincial and district offices, homes and farms, seminars and conferences, and male qāt-chews. For research purposes a qāt-chew amounts to a "focus group," for people speak openly and the guest is entitled to introduce a discussion topic, listen in on other business, and to take discreet notes. In these and other settings I enjoyed the collaboration of Yemeni colleagues who worked with me in the field or on documents, not translating but helping me to translate for myself while offering their own insights and analyses. Finally, I owe a great and genuine debt of gratitude to the Yemeni government, the Yemen Center for Research and Studies, and the foreign and interior ministries for the unfettered access I have enjoyed to all aspects of Yemeni life and politics; and to the countless officials who personally offered documents, permissions, and friendly respect.

Note on transliterations and terminology

Because I record Arabic information in English, I am very conscious of what things are called. Linguists know that translation is not merely a question of comprehension but also of representation, and this issue emerges as soon as one attempts to describe roles and institutions in a place such as Yemen. In composing this work, I tend to use the terminology of the bilingual community of scholars in Sana'a, including both Yemenis and foreigners: the Arabic for short words that fit in English sentences and English abbreviations for other institutions; and tried to provide all synonyms in both English and Arabic at least once. I also spell out transliterations to demonstrate the repetition and development of certain terms in political discourse, and for the sake of clarity for those who read and/or speak Arabic. The lists of Arabic words in the glossary and of abbreviations below include all those that appear in more than one paragraph. Eng Seng Ho inserted the diacritical marks, dots, and dashes of full correct Arabic transliterations, and patiently helped with many final stages of preparation for publication. Names of cities with established English spellings and persons cited in English publications are not necessarily transliterated.

Abbreviations

AA	Aden Association
AI	Amnesty International
AID	Arab Institute for Democracy
AIYS	American Institute for Yemen Studies
ATUC	Aden Trades Union Congress
BSOAS	*Bulletin of the School of Oriental and African Studies*
CDA	community development association
CPO	Central Planning Organization
CYDA	Confederation of Yemeni Development Associations
EY	*Encyclopedia of Yemen*
FLOSY	Front for the Liberation of Occupied South Yemen
GCC	Gulf Cooperation Council
GPC	General People's Congress
ICRC	International Committee of the Red Cross
IDA	International Development Agency
IJMES	*International Journal of Middle East Studies*
LCCD	local councils for cooperative development
LDA	local development association (*hay'at al-ta'āwun al-ahlī li-l-taṭwīr*)
MBC	Middle East Broadcasting Corporation
MEED	*Middle East Economic Digest*
NC	National Conference
NCFE	National Committee for Free Elections
NDF	National Democratic Front
NDI	National Democratic Institute
NGO	non-governmental organization
NLF	National Liberation Front
ODDRL	Organization for the Defense of Democratic Rights and Liberties
PC	Presidential Council
PDRY	People's Democratic Republic of Yemen
PSP	People's Socialist Party

PVO	private voluntary association
RAY	Rābiṭat Abnā' al-Yaman (League of the Sons of Yemen)
SAL	South Arabian League
SEC	Supreme Elections Committee
TOM	al-Takattul al-Waṭanī li-l-Mu'āraḍa
UNF	United National Front
UPF	Union of Popular Forces
USAID	United States Agency for International Development
YAR	Yemen Arab Republic
YCRS	Yemen Center for Research and Studies
YIDD	Yemeni Institute for Democratic Development
YOHR	Yemeni Organization for Human Rights
YSP	Yemeni Socialist Party
YT	*Yemen Times*

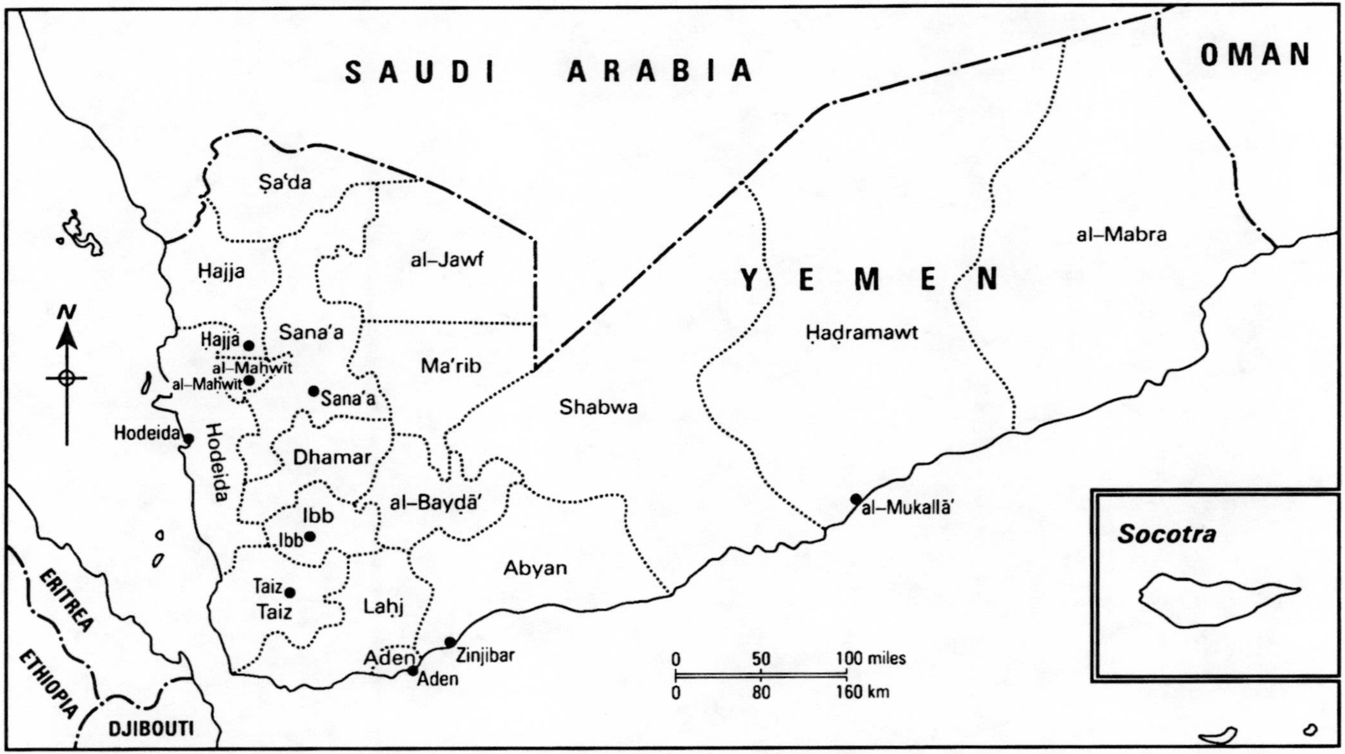

Yemen, with provinces and major towns

1 Civil society in comparative perspective

Heralded for a "third wave of democratization," the 1990s witnessed the collapse of the Berlin Wall, official apartheid, and a host of dictatorships buttressed by the bipolar structures of the cold war. Even in the Arab world, so often seen as uniquely inhospitable to political, economic, and cultural liberalism, noteworthy political openings raised hopes for more tolerant, responsive, rule-based, fair, pluralist governance and greater personal liberty, freedom, and participation in Algeria, Egypt, Jordan, Kuwait, Lebanon, Palestine, Sudan, and Yemen. Among these, the prospects for the newly unified Republic of Yemen – itself partly a product of the end of the cold war – seemed especially dramatic and promising. Alas, however, in Yemen as in several other Arab countries, a brief "democratic experiment" was soon submerged in a counter-current of violence and repression. Is nothing better possible for Arab countries?

Those who contend that nothing better is possible have observed that even high standards of living, bourgeois lifestyles, and Western technology have not produced a relaxation of political controls in the Arab Gulf states. Furthermore, electoral competition in the Arab world seems only to embolden intolerant religious puritans who neither respect basic rights nor tolerate alternative ideologies. According to this argument Islamic civilization in general, and Arab tribal culture in particular, have not and probably will not fertilize the sorts of vibrant civic activism that underlie Western democracies, for deeply imbued cultural values and social structures retard the development of civil society.

Although this argument has been widely critiqued, we have few empirical studies that offer evidence to the contrary. This book, a study of civic activism in twentieth-century Yemen, shows Yemenis participating in labor unions, community self-help projects, political organizations, and other events and associations that seem to flower under some political and economic circumstances and wither under other conditions. Focused on three historical periods of heightened activism in the civic sphere, it offers not simply an argument that "civil society exists" but an exploration of the ways civic activism varies over time. It begins, in this chapter, with a consideration of how the notion of civil society is utilized as an analytical tool in the study of Western and African political economies, contrasting that rich concept with the rather narrow, rigid construct most frequently applied to the Arab world.[1] Subsequent chapters examine how the gradual, tortuous development of the state, economic vicissitudes determined largely in the Arabian Gulf, and regional ideological trends influence participation in civic projects. Mechanisms rooted in Yemeni culture as well as forms imported from abroad are put to various uses in struggles to improve both welfare and freedom.

Western civil society

According to Western social theory, the institutions, associations, and networks of European and North American civil society operate in a pluralistic, continuously contested public space or public civic realm, a zone between the state and private sectors. Distinct from either the coercive and bureaucratic functions of the state public sector or profit-seeking private sector businesses, often said to constitute a layer or buffer between government and households, civil society represents a third, non-governmental, non-profit, voluntary sector of modern society. As such, it seems to contain the moral residue of a primordial, pre-modern civic realm, for many of its organizations and activities valorize ethical responsibilities, communalism, charity, and so-called traditional values. Yet civil society is conceived as a modern, bourgeois, post-Enlightenment phenomenon, characteristic of liberal polities and economies centered on the individual, not the ascribed primordial community. In many countries, women moved from the private domicile into the public sphere and business via civic participation. Such activity engages men and women in joining, communicating, socializing, demonstrating, contributing, organizing, and attending events and projects that cumulatively serve communities and whole societies by offering social services, formulating and expressing public opinion, and legitimizing a political order. The study of civil society encompasses not only voluntary associations but social movements and popular struggles as well.

De Tocqueville's ode to American civic harmony notwithstanding, a concept that merely extols the virtues of social networks in mitigating class conflicts and abuses of state power would be of little analytical utility in the study of Western society. European social historians still debate the precise relationship of civil society to capitalism, democracy, and Christianity. One theory is that a layer of largely urban civic institutions emerged with the transition to capitalism in order to wrest concessions from absolutist states. In the transition from *Gemeinschaft* to *Gesellschaft*, the primordial private sphere was metamorphosed into a modern private sector, where the moral economy was replaced by self-seeking market behavior and political, presumably secular, rationalism. When private becomes separate from public, evidently, there is room for civic. Overall, however, there is no consensus as to which came first: markets, modern states, or the salons, foundations, publications, ceremonies, and associations that collectively comprise civil society.

Westerners writing seriously about their own societies recognize the contingent, contested dynamic between civil society and democracy. Western rights and liberties are the product of long struggles by the bourgeoisie, labor, women, and finally minorities, in the courts, the press, and the streets. Social scientists analyze European and American authoritarian movements, civil unrest, and hate-crimes; the role of civic-philanthropic institutions in consolidating ruling-class hegemony; and the religiosity that permeates charitable and educational foundations and many labor syndicates, political parties, fraternities, and community clubs. Nowadays, pundits bemoan the demise of civil society as embodied in folksy old-fashioned bowling leagues and quilting-bees. The literature clearly distinguishes civil society from the narrower behavioralist notion of civic culture, a construct measured in public opinion surveys of attitudes such as empathy, efficacy, and optimism.[2]

In the 1990s, inspired by the image of a Czech poet and a "New Civic Forum" galvanizing a "velvet revolution," Western enthusiasts seized on the concept of civil society to project a rapid but peaceful transition to political, economic, and cultural liberalism in Eastern Europe. According to this reasoning, a resilient civil society that survived Stalinist totalitarianism in part by retreating into informal, underground, or folk-religious forms would now be free to organize competitive politics and markets and institutions to protect people from unbridled competition. Since the actual experience has not borne out the sanguine early forecasts, debates about the relationship of civic activity to capitalism and democracy in Europe continue.

Given politically complicated, often abstract theoretical discussions of how civic projects function in the West and how they might transform already-modern post-communist Europe, it is not surprising that analysts would differ over how civil society responds to economic and political conditions in Asia and Africa. Even optimists about prospects for globalizing liberal democracy frequently treat Southwest and Central Asia and North Africa as exceptions, or omit the Arab region from comparative volumes and conferences. One prominent scholar argued that whereas in the European republics of the former Soviet Union people "craved civil society," Muslim fellow countrymen did not.[3] Another contends that Islamic culture is peculiarly inclined to "clash" with liberal enlightenment values.[4]

Civil society in the Arab world

In the most widely held Western image of Arab Islamic society, culture defies state-led modernization and secularization because Islamic beliefs and patriarchical tribal social organization obstruct values such as tolerance, civic-spiritedness, and personal freedom. Thus "Arab civil society" is an oxymoron. A related but more nuanced perspective grounded in African economic anthropology portrays a moral economy or primordial civic realm where there is such social, psychological, economic, and political security that people tend to close ranks around patrons when their communities are threatened with the encroachment of modern states and markets. Whether the explanation lies in value systems or political economy, however, the conventional wisdom is that Arab Islamic society reacts atavistically against modernization. Research in this vein in Egypt, for instance, finds little between the household and the state except *rābiṭāt* (translated as "bonds"), *baladī* ("our locality") or *ahlī* ("primordial") associations, Sufi orders, and "mutual aid" networks serving religious, neighborhood, or village communities, all dismissed as lacking civic content. The recent spread of self-declared fundamentalists or puritans advocating "strict" Islamic law is taken as evidence of Muslim resistance to modernity.[5]

Many political scientists writing about the Arab world counter this prevalent view with evidence that Arab states generally block autonomous civic participation. Pervasive state security establishments, centralized economies, and co-optation of independent syndicates, associations, foundations, cooperatives, academies, and other institutions explain the apparent absence of genuinely autonomous civic organizing. The oil-rich rentier states, enjoying material standards of living on a par with those in some Western or Asian democracies, exchange economic perks, physical comfort, and a modicum of political input for near-total acquiescence to absolutist executive or royal authority. The Iraqi, Syrian, and Sudanese governments seem to have virtually obliterated their civil societies. In Egypt, millennia of centralization, decades of one-party, president-for-life rule, and the legacy of Arab "socialism" virtually guarantee that no organization is genuinely non-governmental. Cairo reserves the right to confer legitimacy even on social clubs, mosques, and private charities through ministries and national federations with strict, bureaucratic, manipulative licensing requirements; group economic interests are represented through monolithic national federations that trade autonomy for certain favors from the state; cooperatives, unions, businesses, universities, and other institutions have made a Faustian deal with Cairo. Borrowing a term from analyses of Latin America, political scientists call this process whereby the state dominates economic and civic participation "corporatism."[6] The implication of this reasoning is that for any liberalization to occur governments must take the lead in voluntarily yielding legal latitude.

The third school of thought equates civil society with formal nongovernmental organizations (NGOs) and private voluntary associations (PVOs). International NGOs and development assistance agencies working from what they call a policy perspective hypothesize that NGOs can articulate political liberalism, complement private-sector initiatives, and extend a social safety net to supplement or replace government services. Hoping that with foreign training and technical assistance NGOs can foster liberalization "from the grassroots" without generating social unrest, bilateral and multilateral assistance agencies and international NGOs have designed "civil society institution-building" projects to promote think-tanks, human rights organizations, chambers of commerce, purchasing and marketing cooperatives, environmentalist societies, women's associations, community centers, independent clinics, etc. In Egypt, where many charities and grass-roots organizations operated even before the 1952 revolution, some 16,000 PVOs or NGOs are registered with the Ministry of Social Affairs, the majority of them receiving both government and foreign assistance. An important group of these are community development associations or CDAs. For the NGO literature, formality and paperwork that contain popular action within parameters set by government in consultation with donors define legitimate "civil society," seen as the vehicle of gradual social reform.

There are some translation, transliteration, and representational issues here that will be confronted in depictions of Yemeni civic activity. Something called *al-rābiṭāt al-ahlī* of Fulan village, for instance, can be translated as "primordial bonds," and subsequently referred to in transliteration. Arabists and anthropologists have good linguistic and logical reasons for doing this. By the same token, the impression conveyed to non-Arabic speakers is one of rarified exoticism, a folksy, family affair: the Orient. One would not expect this group to have computer-generated spreadsheets. To non-Arabists, even a formal organization, say *al-majlis al-shūrā* for consultative council, if called by the Arabic, seems like something with no English equivalent, a cultural artifact rather than a modern political institution. Something else happens on the printed page if it is written with upper-case letters, as in *Majlis al-Shūrā*. Very different images are conveyed, however, if one translates these Arabic names into their English-usage equivalents. The consultative council becomes a Senate or House of Lords. Finally, the highest degree of institutional reification comes if one calls *Rābiṭāt Ahl Fulan* the Fulan CDA. For instance, the fifth chapter in this book is about something known in Arabic mostly as *al-ta'āwun al-ahlī li-l-taṭwīr, al-ta'āwun al-ahlī*, or simply *al-ta'āwun*. In written or spoken English this phenomenon is most commonly referred to as an LDA. An LDA or local development association is defined in culture-neutral terms as an inclusive, non-government, non-profit community-level services provider. The folksy informality of *al-ta'āwun al-ahlī* becomes the bureaucratized LDA. In donor parlance, a "civil society project" would mean technical assistance to help institutionalize the LDA, for instance by providing computers, training, and advice on income-generating projects. Savvy bilingual Arabs in the poor Arab countries that receive concessional development assistance know that one way to attract Western sponsorship is to call something by three capital roman letters (e.g., CRLs). Funds-hungry third world governments also know that defining local institutions as LDAs or CDAs helps draw hard currency for their projects.

Some of the English-language studies pertaining to the question of civil society in the Arab world have been translated into Arabic, and Arab scholars, jurists, and journalists writing in Arabic, English, and French have expounded on the idea. In Cairo, thanks largely to the considerable availability of foreign funds for think tanks and liberal interest groups, symposia and journals have been dedicated to discussion of how civil society might or might not play a liberalizing role. This discourse blends the culturalist, corporatist, and policy perspectives identified above with a highly idealized Tocquevillian view of Western civil society. The project of liberal Egyptian intellectuals is to persuade the Mubarak government to loosen the corporatist restrictions on formal modern civic institutions without ceding ground to religious neo-fundamentalist groups who are so active in the Egyptian voluntary sector.

Cairo's Western-educated intellectuals translate civil society as *al-mujtama' al-madanī*, eschewing the alternative *al-mujtama' al-ahlī*. This is a legitimate translation decision, which I have adopted, but one that also embodies both logical and political suppositions. *Madanī*, meaning civil, civic, civilian, and urban, becomes the antonym of *ahlī*, which can also mean civic but further suggests local, private, community, parochial, and primordial. This rendering consciously accommodates cultural-essentialist assumptions about the incapacity of local, indigenous, or religious traditions to enter the civic arena. Social and religious conservatives tend to prefer the translation *al-mujtama' al-ahlī*, defined as the modern sector where a moral economy guarantees social, economic, and political security. But for secular intellectuals what is *ahlī* cannot also be *madanī* or constitute a component of *al-mujtama' al-madanī*. Nor does there seem to be any potential for the dialectical transformation of *al-mujtama' al-ahlī*, say a primordial civic realm, in the direction of civil society. Looking from afar at events in Yemen, Caireen theorists write and speak derisively of Yemen as a primitive place where primordial traditions of tribe and religion preclude "*madanī*" institutions.

For Egypt, the Cairo school assumes pervasive central control but appeals to the government to empower civil society. For instance, a prominent jurist identified the elements of civil society as "government of, by, and for the people"; popular right to legislate through democratic institutions; separation of religion from politics; free, individual participation; citizenship as the basis of all rights and obligations; social, political, and legal justice; and welfare systems ensuring "contentment of the individual."[7] These criteria refer more to the constitutional, judicial, and public service aspects of the state than to any quality of or initiative from society. Other Arab and Arabist writers contend that only legally licensed, registered organizations, or only those that are internally democratic, can be counted as part of civil society. Before we can conclude that a society is civil, says a widely cited recipe, three preconditions must be met: formal, democratic, tolerant organizations; government tolerance of peaceful dissent and autonomous activities; and the rule of law as codified in a constitution and enforced by the courts.[8]

Thus there is an effort to persuade the government that formal, modern, registered, but relatively autonomous business associations, trade unions, professional syndicates, social clubs, interest groups, and political parties can promote state interests.[9] Although most existing associations in Egypt are still in skeletal and formative stage, incapable of serving fully as an outlet to participation and distribution, voluntary energies can potentially boost national economies through "*al-qiṭ'a ghayr al-hadaf al-ribḥ*" (an awkward rendering for the "non-profit sector") – which is a significant, socially valuable source of employment and investment in industrialized nations.[10] In addition, civil society can help protect the state against extremist movements' random violence;[11]

most civic groups are led by middle-class professionals,[12] a natural constituency for the regime. Autonomous organizations benefit state interests by relieving the burden shouldered by the state in providing services, complementing the actions of the state by mobilizing additional resources, or by preparing the ground for political change where consensus is lacking.[13]

Overall, then, much of the literature on civil society in the Arab world insists on cultural modernization, institutional formality, and governmental democratization as prerequisites for civil society. Associations, networks, and activities whose Western or African counterparts would easily classify as part of a broadly defined, pluralist, contested civic space are disqualified as religious, traditional, or exclusivist. Movements not much different from those valorized as "pro-democracy" or "charitable" in other contexts are vilified as "terrorist fronts." Individual organizations must further pass tests of civility and internal democracy. Moreover, many scholars writing about the Arab world insist that the government must first establish a congenial legal and institutional environment before civil society can exist. Some contend that an activity must be legal before it can be civil. This position resolves for the Arab world a question that still stirs debate in the West by asserting that the state comes first and regimes' political will is a "prerequisite" for civil society.[14] Because there is so little faith in the potential of Arab civil society, the only escape from the authoritarian cul-de-sac seems to be for states voluntarily to cede space to formal interest groups. In many cases, it can only be imagined that foreign pressure in the form of either positive influence or negative sanctions could make this happen.

African civil society

Although twentieth-century Africa on the whole is no less victim to authoritarianism, political violence, intra-communal strife, and what some observers have called (misleadingly, in the African context) "retribalization" than Arab Africa and Southwest Asia, discussion of African civil society contrasts markedly from discussion of Arab civil society. Students of African political economy eschew either-or questions about cultural essences, instead adapting a theoretically rich concept to situations where state–market–society relationships are quite different from those in Europe. The question of whether culture and beliefs impair civil society is not seriously entertained. Instead, the main concern is how civil society counters authoritarian violence and absolutist corruption.

In Africa, whatever arguments are made against the existence of "civil society" are embedded in a construct of "moral economy" or "primordial civic realm." In pre-market communities, the argument goes, mechanisms of reciprocity and solidarity insulate tradition against assault by states and markets. Peasant communities resist penetration by strengthening traditional bonds or engaging in primitive rebellion, a phenomenon also well analyzed in Europe.[15] Thus Kenyan Harambee (self-help) and Sierra Leonian peasant protests (banditry) are different responses to outside penetration, both aimed at holding the state at bay. A strong sense of community within the primordial civic realm does promote self-help as one way of shoring up traditional bonds under attack from larger structures. One would not confuse this primordial civic realm, embedded in a communal mode of production, with civil society; but neither would one rule out a dialectical transformation of the civic realm.

Many students of Africa apply the term "civil society" routinely, turning their attention to more complex questions of its relationship to the state and ruling classes. Civil society is characterized as the "process" whereby society seeks to "breach" or "counteract" state totalization. It encompasses both "popular modes of political action" and "claims of . . . socially dominant groups" such as businessmen and clergy. It is "an autonomous space of mass expression."[16] While we should avoid assigning civil society a "teleological virtue" whose advance necessarily results in a "glorious counter-hegemonic project," neither should we underestimate society's capacity to "invent democracy" and eventually bridge "epistemic gulfs."[17] Civil society is not necessarily formal, much less legal. It may be "that segment of society that interacts with the state, influences the state, and yet is distinct from the state," which helps check authoritarian rulers' abuses, increase accountability, and create a common framework for disparate interests. It is also called the "missing middle," a "benign broker between state interests and local concerns," and a voice for popular demands and culture. These definitions imply that civil society is a bridge between the primordial private sphere and the state sphere. Moreover, we should be wary of any "axiomatic connection" between expansion of the voluntary sector and consolidation of civil society; civil society does not equal NGOs, although NGOs, especially those with specific social welfare objectives, do constitute an important element.[18]

Some Africanists find Arab and Islamic as well as African precedents for civil society. The Sudanese anti-colonial struggle, the Palestinian Intifāḍa, and the Soweto uprisings were models for demonstrating society's "organized strength" through "National Conferences," "Sacred Unions," and other public events."[19] Africanists discover forms of civil society in Sufi brotherhoods, puritanical or reformist movements, and revolutionary Mahdist tendencies.[20] Post-colonial authoritarianism "inspired Africans to devise methods of communicating and acting outside the reach of the state's repressive agencies," through informal networks drawing on pre-colonial customs and institutions. These are among "*les forces vives*," forces of democratization that came together in Benin and elsewhere to form national civic conferences. The national civic conferences are themselves complex, contentious political events that raise all sorts of questions about inclusion and representation and how a new order can encompass the old.[21]

Once a few autonomous conferences were successful, regimes organized others to simulate mass support for their governance projects.

In Africa, therefore, Western scholars see popular organizations with a mass base, a civic conscience, and a potentially constructive political role. The persistence or revitalization of communal, ethnic, and/or religious motifs do not "disqualify" events from being characterized as part of civil society, for as in Europe civic impulses may go underground in the face of a police state. Cultural values, rituals, and oral traditions are given a positive spin. Violence in some parts of society or from within movements such as South Africa's African National Congress does not preclude meaningful civic participation within those societies and movements. Struggle and conflict are not cultural but structural. State civility, legal guarantees, and organizational formality are associated with the civic hegemony of the state; they are not preconditions for civil society.

Activism and civil society in Yemen

The documentation of animated civic activism at the periphery of the Arabian Peninsula may surprise those who associate civil society with state tolerance and Westernized lifestyles. For the data show quite clearly that although modern Yemeni states have never guaranteed democratic rights and liberties, material and educational standards have never been conducive to bourgeois liberalism, and uniquely South Arabian, Muslim cultural motifs dominate the social landscape, in the past couple of generations Yemenis have engaged in progressive labor militancy, strikes, and partisanship in late colonial Aden; in *al-ta'āwun al-ahlī* or "local cooperation" for basic services such as roads, education, and utilities from the 1940s through the 1980s; and, throughout the century but most notably since unification in 1990, in intellectual production, partisanship, and events representing a wide array of political tendencies. In the tumultuous modern history of a remote, colorful corner of the Arab world at its crossroads with East Africa and South Asia, popular and oppositional activities spanning diverse organizational and political spectrums have addressed major, basic issues of social welfare and human rights.

The extent and range of activism in Yemen challenges stereotypes of inherent conservatism usually attributed to tribalism and Islam. South Yemen, of course, was home to the Arab world's lone "proletarian" revolution, where a radical faction of the independence movement swept foreign companies from Aden and sultans from the hinterland, while the insular conservative thousand-year-old theocratic imamate of North Yemen fell to largely homegrown modernizing opposition. Both the imamate and subsequent military regimes left the capitalist transformation of the countryside to *ad hoc* private and voluntary efforts. During the cold war two Yemens represented Socialism and liberalism, respectively, and only in the mid-1980s did a neo-fundamentalist movement gain momentum. Even today, when, as throughout the region, religious neo-conservatives have stolen the political stage from either Arab nationalists or Marxist revolutionaries, a plethora of historically rooted political tendencies are represented. Neo-Islamist parties and welfare associations are only one significant contemporary innovation. Although there are interesting, important constants and continuities, there is a discernible ebb, flow, and recreation of civil society reflecting broader economic trends and ideological currents as well as the political will of the state. By definition, activism responds to concrete, often local, material and political circumstances, and is embedded in wider struggles over the allocation of resources in society. For instance, control of education has been continuously contested. Dramatic shifts in both the nature of governance and access to aid, remittances, or investments from abroad over the past fifty years prompt particular sorts of responses. Passivity and violence are two possibilities; between these extremes is a good deal of civilized activity.

The civic realm occupies the interstices of the government's public sphere, the private profit sector of business, and the private affectionate space of families. While part of the argument of this study is that prior to the quite recent, uneven development of modern state institutions, mechanisms rooted in Islam and tribalism provided social and legal services normally associated with the state, care is also taken to distinguish, first, contradictions within the primordial civic realm, and second, how modern activism differs from "tradition." The modern civic realm, a contested interface beyond the state, above the family, and parallel to the private business sector is the public arena for certain sorts of quite modern behavior. First, and most obviously, one form of civic participation is membership in formal autonomous literary societies, labor unions, professional associations, village committees, interest groups, charitable societies, sporting clubs, political organizations, and the like. Secondly, an important form of activism at both the elite and popular levels comes in the form of material contributions to private or cooperative non-profit modern social services, especially schools, water supplies, electrification, clinics, and welfare. Thirdly, independent intellectual production, including newspapers, poetry, and salons, is certainly part of what Europeanists mean by the civic realm, and is a key outlet for the dissemination of ideas and the creation of public opinion. Finally, activism in the civic sphere includes organizing or attending public non-governmental non-commercial events such as seminars, conventions, meetings, artistic presentations, demonstrations, and celebrations. Civic activism, it should be noted, incorporates the narrower phenomenon of specifically political participation which is activity directed towards influencing the composition or policies of the state – voting, canvassing, campaigning, lobbying, and so forth. While political participation is central to the operation of full-blown democracy, in other circumstances other sorts of activism, some of it informal and some of it illegal, may be more significant than participating in polls or referenda whose outcome is known in advance. In such circumstances especially, civil society constitutes the benign broker, the popular voice, the missing middle.

Civil society is not a binomial element, either there or not, but a variable that assumes different forms under different circumstances. Rates of activism – of joining, building, publishing, and meeting in the civic realm – expand and contract. In the mid- to late twentieth century there have been three distinct civic openings, as it were, three periods of civic renaissance, when rates of project activity were high. Each began in a period of economic expansion with liberalizing experiments on the part of fledgling governments seeking to marshal social legitimacy and private investments. The first was concentrated in the modern enclave of late colonial Aden amidst heavy immigration, but also had significant manifestations in the protectorates and the imamate. Activism peaked a second time in North Yemen during the 1970s, with very little central control but exceptional affluence thanks to remittances from the Gulf. The third opening, coincident with the "third wave of democratization," following Yemeni unification in 1990, occasioned more formal political participation and specifically human rights activism. Civil society is not credited with "causing" the civic openings, periods of tolerance for public activism, but quickly animates to fill and transcend the narrow legal autonomy granted by a fledgling government in contingent enabling legislation. Among the ironies explored in this study are how religious and tribal mechanisms or ideas are applied to novel purposes; and how activism generates social capital that may indeed fall prey to state appropriation. Indeed states, never hegemonic and constantly in search of legitimacy and control, continually strive to "incorporate" or "corporatize" civil society. Although Yemen's openings are something short of "democratic movements," and activism is ultimately no match for either military governments or economic dependency, the civic sphere is a zone for provision of services and the protection of rights.

It is not clear whether this study of activism in Arabia is exceptional mainly because of the way we have been looking at Arab politics or because Yemen is truely unique. Yemen certainly has a history all its own. Unlike the arid interior of the Peninsula, Indian Ocean monsoons wash the southwest highlands and valleys, a territory always densely settled by farmers and shepherds. With a historical memory extending back to the Marib dam and the frankincense trail, and continuously inhabited cities as old as any in the Middle East, the current nation-state emerged only at the end of the cold war. It is almost as new as the Palestinian Authority or the Eritrean government. In the number of different states or state-like entities – an imamate, a colony, sultanates and tribes, socialist and military republics – that have occupied its territory in recent memory, Yemen rivals Yugoslavia. Furthermore, despite colonization of the South, what used to be North Yemen retained an extraordinary insulation from Western influence, perhaps even greater than two comparable rugged mountainous autonomous kingdoms, Ethiopia and Afghanistan. And whereas the other monarchies of the Arabian Peninsula were established in the nineteenth or twentieth centuries, the Mutawakkilite Kingdom of Yemen claimed an unbroken legacy of a Zaydī imamate traced to the eleventh century; whereas the Gulf kingdoms had strong relations with foreign oil companies, oil was discovered in Yemen only in the mid-1980s.

On the other hand, colonialism and other international forces have certainly influenced political history. Wrested from the sultans of Laḥj in the nineteenth century, Aden became a Crown Colony, and with its hinterland remained under British control until 1968, later than most Arab and African territories. Aden and the rest of South Yemen experienced a radical revolution along the lines of those in Mozambique or Angola, and the People's Democratic Republic of Yemen (PDRY) became the sole Marxist state and Soviet ally in the Arab region. More or less concurrently, the death of the last imam marked the birth of the Yemen Arab Republic (YAR). Thus, like Vietnam and Korea, Yemen was divided by the cold war, although the YAR's anti-communism and its relationship to the West were mediated by Saudi Arabia, with a minimum of Western military involvement. With unification in the 1990s, Yemen is undergoing a partly post-Socialist structural adjustment monitored by external creditors. In different ways, therefore, it also shares some commonalities with Germany, with the Asian republics of the former USSR, and with many third world countries. With a population of about fifteen million in 1996, Yemen ranks as a lower-middle-income, least-developed nation. It has exceptionally high birth rates, low literacy especially among women, and low productivity in the farm and services sectors where most people work. Throughout this century, remittances from migrant laborers or entrepreneurs supplied the bulk of earned foreign exchange; nowadays, although it exports modest amounts of oil, its balance of payments deficits are catastrophic.

It has been a century racked by political instability and violence. States have never possessed what political scientists call "a monopoly over the use of violence," but they have nonetheless claimed the lion's share. The century dawned with Ottoman and British forces attempting to impose "law and order," and in the 1920s and 1930s colonial and imamic armies, recruited from the tribes, waged pacification campaigns against strategically or economically valuable valleys. From the early 1960s through the early 1970s two civil wars pitted colonial and royalist forces against revolutionaries and republicans, all prey to the regional conflict between Egypt's 'Abd al-Nāṣir and Saudi King Faysal. Inside the two republics of the cold war era, military and party elites engaged in murderous internecine struggles – coups, counter-coups, factional civil wars. Most recently, what had been the army of the Yemen Arab Republic defeated what remained of the People's Democratic Republic army. There have also been skirmishes along the mostly undefined border with Saudi Arabia. Although the noisiest, bloodiest clashes occurred among contending regimes and their armies, tribally based resistance to military policing and state taxes has taken the form of banditry (kidnappings, car hijackings, and road blockages) or, occasionally, kaliznikov or bazooka exchanges. It warrants specific mention that even amidst a heavily armed population, arbitrary policing, disregard for human rights, and considerable political tumult, warfare has *not* turned against the population with horrific village massacres, mass executions, or physical punishment of women and children; with few exceptions, warfare has mainly been conventional, among armed combatants, and has not resorted to terrorism or community retribution as in, for instance, Lebanon, Somalia, Bosnia, Algeria, or Sudan. Still, wars and coups have been endemic.

It is not within the general context of Yemen, then, but rather in more specific historical contexts that we seek to explain the periodic renaissance of activism in the civic sphere. This question is addressed in a general way in the next chapter, through a historical overview of the political economy of twentieth-century Yemen. Specifically, chapter 2 hypothesizes that the space open to civic activism depends on an interrelated cluster of factors: regimes and their power bases, which in turn determine decisions and capacities to suppress, tolerate or co-opt autonomous action; courts, legal systems, policing, and related questions of constitutionalism and the role of various judicial philosophies; public infrastructure, especially in the areas of information and communication, and the related question of who owns, operates, and uses their services; and, finally, economic resources available for various sorts of public-, private-, and voluntary-sector investment. In interaction, these four sets of factors seem to set the parameters of civic space, within which activists then press for greater tolerance, expanded services, and clearer separation of private from public wealth.

Following this chronological overview, subsequent chapters take a closer look at activism in a series of historical periods, starting in chapter 3 with an examination of the "*ahlī*" civic realm in early twentieth-century South Arabia. Here cultural motifs display a range of permutations. Non-state mechanisms supplying water, basic religious instruction, legal services, market facilities, and other infrastructure, embedded in local structures of wealth, power, and expropriation, not only challenged absolutism but generated some novel protest and direct-action projects such as theatrical displays, "open" schools, and community betterment drives. Chapter 4 is a case study of the first period of vibrant public participation, centered in the expansive, relatively open climate of Aden in the 1950s and 1960s, where laborers, traders, and intellectuals from all over the country gathered, and where a wide range of largely class-based political tendencies from Marxism and Nasirism to mercantilism and the Muslim Brotherhood established themselves in unions, parties, newspapers, and other fora. This distinctly modern behavior intersects with anterior social configurations in complex ways, as does the next episode of voluntarism in the 1970s. Chapter 5 shows how mechanisms recognizable from traditional practices and pre-revolutionary community betterment, invigorated by massive infusions of remitted earnings and innovative technologies, transformed the towns and regions of North Yemen with thousands of schools, roads, utilities, and other services by *ad hoc* "LDAs." Together, the details in these three chapters present a powerful case study in the veritable auto-transformation of a traditional, tribal, predominantly Muslim society.

Table 1.1. *A snapshot of three political openings in Yemen*

location and time period	political circumstances	economic conditions	civil society activity
Aden and protectorates, 1950s–1960s	British colonial authorities authorize syndicates, propose constitutions, elections for minority of Legislative Council seats; restrict political organizing, strikes, opposition press	foreign currency investment in transport, commerce, utilities, health care, education, military; high inflation in post-WWII recession	labor unions, cultural clubs, independent presses, labor political parties, rural movements, local self-help; independence movement
Yemen Arab Republic, 1970s–early 1980s	military corrective movement suspends constitution; no press, party, labor rights; accedes to demands for local autonomy and local elections	aid and labor migrants' remittances finance consumption, commerce, infrastructure; second-hand prosperity ends in early 1980s	self-help roads, schools, water supplies; pressure for release of taxes for local services to elected bodies; local elections
Republic of Yemen, 1990–1994	new constitution and legislation permit independent parties, presses, associations; civil war and constitutional amendments retract freedoms	development of Yemeni oil industry attracts investment, raises expectations; fallout from Gulf Crisis causes unemployment, inflation; structural adjustment	multiparty competition, press, conferences, organizing provide multiple forums to pressure for political and constitutional reform human rights

By the same token, both expansions of civic space ended in police repression. Each occurred against the backdrop of a capricious, unconstitutional system wherein most autonomous initiatives were subsumed under tribal, religious, or informal mechanisms that nonetheless challenged fragile government authority indirectly. In order to relax social tension, fortify their own shallow power blocs, and mobilize financial investments in the economy, two very different sorts of governments permitted certain forms of independent economic organizations, scheduled non-partisan elections to public office, and adopted some pro-business policies. In both cases infrastructure and investments were expanding. Given an opening and some private resources, civic activism spanning both left–right and local–national spectrums soon transcended the narrow boundaries of legal autonomous space. Each government, dismayed by its failure to secure an electoral mandate in limited elections, began to retract its license to civic, political, and even business participation. In each case an economic downturn caused by exogenous factors added to the zero–sum reasoning of a military-security organization that attempted to block autonomous projects even as it endeavored to build upon their legitimacy. Imperial governors in slow retreat and a coup-ridden military regime struggling to gain control each granted and gradually retracted license to counter-hegemonic but non-violent, largely popular, forces. Contingent liberalization gave way to totalization not because civil society turned to banditry or armed resistance but because peaceful activism was ruled out by extra-legal police action. In the end, armies won military contests, and civil society retreated. The projects of the civic sphere – both the social capital, the schools, libraries, fountains, clubs, roads, clinics, and other facilities, and the discourses and principles of justice, equality, representation, intellectual freedom, basic rights, and common good – are co-opted to the state sector and its legitimizing pronouncements. On the other hand, regimes that suppress civil society have not fared well. So while it is true on the one hand that each opening ended in repression, it is equally true that each period of repression yielded a new regime needful of civic state-building efforts to fortify itself. In other words, Yemeni states, lacking major outside benefactors or domestic wealth, may be unique in the region in their need for civil society.

The "democratic experiment" of the early 1990s replicated some of these patterns, but also had special characteristics. The expansion of civic space was palpable as the many barriers to assembly, publication, speech, travel, investment, and open partisanship were lifted. A discernible, diverse realm of public opinion dealing with broad issues concerning the constitution, the judiciary, education, the very conception of the public arena, was defined and debated in the press, symposia, and conferences, replete with references to the full range of recent Yemeni political experiences. Activism quickly tested its narrow legal limitations, seeking explicitly to expand and codify some basic rights and liberties, pressing for transparency in the disposition of public-sector assets, and finally crystallizing along the lines of a pro-democracy, anti-war effort to dissuade army commanders from fighting for control of the state apparatus. When this last-ditch plea for civility failed, and in the face of deepening economic recession and fiscal crisis, military action justified new restrictions on public activism. Two chapters are devoted to the 1990s, one to the civic opening surrounding political participation in the 1993 elections, and the second to civic responses to the new totalitarian effort surrounding the 1994 civil war. While the fact that each period of relative liberalization ended in political repression stops the argument short of sanguine predictions for the future of democracy in the Arabian Peninsula, the evidence from twentieth-century Yemen is sufficient to refute the null hypothesis that Arab society cannot be civil. It encourages us to replace the static view of civil society as a particular set of institutional arrangements with a more dynamic view of how people act on their own history. It allows us to imagine a tolerant, democratic order on the Arabian Peninsula.

2 Twentieth-century states and economies

While it is tempting to conceptualize states as fixed entities possessing hegemonic control over the civic sphere, in twentieth-century Yemen "the state" has been a variable rather than a constant. Three generations of states have ruled parts of Yemen during the past century: a motley mixture of semi-feudal and colonial systems through the 1960s; two republics associated with opposite sides of the cold war during the 1970s and 1980s; and, since May 22 1990, the Republic of Yemen. The civil war of 1994 culminated a hundred years of struggle over the composition and power of the state, and the current government recognizes quite well the limits of is own constitutional, judicial, institutional, and fiscal capacities. Although it commands international diplomatic recognition, membership in the United Nations and other international institutions, military and police forces, a national budget, a civil service, substantial foreign debt, weighty physical infrastructure, and other attributes of state-ness, and although a common national conscious helps bind more than fifteen million Yemenis together, the Republic of Yemen is a new state, still in the process of formation. The gradual, uneven development of the contemporary Yemeni nation-state, sketched in table 2.1, is the timeline against which the variable, dynamic relationship between states and civil society must be viewed.

Civilian state construction is in part a quest for constitutional order and legal hegemony, an effort to centralize judicial practices, co-opt interpretations, and impose the "rule of law." A diverse, semi-sequential mixture of legal traditions – Ottoman, Zaydī, Shafa'i, British civil and martial, Socialist, Egyptian, various tribal principles, internationally recommended commercial codes – complicates this quest. Legal principles embedded in judges' educations, precedent, court practices, and dispute-settlement mechanisms carry over despite revolutions in executive authority, contributing to a modicum of judicial autonomy from regimes and police who often disregard their own laws. Divergent legal traditions were a major difference between South Yemen, where English and Stalinist models were quite thoroughly institutionalized, and the

Table 2.1. *States and economic conditions, three historical periods*

	North Yemen	Aden	Protectorates
1910s–1960s	– traditional Zaydī imamate – tribute-collecting state – Islamic and tribal law	– British Crown Colony – elective Legislative Council – British civil and martial law	– British "protection" of sultanates and shaykhdoms – Islamic and tribal law
	– minimal state services	– modern urban infrastructure	– modest infrastructure
	– investment and trade discouraged – family and semi-feudal agriculture – emigration to Aden	– foreign public and private investment – major transport/naval hub	– limited capitalist development – emigration to Aden and Asia
	Yemen Arab Republic	People's Democratic Republic of Yemen	
1960s–1980s	– civil war and political instability – conflicts w/PDRY 1972, 1979 – Islamic, tribal, civil, and military law	– civil war and political instability – conflicts w/Oman, YAR – socialist constitution and law	
	– donor-driven public construction – aid from Gulf, East, West, and multilateral institutions	– donor-driven extension of colonial infrastructure and services – aid mainly from East and multilateral institutions	
	– free-market economy – labor emigration and remittances – high consumption, low investment – oil discovered 1986	– nationalization of colonial and capitalist property – labor emigration and remittances – low consumption and investment – oil discovered 1987	
	Republic of Yemen		
1990s	– unity in May 1990 creates coalition government of two former executives, cabinets, leglislators, courts – Gulf Crisis disrupts foreign aid and labor remittances – problems merging armies, public sectors, courts – compromise unity constitution		
	– May 1994 civil war maintains unity, defeats former PDRY Socialist leadership – constitution amended – budget and payments deficits lead to financial collapse, debt rescheduling – parliamentary elections, 1993 and 1997		

states of the North, where Islamic and tribal models were only gradually accommodated to modern commercial, civil, and criminal codes. Yemenis express this as the difference between "*qānūn wa-niẓām*" or "law and order" in the South and "*fawḍā*," "chaos" or perhaps "anarchy," in the North. Moreover, the legal community has periodically offered constitutional proposals expressive of popular demands to counteract government campaigns to "corporatize" legal education, judgments, and prosecution, and constitutional debates continue today.

Public works are also a very important element in the power of modern states. Infrastructural projects create a "national" market linked to international commerce, legitimize the government through education and social services, represent an impressive share of all fixed capital investment, and provide the largest single source of employment. Control of education on the one hand and "the streets" on the other have important implications for the development of both the state and civil society, for civic spaces are in some sense public places, expanding with public schools, campuses, courts, transport, parks, stadiums, offices, hospitals, lights, and airwaves. "The state" becomes not only the government and the army but the bureaucracy that manages and regulates these spaces. In Yemen, as in many third world nations, states have relied almost exclusively on other states to finance construction of national infrastructure. Among them, the United Kingdom and then a range of Arab, communist, Western, and multilateral assistance agencies have built everything from port facilities to agricultural research centers, and trained the civil servants and technocrats who run the ministries and agencies of government.

Access to wealth affects the power of the state and the autonomy of civil society. Twentieth-century Yemen is surely an example of "dependent development," where major swings in economic fortunes are determined by changes in the world market. Aden flourished as the British naval hub between Suez and India and suffered from Arab–Israeli wars. During the "oil boom" in neighboring Arab Gulf countries, all of Yemen, but especially the North, enjoyed a second-hand affluence thanks to labor remittances and foreign aid. Its vibrant commercial markets are skewed toward retail trade in imported commodities. Throughout the twentieth century, the country's major export has been unskilled labor. The disappearance of communist donors, the decline of oil prices, and especially the Gulf War sent the dependent economy into a tail-spin. The discovery and production of oil by multinational corporations in the past decade has only partly offset massive import dependency, balance-of-payments deficits, and fiscal crisis.

Within the country, the agricultural sector that still supports half the population has remained mostly stagnant throughout the century, and industrialization has been limited. Most families live from a combination of farming, petty enterprise, and remittances. Political instability, infrastructural inadequacy, and administrative inefficiency have warded off major private investors, even in the Yemen Arab Republic and the Republic of Yemen where they have always been welcome. Thus there is a rather contradictory situation wherein, on the one hand, a series of processes – colonial and imamic economic policies, revolutionary expropriations in the PDRY, international loans and grants to the public sectors, the emergence of state-owned oil and gas industries, and corruption on the part of public officials – have tended to accumulate modern assets in the hands of the state. This dynamic was an important force for unification, and a salient factor in recent struggles for control of the state apparatus. Even now that socialism has been defeated and international creditors led by the IMF are relatively satisfied with Sana'a's pro-market policies, the government (and within the government, the army) is the country's single largest employer, investor, and property owner. On the other hand, the uncaptured, informal sector is very large, for it includes small farmers, traders, drivers, and individual service providers, an important "parallel market" in currencies, and a not insignificant smuggling industry. Moreover, many Yemenis, rich and poor, have family or property abroad that affords them an income that bypasses the state, and private-sector wealth is concentrated in either real estate or mobile liquid assets. The government and its officers control an important share of the nation's physical plant and the national bank accounts, but beyond this sector are a significant autonomous commercial class and millions of smallholders, traders, and semi-skilled laborers with no stake in the system.

This chapter traces political–military, constitutional, legal, infrastructural, and economic developments in order to demonstrate, on the one hand, the real limits on state authority, and, on the other hand, the absence of limitations on how state power is wielded. Overall, progress toward state building is mainly infrastructural and technocratic–institutional, and even that is sporadic, uneven, and incomplete. In each period power ploys within ruling circles play havoc with institutional development, legal formalities are overridden by security considerations, infrastructural progress is determined by foreign donors, and economic fortunes depend on circumstances elsewhere. Indeed, the past hundred years have seen continued struggles in military and civic arenas over the composition and constitution of the state, and episodes of liberalization alternate with military engagements.

Colonialism, tradition, and revolution

Turn-of-the-century South Arabia consisted of Aden, the protectorates, and North Yemen. Under the British, cosmopolitan Aden was isolated from a hinterland where, to discourage alignment with "foreign powers," notably Yemen, the colonial office subsidized twenty-odd local sultans and *shaykhs*. The western protectorates around Aden included some sultanates, notably those in Laḥj and Zinjibār, and nine tribes. The eastern protectorates included the powerful Qa'ayṭī sultanate, seated in the seaside town al-Mukallā', and the Kathīrī sultan in the Wadi Ḥaḍramawt. To the north, the Kingdom of Yemen's southern uplands and coastal Tihama region were partly occupied by the Ottomans until 1912, when the imams of Sana'a gained nominal control. During the next couple of decades, the imams established North Yemen's borders with the protectorates to the south and Saudi Arabia to the north. Long after capitalist markets and classes developed in Aden, North Yemen's rulers actively discouraged modernization. Over the course of the next five decades, opposition to colonialism in the South and tyranny in the North catalyzed into two revolutions, one Socialist and the other bourgeois.[1]

Aden colony, the free port

Situated near the intersection of the Red Sea with the Indian Ocean, shielded from monsoons by the Horn of Africa and local topography, Aden was the mid-point on a shortened journey from the Mediterranean to Asia via the Suez Canal. The British navy put in a coaling station in 1839, wresting a small seafront enclave from the sultan of Laḥj. Over the next century, the British rebuilt the entire seafront. The 1869 Shaykh 'Uthmān water scheme, comprising wells, reservoirs, and a six-mile aqueduct, was later expanded with wells to pump water from Little Aden and as far away as Laḥj.[2] Aden expanded across the man-made Khūrmaksar causeway onto the mainland, eventually covering an eighty-square-mile area. Several public and private hospitals were built. The Aden settlement grew from a cluster of fishing villages to a city of 20,000 in the 1850s, nearly 150,000 a century later, and almost twice that number by 1968. By then Aden was served by an international airport, a power station, a network of streets and highways, and telephone and telegraph service; one could study in Urdu, Hebrew, Gujarati, English, Arabic, and probably Somali. The government brought in at least 2,000 Indian teachers and wholly or partially subsidized several dozen schools, a technical institute, a men's teachers' training center, a girls' college, private evening classes, and several public libraries. Students sat for London City and Cambridge School exams, like British subjects elsewhere.[3] Although its barren landscape and steamy climate never attracted European settlers, it was easily the most cosmopolitan spot on the Peninsula.

An entrepot hub, Aden became a "resort for traders," where, except during World War II, markets were "virtually uncontrolled" and "often uncontrollable."[4] As one of the world's busiest ports in the 1950s, Aden attracted significant investments: British Petroleum spent $45,000,000 on a refinery at Little Aden, and over $1,000,000 was invested in power, water, and telephone systems. Migrants poured in: 2,000 Arabs worked at the port, and thousands of others found jobs in and around the shipyards. Then, after the 1956 Suez invasion, British troops were permanently stationed at an enlarged base. Military installations were expanded further after the successful operation to dislodge Iraq from Kuwait after its first invasion in 1961. In its last decade, the naval installation, covering a quarter of the city's land, generated up to 25,000 jobs and a quarter of the colony's GNP.[5] Multinational banks, shippers, and insurance companies opened branch offices, while East African, South Asian, and Yemeni merchants traded across the lower Red Sea. The local commercial class were predominantly Indian subcontinent Muslims. Some Yemenis ran taxis or corner shops, and many were students, but the majority of 50,000–80,000 Yemenis worked for the army, the port, the refinery, or other foreign-owned enterprises.

For all its massive military, infrastructural, and financial investments, the United Kingdom never decided how to govern Aden. It was incorporated as a fortress, a municipality, a settlement, and finally, in 1939, a Crown Colony; ruled from Bombay and then London; separated from the hinterland (whose people were treated as aliens in the city) and then urged to federate with the protectorates. Until World War II, the government owned all the land on and beyond the Aden peninsula; even after land was privatized, the port trust power and water industries were made public. It was only in the late colonial period, while attempting to make Aden self-financing by privatizing its extensive land holdings, nationalizing power and water systems, and raising land, property, license, market, and other sundry taxes, that the government proposed constitutional rule and elections. Policy was coordinated with bankers and the major English- or Indian-owned trading companies through the chamber of commerce. In this context, propertied male Adenis were allowed to vote for a few seats on an Aden municipal council in 1949, and for a majority of seats on a reconstituted Aden legislative council in 1959.

Also in 1959, a series of ill-fated constitutional projects was launched. The Aden constitution codified the selection and limited authority of the Aden legislative council, while a separate federal constitution called for a council of the sultans and *shaykhs* of the protectorates. Both constitutions were amended in 1963, when Aden joined the federation. More legislative council elections were finally held in 1964 after many postponements. A year later, however, the Aden constitution was suspended and the council dismissed under a state of emergency. Still in the late 1950s the British government intended to retain the Crown Colony and form a federation of the protectorates. By 1964 it was decided to grant independence by 1968 to a federation comprising both Aden and the protectorates, under a plan that would allow the UK to retain its naval base at Aden.

Independent of any constitutional arrangement, the civil court system was one of Britain's hardiest legacies in Aden, where the two-tiered judicial system headed by a chief justice and supreme court also included magistrates' courts that heard criminal, civil, and traffic cases. Appeals went to higher courts in Bombay and later (after 1947) the Court of Appeal for Eastern Africa in Nairobi. Attorneys, practicing in Aden since the 1920s, were organized into a Council of Legal Practitioners in 1954. English-style, English-language courts operated from court houses in Crater, Steamer Point, Shaykh 'Uthmān, and Little Aden. They applied a corpulent corpus of British and Indian statutory codes and ordinances published in five volumes in 1955. Courts were backed up by a municipal police force whose ranks rose to 1,111 in 1958 under the state of emergency.[6] Hundreds of political activists were detained, and the courts did not protect civil liberties.

The late colonial "opening" was defective, incomplete, and fraught at every turn with manipulation, restrictions, and repression. Compared with autocratic North Yemen at the time, however, the space for activism was relatively expansive, like the wide-open physical spaces and the relatively easy money. Certain associations and publications were encouraged, labor was given the right to organize (though not to strike), and other groups found ways around restrictive legislation. Under these circumstances, and given irresolvable Yemeni grievances with the colonial administration, activism spilled well beyond its narrow legal scope.

By mid-century, the tens of thousands of mostly male Yemenis in Aden, treated as temporary alien workers, were politicized by the combination of a massive foreign military presence, expansion of education, rampant inflation, employment recessions when the major construction projects ended, labor surges due to rural droughts, the trend toward large public and private enterprises, the devastation of crafts, the breakdown of the old labor brokerage system, and growing access to information. The first union strike occurred in 1948, amidst rapid cost-of-living increases not matched by improved earnings. In the face of labor restiveness, merchant trading houses organized to protect their own interests through the Aden Association, whose pro-colonial members got themselves appointed or elected to municipal, legislative, and federal councils. Labor militancy escalated commensurately. Nationalism and anti-colonialism, fanned by Arab–Israeli confrontations, the Egyptian revolution, Mosaddeq's nationalization of Iranian oil, Indian, Kenyan, and Kuwaiti independence, and the coups against the imams of North Yemen, all reverberated in the colony, crystallizing nascent activism into a range of political parties and organizations.

The protectorates of South Arabia

In the protectorates, the UK left a convoluted constitutional and political legacy marked simultaneously by highly formalized legalism and opportunist inconsistency. In order to protect the Adeni hinterland, the empire made treaties with local leaders, similar to arrangements in the Gulf: recognizing the "sovereignty" of sultans, amirs, and *shaykhs* in vassal statelets, freezing preexisting arrangements for leadership selection, and occasionally deposing recalcitrant rulers. The sultanates and tribal regions of South Yemen differed in their internal structures, economic wherewithal, legal practices, and treaty relationships with Britain. In South Yemen this decentralized, little-rationalized system foiled rather than facilitated state building. By the same token, the protectorate treaties, constitutional proposals, and thousands of ordinances inculcated a certain Western-style legalism into a legislative and judicial culture in Aden and the entire South. For instance, by 1954 there were thirty-one major treaties of protection and some ninety conventions including thirteen advisory agreements.[7] The principle of governance based on codified law was relatively well understood.

Whereas the western protectorates were the immediate periphery of the capitalist enclave in Aden, the eastern protectorates were far more remote. Near Aden the two major sultanates of Laḥj and Abyan, whose traditional wealth derived from a combination of wadi agriculture and seafaring, were transformed by sub-urban connections into capitalist farm regions supplying the Aden market. By contrast, in the east the Ḥaḍramī economy was relatively autonomous from the colonial system, thanks to migrants and their remittances. Long before the British arrival

Ḥaḍramīs commanded the army of the Hyderabad Nizam in India, amassing fortunes that accrued to the homeland. Between the two world wars an estimated 20 to 30 percent of the Ḥaḍramī population, mostly from its upper crust, lived in India, Singapore, Indonesia, or East Africa; in Java alone there were 70,000 Yemenis. In 1936 remittances to Ḥaḍramawt were estimated at nearly $650,000.[8] Leading families invested in private and public construction, and markets for imported clothes, food, and luxuries flourished. Unlike Aden-based merchants of foreign origins, Ḥaḍramī traders' Asia-oriented fortunes were independent of British favor. These factors, together with oil explorations in the region, help explain both the efflorescence of community betterment activities in the Ḥaḍramawt and the reluctance of the Qa'ayṭī and Kathīrī sultanates to join the South Arabian Federation.

In the eastern and western protectorates, some modern services were built. The British provided partial or full funding for 133 elementary or secondary schools serving a total protectorates population (excluding Aden) of nearly a million people. The minor Indian Ocean port of al-Mukallā', seat of the eastern protectorates and one of the two Ḥaḍramī sultanates, boasted several schools, a teacher-training institute, and Sharī'a instruction at the nearby Ghayl Bā Wazīr religious institute. It was connected to some 2,680 miles of locally or British-built unpaved but motorable tracks, and served by Aden Airways. Electricity and public water supplies were available.[9] Funds for health services came from the Colonial Development and Welfare Fund, the Nuffield Foundation, and UNICEF.[10] There were hospitals in Eastern towns such as Makhzan, al-Mukallā', Say'ūn, Shibām, and Tarīm. In Tarīm and al-Mukallā' local rulers paid physicians' salaries, the Church of Scotland and Danish missions each sent small medical teams, and there were "in each protectorate some 35 health units."[11]

Another study will have to consider whether oil alone explains the success in the Gulf of institutional arrangements that failed in South Arabia. For whereas "Kuwait for the Kuwaitis" holds to this day, "Aden for the Adenis" could not separate propertied second-generation men from other Yemenis in the port, and the protectorate governments, each with its own unique peccadilloes, fell to the wider revolution in South Arabia. That political action eventually gave way to guerrilla warfare says less about local culture than it does about imperialism. There are some obvious parallels to Vietnam: a historical cultural entity was divided by colonial rule; legitimate national aspirations were denied well after so many other colonies had gained independence; and the liberation struggle unleashed societal-wide violence even after the departure of foreign troops. Like other third world countries where colonial powers long overstayed their welcome – Algeria, Angola, Mozambique, and in another way Cuba – the outcome was a radical revolutionary regime. Having failed to quell either rural rebellion or labor militancy, instead of handing over power to its erstwhile clients in the Aden and protectorate councils, the United Kingdom relinquished governance to the National Liberation Front (NLF).

The North Yemeni imamate

North Yemen's semi-feudal, isolationist theocracy, based in a rugged mountainous region, was one of the most backward, remote enclaves in the world. Imams Yaḥyā (r. 1911–48) and his son Aḥmad (r. 1948–62) claimed the mantle of the tradition of the Zaydī school of Shī'a Islam which predominates in the north-central Yemeni highlands. Followers of the Shāfi'ī sect of Sunnī Islam, a numerical majority concentrated in the densely cultivated and populated southern uplands and Tihama regions, resented the Zaydī imams' dictates, as did members of the minority Ismā'īlī sect. Indeed, many Zaydīs also questioned the legitimacy of the thousand-year-old imamate's *bay'a*, or summons. Tribes of the interior highlands sometimes contended that tribal law, leadership, and sovereignty was a viable alternative to the institution of the imamate; any loyalty was won by either giving subsidies and guns or taking *shaykhs*' sons hostage. Even Zaydī *sayyid* men, technically the base of the imamate's support, dissented from the latter-day imamate's abuses of Zaydī doctrine,[12] staging coup attempts in 1948 and 1955. The class dimension of these conflicts – the radicalization of Shāfi'ī sharecroppers, liberalism of upper-and-middle merchants and technocrats, and populist- or libertarian-style conservatism of tribal smallholders – would only subsequently be revealed.

By and large, North Yemen remained a land of peasant sharecroppers and independent farmer-herders, a pre-capitalist agrarian formation where a tribute-collecting system coexisted with a communal mode of production, as explored more fully in the next chapter. Strict trade and investment restrictions protected a few monopoly importers, coffee exporters, and large landowners, but inhibited other investments and foreign trade. Austrian-minted Maria Theresa silver thaler and Saudi riyāls served in the absence of a national currency. Consequently, the would-be bourgeoisie and working class escaped to Aden, while their families continued farming but spent cash remittances on imports. By the 1950s most farms within a couple of hundred kilometers of Aden, including Laḥj and Abyan in the protectorates and Taiz and Ibb provinces in the north, were selling grain, ghee, qāt, vegetables, honey, saffron, eggs, milk, meat, and skins to Aden-based brokers. Barter, production for use, and semi-feudal rent payments gave way to market-oriented production, exchange, and consumption.[13] Eventually even erstwhile beneficiaries of the *ancien régime,* landowners and tax collectors, bridled under its constraints on investment and trade.

Services for 5,000,000 predominantly rural North Yemenis were primitive by any standard. "Urban" amenities included neighborhood wells, fountains, cisterns, or *qānāt,* often connected to mosques or public baths; and some academies, libraries, poorhouses, and orphanages; and caravansaries, town gates, and municipal watchmen. In 1962 North Yemen had six hundred local mosque schools and sixteen Islamic institutes. Modern, state education was offered in forty one-room secular schools, ten full primary schools, a half-dozen intermediate and secondary schools, and twelve technical training courses – virtually all in Sana'a, Taiz, and Hodeida.[14] There were sick-wards in a couple of garrison towns, low-standard clinics in Sana'a and Hodeida, and a tuberculosis hospital in Taiz. Diesel generators operated for the hospitals and the royal palaces at Sana'a, Taiz, and Ḥajja, and in 1960 work began on a 300-kilowatt power station for Sana'a. Telegraph lines were for military, not public, use. There was a dirt airstrip at Taiz. These services were mostly the work of foreigners, especially the Turks before World War I and the Italians afterwards. Around 1960, the USSR constructed a deep channel and breakwater for Hodeida, a thousand Chinese began rebuilding the Turkish camel-trail from Hodeida to Sana'a, and the Americans laid a roadbed connecting al-Makhā' with Taiz and engineered Taiz's public water supply.[15] UNICEF began an educational assistance program.

Ideological statements from traditionalist and neo-fundamentalist Islamists notwithstanding, the Holy Quran and/or Sharī'a do not represent a formal constitution, but rather a general set of principles coupled with specific rules for taxation and in areas of family, property, and criminal law. Shāfi'ī sultans and Zaydī imams, professing Islamic rule, nonetheless took liberties with some of its tenets. Each sat atop institutional pyramids comprising little more than a *bayt al-māl* (treasury), collecting the Islamic tithe via an abusive system adopted from the Turks, tending personally to expenditures, judicial review, and petitions. Local administrators, judicial appointees, tax collectors, and finally ministers were their cousins or clients. Among the few clear constitutional principles was that of *shūrā* or consultation, obliging the ruler to consult with Muslim scholars and be confirmed in office by an electoral college. Although modern Islamists would dispute them, the imams and sultans of Yemen contended that members of the *sayyid* aristocracy, descendants of the Prophet, had God-given privileges including fitness to rule. Yet the aging Imam Yaḥyā violated their electoral authority when he designated his son as his successor, prompting a revolt among his own base of support that took the form of a proposal for a Sacred National Pact (*al-Mīthāq al-Waṭanī al-Muqaddas*). Around the same time, in the Ḥaḍramawt neo-Islamists were questioning the very doctrine of *sayyid* superiority.

Thus resistance mounted against both repressive traditionalism and exploitive modernization. As explored more thoroughly in chapter 4, activism based in Aden gave rise to republican and revolutionary movements. The second phase of Yemen's modern history began with two concomitant, intertwined revolutions: a republican or bourgeois revolution against the imamate[16] and an anti-imperialist, radical Socialist upheaval in the South. Known by the dates their respective civil wars began – September 26 1962, when the palace guard announced the death of the imam and creation of the YAR, and October 14 1963, the date associated with the onset of armed rebellion in the South – these revolutions encompassed mutual, regional, and global power struggles. Activism in Aden threatened the imamate; the latter's collapse drove a nail into the coffin of the Federation of South Arabia by raising, if only temporarily, the prospect of pan-Yemeni unity. In the 1960s ʻAbd al-Nāṣir's Egypt backed one revolutionary faction in the South (known in English by the acronym FLOSY) and the YAR's republican officers in their respective battles against Saudi-financed royal families. The YAR's civil war, stalemated by Saudi–Egyptian rivalry between 1962 and 1967, was negotiated under the pan-Arab rapprochement in the wake of the Six Day War with Israel. Once the Egyptians withdrew from North Yemen, Britain agreed to remove its military bases in the South. Henceforth Saudi Arabia endeavored to extend its hegemony over the populous southern part of the Peninsula.[17]

State institutions and state sectors in two Yemeni republics

About eighty thousand people left Aden after 1967, perhaps half foreigners (mainly Asians and Africans), and the other half Yemeni. No wonder the rural faction of the National Liberation Front won: urban labor and property owners deserted the city. Aden's assets were redivided. Revolutionaries seized a port and commercial sector whose custom were decimated by closure of the Suez Canal, public buildings and institutions, power and water plants, and most urban housing.[18] Red Sea traders moved to Mombasa, Asmara, Mogadishu, or other East

African cities, from where many would remigrate to North Yemen in the 1970s; Southern merchants and aristocrats went to Saudi Arabia. Northern businessmen, most of them originally from the southern uplands or the Tihama, relocated to Taiz or Hodeida. Petty traders and drivers dispersed. Consequently, Taiz, Hodeida, and Sana'a acquired the core of a national bourgeoisie and soon burst beyond their medieval walls in a frenzy of suburban construction financed partly from late colonial Aden, partly from foreign aid, and partly from private remittances.

The People's Democratic Republic of Yemen

Of the two cold-war-era Yemeni republics, the PDRY built the stronger state order, one based on a constitution that outlived several regimes. The 1970 PDRY constitution, with traces of Islamic and British as well as Marxist legal principles, enshrined a unified, Arab, Muslim, Socialist Yemen where sovereignty rested with the "working people." Special privileges of sultans, *sayyids*, men, foreigners, and property owners were replaced by universal rights to housing, education, health care, and social security. Authority was vested in a 101-member Supreme Popular Council (*Majlis al-Sha'b al-'Ulyā*) and an eleven-member Presidential Council. Amended once, in 1978 (after the NLF Political Organization became the Yemeni Socialist Party), to replace the Presidential Council with a Presidium and seat them in the now 111-member parliament, this single document did lay out a blueprint for the structure of formal state and ruling party authority. Unlike the YAR constitution, it defined governing institutions and served as the basis of legislation on matters pertaining to the judiciary itself, education, family law, and economic issues.

What remained of the Southern economy was nationalized or redistributed. Agrarian reform expropriated feudal estates, religious endowments, and, later, some family-sized holdings that ought legally to have remained with previous owners. Expropriated estates became state farms, and other parcels were redistributed to small farmers through purchasing and supply cooperatives. In the leading export sector, Indian Ocean fishing, colonial loans had hastened replacement of old-fashioned, locally crafted oar-and-sail-powered *sunbuk*s with crews of fifteen by mechanized, refrigerated vessels with crews of six, cash credits, and inputs from the quasi-governmental Fishermen's Credit Cooperative Society, Ltd. and Fishing Gear Supply Cooperative.[19] Revolutionaries either nationalized these enterprises outright or reorganized them as cooperatives selling to a state marketing board.

Household and micro-enterprise trade in domestic fish, honey, grain, fresh produce, and qāt persisted; half of all households were still engaged in subsistence farming on small plots.

The People's Democratic notion of representation included "mass" or "popular" as well as government institutions. After the *intifāḍāt* (uprisings) of the early 1970s, neighborhood defense committees on the Cuban model were set up. Law 18 of 1978 entitled them to nominate representatives to *Majlis al-Sha'b*; 1978 constitutional amendments defined separately elected local popular councils (also *majlis al-sha'b*). Cadres of village or neighborhood councils and defense committees represented them at governorate and national levels. At party conventions they elected the central committee (*al-lajna al-markaziyya*), which in turn elected the politburo (*maktab siyāsī*) and, theoretically, the top party leadership. Local elections were held in 1976 and 1977. Elections to the Supreme Popular Council in 1978 were held in each of eighty-six constituencies, the other fifteen seats being filled from the mass organizations. In the two rounds some 10 percent of those elected and/or appointed were women. In the 1978 elections, forty non-Socialists were elected.[20]

On Independence Day in 1967, the NLF's fifth decree provided for the continuity of all urban (British) and rural (Islamic) courts, practitioners, codes, and procedures until specifically amended by law. The 1970 constitution placed all courts under the Ministry of Justice. As in the Soviet legal system, the separation of judicial and executive powers was rejected on the grounds that state power and policy originated from popular elections. Far from being neutral, courts were conceived as instruments of societal transformation. Gradually, therefore, the old courts were replaced by a three-tiered system of divisional, provincial, and national courts presided over initially by young revolutionaries and later by graduates of Aden University's law faculty. The system was further elaborated through supreme court decisions, the 1973 penal code, and laws on courts, the legal profession, and criminal and civil procedure in the early 1980s. Several laws and the 1978 amendments to the constitution described the procedures for prosecution. Legal defense and a jury trial were stipulated.[21]

The judiciary implemented social policy in areas of family and property law. The PDRY's 1974 family law, always acknowledged as the Arab world's strongest legislative protection of women's rights, helped win women's political support for the revolution, mobilize their energies for economic development, and reform the conservative patriarchal family. An important feature of the law, granting most divorced women custody of the children and possession of the marital home, was given teeth by the fact that urban housing was public and could be disposed by the courts.[22] In real-estate law, people's courts and land reform tribunals pressed claims against former elites during the early 1970s, and transferred urban publicly owned villas to new tenants after changes in leadership.

The Yemen Arab Republic

In North Yemen, no republican constitutional or legal system was established to replace the imamate. Free Officers seized the reins of power 1962, after the last imam's natural death, and issued a constitution based on the Egyptian model in 1963 amidst a civil war. In 1965, prominent Yemeni republicans of every political stripe met at Khamir, seat of the Ḥāshid tribal confederation, where *'ulamā'*, modern scholars (*muthaqqafūn*), and tribal leaders advanced proposals drawn from the earlier Sacred National Pact, *'urf* notions of local self-governance, and some liberal language. Yet the 1970 YAR "permanent" constitution, in effect a compromise between Saudi Arabia and Egypt, overruled most popular proposals, and did not prove to be an effective blueprint for governance. It did serve to establish, temporarily, a parliamentary system with a 159-man *majlis al-shūrā* and a prime minister, a governmental system with some legitimacy based on the stature of its leaders but not on a constitutional consensus. Stipulations for a lower house or *majlis al-sha'b* to constitute a bicameral *majlis al-nuwwāb* (chamber of deputies) were never implemented.

Moreover, the constitution was suspended in the June 1994 "corrective movement." This movement, headed by a populist officer, Ibrāhīm al-Ḥamdī, the elected chairman of the fledgling confederation of local development associations (known in English as LDAs), embodied some popular demands and afforded considerable latitude to local and regional betterment efforts through legally empowered, elected LDAs. On the other hand, it was an anti-constitutional ploy that permanently instituted praetorian rule under a military command council. The next command council replaced the consultative council with ninety-nine appointees to a People's Constituent Assembly. Finally, President 'Alī 'Abd Allāh Ṣāliḥ reinstituted the 159-man *Majlis al-Shūrā* and erected a quasi-party "mass" institution, the General People's Congress (GPC), which attempted to marshal the energies and resources invested through the LDAs. Ironically, then, elections in the YAR were extra-constitutional and extra-parliamentary.

Unlike the PDRY, the YAR never set out to reorganize the judiciary as an instrument of social transformation. Imamic decrees were repealed, but new Egyptian-model laws were rarely implemented. In the absence of modern prosecution, torts, insurance, practicing attorneys, or even a penal code, state-appointed Sharīʿa-trained judges heard some cases in new court buildings, but most litigation still took place in private *dīwāns*. A bastion of traditional, predominantly Zaydī, legal conservatism, the Ministry of Justice exercised a certain independence, and within the judiciary there was evolution in legal competence. The University of Sana'a opened a Sharīʿa college where many faculty members were graduates of al-Azhar in Cairo. In Sana'a, Taiz, and other provincial capitals the elaboration of the legal process was slow, gradual, and uneven.[23] Modern commercial and traffic courts first appeared about 1976, with the assistance of Sudanese legal advisors. Prosecutors' offices came later. On the other hand, defense attorneys and appellate courts were unknown, death-penalty appeals rested with the president, plaintiffs could appeal directly to police to arrest adversaries, detainees could be billed for police and prison services, [24] and there were known to be private prisons.

If the PDRY revolution was socialist, the YAR's was bourgeois, laissez-faire in the extreme. The monarchy was overthrown, its estates appropriated, and aristocratic privileges revoked. Suddenly released from anachronistic autarchy, North Yemen became a "no doors" economy with few legal barriers to imports, domestic trade, investments, speculation, transportation, or construction. Traditional taxes were either repealed or made voluntary, but not rewritten. Four-wheel-drive vehicles easily evaded remote customs posts on undemarcated borders. Consequently, especially since the riyāl was subsidized at an artificially high rate of 4.5 to the dollar, service sectors exploded. Yemeni merchants driven from Aden established their businesses in the North.

After the rise in oil prices in 1973, rural men increasingly abandoned farming or traditional trades in search of employment in the Gulf's construction, trade, and services. A third of the male workforce, or as people told surveyors, "one from every family," spent part of the following decade in Saudi Arabia. Over a billion dollars a year sent home to ten million Northerners enriched remittance-agents, inflated wages, and stimulated retail consumption. In the PDRY, too, in 1982 remittances accounted for half of gross national product. Combined with traditional farming that still accounted for 55 to 60 percent of domestic production,[25] this afforded households autonomy from either Yemeni government. The YAR's remitted earnings ($428 million in 1987) were untaxed, and two-thirds of the riyāls in circulation were outside the formal banking system. The overall result was a "labor-short, capital-surplus" developing economy.[26] Despite the healthy rate of GNP growth and rapidly rising living standards, these factors inhibited productive investment.[27] Instead, the YAR's laissez-faire commodity markets contributed to heavy private consumption of imported goods, everything from the finest Indian silks to Czech weapons to Japanese electronics. Aden merchants, northern migrants to the Gulf, and immigrants from East Africa gravitated to the currency-exchange, real-estate, and import commerce in Hodeida, Taiz, and Sana'a. Wholesale and retail trade, construction contracting, money-changing, and other "services" flourished because migrants and their families spent remitted savings on consumer goods. The relatively high cost of unskilled labor – in Sana'a, YR150 a day (around $7) in 1978 – was a mighty disincentive to large-scale productive ventures.

Family farms, still the largest category of ownership, employment, and production, generated little new investment. Instead, marginal land (i.e., narrow, inaccessible, dryland terraces) went out of production in both halves of the country. New irrigation technology spread rapidly in the North at the hands of private, cooperative, and public-sector incentives, but it was applied mainly to traditional crops grown for the domestic market: sorghum, other grains, alfalfa, other fodder crops, and, in the highlands, qāt. Qāt, a semi-narcotic shrub whose leaves produce a mild euphoria, was the alpine farmer's best financial investment.[28] The labor shortage, easy-money opportunities off-farm, topographical limitations on mechanization, consumer preferences for local meat, honey, and cereals, and uncertain growing conditions and markets for exotic crops limited their appeal to farmers. Thus there was relatively little new rural productive capital formation, despite domestic capital investment in cooperative (*ta'āwun*) feeder roads, utilities, schools, and other services necessary to fully commercialize the agrarian economy.

Overall, then, the two revolutions thus produced two quite different Yemens. The Marxist PDRY was a third world version of a partly Stalinist, partly Maoist state. Private property was confined to micro-enterprises, especially traditional production; mass and legal institutions supported the party-state; a Socialist leadership vowed to export revolution elsewhere on the Peninsula, notably Oman; close relationships were forged with the USSR and other Socialist governments; most native English speakers were not welcome. Aden extended education, medical care, and other social services to most of its population, and made notable progress toward liberating women from patriarchical constraints. By contrast, the YAR, though neither democratic nor a military ally of the West, exemplified a free market for investment, trade, and consumption, and eschewed policies of social reform. The border between North and South Yemen, originally drawn between the Turkish and British empires, became a cold-war border, and the PDRY and the YAR, respectively, seemed to represent microcosms of the differences between peripheral capitalism and third world socialism.

For all their evident differences, however, there were connections and elements of convergence between the YAR and the PDRY that would keep the prospect of unification alive. Commonalities derived from and were perpetuated by specific political events that reverberated throughout the country and the region, and shared environmental and economic niches at the periphery of the Arabian Peninsula. In other words, they converged on a common pattern of instability and dependency.

Political violence and political order

A vicious cycle of political violence gripped both republics. Two civil wars raged in the 1960s. Subsequent power struggles produced seven irregular leadership transitions, three more internecine wars, three inter-Yemeni border confrontations, and several regional uprisings, as summarized in table 2.2. Each government, positioning itself as the legitimate ruler of the whole, gave refuge and arms to the other's chronic oppositions-in-exile. A short-lived inter-Yemeni border clash in 1972 ended in Arab League mediation and the first of several official declarations of intent to unify. A few years later, three assassinations embroiled Sana'a and Aden in a cycle of intrigue. In late 1977, the body of then command council chairman, Ibrāhīm al-Ḥamdī, was found with the corpses of his brother and two unnamed French women. His successor, Aḥmad al-Ghashmī, died six months later when an Adeni emissary's briefcase exploded in his office. The following morning, amidst power struggles within the South's ruling party, a PDRY firing squad executed its own leader, Sālim Rubayi' 'Alī.

Unresolved domestic issues were aggravated by cold-war and regional politics. A peasant rebellion headed by pro-unity progressives under the banner of a National Democratic Front (NDF or *al-Jabha al-Waṭaniyya al-Dīmuqrāṭiyya*) won widespread if covert support in the YAR, especially among Shāfi'ī sharecroppers, workers, and students in the southern uplands (the Aden hinterland). The PDRY under 'Abd al-Fattāḥ Ismā'īl backed the NDF, sparking border skirmishes in early 1979. More Arab mediation produced a Kuwait Pact declaring the Yemens' intent to unify. At the height of tensions, the USA, with an eye on events in Iran and Afghanistan and eager to strengthen relations with Saudi Arabia, transferred weapons to Sana'a via Riyadh to repel the presumed communist advance from the South. Subsequently with both

Table 2.2. *Regime changes in the YAR and PDRY*

Date	Event	Deposed	Inaugurated
The YAR, 1962–1990			
September 26 1962	Free Officer coup, YAR declared	Imam Aḥmad	ʻAbd Allāh al-Sallāl
November 1968	compromise ends civil war	ʻAbd Allāh al-Sallāl	ʻAbd al-Raḥmān al-Iryānī
June 13 1974	corrective coup	ʻAbd al-Raḥmān al-Iryānī	Ibrāhīm al-Ḥamdī
October 1977	mysterious assassination	Ibrāhīm al-Ḥamdī	Aḥmad al-Ghashmī
June 1978	briefcase of PDRY emissary explodes	Aḥmad al-Ghashmī	ʻAlīʻAbd Allāh Ṣāliḥ
The PDRY, 1967–1990			
November 30 1967	Independence day, NLF assumes power	colonial system	Qaḥṭān al-Shaʻbī
June 1969	corrective move	Qaḥṭān al-Shaʻbī	Sālim Rubayiʻ ʻAlī
June 26 1978	death by firing squad	Sālim Rubayiʻ ʻAlī	ʻAbd al-Fattāḥ Ismāʻīl
April 1980	"retirement for health reasons"	ʻAbd al-Fattāḥ Ismāʻīl	ʻAlī Nāṣir Muḥammad
January 1986	thirteen-day civil war, ʻAbd al-Fattāḥ Ismāʻīl and others killed	ʻAlī Nāṣir Muḥammad	ʻAlī Sālim al-Bīḍ Ḥaydar Abū Bakr al-ʻAṭṭās Yāsīn Saʻīd Nuʻmān

American and Soviet arms the YAR army, backed by tribal irregulars and a shadowy Saudi-funded Islamic Front (*al-Jabha al-Islāmiyya*), chased the insurgents into the South. There was now another significant opposition-in-exile. The *al-Jabha al-Islāmiyya*, some of whom were later recruited to join the Afghan *mujāhidīn* as part of a group known colloquially as *Afghān al-'Arab*, saw the PDRY as another instance of Soviet imperialism.

From 1978 onward, President 'Alī 'Abd Allāh Ṣāliḥ surrounded himself with an elite Republican Guard commanded by his brothers and cousins from the Sanḥān tribe of the Ḥāshid confederation. He pulled key Ḥāshid and Bakīl figures into Sana'a's orbit, enforced the draft to bring most men into national service, forged key alliances among the urban bourgeoisie, fortified the security establishment, flattered friendly intellectuals, and constructed some new civilian institutions. Ṣāliḥ's government maintained good relations with Saudi Arabia, Kuwait, and Iraq, as well as with both halves of Europe. The 1986 state visit of then Vice President George Bush, occasioned by the discovery of oil in Ma'rib by the Texas-based Hunt oil company, was taken as a measure of support for the regime.

In the 1980s, President Ṣāliḥ unveiled a new institutional–constitutional arrangement under the General People's Congress (or perhaps general popular conference *al-mu'tamar al-sha'bī al-'āmm*). In 1982 700 delegates, including significant numbers of associates of the Islamic Front, were elected to the GPC through the LDA election process; another 300 deputies were appointed by the president. The *Mu'tamar*, casting itself as the non-partisan, all-inclusive bearer of the banner of early nationalist, third-force, and cooperative conferences,[29] unanimously approved a quasi-constitutional document called the National Pact (*al-Mīthāq al-Waṭanī*). The *Mīthāq* called for a sort of representative consultation through non-partisan annual popular conferences as well as a parliament. Henceforth the GPC's fifty-man "permanent committee" set its goals as state building, democracy, constitutional rule, modernization, and "building military and security institutions."[30] In 1986, new legislation transformed the LDAs into local councils for cooperative development (LCCDs), now responsible to the Ministry of Local Administration. Elections for the LCCDs constituted a new GPC. This time the Islamic Front did not do as well, but Islamists were permitted to publish a newspaper and given university and security posts. Finally, in 1988, candidates elected in 128 local districts joined thirty-one presidential appointees in a reconstituted *Majlis al-Shūrā*. This 159-member body, along with the last PDRY parliament of 111 delegates, would later ratify the unification accords.

Meanwhile, two more Southern leaders came and went. The latter of these, ʻAlī Nāṣir Muḥammad, lost a gamble to eliminate rivals in the ruling Yemeni Socialist Party (YSP) in January 1986. The ensuing two-week gun-battle in Aden, Abyan, and other locations killed off thousands of party cadres, leaving the PDRY physically, psychologically, and socially scarred.[31] ʻAlī Nāṣir himself and tens of thousands of his followers, including many soldiers, fled North or abroad. The party leadership was decimated. A group of civilian Ḥaḍramīs left standing when the smoke cleared – ʻAlī Sālim al-Bīḍ, Ḥaydar Abū Bakr al-ʻAṭṭās, and Yāsīn Saʻīd Nuʻmān – assumed leadership of the party-state while top military commands went to Radfān tribesmen. In 1988, the YAR and PDRY armies clashed again, in the semi-desert easternmost frontier between Ma'rib (in the YAR) and Shabwa (in the South), where oil production was then in its infancy.[32]

Despite the contrasts between "law and order" in the South and "chaos" in the YAR, the two legal systems shared a common trait: the presence of extra-judicial military and security courts who needed no charge, warrant, or hearing to detain, imprison, or even execute dissidents. Security forces (*al-amn*), trained and equipped on both sides of the border by East Germany and Iraq, among others, captured an important share of state budgets and employed thousands of agents to monitor citizens. A parallel, extra-legal police force-cum-judiciary wielded tremendous influence in each state structure. Over half of both budgets went to general administration and the military. In the YAR, security alone was over half of all state spending. These are indicators of the overdevelopment of the armed forces at the expense of civilian government. Moreover, YAR–PDRY military rivalry justified both army and security expenditures.

Human rights records in both states were poor. The concerns of Amnesty International (AI) in the YAR centered around the unlawful detention and possible torture of political prisoners accused of cooperation with the NDF, even after the cease-fire and general amnesty in 1982.[33] Other journalists, intellectuals, and political activists were detained without charge at the *al-Amn al-Markazī* building beyond the ring road for periods from twenty-four hours to several years; some were tortured. The military conducted its own tribunals. Although most of these abuses were beyond control of the courts, in the 1980s neo-fundamentalists brought suit against secular writers for "blasphemous" writings. At least one Sana'a University professor fled to Aden after being sentenced to death on these fraudulent grounds. Also, some state-authorized public floggings, mutilations, and hangings in the 1980s by self-declared enforcers of Sharīʻa were little more than mob lynchings.

Table 2.3. *Basic economic indicators, YAR and PDRY, 1987*

	YAR	PDRY
population (mil)	8.5	2.3
GNP per capita ($)	590	420
life expectancy at birth	51	51
current account balance ($mil.)	−607	−122
net workers' remittances ($mil.)	428	303
ODA as % of GNP	8.1	8.2
external debt ($mil.)	2,389	1,724
GDP ($mil)	4,270	840
– % agriculture	28%	16%
– % industry	17%	23%
– % services, etc.	55%	61%

Source: World Bank, *World Development Report 1989*, pp. 164–66, 198, 202

Thousands of Southerners fled the PDRY: eventually as many as 500,000 former colonial civil servants, officers, and conservative business, tribal, and feudal families.[34] The victorious NLF launched a "reign of terror," as it is known in the literature on comparative revolutions. Uncounted numbers of its opponents died, languished in security prison, or simply disappeared. Some egregious abuses originated in the popular and land reform courts of the 1970s, others in *ad hoc* tribunals, and still others by order of military or party officers. The most hated and feared man in the country was the notorious security chief "Muḥsin." Because every new regime issued a new list of state criminals, security prisons remained full even after the periodic amnesties. Fifteen hundred people were detained after the events of 1986, and much was made of trials of a hundred traitors. Whereas the YAR permitted the International Committee of the Red Cross to inspect its admittedly medieval and rat-infested jails, Aden denied access to al-Fatḥ and al-Manṣūra prisons, and other detention centers.

Dependence on foreign aid

For at least two thousand years Yemen has been known as Arabia Felix, the most temperate, verdant, productive region of the Peninsula, exporting to the Levant, Africa, and Asia. Yet in the late twentieth century the agrarian southwest corner of Arabia became a dependent, least-developed economy. Statistics on literacy, infant mortality, access to safe water supply, and so forth showed that standards of living were among the worst in the region, nay the world. Its relationship to the world economy was as supplier of cheap labor to Saudi Arabia, and its position in the global balance of power was as a peripheral front line in the cold war. In the short term this position afforded some affluence in the form of remittances and foreign aid. Together with a common, if varied, ecological base, moreover, these circumstances molded both economies in similar ways. While private transfers financed private consumption, public transfers enriched the public sectors of both economies. Thus although real-estate and retail markets were private in the North and nationalized in the South, patterns of new investment in the wishful-capitalist YAR and the socialist-oriented PDRY were such that the two economies converged on a common pattern: fixed capital investment was concentrated in the state and "mixed" sectors of both economies.[35]

During the early 1970s both the YAR and the PDRY joined the International Monetary Fund and the World Bank. In the process the YAR established a semi-public central bank, issued a national currency, the riyāl, and created a Central Planning Organization (CPO) to draw up budgets and loan proposals. At about the same time, the Planning Ministry in the PDRY took control of a budget now denominated in PDRY dinārs, also with help from the World Bank. The CPO and the Planning Ministry coordinated the technocratic functions of the respective states, following common strategies proposed by the multilateral lending agencies (national transport, basic industry, integrated rural development, joint ventures, oil exploration).

Grants and loans from a wide range of international and regional donors financed the North's belated modernization. Between 1974 and 1984, the foundations of a national infrastructure was built: a 2,000-kilometer grid of two-lane tarmac highways; urban water, sewerage, and power for the five cities; Hodeida harbor and three airports; modern urban public hospitals and some provincial clinics; and campuses for university, technical, and secondary education. These construction projects, executed by Chinese, South Korean, and Italian contractors and work-crews, contributed to rapid urbanization and high rates of growth in the services sector. Somewhat counter-intuitively, international assistance from both the socialist and the capitalist worlds contributed to the accumulation of assets in the public sectors of both the PDRY and the YAR.

The World Bank, the UN, and Europeans trained a technocratic elite speaking English, German, Czech, or Russian to manage the YAR, while Kuwait and other donors built up the public education system. The public university, health workers', teachers' training, and research institutes made Sana'a look more like a modern city, while roomy contemporary Gulf-style structures gave a suburban air to small towns. In the mid-1980s some 20,000 Arab expatriates, mostly Egyptians or

Table 2.4. *Central government expenditures, YAR and PDRY, 1977*

	YAR	PDRY
general administration	20%	16%
defense and security	54%	43%
education	9%	17%
health	3%	6%
construction and communications	9%	2%
agriculture	2%	2%
other services	3%	5%
finance (debt service)	–	9%
Total	100%	100%

Sources: World Bank 1979 (PDRY) p. 104; World Bank 1979 (YAR) p. 245

Sudanese, with little appreciation of Yemeni history, nationalism, or even dialect were teaching in Yemen. Many were religious conservatives recruited by Saudi Arabia to reflect the kingdom's political ideology. The well-endowed colleges of science and Sharī'a at Sana'a University attracted the most conservative scholars. 'Abd al-Majīd al-Zindānī, a frequent visitor to Saudi *'ulamā'*, zealot for the Afghan jihad, and advocate of a puritan ethic, gender segregation, and Islamic science, was a popular guest speaker at the university. In addition, Saudi money helped finance a string of Wahhabi-oriented "scientific institutes" built by the Islamic Front in the early 1980s.

Southerners built on their colonial infrastructural legacy. Water, power, transport, health, and schooling systems were expanded with foreign assistance. Radical critics of elitist colonial schooling made a concerted effort to boost literacy through heavy expenditures on general, technical, and specialized academic training.[36] The PDRY was far more self-sufficient in training than the YAR; its teachers, university faculty, nurses, all more numerous, per thousand head of population, than in the North, were mostly Yemeni. Often YSP members, they taught an official history that affected the way the next generation thought about politics. Overall, as measured by variables such as literacy, child mortality, or women's participation, the PDRY started out and remained well ahead of the YAR. The latter was spending heavily on services and communications,[37] while the PDRY pursued a more sector-balanced development investment strategy.

The differences in sources of concessional finance were not what might be guessed from cold-war orientation. The withdrawal of UK subsidies that covered about two-thirds of Aden's budget, coupled with the flight of private capital and closure of the Suez Canal, nearly bankrupted Aden. True, during the revolutionary period, while the West and the conservative states of the Peninsula shunned the "outpost of socialist development in Arabia," the USSR, its allies, and China became the PDRY's primary bilateral benefactors. Eastern technology and management therefore permeated the dominant public sector. In addition, however, global multilateral agencies, led by the World Bank's International Development Agency (IDA), all apostles of economic liberalism, made major commitments even in the 1970s. Moreover, by 1980 Saudi Arabia, Kuwait, and Abu Dhabi joined Libya, Algeria, and Iraq in offering concessional credit. Official grants from Arab countries alone peaked at $126 million in 1982, and loans and grants combined from Arab sources of $600 million a year in the mid-1980s surpassed total Soviet assistance that was worth only $50 million in its last year, 1989.[38] By then, partly because the USSR evidently distanced itself from Aden after January 1986 and partly because of its own problems, Soviet influence was very much on the wane,[39] whereas the PDRY had partly mended its fences with neighboring countries.

North Yemen's unregulated economy, global non-alignment, and position as a "buffer" between the PDRY and the Peninsula's oil fields privileged it to aid from powers as divergent as Kuwait, Iraq, the Netherlands, the USSR, and China. Virtually every global, bilateral, and Middle Eastern donor, regardless of ideology, contributed to a level of official development assistance which rose to well over a billion dollars a year around 1980. After that, it fell to about half a billion dollars a year in 1985 and less than $100 million in 1988.

By the end, then, both Yemens relied on a similar list of creditors. The World Bank and other multilateral lenders advised both Yemens, and both owed 45 or 46 percent of their foreign debt to the USSR, mostly long-term credit for military equipment. Apart from the Soviet Union, the YAR borrowed from Saudi Arabia, Iraq, Kuwait, the Netherlands, and China, and the PDRY from China, Kuwait, Bulgaria, the GDR, Abu Dhabi, Czechoslovakia, Algeria, and Iraq. Sana'a owed 31 percent of its debt to Arab sources, compared to 22 percent for Aden. The PDRY's debt to China and Warsaw Pact countries other than the USSR was 19 percent of its total compared to only 4 percent for the YAR. Japan and some European nations lent only to Sana'a, and the YAR was a special beneficiary of Netherlands and West German development efforts, but several Western donors and lenders had programs in both Yemens.[40] These figures exclude grants, whether the substantial cash subsidies from the rich Arab countries or soft assistance from industrial states in the form of scholarships and technical experts. All in all, differences were less stark than one might imagine.

Public and private sectors

In the PDRY, the nationalizations of 1969–77 coincided with a deep recession due to the port's virtual closure and the flight of private capital. Donor funding became the principal source of investment, reinforcing the dominance of the public sector in manufacturing and industrial services. China and East Germany set up agricultural product processing plants, flour mills, textiles, and canneries, and the state fishing corporation received Soviet, World Bank, Danish, and Kuwaiti assistance. Industry represented nearly a quarter of GDP by 1980 and about 15 percent of employment; the public sector managed about 70 percent of the industrial sector[41]: power and water, the Aden refinery, publishing construction, several clothing and food-processing plants, and toolmakers. Mixed companies, some of them joint ventures with foreign corporations, produced cigarettes, batteries, and aluminum utensils. Private manufacturers were mostly in smaller-scale plastic, knitwear, glass, food, and paper-goods industries, or traditional crafts. The state managed docks, shipping, trucking, busing, and the airline, and left only small retail services to the private sector.

Private investment and capital were not entirely absent from the PDRY, however, which began "on the road to socialism" but never arrived. Most land in Aden governorate and nearly a third in Laḥj became state farms, but well over half of all farm land was classified as cooperative, and up to a quarter as private.[42] Informal-household sector farms and crafts subsidized by private remittances still characterized many villages.[43] British Petroleum stayed on as a contractor for the refinery, and other foreign firms provided other high-tech services.[44] In 1980, private concerns generated over half the value of agriculture, construction, and trade, while the public sector dominated fisheries, industry, and, by a small margin, transport; the cooperative sector contributed a third of the value of agricultural production, but in fishing it was about the same as that of the private sector.[45] Foreign (Japanese) companies' share of fish catches rose from 9 percent in 1978 to 25 percent in 1982, and domestic private catches from zero to 15 percent during the same period.[46]

As World Bank calculations in table 2.5 illustrate, the public and planned "mixed" sectors generated less than half of GDP in 1982, and it was only in industry and air-and-sea transport that the state was dominant. Although the number of highly mechanized state farms had increased from eighteen in 1975 to forty-seven in 1982, farm production was nearly two-thirds private. In construction, public planned projects generated more than two-thirds of demand, but local and sometimes

Table 2.5. *Proportional value of production by ownership and sector, PDRY, 1982*

	Private	Public/Mixed	Cooperative
agriculture	58%	11%	31%
fisheries	45%	14%	34%
industry	25%	75%	0%
construction	63%	37%	0%
transport	46%	54%	1%
trade	63%	30%	7%
Total	47%	45%	8%

Source: World Bank, 1979 *PDRY, Special Economic Report*, p. 9, table 1.4

foreign private capital did over half the work.[47] During the subsequent recession, moreover, and after the 1986 debacle, the economy was decentralized further. According to the 1988 census, of nearly 35,000 establishments, 75 percent were private, 21 percent governmental, and the remainder cooperative or joint ventures. Just over a quarter of the workforce was in the government sector.[48] All in all, the ruling YSP controlled most large modern enterprises and real estate in Aden and some other towns, but a significant sphere of informal, traditional, and micro-enterprise activity endured, some foreign and local firms contracted for the state, and both laborers and investors remitted earnings from abroad.

North Yemen's liberal private investment incentives had limited impact on manufacturing: even counting small workshops, industry contributed less than 20 percent of GDP and only a tenth of employment. Foreign investors such as Rothmans and Canada Dry preferred licensing arrangements with state corporations wherein they lent their names, equipment, and expertise to the YAR's "mixed" sector plants on a contractual basis.[49] Most global corporations were scared off by the high cost of unskilled labor, six-and-nine month backlogs at Hodeida port, political instability, poor infrastructure, and the chaotic state of commercial law. Instead, international publicly guaranteed loans financed the large-scale power and water, national tobacco, cotton, cement, textiles, milk, publishing, and petroleum companies. The USSR and China built cement and textile factories, mills, and bakeries, the World Bank backed a battery plant and the electricity corporation, Saudi airlines invested in Yemenia, and a joint YAR–PRC Yemen–China Construction Engineering Corporation was formed. The Hayel Sayeed industrial complex outside Taiz, producing soaps, plastics, and sweets mainly for the domestic market, dominated private manufacturing. Otherwise private industry consisted of "workshops," mostly construction-related producers of stained-glass windows, wood or metal doors, and bricks; or automotive repair shops. Retail construction contractors, equipment and commodity importers, and currency dealers helped round out the nascent national bourgeoisie resident in the North.

Despite overwhelmingly private land ownership in the YAR, where farming still employed three-quarters of the domestic labor force, public investments nonetheless dwarfed private capital formation in the farm sector. Bilateral and World Bank financing engorged the Ministry of Agriculture, dubbed by one consultant a "clearing-house for foreign aid." The largest projects such as the Tihama Development Authority and the Southern Uplands Rural Development Program involved heavy public investment in irrigation, roads, electrification, extension centers, equipment support, and credit schemes. Other important projects irrigated the semi-desert eastern regions around Ma'rib and the Jawf, where military officers bought land and took advantage of cheap credit. These projects failed in the effort to foster heavy private investment, however. Whereas investments in YAR farms was more than three-quarters private in 1974/75, by 1982 the public sector accounted for 61 percent of gross fixed capital formation in agriculture.[50]

Basic communications, utilities, education, and health facilities dominated YAR civilian development projects in the first two decades after 1962. By 1982, services and communications claimed two-thirds of gross fixed capital formation. Investment in services was 86 percent public, and in communications half public. Power and water were 95 percent public. These infrastructural investments contributed to the growth of the public sector's share in the economy: private investors generated two-thirds of recorded fixed capital formation in 1975 but only one-third seven years later.[51]

In the mid-1980s, declining aid and remittances, inflation, uncontrolled currency exchange, soaring balance-of-trade deficits, and the disastrous effects of unfettered import of food on domestic agriculture forced Sana'a's technocrats, heretofore models of "hands-off" economic management, to change strategies. To protect what remained of a formerly substantial cushion of foreign currency reserves from the ravages of recession, the YAR enacted sweeping policy changes. The riyāl, stable at 4.5 to the dollar during the boom years, was pulled downward by the decline in aid and remittances and the printing of new bills to cover shortfalls in the state budget. When it dipped to 18 to the dollar in early 1987, the Central Bank shut down private money-lenders who normally sit publicly in Sana'a shopfronts counting thick stacks of

Table 2.6. *Investments by ownership and sector, YAR, 1974–1986*

	1974/5		1982		1982–86	
	Public	Private	Public	Private	Public	Private
agriculture and fisheries	22%	78%	61%	39%	75%	25%
mining*			89%	11%	97%	3%
manufacturing	62%	38%	39%	61%	31%	69%
electricity and water*			95%	5%	94%	6%
construction	0	100%	0	100%	0	100%
trade and hotels**					11%	89%
transport and communications	51%	49%	68%	32%	73%	27%
financial institutions**					64%	5%
Total	35%	65%	68%	32%	66%	33%

* mining, power, and water were included under manufacturing in 1975

** trade, hotels, financial services included under services in 1975, 1982

Between 1976 and 1981, the cooperative sector generated one-third of investments in transport, 11% of investments in water supply, and 24% of investments in health and education. (Carapico, "Political Economy of Self-Help," table 8.10).

Source: World Bank. 1979 *Yemen Arab Republic, Current Position and Prospects* (cooperative sector counted as private)

CPO, "Evaluation of the Second Five-Year Plan, April 1987," pp. 33–37 (cooperative sector counted as public)

Saudi and American notes. This was the first of many brief periodic shut-downs of the currency traders, including one who controlled some 75 percent of labor remittance transfers. Simultaneously, all imports were banned temporarily, and fruit and vegetable imports suspended indefinitely. Finally, "presumably to stem the effects of the import ban on the prices of basic necessities, the government reserved 60 percent of all imports for the newly merged Foreign Trade, Grain, and Military Corporations."[52] The Military Economic Corporation, already a trade and agricultural giant, prospered under new management, the Ministry of Supply. To compensate for the collapse of customs revenues, the government centralized the municipal and farm taxes heretofore used for rural infrastructure.

Massive government intervention into currency markets, tougher taxation, import licensing, incorporation of the chambers of commerce into the regime, and other measures alienated much of the autonomous commercial elite. The new policies simultaneously drove some traders underground and offered others new earnings from within the enlarged government-managed sector. Consequences included on the one hand a buoyant trade in smuggling currency, arms, and drugs into Saudi Arabia; and, on the other hand, enhanced opportunities for government clients through the awarding of import contracts, subsidized credit, and outright graft.[53]

Although neither Yemen faced debt restructuring during the 1980s, the post-1983 oil recessions, experienced second hand, put them both in increasingly dire economic straits. The general malaise in industrialized socialist economies also trickled down. As migration and aid leveled off while population and social needs continued to grow, both states faced acute fiscal crisis. At the darkest hour, the discovery of oil offered to save them from economic collapse by offering a source of earned revenue for public coffers.

The oil industry and the fall of the iron curtain

Despite radically different cold war orientations, therefore, a confluence of global, regional, and domestic political and economic forces put them on a convergence course. The balance of forces in favor of unity was tipped by a series of further developments. First and foremost, discovery of oil in the inter-Yemen border region sparked hopes of a potential "take-off" and created incentives for cooperation. In 1984, when the Dallas-based Hunt Oil company found commercially viable petroleum deposits near Ma'rib in the southeastern YAR, prospects for attracting foreign private investment improved for the first time since 1968. Soon

Exxon, and then a consortium of South Korean firms, bought into Yemen Hunt. Texaco, Elf Aquitaine, Total, Canadian Occidental, and USSR firms paid to drill for Yemeni oil. The Soviet company Technoexport made a major find in 1986 at Shabwa across the border from Ma'rib, and launched production. There were new commercial finds in 1987, 1988, and 1989, mostly south of the border, including the ultimately lucrative Ḥaḍramawt concession to Canadian Occidental.

Realization of the commercial potential below the Ma'rib–Shabwa basin required both inter-Yemeni cooperation and foreign technology. The last armed clashes between the YAR and the PDRY occurred in the border region around oil fields.[54] Joint production was an alternative to fighting it out. In addition, the YAR hoped to utilize Aden's port and the refurbished British Petroleum refinery. Therefore, the two national petroleum companies merged into a joint Yemen Company for Investment in Oil and Mineral Resources. Its 1989 joint production agreement with an international consortium consisting of Hunt and Exxon, the Kuwait Foreign Petroleum Exploration Corporation, Total, and two Technoexport subsidiaries[55] signified the economic merger of the formerly "socialist" South and the "capitalist" North.

Unity also offered other potential economic benefits. International development banks, anticipating economies of scale, had already approved loans for unification of the electrical grid, and for joint projects in the fields of agricultural export, port facilities, and tourism. Unity favored the interests of Yemen's traders, financiers, and manufacturers in much the same way as German unity, for it heralded new private investment opportunities. Although some Yemeni "capitalists" in Sana'a, Hodeida, Taiz, Saudi Arabia, and abroad still harbored a residual hatred of the revolutionaries for expropriating parts of their Adeni fortunes, others saw in Aden, the Ḥaḍramawt, and the rest of the South new frontiers for commercial and private construction, retail trade, and consumer services. Yemenis abroad seemed ready to invest, and planners on both sides were anxious to welcome them. With the reopening of the Suez Canal and developments in the oil sector, Aden's underutilized port and refining facilities would have more business than at any time in a generation. Expectations were high that Aden would be restored to its former glory, as a free port rivaling Hong Kong. The investment capital available in the North and abroad, combined with Southern human resources, would create new enterprises in the private, public, and mixed sectors to sell foodstuff to the Gulf. Large state enterprises would coexist with the private sector and with state–private partnerships in oil and gas production; farmland would be privatized gradually, region by region. Traders quickly flooded Southern markets with goods, mostly imports. Finally, with a GNP per capita of about $600 annually, the YAR was at risk of "graduating" from eligibility for concessional finance, so unity was a way of prolonging aid targeted for low-income countries, especially from the World Bank.

In the international arena, to the extent that friction between the two Yemens was a function of cold-war politics, changes in the Soviet Union and Central Europe were necessary for Yemeni unity. The heretofore insurmountable obstacle of cold-war competition in the third world was removed. Although scholars who examined the PDRY discredited the facile portrait of Aden as a mere puppet of Moscow,[56] and Sana'a was hardly a darling of the West, through the mid-to-late 1980s any move toward Yemeni unity would have sounded alarms about the potential destabilization of the balance of power in the Red Sea/Horn of Africa/Arabian Peninsula region. In the event, the Yemens actually unified just ahead of the Germanys, but the two mergers were part of global transformation.

Regional trends played a more contradictory role. In 1986, after the fighting in Aden and amidst oil discoveries in the region where the PDRY and the YAR met Saudi Arabia near the empty quarter, Saudi Arabia made a claim to areas of Shabwa and Ḥaḍramawt. This territorial claim included the bloc managed by the Saudi-based Nimr petroleum group, owned by Bin Mahfuz, a family of Ḥaḍramī origin that also owns Saudi Arabia's National Commercial Bank.[57] Although Riyadh's claim was directed mainly against the PDRY, it also included some Northern territory. In response to this gesture and its exclusion from the Gulf Cooperation Council, the YAR joined the Arab Cooperation Council with Egypt, Jordan, and Iraq.[58] In addition, the dwindling cash flow from the Gulf to Sana'a gave the YAR greater latitude from Saudi Arabia and also Kuwait than previously. The kingdoms still regarded Yemeni unity as anathema in many ways, and Saudi Arabia would press its claims in a brief skirmish with the PDRY in 1989, and later by warning foreign companies out of the "disputed" zone and offering Saudi passports to Ḥaḍramīs in the Ḥaḍramawt. But at the time, perhaps because they anticipated an Iraqi threat, while Iraq and Libya praised Yemeni unity, the Gulf kingdoms did not block it. Inside Yemen, Saudi influence seemed to flow through a new political party, the Yemeni Reform Grouping, heir to the Islamic Front.

Additional impetus sprang from domestic considerations. Unity was an ever-popular cause long valorized by all pretenders to power. "Yemen," not the YAR or the PDRY, inspired patriotism. The two states were each in their own way so flimsy, flawed, and illegitimate that merger was each leadership's best option. This point is often made with respect to the PDRY, whose very *raison d'être*, not to mention most of its bilateral assistance, seemed to evaporate with the demise of socialist party-states in Europe and the move toward German unification. Its own last internal bloodbath in 1986 drained the last dredges of genuine revolutionary fervor.

After January 1986, a reformist movement took shape in Aden as a weakened regime desperate for hard currency tolerated the beginnings of the third political opening. There were clear overtures toward the absentee bourgeoisie in the North and the Gulf. New policies welcomed private investments in tourism and liberalized terms of fishing and oil concessions. Show trials became a forum for legal defense, while elsewhere constraints on speech, press, and association loosened. The impetus for this tentative but unmistakable liberalization evidently came from within and beyond the party. Northern Socialists in exile in the PDRY, members of the party but not the power structure, urged the YSP towards party pluralism, (*ta'addudiyya)* human rights (*ḥuqūq al-insān)*, citizen rights, freedom of intellectual pursuits, and other liberties. As a first step, intellectuals, capitalist businessmen, and popular organizations should be engaged in the ongoing constitutional and unity negotiations.[59] In view of *perestroika* in the USSR, the events of January 1986 in the PDRY, and political currents in the YAR, one Northern exile argued, it was time for tolerance of opposition parties and relaxation of restrictions on the press.[60]

Although the official YSP line was still that the party controlled democracy, these issues were debated within and beyond the ruling cadre. The Yemeni Writers' Guild, a unified organization of intellectuals, held seminars and published essays on unity and democracy. A new PDRY elections law, promulgated on the eve of unification, relaxed nomination and polling supervision and redrew constituency lines.[61] Local popular councils were given authority and budgetary discretion beyond the vague functions outlined in the constitution, and significant numbers of non-Socialists not only got onto candidate lists but won in local elections. The government, according to then-US ambassador to Sana'a Charles Dunbar, seemed to reach a "tacit agreement" with newspapers to allow "freer journalistic expression": the spring of 1990 saw "considerable ferment" in the PDRY media, "in contrast to the silence of the still highly disciplined" fourth estate in the YAR – as well as "the first stirrings of political demonstrations and strikes."[62] *Ṣawt al-'Ummāl*, the technically independent organ of the trades unions congress, having survived since colonial days, now exercised reborn editorial autonomy.

The YAR was tottering, too, although it was not yet liberalizing. Lacking any moral vision, the GPC enjoyed little support beyond the civil service and the army. Businesses and consumers resented economic austerity measures and the recession that deepened after Gulf donors further trimmed aid budgets. As discontent spread, the government became obsessed with internal security. Tensions were so high that by the summer of 1989, a relatively trivial altercation that began when a soldier at a Ma'rib checkpoint slapped a tribeswoman driving an unlicensed truck escalated into a small-scale war between the army and her tribe. The army first engaged her kinsfolk in tribal-style retaliation, then violated tribal principles by opening fire on a dozen *shaykhs* who came to negotiate. A petrol shortage in Sana'a that week, which happened to be a holiday, was credited to some Bakīlī tribes having "cut" the pipeline from the Ma'rib oil fields. Even as the president rushed to Ma'rib to contain the damage, the city-dwellers, tribesmen, and security forces braced for further political violence. It seemed at the time that only a dramatic gesture could preserve the regime.

The YAR state was just as ideologically and financially bankrupt as the PDRY, and administratively much weaker. The contrast between the "soft" YAR state and its relatively more orderly Southern counterpart went well beyond Jeanne Kirkpatrick's "authoritarian/totalitarian" definition of socialist dictatorships as more repressive than free-market authoritarian dictatorships. By almost any indicator – proportion of girls or boys in school, taxation capacity, command of the economy, recruitment of soldiers, policing capacity, the hegemony of state law, ideological coherence – the YAR was far less able to exert control of society than the PDRY.[63] Indeed, the YAR came up short on most of the standard definitions of a state. It lacked a "monopoly over the use of violence," clearly defined borders, an operative constitution, autonomy from outside powers, especially Saudi Arabia, and a legitimizing ideology.[64] And the YAR leadership was decidedly illiberal: on the eve of unification its president denounced pluralism and cited the military as an example of a democratic institution.

This merger, then, was not like Germany's, where a rich democratic powerhouse absorbed a failed system and sent socialists into disgruntled opposition. The distribution of power in the first unity government, the constitution, other documents and public statements treated the two sides as equal partners despite the North's fourfold population majority. Based on past performance, they seemed to have military parity. Each fancied itself capable of out-maneuvering the other.

The unity accords

In short, everything – global transformations, economic factors, popular sentiments, and their own self-interests – propelled Sana'a's military command and Aden's politbureau toward unity.[65] Even after two decades of committee work on a draft constitution, the announcement in November 1989 that full-scale unification was nigh, and the concomitant partial exchange of army divisions to guard each other's capitals,[66] took most Yemenis and diplomats by surprise. Under the unification accords, during a transition period formal power was shared equally between the partners. The five-man Presidential Council consisted of President 'Alī'Abd Allāh Ṣāliḥ and two other members of his General People's Congress (GPC) and (unofficial) vice president 'Alī Sālim al-Bīḍ and one other Socialist. Prime Minister Ḥaydar Abū Bakr al-'Aṭṭās and speaker of Parliament Yāsīn Sa'īd Nu'mān were both Southern Socialists. The 301-man Chamber of Deputies comprised the two preexisting, quasi-elected parliaments (159 from the YAR and 111 from the PDRY), plus thirty-one appointees from beyond the two political establishments. At the end of the thirty-month transition period, by November 1992, a popularly elected Parliament would select a new five-man Presidential Council that would, in turn, invite a prime minister to form a new government.

The Republic of Yemen's constitution was drafted by a committee of jurists who wove together Arab, Western, and socialist legal principles, drawing among other things on model Arab constitutions developed in Tunis. When approved by referendum in May 1991, it guaranteed more rights and liberties than most Arab constitutions. Constituency-based elections would create a 301-seat Chamber of Deputies and, indirectly, the Ministerial and Presidential Councils. In addition to universal adult suffrage, the constitution guaranteed freedom of thought and expression by speech, writing, or pictures within the law (Article 26), "equal treatment" without discrimination due to "sex, color, racial origin, language, occupation, social status, or religious beliefs" (Article 27); rights to legal defense and a presumption of innocence (Article 32); and political rights including the right to vote and freedom of association "inasmuch as it is not contrary to the constitution" (Article 39). It guaranteed the right to work (Article 21) and promised both private property rights and state ownership of wealth on behalf of the public (Article 6).

The two-party balance of power left extraordinary latitude for autonomous organizing in expanded public space, as discussed in chapter 6. Even as new press and party legislation was being written, some forty political organizations and a hundred new publications flooded the arena of public expression. Surveillance was curtailed, political prisoners released, many exiles permitted to return. The post-unity political euphoria crested in the parliamentary elections of April 27 1993, relatively the most open, free, and fair polling experience ever in the Arabian Peninsula. In these hotly contested, multiparty elections, a system of 301 winner-take-all districts each representing just under 50,000 inhabitants guaranteed that some four-fifths of the parliamentary seats would go to Northerners. Thus although the YSP virtually swept the South and picked up a few Northern seats and the GPC lost in many Northern districts to the more conservative Reform Grouping (Iṣlāḥ), independents, or members of small parties, the result was that in the elected government the YSP controlled far fewer votes than in the transition arrangements.

Unity and discord in the Republic of Yemen

Neither the constitution nor the elections proved binding on former ruling cliques who clung tenaciously to their armies, security forces, and public sectors. As rivalry between them intensified, their accords and arrangements unraveled, the troop exchange simply put opposing armies in easy shooting range, and discord over power sharing was such that Vice President ʿAlī Sālim al-Bīḍ and his colleagues ensconced themselves back in Aden. Finally, they declared a separate Democratic Republic of Yemen in what had been the PDRY. By July 1994, after two months of slow-moving conventional warfare, Sana'a's forces encircled and defeated a half-hearted resistance by what remained of the PDRY army. This civil war, now known as the war to preserve the union, had socio-economic as well as political causes.

Economic crisis

The economic aspirations attached to unity were dashed by disrupted external financial flows, a drought in 1990/91, and the financial costs of moving Southern politicians and institutions to Sana'a. The economy reeled from suspension of most bilateral aid, pressures of absorbing over three-quarters-of-a-million Gulf War returnees, and the subsequent precipitous drop in remittances. By 1993, despite oil-sector growth, real per capita income was 10 percent lower than in 1989. Unemployment was over 25 percent. The inflation rate was 35 percent in 1990, 50 percent in the first half of 1993. The balance of payments deficit for 1990–93 totaled $3.1 billion. Central Bank reserves plummeted to the equivalent of a month's import bills. The debt overhang, measured by the ratio of debt to GDP, was 200 percent – among the highest in the world. Not surprisingly, the IMF was recommending stringent adjustment measures.[67]

Now that oil rents deposited directly into state coffers constituted the main source of foreign exchange, the petrocarbon industry represented high political stakes. Rents constituted a new, substantial source of state revenue. New fixed assets of the state oil corporations and the mixed associated ventures – wells, rigs, pipelines, etc. – constituted a significant addition to public, indeed to total, productive fixed capital. Political competition over these assets ensued. Most oil and gas reserves proved to lie under the former PDRY's territory. The single largest field was Canadian Occidental's al-Masīla field in Ḥaḍramawt governorate, pumping at least 120,000 barrels a day. The Socialists claimed that Sana'a was centralizing all the revenues, thus profiting from "their" oil. Some Southerners now said that if only they had held out another couple of years the PDRY's economic woes would have been solved. Additionally, by 1994 earlier estimates of total reserves had been revised downward, and production was expected to stabilize at current levels of around 350,000 barrels per day. Dry holes, Saudi warnings to foreign firms not to do business in Yemen, and banditry in the Ma'rib–Shabwa region discouraged the major multinational firms from further commitments. Ultimately, the level of prosperity fantasized after the first strikes was not forthcoming. Popular material aspirations, based mostly on Saudi living standards, were not fulfilled.

Like the imams, the regime could now bestow private fortunes through government contracts. For instance, grain and sugar contracts went to powerful tribal families, notably al-Aḥmar and Abū Luḥūm,[68] while army officers prospered from their affiliation with the Military Economic Corporation and subsidized credits for irrigated cash farming in Ma'rib and al-Jawf. Independent entrepreneurs found themselves in an ambivalent relationship with the state, on the one hand given lucrative licenses but on the other hand taxed retroactively and pressed for donations to favored state causes. Inheritance of the PDRY estate prevented the YSP from going into political opposition, for doing so meant relinquishing public-sector housing and investments as well as military commands. Under worsening political and economic conditions, the YSP's financial portfolio and revenues from southern and eastern oil concessions were contested between the Aden and Sana'a leaderships in a zero–sum, or even a negative–sum, game.

Household resources were stretched to breaking point. Young men took to the streets in October 1991, when one economist estimated that the proportion of the population living below the poverty line had risen from 15 to 35 percent since the end of the Gulf War.[69] Frustrations erupted into urban consumer riots again in December 1992, when the riyāl, which had traded at fourteen to the dollar in May 1990, hit forty-two to the dollar. Demonstrators vandalized shops to protest at rising prices and political paralysis. By the time elections were held in April 1993, Southerners complained that the price of milk had quadrupled since unity while earnings dwindled. A year later, on the eve of the war, Sana'anī families protested that a fifty-kilogram sack of rice (economically priced in May 1990, at YR350) now cost 2,000 riyāls.[70] Virtually the whole price increase (some 575 percent) was accounted for by the collapse of the riyāl to more than seventy to the dollar. Families with riyāl-denominated incomes were reduced to buying rice in small quantities, often on credit from corner grocers, for the much higher retail price of about 60 riyāls a kilogram.

While most households could barely afford staples, the *nouveaux riches* state class lived in luxury. In Aden, YSP leaders enjoyed forty or fifty spacious, up-scale, air-conditioned public-sector homes. Sana'a's top political, military, and security elite owned lavish, walled, guarded, electronically equipped, cut-granite villas, and rode in chauffeur-driven top-of-the-line Toyota Land Cruisers with bullet-proof windows given out as favors by the Republican Palace. While working people waited in long lines for dirty beds in overcrowded, understaffed, underequipped public hospitals, the families of the political elite jetted to Jordan or Germany for treatment at public expense.

The 1994 civil war

Although the Saudi press and separatist propaganda emphasized cultural differences between North and South, the real divisions were between bureaucracies, armies, and ruling cliques. The Adeni professional class was appalled at how YAR ministries were run. The courts, in particular, could not have been much more different: British-trained judges pleaded with Northern jurists seeped in calligraphic tradition to have their judgments typed. Worse, the North seemed lawless: prosecutors winked at hijackings, kidnappings, assassination of Southern politicians, and unconcealed bearing of weapons. Yet even these sorts of legal-organizational issues were not the real problem, for within the judiciary was a common interest in the law, supported from civil society by attorneys, journalists, academics, and human rights groups. From the point of view of Northerners, *niẓām* began to supplant *fawḍā* within the courts and the justice department. No, the real disjuncture was within the two armed forces and the top leadership coteries, whose cultures were more similar than different.

While the two sides prepared to fight for control of the state, non-governing elites and popular organizations attempted to preserve unity with civility. The post-election impasse between Sana'a and Aden generated the impetus for an extra-constitutional multiparty committee to draft a new, more democratic constitutional proposal. In November 1993, prominent national figures outside the two ruling cliques initiated a national dialogue of political forces to hammer out a document of contract and accord. Signed by Ṣāliḥ, al-Aḥmar, al-Bīḍ, and the members of the Dialogue Committee on February 20 1994, it stipulated limits on executive powers, depoliticization of the military, administrative and financial decentralization, a bicameral legislature, judicial autonomy, and other reforms. The same night, the first skirmish in what would be the 1994 civil war occurred in Abyan.

Soon after full-scale war errupted on the night of May 4, Sana'a's forces were on the offensive. The victors broke through separatist lines in early July, and entered Aden flanked by remnants of the followers of 'Alī Nāṣir Muḥammad who had fled Aden and Abyan in 1986 and by some irregulars and volunteers recruited by Iṣlāḥ. In the process, they destroyed the public sector that had belonged to the PDRY. It may be true, as Sana'a asserted, that the mutineers made off with bank-books. Nonetheless, fixed assets were pillaged by victorious forces. Many villas were reoccupied by their pre-1986 tenants. Angry Adenis blamed this wanton destruction on vengeful people whose property had been confiscated twenty-five years earlier or reassigned after 1986, and on the Northern Military Economic Company anxious to wipe out competition. Damage in Aden was estimated by the UN at one to two hundred million dollars.[71]

The 1994 war resonated with unfinished business from Aden's 1986 intra-party bloodbath and Ṣāliḥ's campaign against the NDF which had officially ended the same year. Not only separatists but hundreds of other Socialists, dissidents, critics, and liberals fled the country, enlarging the counter-elite-in-exile. The top leadership in Sana'a in 1995 was virtually identical to what it had been in 1985, with the addition only of a few self-declared Islamists and a couple of token pro-Sana'a Socialists. Among the ironies were Saudi backing for elements of the Socialist leadership against former Saudi clients in Sana'a, the participation of 1986 exiles in the sacking of Aden, and the ways various "third" parties within Yemen reacted to the bipolar confrontation.

During the civil war, the Republican Palace appealed to a pliant, truncated parliamentary quorum for permission to extend the (extra-constitutional) state of emergency. On October 1 1994, this parliament rubber-stamped extensive amendments formally concentrating unprecedented constitutional power in the hands of the president. The collective Presidential Council was abolished in favor of a strong president empowered to appoint the vice president, a consultative council, and other officials, dissolve Parliament, declare states of emergency, etc. (Articles 105–26). Ground was lost on other fronts as well. The language of freedoms and social equality from the 1991 constitution were retained, but new provisions made the "family the basis of society" (Article 26), called on the state to "protect mothers and children" (Article 30) and called women the "sisters of men" (Article 31). Local administrative units and local councils are an "inseparable part of the power of the state" and "obligated" to execute the decisions of the president and the council of ministers "in all cases" (Article 145). New rules for the 1997 parliamentary elections prompted most parties to threaten a boycott, the press was restricted, and presidential elections were promised but not planned.

As the government resumed negotiations with the IMF to schedule eight to ten billion dollars in debt arrears, long-delayed economic reforms were announced. Socialist civil servants were laid off in the name of streamlining. "Communist" enterprises were "privatized" at fire-sale prices to carpet-baggers and scalawags; public utilities and hospitals were converted to money-making operations. When the riyāl slid to a new all-time low on the parallel market in late March 1995, Prime Minister ʻAbd al-ʻAzīz ʻAbd al-Ghanī instructed private traders to buy and sell riyāls within a percentage margin of the new official rate of YR60 to the dollar.[72] By summer steps toward debt rescheduling, rapprochement with Saudi Arabia, and a politically motivated sale of dollars in the private *sūq* halted the riyāl's free-fall. In September, a meeting of creditors in The Hague agreed to a plan to close the substantial financing gap of about half a billion dollars. The Paris Club renegotiated and extended structural adjustment loans: $200 million in standby credits at 6 percent interest from the IMF, and $160 million from the World Bank. The Netherlands and Germany also made deficit financing available, and the board of the IMF approved the package in March. Removal of subsidies doubled energy prices, notably petrol (from YR6 to YR12 per liter, still well below world market prices), cooking gas, and electricity. Import tariffs of 200 percent were imposed. In response, wholesalers withheld bulk quantities of grain, ghee, and sugar, causing even steeper price increases. These effects of economic adjustment prompted demonstrators to "shake the streets" again in April. Among those detained in connection with these disturbances were at least three dozen money-changers.

The war brought to the surface neo-Islamist and neo-tribal currents along with a security crackdown. Religion was wielded as a political weapon. When the mutineers retreated inside Aden with their weapons, the attackers obtained a *fatwā*, a revisionist legal opinion, from a right-wing jurist, ʻAbd Allāh al-Daylamī, to the effect that under such circumstances the rebels, not the attackers, are responsible for any harm to women and children. When vacant Cabinet posts were filled after the war, al-Daylamī was appointed minister of justice. The official Sana'a press took to legitimizing hijackings and even murder as "tribal custom," implying that such acts are immune from prosecution. After over a decade of incarceration the most famous Northern prisoner of conscience was invited by the speaker of Parliament to pursue tribal channels for his release. A reconstituted Political Security Organization resumed extra-judicial detentions during the state of emergency and reasserted a high public profile afterwards. Regime critics happened to be mugged in broad daylight in Sana'a, and "tribal" elements looted or firebombed newspaper and party offices. Challenges to defenders of human rights and liberties were formidable. Even the 1997 parliamentary elections, which allowed the GPC to restore fully its pre-unity control of governing institutions, were followed by yet another security round-up of regime critics.

Many of the rhetorical claims of the post-1994 government have revered religious and folk beliefs and customs, the same practices reviled in the negative propaganda of the exiled counter-elite. Government spokespersons, their critics, and outsiders all explain political behavior in terms of the enduring hold of Islamic and tribal values on the hearts and minds of Yemenis. By reviewing the full sweep of twentieth-century history, this chapter has shown that while it is true that the state has yet to replace traditional values with its own brand of civility, "traditionalism" is political conservatism in a 1990s context. The past hundred years have seen nearly continual upheaval, a long, complex, dramatic, uneven struggle easily presented in the teleology of unification, capitalism, and a sort of democracy. The reinvention of Islam and tribalism as political ideology in the 1990s is the product of societal transformation, of regional trends, and of post-socialism, not a resurrection of the actual past but its recreation in an affinity for privatization and an antipathy toward women, minorities, the press, and civil liberties. Having established the longer timeline, we now return to the pre-revolutionary stage of twentieth-century Yemeni history to explore more fully traditions that have not always inspired affection or been used for purely conservative purposes. It will be shown how the "primordial civic realm" gave rise to the sorts of political activism and community betterment activities analyzed in chapters 4 and 5.

3 Islam, tribes, and social services

The trajectories of state and market operate on a historically derived socio-cultural base, or anterior social formation, that we normally refer to as "traditional" or "primordial" society. The purpose of this chapter is to explore this customary, or *ahlī*, character of society in its political and economic dimensions. The focus is not on historical developments per se but on change. As the ethnographic literature shows, traditions are variable and contested. The anterior social formation, where politics and economics are embedded in a *Gemeinschaft*, reacted to political and economic transformations by adapting customary mechanisms to bridge the gap between the primordial civic realm and modern Yemeni civil society. By and large, this was a struggle over creation and control of public social capital.

The argument here is that there was a discernible "primordial civic realm" wherein religious and tribal mechanisms provided for public welfare and protected public spaces. These mechanisms are of two sorts, tribal–communal and religious–philanthropic. To understand these mechanisms it is necessary to look at both their ideological and their material content. The ideologies of tribalism and Islam depict moral economies assigning rights and responsibilities to individuals according to their status, and they contain ideas about equality, election, consultation, even rights of dissent. Nonetheless, the material basis of the public welfare mechanisms is based at least in part on deprivation and exploitation. Not surprisingly, people did not cling all that tenaciously to conditions of scarcity and appropriation. Rather, once material conditions changed, they transformed indigenous welfare mechanisms and the morality on which they were supposedly based. This was the beginning of a bourgeois civic realm – cash based, defining public spaces and public services in a new way. In other words, it represented the beginnings of civil society.

The political scientist addressing these issues treads gingerly on ethnographic generalization, all the more so when the thickly descriptive detail of the anthropological studies reveals each community's uniqueness. The role and meaning of "*shaykh*," the relationship between tribes and sanctuaries, patterns of land ownership and tenancy, legal and economic positions of women, and the material aspects of daily life all differ from one region to the next. Regional differences are material and ecological as well as ideological and historical. The sectarian split between Zaydīs and Shāfi'īs, the one Shī'a and the other Sunnī, for instance, is a doctrinal difference rooted in the history of conquests and dynasties.[1] It is also very much a geographical descriptor, with obvious topographical and accent markers (Shāfi'īs say *gīm*, Zaydīs say *jīm*). Zaydīs populate the rather spartan north-central highlands: the high semi-arid plateau of which Sana'a is the center; and the rugged, relatively verdant western mountains on the Red Sea side of the plateau. Many imams have risen and fallen in this territory in the past thousand years. This is also known as tribal territory, home to the powerful Ḥāshid and Bakīl tribal confederations who protected it from foreign conquest. Shāfi'īs predominate in the remainder of the country, that is, all along the coastal plains, in the southern uplands or "middle regions," and in the far east. Thus the Shāfi'ī areas contained the country's richest agricultural regions – the Ḥaḍramawt, Laḥj, and Red Sea Tihama wadis and the southern uplands of Taiz and Ibb, areas coveted and conquered by Rasulids, Ottomans, Englishmen, and Zaydīs at various times. As their irrigated gardens became large estates, sharecroppers, disarmed and deprived of property, all but lost their tribal identity; on the other hand within this region mountainous and desert regions remained quite "tribal." Merchant houses were situated in the ports, all Shāfi'ī – Aden, al-Mukallā', Hodeida, the smaller ports – or Taiz. Sectarian differences were simultaneously regional economic differences.

Within regions, ascribed status and economic position cross-cut one another. There is a well-known tripartite status hierarchy, socially relevant but not to be confused with class position. Families tracing their lineages to the Prophet, known as *sayyids*, constituted a small religious aristocracy including the imams and sultans. The vast majority of the population were tribespeople, mostly farmers and soldiers. Several low-status service groups of Muslims and Jews occupied the bottom of the social ladder. Within tribes, certain families trained their sons as *shaykhs* (tribal chiefs), and others as *qāḍīs* (judges qualified in Islamic law). Although these status categories were politically important, status alone brought neither wealth nor poverty, and relationships among the groups depended very much on local history, ecology, and socio-economic structures. The semi-feudal landowning elite contained members of both sects and all three "castes."

In this context, the issues of tribalism, traditionalism, and Islam are not general but specific. Part of the historical experience of theocracy is of an autocratic, atavistic imamate or the tyranny of quasi-feudal sultans and *sayyids*. Early twentieth-century political Islam in the sultanates, Shāfiʿī consciousness within the imamate, and some Northern tribes challenged traditional ruling interpretations of Islam based on *sayyid* privilege and the payment of tribute to imams or sultans. On the other hand, tribes' relationship to either theocratic rulers or colonial authorities was one of deep ambivalence. The imams and the British simultaneously feared the tribes, whom they depicted as warlike wild-men; and recruited tribal levies to pacify the fertile wadis. Nor did "the tribes" constitute a meaningful political bloc, as illustrated in both revolutions when different tribes even within the same confederation fought on different sides. Similarly, political Islam in twentieth-century Yemen has had royalist and populist elements, Shāfiʿī, Zaydī, or Wahhabi tendencies, and moments when it represented radical egalitarianism.

Cultural symbols and mechanisms can be applied differently under different circumstances. For example, tribes traditionally guard the territory bearing their name (including any *sayyid* or market enclaves); they may guarantee safe passage to travelers and guests, even providing water and lodging; extract a duty from traders; or refuse passage, a mechanism known as "cutting" the trail. When the British first started building motor-roads they encountered resistance from tribes protecting an important source of revenue. Even today tribes periodically "cut" routes in their territory in protest at government actions. Such actions could be read as resisting the penetration of the state and/or capitalism. On other occasions, however, tribes activated mechanisms such as "summons" and "subscription" to build their own roads, or used roadblocks to force the government to provide them with highways.

At mid-century most Yemenis lived in squalid, isolated ignorance. Rural surpluses financed superior public works in medieval towns, where elites lived surrounded by artisans and tradespeople, but even those were woefully inadequate. At the end of the pre-revolutionary period some of the customary mechanisms of philanthropy and community were turned toward the improvement of material standards of living. This chapter closes with a look at charitable and community projects in urban and rural areas where the penetration of new forms of trade was facilitated by local self-help. It is clear that these mechanisms carry over directly into the political activism in colonial South Yemen and "development cooperation" projects in scores of towns of these regions. Sometimes, these projects got mixed up with socialist, Baʿthī, Nāṣirī, or Islamist politics.

For a long time, Western scholars asked few questions about the historical allocation of resources for public works in the Arab world, in part because our construct of "traditional Islamic society" blurred the distinction between "public" and "private." Although we recognized that historically Arab or Islamic states offered few public services, and that public works were endowed by families or financed from community trusts, the political implications of this circumstance were not explored. Only a couple of scholars recognized that the region's pre-capitalist municipal, tribal, neighborhood, associational, and philanthropic networks wielded power and material resources rivaling those of the state,[2] and that the "*laissez-faire* attitude of the state" left social services to "pluralistic civic networks" with tremendous neighborhood-level strength and vitality.[3] Thus the private and community resources of traditional, decentralized Arab polities filled a large gap between government infrastructure and social needs. In early twentieth-century Yemen, before foreign capital financed modern infrastructure, most schools, water supplies, and other services were filled by semi-public, semi-private initiatives rooted in tribal and/or religious mechanisms.

True to Ibn Khaldūn, Yemen has an urban history of Islamic states and principalities, of fine architecture, and of scholarship; and a rural history of valor, tribes, and warfare. The symbiotic relationship between the urban-religious and rural-tribal orders has historically been one of profound ambivalence as one conquers the other, or, alternatively, tribes fight for and against rival sultanates. In the Islamic history of Yemen, sultanates and imamates endowed their various capital cities with fine mosques, academies, and public spaces. The tribal-communal order, more enduring but under the *ancien régime* less wealthy, provided far more modest services to villages and hamlets.

Institutions of community and tribute

The turn-of-the-century agrarian formation contained two modes of production. One consisted mainly of independent farm households loosely organized into larger circles of tribal identity and responsibility. Indigenous craft production and periodic markets articulated this system with a second, tribute-collecting system wherein landowner-tax collectors collected crop-shares from peasants. The tribute-collecting mode was integrated into traditional long-distance trade in export commodities such as coffee and incense. Well into the twentieth century, the former predominated in the semi-arid steppes of the interior, whereas the seaward mountains and the coastal valleys were most feudal. Not surprisingly, smallholders (tribesmen) tend to be more politically conservative (all other things being equal), whereas landless or indentured peasants join agrarian reform movements such as the National Liberation and National Democratic Fronts (the NLF and the NDF).

Roughly three-quarters of the Yemeni population were originally tribespeople who earned their livings from the land. The predominant household-based cereal-and-livestock-based agricultural system depended heavily on the ecological balance of water, grain, livestock, and labor.[4] Within extended, patrilocal, landowning households, men specialized in land management, and women in livestock husbandry, water and fuel collection, and food processing. Families consumed or recycled most of what they produced. Far from being self-sufficient, however, domestic units were integrated into community exchanges and interdependencies mandated by common use of water harvesting or irrigation systems, threshing floors, grazing, and woodlands as well as by common defense, disaster relief, and certain limited forms of labor exchange. While most farm tasks were performed by household labor, irrigation[5] management, natural disasters, even meeting state tax obligations – entailed collective action. This was organized through the tribe, led by someone called *shaykh*.

Tribespeople shared a form of common law (*'urf* or *ḥukm 'urfi*), leadership roles (especially *shaykh*), a sense of identity for members, and a code of ethical behavior (*qabyala*). Tribalism was a decentralized socio-political organization that presented itself as an alternative to the authority of the state: it helped organize production, group protection, dispute management, and relations with non-tribal groups. Within its territory, the tribe was responsible for defense, keeping the peace, guaranteeing the sanctity of local markets,[6] and either protecting or preventing the passage of travelers. Armed with the *janbiyya* (dagger) and, by the turn of the century, with rifles, tribesmen bore responsibility for protecting non-tribal groups and their physical spaces – the descendants of the Prophet and their protected (*ḥaram*, *hijra*, or *ḥawṭa*) villages or towns, and artisans or traders and their market-places. Along with women, all these groups were called "weak." In the inter-community competition for scarce resources, especially water, small wars occurred, but the main function of tribal law was to protect the peace. *Qabyala* accented collective responsibility within the concentric circles of tribal fraternity to come to one another's aid for these purposes.[7] The notions of equality, cooperation, and charity were obviously tribal ideals rather than models for daily behavior, for even within small groups there were bases for antagonism as well as fraternity, but *'urf* and *qabyala* provided both ethical codes and mechanisms for the peaceful resolution of disputes.

Most artisans and traders were neither tribal nor *sayyid.* Yemen's Jews, famed for their fine silverwork and other artistic crafts, as well as many Muslims, occupied a lower status. Specialized as butchers, barbers, male and female entertainers or healers, blacksmiths, silversmiths, weavers, potters, tanners, builders, carpenters, traders, bath- or inn-keepers, qāt or vegetable- (as opposed to grain-) growers, porters, and laborers, artisans and merchants were unarmed and "protected" by the tribes, but unlike the superior groups they were considered (in different degrees depending on occupation and wealth) "deficient" in honor. In the pre-cash economy that still dominated parts of Yemen in the early twentieth century, most of them contracted with farm communities or urban families to barter goods for grain and other necessities. Their domain was the *sūq*, or market. At the bottom of the social ladder were the so-called *akhdām*, literally "servants," working as urban street-sweepers or migrant harvest workers.

The "superior" social category, the *sayyid* (also called Hashemite or *sharīf*) lineages, could trace their genealogies back to the family of the Prophet Muḥammad. Women veiled, learned the Quran, and would marry only other *sayyids*; men were unarmed (or wore only a decorative dagger), often served as arbiters in tribal disputes, and were at least technically eligible for rulership of the Muslim community. Unlike the other two categories defined in large measure by occupation or relationship to the means of production, this was a purely honorific category, an ascribed position that qualified men for but did not guarantee them political influence. The twentieth-century Zaydī imamate and several Southern sultanates relied on the ideology of aristocratic fitness to rule and the assent of learned elder *sayyid* men as their legitimacy formula.

Religious and customary law

Traditional formal education revolved around the study of Sharī'a, or Islamic law. Young men and, more rarely, women, usually of the *sayyid* strata, studied the Quran, the Ḥadīth, and then the works of Yemeni and Arab jurists. A tribesman who studied Islamic law became a *qāḍī* or *'ālim* (singular of *'ulamā'*, scholars), elevating himself and his family to a status nearly equal to that of *sayyid* judges and scholars. Whether or not appointed "*ḥākim*" by the government, judges were qualified to mediate, adjudicate, or arbitrate cases brought to them by mutual consent of parties who agreed to pay for the service. The practice of Islamic law from judges' *dīwāns* depended, therefore, on their discretion, schooling, and reputations, rather than police, prisons, or the administrative power of the state.

In their domains, imams and sultans attempted to control legal scholarship and practice. The imamate's guiding doctrine was the Hādawī *al-Aḥkām* (rules or principles), a Zaydī school of jurisprudence said to most closely approximate Shāfi'ī Sunnī judicial doctrine. One of Imam Yaḥyā's main policy objectives, shared with some Shāfi'ī sultans, was to expand the application of Sharī'a – "that is, to limit the occasions in public and private life when *'urf* was used."[8] Theocratic rulers, not unlike the British, disparaged *'urf* or tribal law as *tāghūt* (barbarism). Geared toward settlement (by agreement, compensation, or, all else failing, retribution) and the maintenance of order (by protecting towns, holy sites, water sources, grazing- and wood-lands, and markets), various tribal codes, such as "Bedouin law," peasant versions of tribal law, law concerned with protection of "*corporatif*" status groups (the so-called *jār* or neighbor law), and inter-tribal law,[9] were copiously documented in quasi-constitutional "principles" (*aḥkām*) that included a code of chivalry obliging armed landowning men to protect "the weak," markets, and common interests. In a rural decentralized system wherein *shaykh*ship was measured in large part by ability to reconcile otherwise disputing parties, tribal law needed neither courts nor a state for its implementation. Like Islamic law, in this century common law found new applications in rapidly changing socio-economic conditions – for instance, water rights were affected by pumps and motors, and personal injury cases by traffic accidents.

The imams also attempted, even more fervently, to substitute the Hādawī *al-Aḥkām* and Zaydī interpretations in lieu of Shāfi'ī Sunnī law in the southern uplands and the Tihama. One way of doing this was de-funding Shāfi'ī academies and institutions and centralizing their endowments; another was replacing Shāfi'ī judges with Zaydīs. In addition, imams attempted to gain control of the *zakat* from the verdant coastal Tihama and southern agricultural regions, in violation of what Shāfi'īs considered the Islamic mandate to spend the tithe in the area where it is collected. At the same time, the imamate imposed or adopted from the Ottomans non-Islamic market taxes to discourage the entrepreneurship of Shāfi'ī merchants in Taiz, Ibb, and Hodeida.

Zaydī aristocrats and *'ulamā'* were theoretically the constituency of the imamate, which endeavored to co-opt their religious interpretations, instruction, and consultation. Even this group lost faith in the system, however. Zaydī *sayyid* male elites (including one of the imam's own sons) tried to overthrow the monarchy in 1948 and 1955, saying they wanted to bring the imamate more in line with Zaydī precepts as well as twentieth-century realities. Leaders of the 1948 coup, including dissident *'ulamā'*, judges, and other Sana'a notables, seized the apparent opportunity of Imam Yaḥyā's death to "elect" 'Abd Allāh al-Wazīr. Although this ostensibly constitutional movement failed when it was learned that Yaḥyā had been assassinated, the constitutional proposal, the Sacred National Pact *(al-Mīthāq al-Waṭanī al-Muqaddas)*, calling for a legislative consultative council with representation from cities, tribes, judges, and Yemenis living abroad,[10] represented an indigenous model still cited in contemporary political discourse.

Taxation and exploitation

Influence over legal interpretations had financial implications. As the "commanders of the faithful," imams and sultans claimed the prerogative to collect the *zakat* (literally, alms), the Islamic tithe the holy Quran says should be "taken from the well-to-do in the community and distributed to the poor amongst them." Complex, detailed rates are spelled out: 10 percent of the harvest from rain-fed land, 5 percent on irrigated land, and progressive rates on livestock, beehives, fish, and merchant capital.[11] Practicing Muslims are normally prepared to pay the *zakat*, as a matter of conscience. But it was not a foregone conclusion that they accepted to pay it as tribute to some urban monarch.

By the twentieth century the ostensibly religious tithe was distorted almost beyond recognition. Surcharges on the *zakat* in northern Yemen included a 3 percent "welfare" (*khayrī*) tax and a collection agent's commission. Customs and secular commercial tariffs, such as municipal and market taxes, were also levied by the imams, the British, and local Southern rulers. Under the imams, the Ottomans, and the Ḥaḍramī and Laḥjī sultanates, collection of the *zakat* and market taxes was farmed out to contractors who bid for the tax contract and pocketed a percentage as commission. Finally, for certain undertakings, notably roads, corvée labor was recruited from the community as a whole by local dignitaries or their tax contractors. This taxation-and-levy system, practiced in many parts of the Ottoman empire, was called *iltizām*, literally "obligation." It became the vehicle for the transformation of social relations of production.

Iltizām was most highly developed in the irrigated, semi-tropical wadis of the Tihama Red Sea coast, in Laḥj above Aden, and in the Ḥaḍramawt. It made substantial inroads in the coffee-for-export-producing upper elevations around Taiz and Ibb, and to a lesser extent in parts of the western mountains. In these areas, tax contractors used a combination of coercion and money-lending to wrest land documents from hapless smallholders who eventually sank into debt bondage and land tenancy. The patronage of the imams or the British, or in some cases fortunes amassed abroad in India or Africa, launched local land-and-power-holding estates.

Twentieth-century governments thus contributed to a centuries-long process of consolidation of ownership of the best land. In the northern Tihama, for instance, one family of tax collectors owned 16,000 hectares, and the royal family another 11,000 hectares, all of it prime wadi land producing several crops a year. On such large holdings, also found around Ibb and in the Ḥaḍramawt, owners extracted up to three-quarters of the crop from tenants in the form of rent for land and irrigation, and might collect taxes on top of that. Imams and sultans likewise granted monopoly trade concessions to their relatives or cronies: for instance, the third major Tihama landholder was simultaneously the imamate's largest financier and commercial agent.[12]

Where "feudal" (*iqṭāʿī*) *shaykhs* and sultans ruled, tribalism, based as it was on the twin concepts of land ownership and self-defense, was substantially weakened. Although tenant farmers continued to produce as family units within community networks, they relinquished their arms, their land documents, and the right to elect *shaykhs* from within the community. They were now called "peasants" (*raʿiyya*, also connoting "taxpayer"). As a consequence of the transformation of land ownership in verdant southern and lower regions but not in the north and east where the very paucity of water limited the farm surplus, tribalism remained a much more powerful force in the north-central plateau and the semi-desert of the east than elsewhere. Ḥāshid, based in Khamir, and Bakīl, spread from the western mountains across the plateau to the eastern desert, mounted periodic rebellions (notably in the 1920s and 1930s) against the imam; or else demanded subsidies to respect the royal domain. By contrast, the imam subdued rebellious Tihama and Taiz tribes with the help of tribal militia. The Aden-based colonial authorities ironically found greater ease of administration via an agent at al-Mukallā' of the distant eastern protectorate, where political and economic power rested with the *sayyids*, than of the nearer Ḍāliʿ, Faḍlī, Lower Yāfiʿ, and ʿAwḍalī protectorates which needed tribal guards and government guards to quell the tribal revolts that flared from 1928 to 1938.[13]

The combination of untoward taxation and painful scarcity sparked tax and peasant revolts from the Tihama to Ma'rib and from the Saudi frontier to Laḥj in the first half of the twentieth century.[14] Ḥāshid, Bakīl, and other tribes demanded either self-taxation or subsidies, while in Ibb, Taiz, and the Tihama Shāfiʿīs maintained that it was reprehensible to transport the *zakat* out of the region where it is paid.[15] In the protectorates, resistance mounted on the grounds of tribal prerogative and/or the fact that the religious elite seemed to be in collaboration with the colonial power. Class struggle against the *iqṭā'ī* class became intermingled with resentment of the elite status of the ruling *sayyids* or *shaykhs*.

It is in this context that we turn to the mechanisms of the moral economy, as it were. These mechanisms were very important in several ways. In offering primitive services and forms of social welfare they guaranteed the reproduction of modes of production, defined communities as partners in the ownership of certain public spaces, and legitimized the rulership claims of theocratic city-states and tribal entities. They have both ideological and material dimensions.

Capital, philanthropy, and endowment

The theocratic states were not structured or intended to deliver services to the population. Only in the late 1940s did Imam Aḥmad and the protectorate rulers establish ministries or departments for education, health, or public works. Instead, private Muslim charity was expected to guarantee community welfare. Beyond *zakat*, which had become a tax that enriched royal families, two important forms of philanthropy are *ṣadaqa* or personal charity and *waqf* or endowment. *Ṣadaqa* is redistributed directly to individuals or families, perhaps in the form of meat or grain for religious holidays. *Waqf*, being a perpetual endowment, is a significant form of capital formation.

Imams and sultans made private bequests to schools, orphanages, or fountains rather than budgeting funds for ministries of education, health, and public works. Their beneficence toward seminaries and religious institutions, particularly, was designed to sustain support among clerics and legal experts.[16] They encouraged others to endow public works for local communities. This "moral economy" operated mainly in towns, where poor people benefited from the charity of wealthy neighbors, and where magnificent medieval mosques, libraries, schools, fountains, and squares graced the urban public domain: Tarīm and Say'ūn in Wadi Ḥaḍramawt; al-Mukallā', Hodeida, and other port cities; Zabīd and some other Tihama towns; Taiz, Ibb, and Jibla in the southern uplands; and in the Zaydī northern plateau, Dhamar, Sana'a, and Ṣa'da.

Private philanthropy for Islamic education, water supply, and hospitality represented Muslim piety, but was also a form of political patronage and of pre-capitalist investment for the upper classes. As Imams Yaḥyā and Aḥmad and the protectorate sultans were well aware, the accumulated wealth of Islamic foundations and informal trusts easily rivaled that of the thrones. Tax-exempt endowments, some of them *waqf khayrī* or welfare endowments and others *ahlī* (here "family" or "private") trusts for direct heirs, covered as much as a quarter of all farmland and perhaps over half of urban rental property, with particular concentrations in and around the *sayyid* towns. Welfare endowments generated rent revenue for mosques, aqueducts, institutes, and caravansaries, each according to a detailed *waqfiyya* specifying the type, location, and size of the endowment, its purposes, and the terms for its maintenance. For instance, a woman and her daughter established a foundation to support a *muṣallan* or women's prayer place in Tarīm. The endowment consists of a house and an irrigated date farm in Wadi Ḥaḍramawt and a rented house in Singapore. Under the terms of the *waqfiyya* the woman's sons and grandsons act as guardians and get one-sixth of the proceeds for administration, the other five-sixths going for cleaning, repairs, water, and a shed for donkeys and camels. In the 1940s the rich, famous al-Kāff family created bequests in Singapore, for instance to support distribution of food to needy local families every Thursday or Friday.

Foundations endowed by generations of prominent Yemenis thus owned valuable productive and architectural capital, especially in and around the towns. Their wealth, tenants, employees, legal stipulations, and positive symbolism gave *awqāf* (the plural of *waqf*) foundations considerable visibility, autonomy, and power. Ibb's foundation was a veritable "government unto itself" with separate offices for mosques, education, tombs, and private endowments managing mosques, the town water supply, public baths and latrines, Quran instruction, roads, travelers' facilities, and burial for the poor.[17] *Waqf* fountains, wells, poor-houses, public hot baths, and mosques served each Sana'a neighborhood; another twenty-seven endowed caravansaries and eighteen wells were available to traders[18] in the central market. Zabīd, Kawkabān, and Jibla, among other towns, similarly maintained their fine mosques, schools, and baths with crop shares from *waqf* farmland. Even in more remote rural communities, some Islamic education, water systems, and hostels were supported by *waqf*.[19] Management of foundations gave descendants of the endowers considerable influence in local affairs, and was sometimes the site of political competition.[20]

The most explicitly political service was education, which royal families made a special effort to incorporate. Among the approximately 600 independent mosque schools in North Yemen were major, privately endowed academies in both Shāfi'ī and Zaydī towns, and several public institutes built by the Turks. Claiming that (Shāfi'ī) state schools, orphanages, technical centers, and a printing press established by the

Ottomans "undermined Islamic education," Imam Yaḥyā closed or reduced enrollments at these tax-supported institutions. Resources were redirected into pro-imamic Islamic institutes: the largest, in Sana'a, established in 1925/26 for about 600 students, taught a Zaydī rendition of an al-Azhar-type twelve-year curriculum. This move won the imam support among some Zaydī *'ulamā'*, also the beneficiaries of a mid-1930s reform centralizing revenues from local pious foundations. Funds for some schools including the famous old Shāfi'ī institute at Zabīd and a Taiz library were transferred to imamic seminaries and orphanages.[21] These measures were only partly successful, however, since legally and practically *waqf* properties, revenues, and expenditures remained bound to the almost invariably local intentions of the benefactor.[22] Foundations still represented enough services, jobs, and physical property in the neighborhoods to maintain a higher profile than the state proper while in the countryside its fragile bureaucracy and infrastructure gave the government little control over hundreds of mosque schools and water facilities.

One *waqf* school, probably more exemplary than typical, an academy in one of the fine South Yemeni towns, illustrates the tension between the "state" and endowed academies. The *Ma'had al-Ribāṭ* was established in the mid-1880s. Evidently it was the brain-child of one of the early Ḥaḍramī voluntary associations, *Ḥarakat al-Iṣlāḥ wa-l-Nahḍa al-'Arabiyya*, the Arab Reform and Renaissance movement, at about the same time as a *Madrasat al-Kāff* (a school named for the al-Kāff family) was founded by *Jam'iyyat al-Ḥaqq* (the "Society of Truth"), also in Tarīm. A *waqfiyya* was drawn up by Ḥaḍramī scholars and their lawyers in Singapore where the initial endowment, a rental property, was located. The founding document, reprinted in a booklet on the institute's history, gave detailed but amendable instructions for the construction and maintenance of a school and dormitory in "Tarīm, Ḥaḍramawt, the Arabian Peninsula"; salaries and provisions for teachers schooled in Sharī'a and Islamic sciences; and food and housing for "needy Arab" resident students.[23] The *waqfiyya* further specified the constitution and operations of a board of trustees empowered to appoint school administrators, conditions for admission and expulsion of students, and general curriculum guidelines. Additional endowments to the institute in the twentieth century included properties in Singapore, Malaysia, Mombasa, Jakarta, and Saudi Arabia.

The curriculum of the *Ma'had al-Ribāṭ* contained Arabic and Islamic sciences: *fiqh* (jurisprudence), *tawḥīd* (theology), *tajwīd* (Quran recitation), *ṣarf* (morphology and declension), and grammar. The pedagogy consisted, at least during the school's first decades, of reading, research, and analysis of commentary on the Quran, the traditions of the Prophet, and the writings of medieval Ḥaḍramī scholars, accompanied by biographical and bibliographical notes. Research and discussion sessions, led twice weekly by the leading local scholar, attracted not only students but *'ulamā'*. One example of a study/exposition topic was the status of a local "free water zone."

According to a former faculty member who wrote a booklet about the institute, during its third administration, when supervision passed from the *'ulamā'* to the sultan of the Kathīrī state, the quality of instruction gradually shifted from these innovative, challenging methods to commonplace rote learning and didactic preaching. Leading scholars no longer attended the sessions; the number of students fell from its peak of about 150; and the quality of the students, now more commoners than *sayyids*, declined markedly. The teacher, writing about 1957, worried that the institute had lost its integrity and was in danger of disappearing altogether.

Informal bequests, honored by custom and less open to political interference, maintained many neighborhood and village mosques. A quarter of Ibb's urban mosques, plus fountains, rest-stops, and dormitories, were managed from informal endowments,[24] and there were lands in the western mountains which, although not formal *awqāf*, were encumbered by similar obligations to support mosques, poor relief, and prayers for the dead.[25] Still less formally, in farming, fishing, and artisan communities simple mosques, water facilities, or shelters without income-generating endowments were maintained by heirs or by the community at large. Finally, like the *noblesse oblige*, some modestly well-to-do families offered food, coins, or lodging to infirm or destitute neighbors, allowed the community to drink from family-owned water sources, or invited guests to private tutorials, *dīwāns*, or meals. These least formal acts of largess blended into or combined with community networks, occasionally for new project construction.

Public works were always politicized, as social services always are. Contenders for offices based partly or wholly on acclaim sought popular support through construction of mosques and services. Beneficence was patronage, as imams knew when they subsidized religious scholars and judges. Private largess played prominently in local politics, influence, and loyalties, linking ordinary households to patrons whose wells or schools were central community fixtures. Privately financed public works also served economic interests, for while mosques, religious education, water, alms, and guest-houses reflected pious charity, *waqf* also protected portions of estates from division through inheritance and from taxation; and supported secular, commercial facilities such as caravansaries. Yemeni and Indian traders constructed hostels/wholesale stations in highland coffee regions, the main cities, and the ports – some of them grand, multi-storied hotels with rooms, courtyards, warehouses, weigh stations, stables, and adjacent mosques and baths. North and South Yemeni traders furnished smaller works along rural market routes and in the larger (usually Thursday) *sūqs*. In the 1940s and 1950s cistern, caravansary, and road improvements facilitated southern uplands commerce with Aden.

Private and foundation resources, in short, were crucial to neighborhood services, and constituted a form of redistribution from leading families to their poorer neighbors and clients. At the same time, the process of taxation and voluntary largess tended to transfer rural wealth into urban services, by channeling ground-rent, *zakat*, and market taxes into public works for aristocrats, monopolists, landowners, tax contractors, and officials who built public works near their homes, or in key commercial or political locations, but more rarely and modestly in villages of their tenants, subjects, and debtors. Important *shaykhs* donated cropshares from elsewhere to their own kinspeople. As a means of financing public works, charity left discretion in the sort, size, and location of innovations to the conscience of the rich and powerful.

Cooperation and mutual aid

Rural services were more modest. Hamlets and villages were typically closely built, walled, often hill-top clusters of houses around a small mosque with a place to wash and read. Country women trekked daily to distant streams, wells, or wadis for clean water. Village men or their clients traded at the periodic *sūqs*, collections of stalls around a caravansary and/or mosque that came alive once a week. Transport, too, was primitive. Only the steepest sections of the centuries-old caravan routes from the ports into the highlands were stone paved. Since most traffic was on foot or hoof, stopping-stations were integral to the transport system: caravansaries catered to wholesalers; guest-houses welcomed dignitaries and visitors; roadside huts sheltered strangers for the night or from a storm; and water-fountains or cisterns let passers-by quench their thirst.[26]

These modest services were the product of community self-help that raised labor, grain, materials, or money to guarantee collective survival. Less formal and smaller scale than endowments, cooperation was neither a system nor an institution but a set of mechanisms that operated either alone or in conjunction with tribal, tributary, or philanthropic practices for the maintenance or construction of public works. Mutual aid operated sporadically in virtually every community, as necessary to maintain existing services. New construction normally required a form of labor–capital partnership. The ethnographic record provides instances of such mechanisms in virtually every community studied, embedded in specific social relations and also not uncommonly codified in contractually binding documents.

Yemeni scholars have suggested that mutual aid arose out of necessity, piety, and political resistance. Necessity required households to cooperate at certain points in the agricultural cycle, notably irrigation and harvest; in repairing roads, cisterns, and houses damaged by catastrophe; and in response to social exigencies such as the payment of blood money to protect the group.[27] Ordinary families extended alms to the mosque or to unfortunate neighbors. Community cooperation became a form of resistance when localities diverted taxes or raised funds illegally for service projects.[28] All three forms were embedded in community social relations.[29]

Foreign anthropologists have depicted these mechanisms as a set of cooperative associations that observed among their members principles of election and majority rule. The tribe "as the collective owner of the tribal lands must be understood as a cooperative for the protection of this property."[30] Within tribes and other associations such as markets and artisan communities the heads of constituent economic units elect the *shaykh*, *'aqīl*, or other official who manages collective interests as reflected through committees and annual or bi-annual meetings. The "*ahl al-sūq*," of Sana'a – literally "children of the market," a colloquial expression for traders – were associations of particular markets, such as cloth or lumber markets. Members met and elected an *'aqīl* to represent collective interests: for example, collective purchasing of timber for carpenters. In old Sana'a a *majlis al-tijāra* or council of merchants (replaced by the official *ghurfat al-tijāra* or chamber of commerce in 1963) met annually to elect representatives including a chairman. Foreign merchandise prices, market taxes, and a force of nightwatchmen were overseen by the merchants' association.[31] Tarīm's large trading community, collectively referred to as "*masākīn*" ("impoverished"), including both "respected" merchants and lower-ranking peddlers, were organized by neighborhood "as a protective mechanism that would counter the political and economic dominance" of the *sayyids*.[32] Each town quarter's traders association, with identifying songs and symbols, was governed by a council comprised of one merchant and one peddler to represent each neighborhood. The council determined community projects – for example, flood relief or festivities – and the contribution from each group and neighborhood.

Tribalism contained mechanisms for marshaling men and/or resources toward a common purpose.[33] The largely military "summons," which measures leadership by the numbers of men who respond voluntarily, provides for collective action against a common enemy, in the face of disaster, for other extraordinary communal endeavors, or, indeed, to celebrate good fortune. The principle of corporate subscription in a tribe, extending contractually to client non-tribal groups, contains formulas for dividing responsibility among men, households, or villages to meet expenses associated with the quartering of *iltizām* troops, payment of blood money, stationing of guards, compensation of disaster victims, and other needs. Tribal ideology, valorizing honor, generosity, loyalty, piety, community, and customary law bolstered these overlapping mechanisms. So did folk arts, both those practiced specialized *muzayyin* criers, musicians, and cosmeticians and the tribal arts especially dancing and poetry.[34] Ties of interdependence between tribes and neighboring non-tribal groups, whether or not recorded in legal contracts, involved the latter in specific, practical obligations toward tribal projects in exchange for grain and defense.

Although tribal affinities facilitated cooperation, non-tribal communities also engaged in self-help. Tribal names still mobilized southern uplands and Tihama peasants who, like the non-tribal *sayyid*, Jewish, artisan, and fishing communities raised collections, met emergencies collectively, and maintained some common property. Within neighborhoods, hamlets, and occupational groups, ritualized or informal *i'āna* (aid), *ta'āwun* (cooperation), *jayyish* (collective labor), *ṣadaqa* (charity), *tabarru'āt* (donations) or *musā'ada* (assistance) bound users of common water supplies and other public goods. Sharecroppers on large estates constituted a self-conscious mutual-aid network, sometimes referred to as a formal association, for harvest, taxation, emergencies, and facilities maintenance. In the flood-irrigated Tihama wadis the very high degree of cooperation among farmers needed to maintain a complex spate system was recorded in law, managed by an association, and still the subject of frequent litigation. Throughout the country local dances, music, and verse celebrated collective projects.

After 1948, the vast majority of Yemen's Jewish minority relocated to Israel, where they earned a reputation for strong community ties and mutual-aid networks. Sana'a and other cities lost many of their best craftsmen. The largest Jewish communities, in Aden, Sana'a, and Radā', had lived in discrete quarters, maintaing separate courts, services, and public spaces. Although there were no national-level Jewish organizations, communities practiced auto-taxation to support a range of charitable works and community facilities: assistance for the poor, disabled, and orphaned; and synagogues, baths and cemeteries.[35] A visitor in 1910 found that the equipment and physical conditions in boys' Torah schools attached to synagogues were poor, but they were nonetheless offering instruction in Hebrew, Arabic, Turkish, and French.[36]

The sociological reconstruction of a Jewish weavers' village outside Ibb before their 1948 exodus illustrates the informal combination of resources for community services. Although there was "no formal membership, no formal elections, and no clear cut division of tasks between the various public functionaries, ... communal activities played a vital role in village life." Donations were made in the name of the synagogue, whose physical structure, built and endowed with farmland by an unnamed ancestor, contained former classrooms used as a hospice for travelers, and a ritual bath with a lined spring feeding a cistern. An *'aqīl* ("trusted one") had paid for the cistern from poll taxes not collected by state officials, and a couple of generations later during Passover volunteers built a lining and a pool. In the absence of full-time teachers, craftsman-savants recited aloud to students while working their looms. The community also owned a widows' home and paid disaster relief, individual lawsuits, and taxes communally.[37]

In all communities, Jewish or Muslim, routine maintenance necessitated the informal pooling of labor and/or produce. Tihama well-users, for instance, waited to ensure proper coiling of rope over pulley as the next user led a donkey from the well to draw the bucket; parts and periodic inspection or repair by a specialist were overseen by an *'aqīl* for the well, who collected costs from users or fines from abusers. In 'Amrān, wellsmen for each of four wells earned annual payments of grain.[38] Grain for wellsmen or the annual whitewashing of unendowed mosques came in small scoops from many households or a full sack from someone celebrating good fortune. Monsoon alpine storms annually collapsed hundreds of small local walls, dams, and paths that each took teamwork to repair. Subtle, low-key, sporadic, and minimally organized, action was mobilized by specific exigencies.

Neither the spirit nor the fruits of cooperation should be overestimated. It was no easy task for small farm settlements to build something. Even for 'Amrān town, it was a major, exceptional volunteer undertaking to build the mud town wall, and later to add a gate. Smaller settlements could marshal neither the labor nor the money for a major project. Pure self-help guaranteed emergency relief and necessary maintenance of existing facilities, but it was difficult for poor communities to improve their standards of living without patronage. Moreover, cooperation was at least sometimes mixed up with class struggle, civil disobedience, or highway banditry. Ḥaḍramīs competed to offer the best projects. During tax revolts in the 1920s and 1930s, tribal, Tihama, and southern uplands leaders courted royal wrath and popular acclaim by expending the entire *zakat* on local mosques, water catchments, guest-houses, or welfare funds in the name of the tribe or community. Now and then, tribesmen set up toll stations along roads or tribal borders to warn off unfriendly militia and exact a safe passage fee from outsiders. In extreme circumstances, desert tribes raided the water sources of politically weaker but environmentally favored communities.

When localities managed their own *zakat*, some fraction was deposited in a welfare fund which might be supplemented by individual donations. Although the Free Yemeni critics of the theocracy doubted the imam's tax contractors followed royal directives to establish such funds from their commissions,[39] formal or informal welfare funds handled variously by foundations, municipalities, notables, or communities disbursed poor and disaster relief and occasionally generated support for mosque or cistern repair, teacher stipends, and the like. Sometimes consisting of pledges rather than cash donations, welfare funds mixed large donations with small.

As noted above, sometimes capital from the well-to-do was combined with volunteer labor from the community. In a latter-day example, years after the revolution a *shaykh* in a village not far from Sana'a paid for dynamite, cement, and some skilled labor and rallied village youth to excavate a pit for a cistern near his home, then invited everyone to a fresh lamb lunch when it was complete. After a leading family near Ḥajja had supported a local tutor for many years, villagers expanded the mosque for classroom space. This political partnership of philanthropy and popular cooperation typified communal and tribal traditions.

Yet the connotations of the news "the *shaykh* summoned *jayyish*" (or *'awn*, also known by other expressions in other localities) depended on who designated the *shaykh* and whom the project would serve. Whereas some elected chiefs could mobilize volunteers or contributors using gentle persuasion, the mechanism did not operate on goodwill alone for the entire country. In rural areas such as al-Misrākh below Taiz, the Saḥūl outside Ibb, and Wadi Zabīd in the Tihama, sharecroppers and artisans recoiled in horror from words spoken with affection in the northern tribal areas. Here, *iqṭā'ī shaykhs* co-opted the ritual of the summons – drummers, criers, and all – in the form of conscription to enterprises serving recruits secondarily if at all. *Jayyish* or *'awn* on market roads and state granaries was not voluntarism but corvée, coerced, with sharecroppers, debtors, or market-people slaving to the rhythm of an overseer's chant. The notion that the *shaykh* would donate to community services was laughable.

Whether by military commanders, *baladiyya* officers, landlords, or tax collectors, conscription (also *jayyish*) depended on mutual-aid networks to guarantee compliance. Mutual obligations made it possible to levy manpower from a wide area by quartering militia in a few homes, threatening to punish local spokesmen, etc., because the whole network would come to their relief. Work teams were thus mobilized by notifying the tribe or community of its obligation for a specific number of man-days. Within the community itself, *ta'āwun* or *i'āna* signified mutual aid in meeting the demands of tribute collectors as a special type of community relief. In comparison with communal self-help that accomplished modest local services, corvée was capable of more ambitious undertakings such as the widening of regional military and market roads.

Cooperation too, therefore, operated very much in the realm of political conflicts wherein leading families either stood with their communities against the state or served the state at villagers' expense. When *shaykhs* stood by their communities, holding back the *zakat* or matching voluntary labor with philanthropy, the struggle took the form of a center–periphery conflict between the state and the provinces; when the *shaykh* acted as collector of tribute or agent of colonialism, conflicts coalesced more along class lines between farmers and landlords or tax contractors. In any case, villages and some towns strained for an already pretty paltry local "surplus" – *zakat*, foundations, volunteer labor – to improve or at least maintain local standards of living.

Latter-day community betterment projects

Although the religiously and tribally based mechanisms for the provision of the most rudimentary social services did contain some civic elements, on the other hand the level of education, security, and comfort they provided was very meager. The deficiency of both services and mechanisms for their provision was perhaps the most significant "push" factor in massive male migration to Aden and/or abroad. Their inadequacy was further underscored by a version of the "cooperation of resistance" that emerged hand-in-hand with a capitalist market. More liberal, organized, modernist, and market oriented than traditional self-help, the new community betterment movement adapted familiar fund-raising techniques to a more commercial environment, using cash donations and hired labor for innovative services. Its projects qualitatively changed local standards of living and the standards by which state and other benefactors' services would be appraised.

The influences of a world market were naturally introduced through the ports. Aden attracted youths from a more-than-hundred-kilometer radius, and its burgeoning population created demand for fresh fruits and vegetables, grain, and coffee. During the 1920s and 1930s, Laḥj, Abyan, Taiz, and Ibb provinces experienced not so much the penetration as the seduction of capitalism, as young men fled tedium, physical hardship, economic stagnation, and heavy taxation for the relative political and economic liberty of the big city. Tentatively at first, their parents and neighbors traded some goods to Aden traders, then shifted production to meet metropolitan demand and began purchasing rice, wheat, and canned foods. By mid-century, a lot of families had one foot in the cash economy.

Novel ways of organizing social capital appeared as early as the 1880s in the Ḥaḍramawt, where by the 1930s community-style organization was apparently an explicit response to the political struggles between *sayyids* and commoners. Powerful families such as the al-Kāff, al-ʿAṭṭās, and al-ʿAydarūs, who amassed fortunes abroad, contributed conspicuously to a rather rich built environment of grand architecture and graceful urban landscapes in Tarīm, Sayʾūn, and al-Mukallāʾ and also to schools, roads, and other modernization projects. The al-Kāffs, famous for road building, were vehicle importers. They thus controlled both religious and secular public forums and spaces.

Names of several turn-of-the-century Ḥaḍramī voluntary associations appear in various accounts: the associations backing the Ribāṭ and al-Kāff schools, a *Majlis al-Ishtirāʿ al-Islāmī*, and *al-Jamʿiyya al-Islāmiyya*, said to have sponsored a school with teachers from al-Ahzar in Cairo, a newspaper, a magazine, and translation projects. Some associations, such as a welfare society that operated Arabic Islamic schools after 1903 in Indonesia, operated abroad.[40] In Tarīm in the 1940s there were at least three charitable welfare associations, connected to Ḥaḍramī communities in Asia or Africa, and at least one Ḥaḍramawt cultural club. Over the course of two decades welfare associations built the first primary-middle school, an electricity project (opposed by the sultan), a system for pumping drinking water, a fuel station, a welfare pharmacy, an ambulance, and cooperative stores locally, and maintained a guesthouse for Ḥaḍramīs in Aden. The Society of Brotherhood and Co-operation, *Jamʿiyyat al-Ukhūwa wa-l-Muʿāwana*, founder of the first modern primary-middle school in the Ḥaḍramawt itself, proved controversial. Although education was offered to all social groups, non-*sayyids* claimed the aristocratic founders secretly agreed to educate the sons of peasants only up to a very basic level. This issue was taken up by the *Jamʿiyyat al-Irshād* (Society of Guidance) and a counter-organization, *al-Rābiṭa al-ʿAlawiyya*. The latter appeared related to the older

'Alawī Sufi order (*al-ṭarīqa al-'Alawiyya*). By 1935 the Irshādīs were running over two dozen schools and a scholarship program for Ḥaḍramīs in Indonesia, a newspaper, and several social clubs. The *sayyid* 'Alawī League raised funds among supporters in Singapore and for schools and public works in the Ḥaḍramī towns.[41]

Activities abroad did affect political and social conditions back home. Among these innovations were novel forms of social activism that fused new technologies and information onto customary practices and long-standing demands for local autonomy and local expenditure of the *zakat*. In Aden itself, as discussed in the next chapter, cultural clubs and reform societies spearheaded the Arabic education drive in the 1930s.[42] Village and town betterment associations, founded initially in Aden or among Yemeni communities abroad, became both a mechanism for improving local services and a basis of political movements. As old institutions faced new exigencies and opportunities, they evolved. To cite just one simple example, wherever roads made vehicular traffic possible new associations of drivers collected subscriptions (in cash or work) to cope with road repairs and accidents.

Village or regional clubs opened restaurants, hostels, and employment services for migrants, then moved into providing scholarships and forms of insurance, and finally toward infrastructural projects in home communities. By the mid-1930s, a cultural club called the *Nādī al-Iṣlāḥ* (Reform Club), was founded in Ḥujariyya by the Northern nationalist Aḥmad Nu'mān as a secular school with lectures and books smuggled from Aden.[43] Other village associations appeared in this populous region below Taiz, one of which, the al-Aghābir association, was collecting donations for constructing a school and digging a well for drinking water in Hayfan by 1941.[44] By this time migrants from the Southern region of Yāfi' to the Gulf, Indonesia, and Aden were involved in providing medicine and night classes in those locations, and then in creating a local association in Yāfi' itself.[45] Cash raised in the name of the home village or lineage or its welfare fund purchased generators, pumps, and other equipment, and hired engineers to install them. Within the next decade, quite a few villages between Aden and Taiz upgraded their water-delivery facilities with pipes and cement, and several established small schools teaching a modern curriculum. The town of al-Bayḍā', north of the inter-Yemeni border, began a water-and-electricity supply project. By 1962, the "Sons of al-Madhḥajī" (village) association, with branches in Ḥujariyya, Taiz, and Aden, collected donations to support needy migrants and students and build schools, water-supply projects, and a clinic.

This activity fused traditional mutual aid and charity with the new-found spending power of migrant workers and traders in a distinctive process.[46] Many of these associations convened annually in the village on the occasion of the great feast, with traditional fanfare made more special with novelties such as megaphones, to determine auto-taxation and projects policies.[47] Sponsors – educated *shaykhs*' sons, Aden-based merchants, and prosperous farmers – led with generous pledges, and farmers and lower-class migrants made more modest contributions. A Yemeni scholar argued that these clubs were based on tribal, kinship, or village ties "that placed moral claims" for donations to village welfare projects or interceding with employers or government authorities.[48] While volunteers helped with some of the labor tasks, however, wage labor, salaried employees, or private contractors did most of the work. Graduates of Aden schools, including several maintained by village associations, taught. In Aden itself libraries, scholarships, and college-level classes were funded from self-assessed *zakat*.[49]

These clubs (singular *nādī*) operated somewhat like political parties both in Aden, where, as discussed in the next chapter, they formed an umbrella political forum, the Yemeni Federation, and back home, where authorities regarded self-help projects, voluntary associations, and even (in the North) the growing cash economy as subversive. The liberal call for "eradication of ignorance, poverty, and disease" became a slogan for community action. Village and town betterment activists, a sort of counter-elite, became prominent in the anti-royalist Free Yemeni movement and/or anti-imperialist ferment within the protectorate.[50] Several modern private and community schools, such as the Freedom Elementary School and the New Generation School, symbolized agitation against the imamate. Nor were associations devoid of internal conflicts: political rivalries were played out in the arena of services, and disagreements over assets and projects resulted in the fission of some regional clubs into village associations.

Hodeida, much smaller than Aden, was simultaneously the most commercial and the most squalid of north Yemeni cities, home to rich Yemeni and East African merchants, scores of foreigners, landless peasants, and a large community of street-sweepers and artisans. Its grand mud-brick villas contrasted sharply with conical thatched huts clustered in their midst. Between the old customs and trading houses and the hospital, schools, and streets under construction by the government and foreign donors, Hodeida had especially expansive public spaces and a lively daily market. It flourished, and attracted more poor immigrants, as a result of heightened Red Sea naval activity during World War II.

The "Town Improvements Board" founded in Hodeida after a major fire devastated a large number of thatched huts in the port district was the most formal of the new associations established in the final days of the imamate. Themselves beset with pleas for personal charity and/or public leadership, representatives of eight urban quarters – one *sayyid*, a judge, and six, most likely merchants or scholars, who gave only the title of "pilgrim" (*ḥajj*) – convened to discuss ways of averting disaster and improving the quality of urban life. After appointing a scribe and a treasurer, the board left a paper trail[51] and established some formal funding channels. A handwritten plan called for acquisition of fire-fighting equipment and ambulances; construction of garbage-burning pits and rental of camels to transport refuse; employment of street-sweepers to keep the town clean; and the draining of standing water that bred germs and malaria. The board successfully lobbied tax and provincial authorities for a share from customs duties on kerosene and negotiated with merchants for special imposts on several commodities, including tobacco, on the grounds that municipal services favored trade. The plans were followed through. In 1955 a series of slightly defiant telegrams to the royal family requested customs exemption to import a Ford truck from Aden for garbage disposal. The association hired a driver and garbage collectors, and commissioned a private contractor to build new public toilets.

The Hodeida town improvement board, which operated continuously, if under different names, for the next few decades, symbolized a significant, qualitative shift toward capitalist markets, bureaucratic rationalism, taxation to fund social welfare, and modern urban services – independent of and more progressive than the state. Along with the village associations in the southern uplands and the protectorates, it was indicative of a new form of organization that marked an evolution, rather than a sharp departure, from customary practices and social relations; but was also part of an accumulating revolutionary movement that would soon transform both North and South Yemen.

This chapter both confirms and challenges an Orientalist view of Arab political culture. It confirms that the basic units of loyalty and solidarity were community and tribe rather than nation and state. But it also shows that the basis of community and tribal affiliations has practical and material as well as ideological and ascriptive elements, and entails a rich dynamic that goes well beyond the passivity-or-resistance view of "traditional" society that predominates in much writing on Arab political culture. Though corresponding to neither idealized images of democracy nor romanticized versions of peasant culture, there was indeed a form of voluntary civic activism among various social groups and classes that served the state-like function of providing essential safety and services. Such activism was a thoroughly political struggle over the allocation of scarce values, in which societal forces were more pluralistic, progressive, and perhaps even powerful than the indigenous states. It was closely connected to a vibrant associational life in Aden Colony and the protectorates, and later gave rise in a continuous but also dramatic evolution, to a "cooperative" or "self-help" movement that would play a major role in the political life of the Yemen Arab Republic. The next two chapters deal with these developments in Yemeni "civil society."

4 Colonialism, activism, and resistance

In late colonial Aden economic prosperity coincided with governmental efforts to offset dissent by tolerating some forms of association and expression. Although, as noted, political and economic liberalism were half-hearted and restricted, public spaces were expansive: shops, cafes, businesses, parks, schools, libraries, radio, and publications together formed a sort of free market-place of ideas. In this environment, organizational activity flourished. Aden's relative openness, especially in contrast to Sana'a or Taiz, gave rise to a plethora of projects in the non-governmental public sphere: sports, cultural, and charitable clubs; offices of village associations and their umbrella Yemeni Federation; local, South Yemeni, pan-Yemeni, and pan-Arab political groups; labor unions and the Aden Trades Union Congress; and Adeni as well as pan-Yemeni presses. These projects rather resemble bubbles on the surface of boiling water, appearing and submerging, but they were indeed pluralist, projected public opinion, articulated interests, and offered some state-like social services.

There is a temptation for Westerners to arrange these activities on a traditional–modern or primordial–civic continuum. Associations with religious, tribal, village, or neighborhood names, or called *rābiṭa* something or something *ahlī*, might be dubbed primordial, while urban, intellectual or nationalist initiatives seem more modern. On closer examination, however, the dichotomous distinction between traditional and civic is shown to be a facile heuristic rather than an empirical descriptor.

Yemeni scholars offer other continua that might, but should not, be confused with primordial–civic: local–national, right–left, and rural–urban. Some groups favored narrow localism based on identification with the protectorate statelets or Adeni separatism, others looked to a wider regionalism, on the lines of greater Ḥaḍramī, Yāfiʿī, or Laḥjī unity. South Arabian or South Yemeni nationalism translated into support for a federation. Yemeni nationalism explicitly encompassed both North and South Yemen. Wider pan-Arab nationalism was influenced by the Ba'th, Arab Nationalist, and Nāṣirī movements. Although in the 1960s the latter were associated with the left and the former with the right, most movements were then still devoid of specifically ideological content, or else tried to reconcile Socialism with Islam.[1] And although Socialism was first espoused by urban labor, it was later the rural-based National Liberation Front that radicalized the revolution. Religious guidance associations were distinctively modern and civic (*madanī*).[2] Moreover, tribal fronts became the vanguard of the Marxist revolution, and village committees introduced modern education. Groups organized around specific political and/or class interests.

This chapter is arranged to develop both an argument and a chronology. After an overview of the electoral–constitutional experience, two sections deal with organizing among the Adeni elite and the colony's fluid workforce, respectively. The two most important Adeni organizations, the Aden Association and the Aden Trades Union Congress, represented explicitly class-based responses to the electoral–constitutional experience. Beyond Aden, the fourth section shows, religiosity, tribalism, and status-consciousness permeated localized and even incipient nationalist organizing. The nationalist and pan-Arab politics, also the topic of a separate section, attempted to transcend urban–rural and status divisions. The last two sections deal with aspects of civil society sometimes overlooked in the comparative literature but very relevant to any inquiry into the relationship of associational life and politics: publishing and writing, and meetings and assemblies.

Elections and formal political participation

The Aden opening was no democratic experiment. An intolerant, punitive government brooking little opposition played havoc with its own rules, leaving most people no legal outlet for political expression. Adenis knew that in India, Kenya, and Egypt colonial rule was brutal enough but did institutionalize a sort of parliamentary governance. This did not occur in South Arabia, where Aden and the protectorates were entrusted to minority rule of a fossilized client elite. The United Kingdom had backed into this awkward situation, drove a zigzag policy for more than a century, and eventually abandoned the country to revolutionaries. The opening in the last two decades of its occupation of Aden saw several ill-conceived, short-lived constitutional proposals and a series of bogus elections open only to the elite.[3]

As a Crown Colony Aden was eligible for only limited self-governance. The Aden Legislative Council, "nominated" in 1947 from the comprador bourgeoisie of three Adeni municipalities, was consulted on "eleemosynary" matters.[4] In 1955 elections were conducted for four out of eighteen seats on the Legislative Council, but residency, age, gender, and property limitations on voter eligibility ensured that colonial loyalists were elected. Pro-suffrage and independence demonstrations began soon afterwards. In January 1959, amidst a deteriorating security situation but under a newly promulgated Aden constitution, elections were held for twelve of twenty-three Legislative Council seats. Five to seven candidates ran for the two or three seats in each of five urban districts.[5] Again voter eligibility was limited to 21,500 of Aden's 180,000 inhabitants. Scarcely 6,000 cast ballots. An aging, pro-British, moneyed group of nine Arabs, two Somalis, and an Indian was elected.[6] Even so, the council only very narrowly supported participation in the Federation. Labor, by then organized into the Aden Trades Union Congress, called a protest strike for September 24 1962, the day before the Aden Council was to vote on the federal proposal – and, as it happened, two days before the September 26 *coup d'état* in Sana'a.

The constitution of the Federation of Arab Emirates of the South accepted in 1959 by the six sultans of the eastern protectorates (the area around Aden) was replaced by Federation of South Arabia constitution in early 1963 when Aden and five more eastern protectorates signed on. Soon eighteen protectorates had joined the Federation. The colony, now in a highly ambivalent constitutional arrangement, was to hold twenty-four of eighty-five seats on the Federal Supreme Council, and four out of fourteen ministerial posts in the federal government. The twenty-four were to come from the Aden legislature.[7] Further amendments to the federal constitution were constantly on the table at the much-protested constitutional conferences in London. The Aden constitution was also amended in ways that gradually opened up the process somewhat. Four more Arabs replaced four *ex officio* members of the Aden Legislative Council. Then the Legislative Council became a parliamentary-style government headed by a chief minister. All these steps were meant to bolster support for British policy, which by then was to hand power over to a constitutional federation comprised of Aden and all the protectorates.

Popular support was not forthcoming, however. On the street, protests swelled over voting rights, manipulation of the council, economic concerns, unity with North Yemen, and British actions elsewhere in the Middle East. In December 1963 a grenade explosion welcomed a British delegation at the airport. In response, the Federation's Supreme Council declared a state of emergency. Two years later, facing growing insurrection, the high commissioner suspended the Aden constitution in the name of security and dismissed Aden's government. Even delegates of the supposedly pliant Aden and Federation councils objected. Incredibly, franchise "reform" reduced the eligible electorate to about 10,000,[8] amidst a total, migration-swollen municipal population that had reached 220,000 – among whom 60,000 were born in the colony; another 35,000 in the protectorates; and 80,000 in Yemen. Somali and Indian communities numbered about 20,000 each.[9]

The Aden Legislative Council elections scheduled for 1962 finally took place in October 1964 amidst widespread political detentions and a ban on public meetings. The major parties, most of whose supporters were not qualified to vote anyway, all declared a boycott. Nonetheless, the man imprisoned for the airport bombing won a landslide victory (98 percent) in Crater, and fourteen of the other sixteen elected said they refused to take the oath of office unless he were released from prison and seated on the council.[10] These demands were met, and as a further concession a moderate labor organizer replaced an automobile-dealership owner as chief minister.

Still, within the Aden and Federation councils – labeled "stooges" by Cairo and Sana'a radio – the British were alienating friends. The endless constitutional conferences, now focused on the question of Ḥaḍramī (Qaʿayṭī nd Kathīrī) membership, produced little of substance. The Aden government insisted on repeal of martial law, institution of universal adult suffrage, UN supervision of new elections for all legislative and governing councils, and respect for ordinary freedoms.[11] While the British stepped up work on infrastructural projects, rebels began terrorizing the families of military and colonial personnel. Stricter curfews failed to quell the violence. In 1965, the Aden Council threatened to resign in protest against still stricter emergency measures aimed mainly at their own rivals in the National Liberation Front. Soon thereafter, the Aden constitution was replaced by direct rule and remaining liberties were suspended.

These measures prompted unprecedented protests in a city racked by strikes for over a decade. Tens of thousands of union members shut down the port, the refinery, transportation, and even military installations. The army fired tear gas and then live ammunition on defiant students. Paratroopers patrolling the streets became the target of urban guerrillas. Soon London (in light of English and international politics as well as events in Yemen) was to conclude that Aden was ungovernable and not worth the cost. A Labor Party government decided to withdraw, and in the event handed over the reins of formal authority to the National Liberation Front.[12]

This experience was thus marred on the one hand by an irrational, repressive, and unrepresentative government, and on the other by the resort to armed struggle to achieve independence: a common recipe for revolution. Between the violence of both the state and the underground, however, a space was cleared for civic activity. During the 1950s, Yemenis were affected by events in the wider Middle Eastern arena, especially British policy toward the Arabs. Many traveled to or studied in Cairo. Transistor radios picked up broadcasts from Arab capitals as well as from the Aden BBC. Sudanese and Egyptian teachers affected a new youth culture. Yemeni and Arab nationalism gained popularity; the imam and the British were vilified. Pubescent political hormones surged.

Urban clubs and associations

Political parties as such were banned this whole time in both North and South. In Aden, however, in addition to laws authorizing labor syndicates, permits were available to "clubs," defined as "any community, society, or association ... of at least twenty members for the promotion of a common social, cultural, political, or other object, except the acquisition of gain."[13] Many syndicates and associations took pains to register legally, but eventually most organizations, public gatherings, and press organs were outlawed.

Social clubs and voluntary associations are at the heart of what most writers mean by civil society. As in Egypt and Africa, Yemen's most modern, formal, *madanī* associations were pioneered among urban, well-to-do, educated, male circles. This segment of Aden's Yemeni and foreign communities joined recreational clubs, social welfare associations, and cultural or educational centers. Such activity, well analyzed in modernization theory, could be read as civic, as primordial, as elitist, or as political, and indeed was some of each. Many adopted the rather modern term *nādī*, for club, but others called themselves by names that sounded pretty old fashioned. As elsewhere in this study, the writer can create very different impressions by calling something *al-rābiṭa* or calling the same association SAL.

The most exclusive clubs served the small, mostly transient European community. Yachting, officers', ladies', or church-affiliated clubs afforded recreation for several thousand Europeans. The Aden Chamber of Commerce was headed by the owner of the city's largest commercial firm, an Aden-born Englishman who, like most other chamber members, based extensive Red Sea trading houses in Aden. The chamber, representing financiers and traders, was said to work closely with the commissioner for trade's advisory board. The British Red Cross, the St. John's Ambulance Brigade, a society to prevent tuberculosis, and other mainly European charities almost certainly served some Arabs.[14]

Sports and youth clubs began in the Persian British, Kurdish, and other expatriate communities and spread to Aden's residential districts. Sporting leagues, primarily an athletic, recreational outlet, were simultaneously an important aspect of Aden's cosmopolitan culture and a way of emphasizing ethnic, class, or neighborhood camaraderie: that is, they both unified and divided the city. Administrators thought of sports as healthy, so they organized city-wide games, a combined youth club, and finally a pan-Aden youth association. During the independence movement, however, teenage sports fans filled the streets to demonstrate their political opinions, and after the revolution the youth association became one of the PDRY's "mass" or "corporatized" organizations.

Charities and welfare societies mushroomed in urbanizing Aden, blending European, Asian, and African with indigenous ideas. The British were very proud of Christian philanthropic missions in South Arabia. Aden's diverse Muslim community, too, founded institutions to assist the poor, orphans, and the aged. An old-age home opened in 1906 in Shaykh 'Uthmān. In the changing post-World War II atmosphere, such activity became more modern, secular, institutionalized, and political. In 1942 a Society for the Care of Orphans and Poor Children started catering for homeless children. After the government agreed to a petition submitted around 1950 to support social work, there appeared a students' club to organize volunteers to work among the aged, a Society for the Care of the Blind that opened an Institute of Light for the Blind, a Youth Care Society with an affiliated Sons of the Bodies Club in Crater, and a social center for the youth of Shaykh 'Uthmān.[15]

Educated Yemeni men customarily sit in a *dīwān* to discuss literature, perhaps while chewing qāt. There was also a tradition, discussed earlier, of donating to education. Adeni intellectuals were fascinated by late nineteenth- and early twentieth-century Arab and European literary salons, and styled their discussions after them. Readers of Arabic devoured Muslim revivalist works by Jamāl al-Dīn al-Afghānī, Muḥammad 'Abduh, Ṭāhā Ḥusayn, Rashīd Riḍā'. The most prominent Yemeni writer was the famed Zaydī jurist Muḥammad ibn 'Alī al-Shawkānī, whose work incorporated Shāfi'ī doctrine.[16] Adenis also read Arab nationalist polemics, Frantz Fanon's *The Wretched of the Earth*, translations of Marx, Lenin, and Mao. Interest in the "Arab awakening," heightened by contact with visiting literati, expanding education, and the circulation of books, plays, and magazines, fertilized the drive for Arabic education. Incorporating a range of political orientations, this phase of the Yemeni intellectual awakening, as it is known, culminated in a conference in 1962 and the founding of the Nationalist Writers' League, precursor to the Writers' Guild. After the September 1962 revolution in the North, more cultural and literary associations in Taiz and Sana'a became meeting-places for intellectuals and political fora for the anti-colonial movement.[17]

This activity cleared a space for public discourse. Clubs became "schools for politicians." In 1925 the then sultan of Laḥj invited intellectuals from leading families to form an Arab Literary Club. In 1929 an Arab Reform Club opened in al-Tawāhī, Crater, and Shaykh 'Uthmān. The Abī al-Ṭālib camp in Crater was led by Aden's leading publisher-politician, son of an old family and favorite of the British. He also headed an Arab Islamic Reform Club that asked Arab kings in 1936 for scholarships for poor Adenis to study in Baghdad and Cairo; and lobbied London for local technical training, study abroad opportunities, an Aden college, and schools for girls. A half-dozen literary centers in Aden held seminars on Arab literature, nationalism, education, religion, the status of women, and other topics, and a group called United Youth of Yemen pushed for affiliation in these cultural clubs and access to their libraries.[18]

The government sought to Anglicize political–intellectual discourse beyond business and government circles where a solid command of English was already prerequisite. In 1943 men's and women's branches of the British Council began teaching English culture and language. British schooling socialized a new generation of Adenis. Graduates of Oxford, Cambridge, or London universities would soon constitute the core of a modern, educated, but not necessarily mercantile strata in Adeni society.[19]

Partly in reaction to the promotion of English culture, an Islamic Association was founded in the late 1940s by a Pakistani lawyer and other professionals and merchants active in the cultural clubs. Its goal was to promote the study of religious subjects and the use of Arabic in schools and official circles.[20] The inspiration for this association was an organization by the same name in Pakistan that subsequently played an important role in Pakistani politics. In Aden, the Islamic Association was an early manifestation of comprador merchant interests.

The Aden Association arose from the embers of *al-Jam'iyya al-Islāmiyya* when the Islamic Association fell apart after the death of its Pakistani founder in 1950. Conservative merchants and pro-British civil servants regrouped under the Aden Association. The AA became a major political player in the Legislative Council and in debate over the future of the colony. Its slogan, "Aden for the Adenis," was politically charged, for it implied Adeni separatism from the protectorates and the rest of Yemen. Furthermore, the AA endorsed the narrow UK definition of Adeni, which included Indians, Somalis, and others born, raised, or owning a business in Aden as Adeni, but classified the majority of the urban population as alien Yemeni or protectorate Arabs. Nationalists charged that the 3,000-member AA "tended to serve citizens of the Commonwealth rather than Yemenis."[21]

The strongest local allies of the empire, AA leaders were appointed, then elected, to the Aden municipal and legislative councils. The AA thus functioned both as a sort of chamber of commerce and as a political party. Its three candidates defeated those of the South Arabian League in the by-elections of 1955, when the fourth seat was won by a Somali merchant. In the 1959 elections, when an estimated 73 percent of eligible voters boycotted the elections, the AA won eleven out of twelve seats and formed the government. It actively championed constitutional over tribal law, opposed the immigration of rural Yemenis into Aden, and generally favored Adeni autonomy from the protectorates over independence from Britain. When the federal proposals were advanced, the association split into two partisan factions: one retained the "Aden for the Adenis" platform; the other favored Aden's merger with the protectorates.[22] The latter prevailed in the September 1962 vote on the Federation and in the 1964 election.

Unions and the Aden Trades Union Congress

Aden was home to the Arab world's most militant labor movement. The particular circumstances that led to strong trades unionism included a large but unstable labor force of port, transport, and refinery workers, many of them disenfranchised Yemenis; a disgruntled rising generation of educated Adeni men; and, ironically, a colonial policy of forbidding partisan organizing but encouraging early syndical organization. Eventually, ATUC strikes paralyzed the city.

In one sense, the first workers' organizations were village associations, because networks that found jobs for cousins and neighbors gathered people from the same clan or village in the same workplace, and because some employers made a practice of hiring men from the same tribe through a broker from the region. Migrants' and locality-based associations, furthermore, provided informal insurance and other benefits. As more workers entered larger shops they began to place demands on employers. A labor office was established in the 1930s. In 1942 a unions law anticipated future developments by authorizing labor syndicates but limiting the right to strike. Unions became highly politicized, along the lines of British Labourites with whom they were in regular contact.

Inflation, political discrimination, and resentment of European imperialism all contributed to the radicalization of South Yemeni politics. Facing both high inflation and an influx of workers who kept wages low, Yemenis, the lowest social strata in Aden, were earning no more in 1955 than in 1951, despite cost-of-living inflation of 48 percent.[23] In addition, whereas employers – the base, the port trust, British Petroleum, other foreign companies, and the merchant class – controlled the government, there was no legal outlet for political interest-articulation available to others. Finally, UK policies in Palestine, the Suez invasion, and other regional events catalyzed public opinion against the colonial administration.

Labor unions, one of the few legal organizational outlets, began forming around 1947, when independent car owners and drivers organized. Next industrial workers and then (predominantly European) airline employees formed syndicates. There were a dozen unions in 1955, and that number doubled in the following year when the strikes began. In the spring of 1956 7,000 wage-earners struck, demanding the right to vote, shorter working hours, higher wages, and health/disability insurance, and twice that number stopped working in autumn after the expulsion of a SAL leader from Aden and the three-power invasion of Suez.[24] In the face of syndical pressures the British made what they regarded as reasonable concessions to labor demands in the form of emigration controls and minimum wages and hours legislation,[25] but failed to quell a rising tide of labor unrest.

The Aden Trades Union Conference (ATUC) was founded by twelve syndicates in March 1956, amidst widespread syndical protest, at the initiative of a group of literate Adeni activists mostly from the white-collar syndicates, some of whom were connected to Labour circles in the UK. Thirty-three more unions registered in the next three years. By 1962 nearly a quarter of the 80,000 workers in Aden belonged,[26] and their numbers were still growing, if more slowly. The ATUC catalyzed not only workers' economic demands but also urban protests against immigration policy, the "counterfeit" elections, the South Arabian Federation, and other Yemeni and Arab issues.

Syndical militancy became the trademark form of political activity in Aden during the late colonial period. Within a couple years of its founding the ATUC organized over 200 strikes, documented in many of the accounts cited herein. In March 1958 strikes and bombs led to political arrests and the banning of the unions' newspaper. In 1959 port and refinery workers defied a strike ban to paralyze the port for forty-eight days and the refineries for thirty-four days. When the government outlawed "politically motivated" work stoppages and imposed mandatory mediation, a "go-slow" campaign ensued. Union leaders were imprisoned or deported. In 1963, undeterred by martial law, half the employees of military installations, joined by transport and petroleum workers, practically shut Aden down. In 1964 farmers demonstrated in Laḥj against low cotton prices partly in sympathy with urban protests against the detention of a union leader. Next, 3000 oil depot and port workers walked out to protest at the detention of a union activist. In 1965, after suspension of the Aden constitution, the strike movement involved over 12,000 employees of the army plus thousands more oil workers, stevedores, taxi and bus drivers, clerical staff, and even shopkeepers.

The core of the ATUC leadership were literate Adenis in six "federated" unions.[27] From the outset, they were drafting a "constitution" and starting to publish a newspaper.[28] They were "outsiders," urban graduates with voter rights but little economic clout, the challengers to the power monopoly of the Aden Association. This group formed a partisan affiliate of the ATUC called the People's (or popular) Socialist Party (PSP). It came to represent the disenfranchised amorphous mass of workers and self-employed traders in Aden in their bargaining with the colonial administration. Thus, after the split in the AA and a hefty show of the power of organized labor, a PSP leader – son of three generations of pro-British civil service – became chief minister in 1964.

Several groups organized around the issue of voter rights. Eighteen minor and evidently transient groups held a national congress.[29] A noteworthy group was the United National Front, a conglomeration of social, cultural, professional, labor, and youth organizations that vowed to thwart the elections, oppose "separatist" politics, work toward Yemeni unity in an anticipated post-imamate period, and "stand with the working class" by supporting unions and strikes.[30] Like the more radical People's Democratic Federation, the Marxist party founded in 1961,[31] the UNF later joined the NLF.

Rural activism

Beyond the clear-cut political issues and class divisions of Aden, however, there was nothing comparable to the Aden Legislative Council elections to organize around. There was no pretext of democratization or constitutionalism, no significant unions, no legal outlet for participation. At best, the sultans after 1937 and the imam after 1948 appointed consultative councils. These circumstances gave rise to two sorts of organizations, either very localized or broadly inclusive. Local social clubs and welfare associations concerned themselves mainly with issues directly affecting members. Parties, on the other hand, whether articulating regional, Yemeni, or Arab nationalism, were more like debating clubs than mass movements. That is, they marked significant departures in thinking about politics, but none of them ever developed a popular following. Instead, whatever rural roots or mass following they had depended on networks with local associations.

Voluntary associations for men[32] appeared in many towns and villages. Quasi-political associations of various pursuasions in al-Mukallā', Say'ūn, Muqayras, Shiḥr, Laḥj, and Yāfi' are mentioned in various accounts of the period. In the village of Dīs near al-Mukallā' a local committee relying on voluntary contributions built a water-supply system.[33] The bundle of Ḥaḍramī charities and other rural-based welfare societies will be remembered from the previous chapter.

Migrants' and village associations were as much a part of the life of Aden's "alien Yemenis" as they were of village life. The village associations described previously were often inaugurated with fund-raising drives in Aden – or, for that matter, Jakarta or Cardiff. About fifty village associations in the greater Taiz region, part employment service, part social welfare association, and part recreational club, simultaneously supported members resident in Aden with insurance and educational benefits; and raised funds for wells, schools, or roads back home. Although the village associations were similar in many ways to "*baladī*" associations dismissed as "not civic" in Egypt, in Yemen the *nādīs* were seen as "an integral part of the political arena," and a "symbol of modernity, progress, and opposition."[34]

Two regions whose rural-organizational history has been best recorded, the Yāfi' tribal region of the western protectorates and the Ḥaḍramawt, were politically significant. Yāfi' and the two Ḥaḍramī sultanates – all places where the early colonial authorities blatantly interfered in local politics – refused to join the federation. They were in other respects quite different, however, Yāfi' being a largely tribal rural area and the Ḥaḍramawt a more urban culture.

What became known as the Yāfi' Reform Front was a special but illustrative case of rural organization in a highland region comprising mainly small farmers. Greater Yāfi', a decentralized tribal region further divided by British agreements with several stipendiary *shaykhs* and sultans, had resisted colonial proposals intermittently since 1903. Authorities regarded it as an all-but-ungovernable region of unruly, quarrelsome tribes. Certainly its internal politics were complex, but Europeans familiar with the region also knew they were not lacking in organizational and rule-making efforts.[35] According to one of its founders, the Reform Front emerged in a series of evolutionary stages:

from roots in a migrants' association in Indonesia, there developed a Yāfi' youth club, and then a Yāfi' federation. Then a community betterment association developed a constitution and was reincarnated as the Reform Front. Finally, it joined the revolution.[36]

The initial agenda of *Jabhat al-Iṣlāḥ al-Yāfi'iyya* involved community betterment, tribal reconciliation, and resistance to the colonial authority. A formal organization with an administrative committee representing each sub-tribe and specialized and local subcommittees, it began collecting donations and *zakat*, attending qāt sessions and religious meetings, and meeting with parties to local tribal conflicts. It even advanced a "free Yāfi' constitution." Mediation efforts, employing *'urf* mechanisms such as collecting rifles from each party, produced several cease-fires among the four feuding tribes of the region.[37] In the 1950s, Lower Yāfi'ī demands for more local benefits from the British-instituted Abyan Cotton Board led to a military revolt with arms supplied from al-Bayḍā' in North Yemen. This was partly suppressed with air-power.[38] After it joined the National Liberation Front in 1963, the Yāfi' Front redistributed rifles and became what the government and local sultans regarded as a "terrorist organization." The NLF later adopted the Yāfi' model of "tribal reform committees" and new non-conflict zones.

If Yāfi' was any sort of prototype it was of neo-tribal organization. The Ḥaḍramawt, geographically an island but also connected via its migrants, intellectuals, and merchant families into veritable global networks, and divided administratively into two sultanates and socially into *sayyid* and "common" strata, had a different experience. Its principal towns – al-Mukallā' port and Tarīm and Say'ūn in the wadi, inhabited by landed, merchant, and religious elites and by low-status *masākīn* – had an urban culture distinct from the tribalism of Yāfi' and even rural Ḥaḍramawt. The Ḥaḍramawt produced a multitude of permanent or ephemeral political, social, or welfare associations representing a wide spectrum of political views.

In addition to the welfare-type organizations mentioned previously, *Jam'iyyat al-Irshād*, the Society of Guidance, was born before World War I in Indonesia to represent Ḥaḍramī "commoners." The impetus for the *Irshād* evidently began over differing legal opinions (singular *fatwā*) on whether or not a *sayyida* could legally marry a lower-status man – something forbidden by *sayyid* men but condoned by a locally respected Sudanese law professor. Influenced by Egyptian Islamist modernists Muḥammad 'Abduh and Rashīd Riḍā', the *Irshādīs* claimed the *sayyids* exploited un-Islamic status divisions in Ḥaḍramī society. When this charge was leveled against the schools run by the predominantly *sayyid* Welfare Society, *sayyids* responded by forming the more exclusivist 'Alawī League. This division, wherein the two sides lobbed rival *fatwās* at each other, grew quite rancorous.[39]

Although the Ḥaḍramawt was divided along status lines and between two rival sultans, it also had something like a separate national identity and had often been marked separately on maps. In addition, as noted previously, its connections to Asia gave it commercial autonomy from colonial authorities. One wealthy local family was in the process of founding Saudi Arabia's largest banking empire. These conditions gave rise to several efforts at Ḥaḍramī unity; 1919 saw efforts from the sultans and even al-Azhar university in Cairo to mediate between the *Irshādīs* and the *'Alawīs*. In the late 1920s, a congress of returned Ḥaḍramī exiles met in al-Mukallā' and appealed, without success, to the rival Qa'ayṭī and Kathīrī sultans to convoke a national assembly and unify their two states. Similar meetings in Singapore passed resolutions aimed at promoting Ḥaḍramī economic development. In 1939, shortly after the advisory treaties went into effect, an Indonesia-based Ḥaḍramī Reform Committee appealed (unsuccessfully) to the British to recognize the unity and independence of Ḥaḍramawt.[40] In the early 1950s, *sayyids* and pro-British intellectuals established the Ḥaḍramawt Improvement Society, the Ḥaḍramawt Islamic Cooperative Party, and the Popular League.[41]

The post-war Ḥaḍramī Unity Movement continued to advocate administrative reform, the replacement of foreign "cadres" with educated Ḥaḍramīs, and Ḥaḍramawt unity and independence.[42] It was a distinctly elite movement of the rich, the educated, and the well born, many of whom had spent their lives in Asia. Their aspirations lacked appeal among commoners and farmers. *Irshādīs*, on the other hand, opposed the notion of Ḥaḍramī separatism. Political aspirations for a separate Ḥaḍramī state were nonetheless given impetus in the early 1960s by a concession of a 5,000-square-mile tract to the Pan-American Oil Company, any proceeds from which would be shared (two shares to al-Mukallā' to every share to the Kathīrī) between the two sultanates.[43]

By mid-century other ideological currents coursed in the region, many of them flowing from events in North Africa or the Levant. An incident at the middle school of Ghayl Bā Wazīr, a small oasis town near al-Mukallā', pushed these currents to the surface. It seems that two features of the program of a school celebration infuriated local authorities and their advisor. First, an Egyptian teacher delivered an address in praise of the United Arab Republic, formed between Egypt and Syria and subsequently to include Yemen. The next evening, an Egyptian morality play set in the Arabian Peninsula during the early Islamic era depicted slaves' aspirations for freedom.

Colonial authorities dismissed the school's headmaster, a member of the locally esteemed Bā Wazīr family, and four teachers. When hundreds of primary, middle, and secondary students gathered for a soccer match staged a protest, they were surrounded by armed security forces. The school was closed, sending students home where they spread the story throughout the region. This student "*intifāḍa*" became a *cause célèbre*. Teachers issued a "declaration of public opinion" (*bayān al-ra'y al-'āmm*) that was picked up by the cultural club in al-Mukallā'. The club was closed by the authorities. Now the *shaykhs* of the region responded with a *qaṣīda* (tribal verse), and the students of Aden College issued their own supportive *bayān*. The matter was reported in *al-Fikr*, *al-Janūb al-'Arabī*, and the colonial government press. Locally, it catalyzed formation of a Ḥaḍramī students' union, forerunner to the Union of Students of the Occupied South that appeared in Aden between 1960 and 1965.[44]

Another club in the inland Ḥaḍramī village of al-Ḥurayḍa in the early 1960s was dominated by modernist *sayyids*. The village council president, reportedly a worldly and astute politician, founded a cultural club for the expressed purpose of promoting local culture and fraternity across status lines. He donated a house, furniture, and books for evening classes in Arabic and arithmetic. The club's first event celebrated Algerian independence. The second was an Egyptian morality play about the Prophet's treatment of the black slave Bilāl, performed for about 300 of as many as 10,000 people at a traditional religious festival held in a local market-place. The third, and last, event was a gymnastics display for the sultan. Although the club proper faded at about the time of the YAR revolution, it laid the groundwork for avid support among the common youth for the Free Yemenis. The youth (*al-shabāb*), the new generation (*al-jīl al-jadīd*) had arrived, and they addressed all other men as either "*sayyid*" or "brother."[45]

Nationalist and pan-Arab parties

Political movements and parties became important insofar as opinion leaders and intellectual elites networked with community groups. Such networks were important in both revolutions, although in the North the sort of mass involvement in explicitly political activity recorded in occupied Yemen did not occur. Instead, intellectual associations became a major element of the Free Yemeni movement, and they became connected with village betterment societies. A Reform Society was founded in Ibb in 1944 to promote change in the direction of Egypt and Iraq, then constitutional monarchies.[46] An organization with the same name appeared in the Ḥujariyya around a school called *al-Madrasa al-Ahliyya* ("the primordial school"), not far from the New Generation School. *Hay'at al-Niḍāl*, the Organ of Struggle, was founded in Sana'a in the mid-1930s by the men later considered the fathers of the revolution, several of whom were poets. It spread to circles in Taiz, Ibb, and Dhamar, among *'ulamā'*, *sayyids*, *qāḍīs*, *shaykhs*, merchants, and travelers.

This movement blended liberal and Islamist thought. *Hay'at al-Niḍāl*, which specifically argued the possibility of effecting change without a formal organization, faded when its founders were imprisoned by the imam. It was replaced by an association called *Hay'at al-Amr bi-l-Ma'rūf wa-l-Nahī 'An al-Munkar* (Enjoining Good and Forbidding Evil, after a well-known Islamic slogan used, *inter alia*, by the Egyptian Muslim Brotherhood and the Bayt Ḥamīd al-Dīn imams) which issued pamphlets especially about the famine of 1940–43. These organizations are central to the story of the Free Yemeni movement, but were, like some of the Ḥaḍramī associations, also about competing versions of Islam – Zaydī and Shāfi'ī, old-guard and modernist, elitist and popular.[47]

Political organizing turned partisan in the mid-1940s. North Yemeni reformers in Aden established the *Ḥizb al-Aḥrār al-Yamanī* (the Free Yemeni Party) in 1944. It gained a following among intellectuals, merchants, *shaykhs*, judges, etc. especially in the southern uplands. Out of a nucleus of about thirty mostly Shāfi'ī merchant-class activists emerged *al-Jam'iyya al-Yamaniyya al-Kubrā* in 1945–46. To stay within the letter of Adeni law, this "Greater Yemeni Association" registered as a social and cultural society. For several years it was considered the center of the Free Yemeni movement. Its newspaper, *Ṣawt al-Yaman,* was the "voice" of the movement.[48] Along with another newspaper, and another called *al-Ikhwān al-Muslimūn* in Cairo, it published the Sacred National Charter in early 1948, marking the start of the constitutional revolt. The Free Yemenis' political, intellectual, and business contacts with *al-Ikhwān al-Muslimūn*'s publisher, the Muslim Brotherhood, and its Egyptian leader Ḥasan al-Bannā', led to speculation among Western diplomats that the Brotherhood was a salient force behind the revolt.[49]

On account of the publication of the Sacred National Charter and the subsequent revolt, hundreds of North Yemen's leading poets and men of letters – the *'ulamā'*, or "turbaned" ones – found themselves in the famous Ḥajja prison. They wrote and exchanged pleas for better prison conditions or for leniency, conciliatory compositions to the imams, eulogies for slain colleagues, tributes to other scholars, romantic poetry and secret works (recorded in egg-white or lemon juice) of protest or parody. Discussion sessions within the group were formalized, and they issued two handwritten newspapers.[50] The prison became the incubator for North Yemen's republican movement.

After the Greater Yemeni Association dissolved, some of its leaders re-petitioned the colonial government in 1951 to form an *al-Ittiḥād al-Yamanī* (Yemeni Federation) to serve as an umbrella for village associations. Community groups in Taiz and Ibb provinces were represented on its board, and their achievements were publicized in its newspaper. The federation collected contributions to village associations and their projects, erected a school for Yemeni migrants in Aden, sent students to universities abroad, and sponsored cultural events. But it also actively opposed the imam and the colonial authorities. As such, it is widely recognized as a forebear of the 1962 republican revolution, the independence crusade, and the cause of Yemeni unity,[51] and the later Confederation of Yemeni Development Associations.

One prominent enduring party, founded in occupied Yemen in 1950, was called *Rābiṭat Abnā' al-Janūb al-'Arabī* (literally League of the Sons of South Arabia) or the South Arabian League (SAL). It was a political party based in Laḥj but with some members in Ḥaḍramawt, Shabwa, and Aden. Characterized as "Nāṣirite" by the British, "bourgeois nationalist" by its more radical successors, the "party of deposed sultans" by some observers, and "part of the Islamic-reformist current" by still others, [52] it is almost always portrayed as tragically flawed. Its top leadership included well-known modernizing *sayyids*, sultans, landowners, and graduates of English universities who enjoyed some support among members of youth, cultural, and sports clubs, the Yemeni Federation, the Islamic Association, and at least one white-collar labor union. But it lacked a social base of support for its collage of positions advocating an independent South Arabian federation of the protectorates; national liberation, Arab nationalism, and Islamic social justice; abolition of British laws on foreign emigration; and instruction in Arabic. After its candidates' poor showing in the 1955 Aden elections, conflicts arose within the party over participation in subsequent legislative elections and the proposed South Arabian Federation. SAL joined with and separated from both FLOSY and the NLF. Overall, it did play a prominent part in the late colonial drama, and would re-emerge, as the League of the Sons of Yemen, some three decades later as a political party in unified Yemen.

These early partisan groups expressed an incomplete, inchoate, reformist Yemeni nationalism. A second phase of party formation, given impetus by the creation of Israel in 1948, the Algerian and Egyptian revolutions, the 1956 British–French–Israeli invasion of Suez, Kuwaiti independence and an Iraqi invasion in 1961, and the 1962 revolution in North Yemen, launched Yemeni branches of two influential pan-Arab parties, the Arab Nationalist Movement and the Ba'th. A generation of Yemeni politicians cut their political teeth in the Ba'th, which remained a viable tendency within Yemeni politics through the 1990s. The Muslim Brotherhood, for all its apparent links to both the *Irshādīs* and the Free Yemenis, did not surface as a distinct party inside Yemen in the colonial period.

This phase of party formation also sired two rival independence groups that eventually fought for control of the revolution: the Front for the Liberation of Occupied South Yemen (FLOSY) and the NLF or *al-Jabha al-Qawmiyya*. FLOSY, the more moderate element, incorporated the ATUC-affiliated PSP, elements of the SAL, and assorted Nāṣirīs under the wing of Egyptian military and advisors stationed in Taiz after 1962. Subsequently most of SAL and organized labor defected from FLOSY to the NLF. Except during a temporary merger of FLOSY with the NLF in 1966, the two vied for Aden's educated young men. In the countryside, however, it wasn't much of a contest. The more progressive NLF, which traced its ideological genealogy to egalitarian message of the *Irshādīs*[53] as well as to pan-Arab nationalism, recruited a rural following by cultivating cells among the disgruntled but ambitious youth. Nine shadowy, predominantly rural groups threw their weight behind the NLF: the Yāfi'ī Reform Front, and others, mostly previously unknown, calling themselves by names as different as the Revolutionary Organization of the Youth of Occupied South Yemen and *Tashkīl al-Qabā'il* (the Tribal Formation). This motley assembly of very different organizations from throughout the South began meeting secretly, then held a congress and issued a communiqué in June 1963 from Taiz. It dated the rebellion against the federal army to October 14 1963, when a military incident occurred in the Radfān mountains, north of Aden.

The press

A key way diverse conservative, radical, parochial, and working forces competed, coalesced, and influenced political events was through the press. If civil society represents an autonomous sphere of mass expression and a forum of public and elite opinion, then the press is an important feature of civil society. Its expansion, recording and interpreting of events, and dodging of legal restrictions were important indicators of the Aden opening. In newspapers, pamphlets, poetry, and other media, parties and politicians staked out public positions, and others commented. Authorities waged a continual, losing battle to keep dissident views out of print. Like the press in other Arab capitals, the press began with publications for expatriate audiences and imperial interests; then entered a factional period of competing private, partisan, and government publications; and finally underwent a consolidation when the press became a vehicle for mobilization.[54]

Typesetting began humbly enough with the importation of a press to Aden prison in 1853. In the 1880s Persian and Jewish entrepreneurs published in several languages. An English-language *Aden Weekly Gazette* first appeared in 1900. In the 1930s Singapore had seven Yemeni publications, at least three of them reporting Ḥaḍramī affairs, and Indonesia had thirteen. After World War II Yemenis began publishing in Aden, and by the mid-1960s two dozen Aden newspapers, including two English and four Arabic dailies, documented events.[55] Although few papers printed more than 500 copies per issue, and readership was limited by 80 percent illiteracy, it would be nearly thirty years before the Yemeni press would be so varied and active again. In addition, the Aden market sold a range of foreign newspapers, magazines, and books in Arabic, English, and other languages. In 1940 the mercantile Aden Association published a landmark commercial Arabic paper, *Fatāt al-Jazīra*. Subsequently the AA issued a weekly called *al-Qalam al-ʿAdanī*, and a couple of individual merchants also financed papers dedicated to "Aden for the Adenis." A privately owned newspaper published in the 1960s that would reappear in the 1990s, *al-Ayyām*, also had an English-language version in the colonial era, *The Recorder*.

Inside the Kingdom of Yemen, politics adopted a literary genre. Between 1939 and 1941, the monthly *al-Ḥikma al-Yamaniyya*, produced by the *Niḍāl* group on the imam's presses, published fiction and cultural essays under the title *al-Iṣlāḥ*. These writings defined the early Free Yemeni Movement. Later, the Aden business community and about thirty Yemeni merchants in East Africa bought a press which allowed the Free Yemenis to publish *Ṣawt al-Yaman*, Aden's first partisan newspaper, in 1946. Another Free Yemeni newspaper, *al-Fuḍūl*, devoted particular attention to the movement's leaders incarcerated in Ḥajja prison after the failed 1948 constitutional movement. As noted above, the poets and writers detained in Ḥajja, in turn, smuggled out coded or invisible-ink messages for publication in manuscript copies or the Aden press.

Nascent political parties and organizations all tried to publish, though several were shut down before they got established. SAL founded *al-Nahḍa* around 1949, and when it was banned began publishing *al-Fajr*, and then *al-Janūb al-'Arabī*. *Al-Janūb al-'Arabī* was also closed by British authorities for criticizing their proposals for the South Arabian Federation. The United National Front put out a paper called *al-Ba'th*, edited by the head of the transport workers' union; the Ba'th Party published one called *al-Fikr*. Members of the pro-Federation group in the old AA began two separate weeklies in Aden in 1959. After the first NLF conference, a new newspaper called *al-Thawrī* appeared, which would later be published under the banner of the YSP central committee.

The first issue of the first ATUC organ *al-'Amal* appeared in October 1957, with the same editor and format as *al-Ba'th*, under the slogan "Freedom, Bread, and Peace." Allowed to publish only 1,500 copies a week, *al-'Amal* was banned within a year for inciting labor insubordination, only to resurface as *al-'Ummāl*, under the slogan "Freedom, Unity, and Socialism." Representing views variously characterized as communist, Ba'thī, Nāṣirī, and petit bourgeois (in one issue the ATUC leader admitted that the labor movement's goals and ideology were "ambiguous"[56]), *al-'Ummāl* was the torchbearer of the organized labor, the NLF, and ultimately, the independence movement. In January 1967 its offices were burnt down, reportedly by FLOSY partisans. In one form or another, however, it published for much of the next thirty years.

Episodic meetings and appeals

In addition to the formal NGOs, parties, syndicates, and news organs, less institutionalized activities expressed popular concerns. Many civic projects originated in after-lunch gatherings where schoolfriends huddled around radios. Politicians entertained in their *dīwāns*, migrants raised funds for home-town improvements, and union activists conferred among themselves or with the rank-and-file. Lounging and chatting are not, obviously, "civil society" as such. But the routinization of a cultural mainstay around civic projects and political issues most assuredly helped formulate public opinion. Organized both hierarchically between power-brokers and clients and vertically among equals, meetings disseminated a discourse and constituted a potential basis of political action. That is why they were banned under the state of emergency. Clearly in the 1950s and 1960s the discourse reflected the content of radio messages, perhaps especially Cairo's *Voice of the Arabs*, while the disposition toward action changed from passivity to efficacy. Activism pervaded even apolitical gatherings of tribes, annual folk festivals at Shāfi'ī saints' shrines, some weekly markets, and increasingly popular football matches, other sport competitions, and school-days.

Colonial authorities feared mass gatherings because they recognized their political potential.

The most momentous gatherings of the late colonial era were labor demonstrations and party conferences. When the barely citified tribesmen in Aden's workforce turned out *en masse*, they vastly outnumbered Aden's voters, and shook the streets. Another sort of "popular assembly" were partisan conventions such as the SAL, FLOSY, and the NLF founding conferences. In the absence of voting rights, the number of people attending meetings was a barometer of political support. For clandestine meetings or conferences-in-exile, individuals represented tribal or union constituencies. The claim of a thousand union and tribal leaders at the NLF's founding conference in Taiz in 1963 was, by this reckoning, quite a showing, and it was in this way that other unions, villages, tribes, and guerrilla cells later shifted their backing to the NLF.

From the earliest days until the end, colonial officers blamed widespread popular opposition to their administration on either primitive tribal irrationality or the perfidy, subsidies, or arms supplies of outsiders – Ottomans, and later Nāṣirites or Yemeni republicans. In their search for chronically short intelligence on the subversives and for ways to stem the rising tide of dissent, authorities resorted to raiding meetings, rounding up activists, torturing some of them in prison, and blocking the International Red Cross and Amnesty International from visiting al-Manṣūra and other prisons.[57] In other respects, too, colonial guards established an unfortunate precedent for violation of fundamental rights. Over a century's worth of anti-insurgency campaigns by the eventually 15,000-strong federal army and the Royal Air Force culminated in an operation poetically called "the Nutcracker." Aden's strikes and martial law fed on one another. Even before the onset of the armed struggle, non-violent PSP and SAL leaders were jailed, prompting work stoppages and marches. Repeatedly, strikes or demonstrations turned into riots when police and soldiers aimed their weapons into crowds. Suspected rabble-rousers were rounded up, sometimes by the dozen and sometimes by the hundreds, and then variously released, tried, or deported.[58] Rebels fought back with the weapons of the weak: pipe-bombs, booby-traps, and sabotage.

In those days there were no human rights or legal aid societies, but there were scatter-shot efforts to defend legal and civil liberties. Detentions and deportations were the proximate cause of many strikes. Resorting to a technique from India, 15 of 107 jailed unionists staged a hunger strike in 1963. Students marched, political detainees penned letters, poems, memoranda, satire, and petitions. The Aden government threatened to resign unless martial law was lifted. Versions of these events published by the Aden press were picked up in the Cairo and London media. Essayists, theorists, and journalists aroused elite and foreign opinion. Pamphlets circulated in Crater and al-Tawāhī. Yemeni intellectuals were in touch with UN, Red Cross, and Amnesty International teams investigating conditions. There has been little research on the extent to which Yemeni defendants or Aden's attorneys, mainly Indians and Pakistanis, used colonial courts to defend the rights of the accused.

Revolution and consolidation

The National Liberation Front won the revolutionary struggle because unlike other organizations it secured a mass following within the rank-and-file of the labor federation, in tribal areas such as Yāfi', and inside the federal army. The decisive events came after the June 1967 Arab–Israeli war, when some South Arabian federal troops refused to fight the nationalist guerrillas. Meanwhile closure of the Suez Canal deprived Aden of much of its custom. In November, amidst gun-battles in Crater and Ma'allā, sections of the South Arabian army joined the NLF. The federal government collapsed, and colonial authorities, already closing the naval base, had no alternative but to hand power to the NLF when they departed on November 30 1967. The various movements of the colonial period were consolidated into the NLF and its political organization. As already noted, the NLF took control of a massive public sector, nationalized private fixed property, and drove both political rivals and entrepreneurs abroad.

Social capital was also incorporated into the party-state. All educational establishments were taken over by the state. Sports clubs were reincarnated under names like Solidarity, Victory, and People; in 1973 they were reorganized under a High Sports Council. The Lake Library became the 'Abd Allāh Bā Dhīb Library, for a revolutionary hero.[59] Tarīm's several major private libraries were nationalized as one collection. All *waqf* was expropriated. The ruling party made good use of its cells and cadres among political, cultural, and popular organizations to centralize them under its leadership. The ATUC, its numbers vastly reduced, became the centerpiece of a "corporate" system where syndicates accepted open alliance with the government, also their employer, in exchange for public housing, social insurance, and a say in enterprise management. All schools, regardless of their origins, were nationalized and given a national curriculum. *Al-Thawrī* survived as an official YSP organ, and *al-'Ummāl* reappeared in 1969 as *Ṣawt al-'Ummāl*, the organ of the central council of the Federation of Labor Unions, but virtually all the private and party newspapers vanished soon after the establishment of the official government daily *14 October*. All these institutions were to dedicate themselves to the revolution.

The model for popular participation in the People's Democratic Republic, patterned on Cuban and Maoist models, emphasized mass organizations, cooperatives, and popular defense committees. New "mass" organizations were the Yemeni Democratic Peasants' Union, the General Union of Yemeni Women, and the Yemeni Democratic Youth League. Cooperatives, a way of managing redistributed land and small boats, served mainly as input-suppliers and wholesale purchasing agents and never evolved into full-scale producers' cooperatives. The popular defense committees that appeared spontaneously in Shaykh 'Uthmān in the early 1970s were later established in other townships and some villages to organize volunteers for vaccination or literacy campaigns and to solve social disputes; but eventually their links to the security apparatus made them agents of the state rather than of popular concerns. They represented, in short, GO–NGOs, more part of the state than of civil society.

This chapter has been a video of the main cultural and political activities during the first political opening. The conclusions are fourfold. First, there was certainly pluralism, in the form of groups and publications representing the full range of opinion from conservative, mercantile, and pro-British to radical, Marxist, and liberationist; and from provincial (including Adeni) to Yemeni and pan-Arab nationalist. These positions, moreover, evolved with changing political circumstances, responding to events in the Yemeni and Arab arenas and even to the messages of Muṣaddiq, then Castro, Mao, and Ho Chi Minh.

Secondly, the line between *ahlī* groups and modern civic organizations is so fine that it is virtually indistinguishable. It is, in other words, heuristic rather than empirical distinction. It should not be confused with a community–national–international spectrum, or with a left–right continuum. Not that political rhetoric doesn't incorporate simplistic dichotomies. Revolutionaries themselves, Aden's educated *shabāb*, waged an ideological war against "tribalism" as well as "feudalism." Like the colonial rulers, they labeled tribes as backward (*mutakhallif*). In the revolutionary analysis, tribalism and its analog *sayyid*-ism were vestiges of underdevelopment, part of the constellation of "superstitions" (*khurāfāt*) that inhibited revolutionary consciousness in some parts of the homeland. Politically, this analysis justified undermining the authority of the older generation of local leaders, explained rural resistance to democratic centralism, and required exporting revolution to North Yemen, Oman, and the Gulf.

The South Yemeni experience has several things to say to cultural-essentialist arguments about natural Arab tendencies to Islamism and/or tribalism. First, in the early twentieth century Islamist political thinking was a radical critique of tradition, a modernizing populist movement with an internationalist outlook affected by events in Indonesia, Singapore, Hyderabad, and Cairo, yet emphasizing commonality with Yemeni tribes and *masākīn*. Secondly, plenty of tribesmen, *sayyids*, and *'ulamā'* found common ground with their nephews agitating in the streets of Aden for a radical revolution. Thirty years ago literate Yemenis were reading Marx along with Muḥammad 'Abduh. Grass-roots politics can be either conservative or radical, as we know from the comparative literature.

Thirdly, counting as "civil" only that which is legalized, registered, or recognized by the state introduces some profound biases. Governments authorize client associations, barring others as foreign puppets or terrorist cells. Consequently, legal associations are mostly headed by regime clients, or clever upper-class dissidents who maneuver around the law. There is a worthwhile distinction, empirical as well as normative, between pamphleteering and bomb-throwing; but there is also, as comparative students of revolution know, a point when government repression or downright unreasonableness may push youth and even their fathers to counter guns with grenades. But illegal activities can indeed be civic, as can short-lived or episodic associations and one-time events. Part of the reason that voluntary activities remain informal is that governments either shut them down or take them over.

Finally, there is much in the politics of the mid-twentieth century to presage Yemeni unity: many issues, tendencies, slogans, newspapers, organizations, and parties survived a generation of hibernation only to reemerge after 1990 in the next opening to party competition proper. In the meantime, there would be another civic opening of a very different sort, one drawing on the rural "self-help" or community-betterment movement whose early development was described in the previous chapter and mentioned several times here. This second opening is the subject of the next chapter.

5 Self-help, social capital, and state power

Yemen's second political opening differed from either the first or the third, for the action shifted from national to community politics. The context for this opening was the tenuous rule of an unstable North Yemeni republican state over a society undergoing a profound socio-economic transformation fueled by infusions of foreign capital in the form of remittances and foreign aid. Under these circumstances, and with ample resort to folk mechanisms, *ad hoc* road, school, and utilities projects transformed everyday material life, enhanced the power of the state, and delivered the global market to rural North Yemen. The structural–functional NGO model, as foreign development experts learned, fitted badly, but the impressive project record showed that formal modern organization was not a prerequisite for getting important things done. Furthermore, while legislation and financial allocations certainly influenced the organization of civil society, LDAs not only negotiated with the center from a position of strength but collectively affected the structure of the government as well. The case study of self-help also shows the importance of basic services as the material basis for state hegemony, underscoring how the imposition of legal–rational accounting methods is part of that process. As far as I know, nothing like it has been documented elsewhere in the Arab world.

The various perspectives on Arab civil society identified in the introductory chapter each shed some insight into the phenomenon known in English as LDAs and in Arabic as *taʿāwun al-ahlī*. In comparative cross-national perspective the Yemeni LDAs seemed a remarkable instance of local self-help, although the popular dimension of cooperation also infused its practice with folk idioms cultural essentialists often dismissed as inherently reactionary. Like its precedents in pre-revolutionary community betterment, the "cooperative movement" (*al-ḥaraka al-taʿāwuniyya*) responded to a political and economic opening in ways that adapted custom to changing circumstances. Defying assumptions about institutional formality, cultural essences, and state control, projects in the non-governmental, not-for-profit sector contributed substantially to the material and political transformation of a society characterized journalistically as "galloping from the fourteenth century into the nineteenth." Not unlike social revolutions elsewhere, this process entailed a considerable measure of struggle. Ultimately, however, project activities linked small towns and their hinterlands to commercial markets and the central state.

This chapter tells the story of Yemen's cooperative movement in three narratives, each an application of one way of looking at Arab civil society. The first is a structural–functional, policy-oriented view that attributes projects to formal LDAs. The second interprets *al-ta'āwun al-ahlī* as cultural expression. The third presents the movement as a function of state policy and legislation. Each of these interpretations has its own integrity, supported by empirical evidence and analytical coherence. In combination, however, they direct us toward a more dynamic fourth interpretation of civic activism in a space between the public and the private sectors and between governments and households. Regardless of whether we look at the NGO properties of LDAs, the cultural continuities in *ta'āwun,* the centralizing mission of the state, or efforts to clear and defend an autonomous civic space, however, the substantial effects of projects on everyday life in villages and towns speak for themselves.

Yemeni LDAs from a comparative development perspective

In the mid-1970s, international development consultants visiting North Yemen marveled over sweeping panoramas from cliff-perched towns down terraced slopes to the bucolic thatch-hut villages of the Tihama, all unspoiled by motor-roads, power-lines, or commercial development. Where, however, jeepable tracks, small water projects, or new schools were discovered in the countryside, they were almost invariably credited to "LDAs," local institutions linked through an electoral process to the Confederation of Yemeni Development Associations (CYDA). The LDAs looked like grassroots organizations supportive of donors' "mission" to improve rural infrastructure. A 1981 World Bank report concluded, for instance, that "the Local Development Association (LDA) movement, which is based on local initiative, represents a bottom-up, self-reliant and decentralized mechanism for meeting basic rural infrastructure needs...based on priorities determined at the local level in the rural areas."[1]

During the 1970s alone, local and regional LDAs expanded the intercity triangle of paved roads built by foreign donors for the government with dirt tracks to every provincial, sub-provincial, and market center in the country. They introduced generators and water pumps to small towns and large villages, opened hundreds of primary schools, and literally outspent the government in delivering village and neighborhood services. International development experts familiar with a wide range of third world experiences including, for instance, Harambee in Kenya and Ujamaa in Tanzania, wrote glowingly of Yemeni self-help associations.

Case studies of the Yemeni LDAs commissioned by international development missions in Sana'a corroborated the aggregate project data. Of four LDAs within an easy drive of Sana'a visited by a USAID consultant in 1975, two were quite impressive. The Ānis development association, founded by about 150 men in 1970, elected a board, created committees, wrote a three-year plan (featuring, *inter alia*, 103 village drinking-water projects, schools for every community, and several roads) and completed seven or eight water projects, a school, and roadworks relying mainly on beneficiary donations. Since its founding a couple of years earlier the Khamir LDA, or *Ta'āwun Ḥāshid*, had undertaken a road, a student hostel, a physician's residence (attached to Khamir's Kuwaiti-built hospital), five village schools, and several small water-supply improvements. Although LDAs in the other two locations were considerably less active, hypothesizing that they were at the beginning of a four-stage process of institutionalization, the consultant concluded that "the four LDA's studied are bona fide expressions of local initiative for development."[2]

In comparative perspective, the cooperative movement's accomplishments were noteworthy. Another American study ranked three local-level organizations – agricultural cooperatives near Taiz and Hodeida and a village electrical cooperative in al-Maḥwīt governorate – at the top of forty-one organizations in seven nations in terms of their impact on community development. Although each of these ventures straddled the line between private enterprise and services cooperation, and were beneath the LDA system *per se*, the leadership of "youth *shaykhs*," the availability of cash from remittances, and resourceful management offered exceptionally successful examples of rural self-help.[3] A number of other rural surveys for bilateral and multilateral assistance agencies, including my own, documented further project accomplishments by local development groups particularly in provincial and sub-provincial towns with populations in the range of 5,000–10,000.[4] Still another major, scholarly, cross-national study of rural organizations and participation in developing countries compared the Yemeni LDAs with other multipurpose, inclusive, locality-based, services-oriented associations, and found in the Yemeni associations a rare example of "development from below."[5] Specifically, it seemed that with some central support LDAs successfully mobilized migrants resources by tapping into strong community sentiments.

These studies led to a number of projects designed by Western and multilateral assistance agencies to channel rural development projects through the LDAs. The logic of these programs was that LDAs were able to auto-finance simple construction but required basic technical assistance to improve planning, budgeting, management, and engineering. Their design emphasized institution building and training in skills such as cost-benefit analysis. In addition to rather modest funds for clinics, culverts, small-scale improvements to local water supply, agricultural experimentation stations, and the like, project designers envisioned teams of expatriate specialists in community health, sanitation, and appropriate technology working alongside counterparts in the LDAs. It is part of the argument of this chapter that a major problem with these projects was embedded in assumptions about the necessity of organizational formality, the role of foreign influence, and the nature of community cooperation.

Self-help and local traditions

In the mid-to-late 1970s, North Yemen opened up to Western researchers, offering especially fertile ground for ethnographers. Anthropologists, most but not all of whom worked in tribal, Zaydī communities in the northern highlands, have written exceptions to many essentialist notions of cultural atavism that nonetheless show how difficult it is to translate "*al-taʿāwun al-ahlī*" as "LDA." By and large, in contrast to development practitioners, anthropologists interpreted *al-taʿāwun* as subsuming material innovation within cultural roles, idioms, and mechanisms beyond the formal institutional structure of state-sponsored LDAs.

First, except in the Ḥujariyya and other southern uplands regions where village committees had functioned intermittently since the 1940s and a scattering of administrative towns, LDAs were not visible in rural areas. Most had no office or ongoing institutional presence. One could live in a village for a long time without hearing of one. On the other hand, whereas LDAs were not part of the tangible reality of village life, *taʿāwun* projects, often autonomous from any institutional entity, appeared in virtually every account. For instance, from the perspective of Banī Awwām in the Ḥajja mountains, the LDA was a "government-sponsored democratic institution superimposed on a relatively remote and uneducated population with a strong sense of local autonomy..., a

Table 5.1. *Government and independent roads, schools, and water projects, North Yemen, 1961–1986*

	1961		1976		1981		1986	
	state	parochial	state	LDAs	state	LDAs	state	LDAs
asphalt roads*			765		1578		2296	
other roads*	231	–		5100		17699		21548
schools	56	616	1107	581	2834	1730	4363	1529
water	–	(1000s)	5 urban	684	95	919	1162	267

Sources: Carapico, "Political Economy of Self-Help," tables 8.1–8.5
CPO, *Statistical Yearbook 1987*, table 2/4
* roads: cumulative kilometers
Note: State projects financed primarily from foreign aid

deep-seated suspicion of the central government and no prior experience with either democratic structures or development."[6] Scattered, modest local project initiatives originated with village notables acting autonomously from the "passive and unimaginative" LDA.[7]

Secondly, *ta'āwun* was most frequently interpreted as one among several modern forms of tribal expression. In one verdant basin in the mountains of al-Maḥwīt governorate, the tribal mechanism of *jayyish* (as communal labor is known locally) was applied to clean cisterns, build mosques, and clear tracks. This informal "cooperation," heavily reliant on the cash flow from remittances, was organized according to tribal custom, beyond the formal development association fostered by the government.[8] Although not every farmer joined a jocular triennial morning's *jayyish* to clean debris from an irrigation cistern, apparently, there was little resentment of "free-riders" because of a general belief that others would contribute commensurably another time.[9]

In several cases the LDA seemed subsumed within the responsibilities of local leaders, for better or for worse. Often the district-level LDA was run by someone called *shaykh*, perhaps out of his own *dīwān*. Most notably, the active *Ta'āwun Ḥāshid* was founded, initially run, and subvented financially by the paramount *shaykh* of the Ḥāshid confederation, 'Abd Allāh al-Aḥmar. Ḥāshid unified the six districts of the plateau region where Ḥāshid tribes predominated under a single LDA, and al-Aḥmar and his brother-in-law, Mujāhid Abū Shawārib, enhanced their power through development projects.[10] The tribal summons, customarily calling men to defend or expand their common honor, recruited volunteers and contributions for collective services.[11] In another sort of example from the poor northern Tihama district of al-Mikhlāf, an old *iqṭāʿī-shaykh*, much more a feudal landlord to his sharecroppers than a tribal leader, headed a moribund LDA that neglected to either initiate or support projects.[12]

Tribal practices could facilitate fund-raising. The well-codified "principle of corporate subscription" in Jabal Rāziḥ in the far northwest mountains obligates members of a tribe (*gharīm* or subscriber) to contribute to collective expenses. Tribal leaders would meticulously divide expenses among long lists of names.[13] A comparison of the active LDA in Ānis, with negligible "cooperation" in nearby but more remote Jabal Rayma attributed the difference to Ānis's strong tribal ethic, characteristic of the plateau region, which fortified the range of mechanisms for raising contributions to projects serving one or more villages. By contrast, the formerly royalist semi-feudal Rayma aristocracy resisted modernization. Thus traditional social relations supported the LDA in Ānis but sabotaged Rayma's development association.[14]

While tribal motifs featured prominently in *taʿāwun* leadership and fund-raising, however, by no means was it limited to especially tribal areas. In the Tihama, for instance, including such traditionally non-tribal towns as Zabīd, the port of al-Makhā', and the poverty-stricken fishing community of Khūkha, significant LDA and/or autonomous *taʿāwun* projects were registered. Similarly, projects serving urban neighborhoods in Sana'a, Hodeida, and Taiz utilized other bases of solidarity. Districts populated by tribes belonging to Ḥāshid and Bakīl were neither more nor less likely than other areas to engage in self-help.

Thirdly, even though mobilization campaigns may have manipulated cultural symbols, project activity was about economic change, not the preservation of tradition. The commercially lucrative switch to extensive qāt production in Jabal Rāziḥ, not unlike those in other alpine communities, revealed a "flurry of self-help improvements" by individuals, communities, and sometimes an LDA as qāt farmers and dealers financed road-building projects conducive to their economic interests.[15] Such projects manifested prosperity, consumerism, and market orientation.

Although in many communities traditional leaders took initiatives, LDAs afforded political opportunities to non-elites. For instance, in the plateau town of ʿAmrān, south of Khamir on the road to Sana'a, the 1978 cooperative elections gave half of the twenty-four LDA board seats to two groups not represented in the old power structure: the "youth" (*shabāb*), most dedicated to the idea of cooperative self-help; and merchants, including six of the formerly despised *bayyāʿ* (peddler) strata, most interested in market expansion.[16]

Other scholars saw *ta'āwun* as local struggle over these socio-economic changes. In the Maḥwītī highlands, the questions of whether and where to build roads to connect formerly remote mountain communities led to conflict between modernizing and conservative forces as well as between neighboring tribes, for road projects not only required substantial contributions coordinated among communities but also promised to revolutionize everyday material life in part by making it possible to install electricity, water, and other services. Ḥufāsh's richest *shaykh* headed that district's LDA and spearheaded extensive road building with two LDA and two family-owned bulldozers, while engaged in a murderous feud with a neighboring tribal chief. Among the non-LDA projects were an unused Kuwaiti-built hospital, a small dispensary run out of another *shaykh*'s home, various locally rigged roads, schools, and cisterns, and a failed municipal generator taken over by a pair of butchers as a private enterprise.[17]

The blasting of roads through the rugged northwest mountains occasioned a class conflict between semi-feudal landowners and the republican "*shabāb*." In 1968, the traditional heads of local semi-formal welfare societies in al-Maḥwīt decided to build a track across the shortest distance from the town to the Hodeida–Sana'a road, over an uninhabited rock outcrop. After they formed an LDA and petitioned for al-Maḥwīt to become a province, CYDA provided funds for bulldozer rental, and a cosmopolitan young military governor camped out along the track with semi-voluntary *jayyish* teams from tribes throughout the entire region. No sooner was it finished than communities not served elected their own LDAs and decided to build a second road through agricultural districts. This initiative pitted *shabāb* and migrants against some powerful landlords who refused to yield the right of way. The landlords' men set up a roadblock and arrested the activists. Yet the LDA completed a road planned by Irish Concern engineers working for CYDA. Even the rough-hewn, flood-washed one-lane mud track that opened in 1976 stimulated commerce and further construction of branch roads and other services throughout the province.[18] In one sub-district, a new youth club and local merchants elected a "youth" *shaykh* who temporarily united popular forces. Villagers later built feeder tracks with true-volunteer labor, installed generators in five villages, and built two cisterns, three elementary schools, and a very impressive mosque.[19]

Migrants were occasionally actors on the *ta'āwun* stage, but were less responsible for these changes than we might imagine. Although Aden generation migrants had indeed important innovations, and even in the 1970s there were some good anecdotes about migrants bringing generators on donkey-back to light up the village for Ramaḍān, and it always helped to have a powerful patron in Sana'a, the work was done by those who were there. Moreover, there was no discernible correlation between migration rates and project records at the district level.[20] This suggests an ecological fallacy in assuming that because remittances collectively constituted the capital available for investment, migrants were making investment decisions. If anything, there was an inverse correlation, because poorer districts tended to have high migration rates and wealthy areas averaged higher project expenditures. This point is important in that it addresses the presumed passivity of traditional society.

Legislative basis of the LDAs

One important argument about Arab civil society is that it depends on government to create an enabling environment, and indeed the official history of the LDAs begins and ends with central legislation and mobilization. Each of five YAR administrations issued laws pertaining to the cooperative movement, whose history unfolded in four main phases: informal community betterment prior to the revolution, loose coordination between 1963 and 1974, empowerment and mobilization for the next decade, and reincarnation as the branches of government from the mid-1980s onwards. Thus despite a more localized orientation, the second opening also recapitulates the four stages of license, mobilization, conflict, and co-optation of other civic openings.

In 1962 the Free Officers suspended restrictions on association, made *zakat* payment voluntary, and promised to eradicate ignorance, poverty, and disease. Law 11 and Law 26 of 1963, patterned on Egyptian legislation, legalized cooperatives and associations organized on a simple general assembly/executive board model.[21] Some associations (notably Taiz city's) complied, but the civil war made organizational activity difficult. Overall, however, the repeal of restrictive edicts removed some legal and economic barriers to community betterment projects.

Upon assuming power in 1968, the civilian government established a Department of Youth, Labor, and Social Affairs (DYLSA) within the Ministry of Local Administration to promote cooperative investments, civic institutions, and producers' associations.[22] In the next few years, DYLSA registered several "development" or "cooperative" associations. By the spring of 1973 it oversaw foundation of a confederation of twenty-eight associations: this become known (in English) as CYDA, the Confederation (*Ittiḥād*) of Yemeni Development Associations.[23] The second of two conferences selected Ibrāhīm al-Ḥamdī of the "northwest region cooperative society" to head the twenty-one-member administrative committee.

A year later, in June 1974, Lt.-Col. al-Ḥamdī launched a bloodless military "corrective movement" within which the "cooperative movement" figured prominently. The new president convened a larger CYDA conference of sixty-five associations, promulgated a cooperative law, and scheduled elections for the LDAs, their provincial councils, and the CYDA executive board. Law 35 of 1975 authorized the administrative boards of town or district "local cooperative development associations" to spend half of local *zakat*, a quarter of municipalities' revenues, a new 2 percent cooperative customs duty, cinema taxes, and other modern-sector taxes on community improvement.[24] Accompanying legislation decentralized local administration from the subprovince or *qaḍā'* to the *nāḥiyya* or district, tripling the number of administrative units and undermining the power formerly exercised by the *'āmil al-qaḍā'*. While the Ministry of Local Administration, having earlier replaced the imamic *baladiyya* (municipalities) ministry, was absorbed into the prime minister's office, the DYLSA became an independent ministry, the MYLSA.

Law 35 of 1975 retained the 1963 general assembly/executive board model. Under Law 35, however, the general assembly delegate represented each 500 persons, a hamlet or neighborhood. Each seven-to-nine-man board or "*hay'at al-ta'āwun al-ahlī li-l-taṭwīr*" elected a president, secretary-general, and financial officer. Districts were not required to have LDAs, nor were LDAs necessarily *nāḥiyya*-level associations. The LDAs were granted a high degree of legal autonomy, and said to represent a "legal personality."

The 1975 law was silent on two upper tiers of the LDA/CYDA hierarchy. A committee of all LDA presidents in each governorate, called a coordinating council (CC), was chaired by the (appointed) governor but elected its own secretary-general. Each LDA sent three board members to the general assembly of CYDA, which elected eleven of its members to the serve on the *Ittiḥād* board along with the CCs' secretaries-general. The CYDA board too was to elect a secretary-general and a president (assumed to be the president of the Republic). Under this system, the first-ever YAR-wide elections were held at each level – subdistrict, district, province, and CYDA – in 1976, and a major conference brought three men from every participating locality to Sana'a.

Many of these delegates had never seen a budget or a check-book. CYDA and MYLSA issued mimeographed accounting guidelines for submitting budget proposals to the Central Planning Organization (CPO) and CYDA. These guidelines included a formula for calculating the distribution of costs among beneficiaries, the LDA, and the state. The costs of schools were divided equally in thirds. The government would help provinces with trunk roads but left feeder tracks of less than thirty kilometers to LDAs and localities. Similarly, the state would finance up to 80 percent of urban water supplies but not necessarily get involved in small water projects. Half the cost of clinics would be borne by the locality, a quarter by the LDA, and a quarter by the Ministry of Health.[25] Teachers and health workers would be supplied by the relevant ministry, it was assumed.

Al-Ḥamdī's successors continued to support the cooperative movement. The brief al-Ghashmī administration raised the share of *zakat* earmarked for local development to three-quarters and promoted a second round of elections for late 1978. By this time a new, four-story, stone, aluminum, and glass building housed CYDA. Most importantly, the number of associations registered with the confederation rose from twenty-nine in 1973, to seventy in 1974, to 152 in 1977.[26] Project activity continued apace.

The YAR's last president, 'Alī'Abd Allāh Ṣāliḥ, had even bigger plans for *al-ta'āwun*. Early in his term, in the winter of 1978/79, he oversaw the second round of elections in 187 districts and towns. The election season began when a twenty-five-man Supreme Elections Committee invited 400 election supervisors, mostly students, to a seminar at the National Institute for Public Administration,[27] and ended with a much-publicized general conference of 600 local representatives. Eighty-three candidates announced for the CYDA board, and seventy actually ran for eleven seats. In voting by secret written ballot,[28] the president of the Republic, several CYDA founding fathers, and other members of the military, religious, landowning, and tribal elites were elected to join the eleven CC secretaries-general, nine deputy ministers, and the chairman of the new Cooperative Credit Bank on an expanded CYDA board. The Cooperative Credit Bank, capitalized at a million riyāls ($222,000), was to manage LDA and cooperatives' accounts and to offer credit for income-generating cooperative ventures.[29]

The CYDA law of 1981 formally established the provincial CCs and the national *Ittiḥād*, empowering them to centralize budgets and to create LDAs where they had not formed spontaneously or not worked effectively.[30] Another round of non-partisan nationwide elections was held in the spring of 1982. Unlike previous rounds, candidates registered in advance and the whole nation voted during a two-day period. In the meantime, village committees that had operated intermittently for a couple of decades in the southern uplands were explicitly banned because they tended to "slip-slide" on local rather than national agendas.[31]

Several difficulties remained embedded in the system: CYDA was stronger than its parent ministry, MYLSA; the LDAs were more influential but less authoritative than appointed district directors; planning, budgeting, financing, and accounting processes, the electoral system, and methods of project execution were chaotic. Its hands full with major national infrastructure, the government could not pay its promised share of hundreds of road, school, and water projects. In 1984, Sana'a suspended all new project initiatives and froze all bank accounts pending reorganization: local groups were to finish what they had started, and new projects would be better planned.[32]

Laws 12 and 27 of 1985 and subsequent decrees resolved the division of authority between the LDAs and local administration by merging them into local councils for cooperative cevelopment (LCCDs). LCCD elections were better organized than LDA–CYDA elections, and expanded on the LDA system. A two-day holiday freed schools and other public buildings as polling stations, and election committees registered candidates and chaperoned the voting. Provincial coordinating councils were made official, under the governor's administration. CYDA, renamed the general secretariat of LCCDs to reflect the inclusion of more appointees on its board, later became a Cabinet-level organization headed by a minister.[33]

Under President Ṣāliḥ's National Pact, general assemblies (with one representative for each 500 persons) would elect both LCCD officers and delegates to the national permanent committee of the General People's Congress; 30 percent of delegates would be appointed by the president. This enhanced cooperative democracy and electoral representation. Appointments ensured that intellectuals and experts joined local leaders and clansmen in deliberations. Supervised by a Supreme Elections Committee, 1823 delegates were elected to the congress in December 1988.[34]

In the reorganization, the district and town boards were simultaneously empowered and reined in. The LCCDs were given larger budgets but less leeway in expenditure.[35] All funds had to be deposited in the Cooperative Bank, which could refuse disbursements or freeze accounts. The existing *nāḥiyya* structure, overlapping with expanding municipalities, was replaced with an "administrative unit," either a district or a town. District administrators, provincial governors, and officers of the general secretariat-LCCDs including the last head of CYDA, Minister Ṣādiq Amīn Abū Ra's, all military appointees, had absolute administrative authority. Elected delegates, now well screened, were to offer consultation.

This process radically democratized the government while disempowering the localities. It democratized the government by electing representatives for the first time, through a hierarchical bottom-to-top system wherein local elections were simultaneously elections to the GPC. This was the reform introduced in *al-Mīthāq al-Waṭanī,* the National Pact, which utilized the cooperative experience to bolster the legitimacy and the hegemony of a mass conference headed by a military regime. Whereas previous cooperative elections were *outside* government, the LCCD elections were *for* government.

Civic initiative and central response

The ultimate success of the corporatist project of the state notwithstanding, closer examination reveals that no regime simply mandated or successfully mobilized popular participation. Laws and centralizing measures largely responded to societal initiatives to improve services, increase administrators' accountability, and carve out an autonomous participatory space in the interstices between the state and primordial or commercial private spheres. If one looks at this dynamic as students of self-help and civil society in Africa or America would, one sees elements of both cooperation and struggle.

The roots of self-help have already been traced to small-scale, *ad hoc* improvements in community services; to liberal discontent with deliberately maintained backwardness; and to popular aspirations for better living standards, a measure of local autonomy, and rudimentary rights of association, expression, and investment. Not only were taxes extracted without services being extended in return, but local initiatives to ameliorate the situation were seen as brazen acts of insubordination. Community projects constituted political mobilization. This "revolutionary" movement surrendered neither initiative nor control after 1962. Rather, through projects and direct action, it challenged the regime by establishing alternative public services. Far from taking the lead, the state consistently reacted to local initiatives, and ultimately drew its own legitimacy from them.

The 1963 laws legalized existing project activity and associations on the condition of an organizational structure to which few conformed.[36] Little more than a resolution of sentiment by a fledgling military regime facing counter-revolution and the gradual disaffection of even republican forces, the new laws merely ratified the precedents set in Hodeida town and the villages of Taiz and Ibb.[37] Nor was the intent to promote local public works projects, for while encouraging association in principle, government itself was to "erase the specter of poverty, ignorance, and disease"; if anything, Egyptian advisors urged the foundation of cooperatives for agriculture and fishing, not services.

Immediately after the fall of the first YAR regime, in 1968 the royalists staged a last-ditch siege of Sana'a that was only broken by leftist forces after two-and-a-half months. The second regime's concession to the left, who were allied with the Ba'th and/or the Arab Nationalist Movement in Aden, was DYLSA. Its small staff of progressive intellectuals took particular interest in labor unions and productive cooperatives, especially in the poor coastal regions, and also in the preparation of social legislation on matters such as labor and family law.

Already in 1968, when the Department of Youth, Labor, and Social Affairs was created, there were some thirty associations. When DYLSA formulated guidelines for their organization, some associations chafed; the guidelines were rarely observed "except the case of urgent need," and local projects were "planned and carried out according to the practical needs and necessities and ... not subject to organizational rules."[38] Hampered by a small staff, low budget, and limited legal authority, officers could scarcely visit, much less manage, the scores of local projects proposed to it.

Yet feeder roads fanned out from the paved inter-city triangle, secondary towns acquired urban utilities, and new schools dotted the countryside. More precedent was set in the process of founding associations, raising money, and spending it for public works. In Taiz city's LDA, the first established after the 1963 laws, sons of merchants and other prominent families were elected in a public forum to a board that enacted the transport and cinema taxes later specified in the 1975 *ta'āwun* law, plus a surcharge on *zakat* and on utility bills. Ḥajja and Hodeida governors released funds and set priorities for provincial development. Zabīd's association, having contributed to two clinics and two schools, established budgetary guidelines: 30 percent for education, 15 percent for health, 25 percent for water, 5 percent for flood or fire disaster relief, 5 percent for antiquities preservation, and 20 percent for administration and contingencies.[39] Ānis and others instituted *zakat* surcharges, applied the principle of tribal per-household assessments to raise labor and funds, and lobbied for retention of *zakat* for local development projects.[40] In the decrepit secondary port of al-Makhā', a customs surcharge was introduced.

Whereas writing and publishing were major features of the Aden and unity openings, the self-help movement generated a paucity of written documentation. At that time, the official daily *al-Thawra* and its Taiz counterpart *al-Jumhūriyya* printed rhetorical accounts of official government events, ignoring even assassinations and wars. The semi-official Union of Yemeni Migrants, one of the few "popular" organizations, published a solidarity-building magazine, *al-Waṭan*, and the emerging

Yemen Center for Research and Studies began issuing *Dirāsāt Yamaniyya*. The most scholarly production was the Writers' Guild's irregularly available journal *al-Ḥikma*.

In this context, the semi-autonomous CYDA press, comprising a newspaper and a magazine both called *al-Ta'āwun*, a series of booklets with some English editions, and an academic-style journal called *al-Ghad*, were important outlets for intellectual expression by faculty, journalists, and activists. The cooperative press provided analysis of the movement, some of it from a Marxist perspective, and documented some activities with extraordinary specificity: the names of sixty-six contributors to the Ḥūth water project, province-by-province and sector-by-sector project reports (inaccurate arithmetic, evidence of government shortcomings, and all), and several detailed, sometimes very frank, case studies.

Regionalism and decentralization

When the more vocal leaders of town, provincial, and sub-province associations met in the spring of 1973, the message that won Ibrāhīm al-Ḥamdī presidency of the new confederation extolled decentralization, local autonomy, self-governance, and auto-taxation. The idea of a confederation itself was regarded in some quarters as excessive centralization. Hodeida governor Sinān Abū Luḥūm urged a boycott of the second confederation conference in 1974,[41] observed by all groups in the province except Zabīd – which in turn flouted the governor's authority. The loose village committees of the southern uplands resented their usurpation by regional LDAs under *shaykh*ly families.[42]

Two of the larger, better-organized, better-networked organizations, both led by prominent nationalists, produced booklets commemorating their efforts. A member of the prominent Ḥujariyya family, known for its activism in the Free Yemeni movement and the earlier, Aden-based *al-Ittiḥād al-Yamanī*, initiated the "War on Thirst:" a water-supply project for the small town of Turba. The book opens with a quotation from the Quran that "God helps those who rely on their own strength" and reminders of religious injunctions to develop and share water resources. Tribal music, dancing, and gun-salutes introduced a speech by 'Abd al-Raḥmān Nu'mān on May 21 1973. Citing the address by Ibrāhīm al-Ḥamdī at the March CYDA founders' meeting, he criticized the "beleaguered government's" incapacity to deliver services and called on all the sons of the region to contribute to the water project.[43] Evidently God smiled on these efforts, for on the day ground was broken for the Turba water project the long drought that had given impetus to the initiative was broken with a sweet, soaking rain. The help of foreign donors was also highlighted; the Turba water project obtained assistance from Oxfam, Catholic Relief Services, UNICEF, Kuwait, UNDP, and other agencies totaling over twice the value of local contributions.

This booklet also relates a debate among the CYDA founders over what to call the confederation and its member associations. Sana'a and Hodeida towns and the regional groups in Ibb, Ānis, and greater Wuṣāb called themselves *al-ta'āwun al-ahlī*, whereas Rayma, Ḥujariyya, and the "northwest areas" used the name *hay'at al-taṭwīr*, development association or board. Nu'mān, the only fluent English speaker in the group, observed that while *al-ta'āwun al-ahlī* had stronger emotional appeal in Arabic, foreign donors preferred "development association." This argument won the moment. The English designations LDA and CYDA stuck, but in 1975 a larger conference chose the compromise *hay'at al-ta'āwun al-ahlī li-l-taṭwīr*.[44]

The second booklet, "Miracle on Ḥajja Mountain," also boasted of a water project for the northwest highland town, a long-time royalist stronghold that had continued to pay its *zakat* to the imam for the duration of the civil war. Ironically, in 1955 Imam Aḥmad had rejected a proposal for a water system to serve the Ḥajja palace complex as too expensive. After the republican army upgraded the old caravan route from the Tihama for vehicular traffic, the commander of the region's republican forces, Mujāhid Abū Shawārib, newly appointed as governor, initiated a multi-million-riyāl project to pump wadi water eight kilometers up to the walled mountain-top town. This undertaking, the pilot project of the province's LDA, first required the building of a feeder road and the installation of a power station. Now *zakat*, sale of shares, contributions from leading families, and government co-sponsored the utilities project. Upgrading and extension of the road entailed financial and labor contributions from communities along the route, provincial funds from Ḥajja and Hodeida, and central government money. An integrated provincial development plans called for roads to every *qaḍā'*, schools and clinics in all districts, and establishment of agricultural cooperatives.[45]

The major modernization drive of the Ḥajja provincial development association was partly a republican-organized effort to woo Ḥajja, to be sure, but in another way it was a form of "cooperation of resistance," for when the governor fell out with Sana'a, the LDA became an alternative locus of power, exercising the capacity to withhold *zakat* from the center, raise funds from local merchants and landowners, and implement projects only planned in the center, this provincial LDA challenged central authority. Neither of the regime nor a grassroots initiative, this was a middle-bothways venture to wrest resources from the state. Because of the *shaykh*ly charisma of the governor, great resort was made to tribal appeals, celebrations, and hospitality in the raising of community contributions. At the same time, as in Turba, regional cooperation entailed rural contributions to projects in a central, urbanizing place: a circumstance that subsequently provoked a more rural sort of resistance.

The 1975 law recognized the complex realities on the ground. It released taxes already being withheld in some regions, authorized others already being collected by some *ta'āwun* boards, and recognized existing general assemblies as the "highest authority" in the system. Although elements of existing practice in local taxation were explicitly incorporated and considerable autonomy granted, nothing was mandated. Where they were founded, development cooperatives were to mobilize, guide, and support, but not control, independent project initiatives. There was no mention of CYDA, the provincial CCs, or other outside constraints, at least in the law itself.

Even so, al-Ḥamdī miscalculated in thinking of CYDA as his own constituency. In the much-publicized 1975/76 elections, culminating in a conference of the *Ittiḥād*'s general assembly to elect its administrative board, he was nearly defeated in a simple majority vote for confederation president; only a last-minute adjustment of the rules extended his titular leadership of the Cooperative Confederation. His rival, Abū Shawārib, having been removed from the governor's quarters in the old Ḥajja palace only to be elected to head *Ta'āwun Ḥāshid*, retreated north of the capital and, along with 'Abd Allāh al-Aḥmar,who had been speaker of Parliament in 1973, sealed off an entire region from central government forces. Mujāhid's many supporters said in praise: "He obeys neither the government nor anyone else." Hodeida governor Abū Luḥūm, a republican *shaykh* from a prominent highlands lineage in the other major tribal confederation, also openly flouted central authority. In these regions and others, Law 35 empowered localities to hold out for project assistance before submitting to central administration.

Although al-Ḥamdī initially "intended to use the co-operatives movement as the base for a regime-reinforcing mass political organization," the effective vote of no confidence for the president in the 1975 CYDA elections "dampened his enthusiasm for the LDA movement and caused him to rethink the prudence and efficacy of using it as the basis of a grass-roots political organization."[46] Local elections weakened the power of certain traditional elites, as hoped, but regime supporters were defeated in some places by avid proponents of local autonomy. Elsewhere, especially in the southern uplands, they lost to left-leaning partisans of the nascent National Democratic Front who favored "a more autonomous and spontaneous process of political construction from below."[47] These issues became more complex when, subsequently, other prominent individuals and/or localities went into opposition.

The confederation's founder and first president thus backed off from plans to create a mass political organization along the lines of, say, the Arab Socialist Union in Egypt. Subsequently, while remaining "stubbornly resistant to political subordination," the movement, and the *Ittiḥād*, not merely survived but flourished, making "well-publicized Presidential concern for the activities and achievements of the LDAs ... requisite for al-Ḥamdī's successors."[48]

The suspicion of mobilized participation extended beyond the Command Council to many Western-educated technocrats who opposed what they regarded as "premature introduction of parties, popular organizations, and representative bodies" that could be dominated by "traditionalist opponents of modernization or by well-meaning radical modernizers."[49] Technocrats regarded the LDAs with "skepticism if not hostility," as "an attempt to create local power bases and political pressure groups rather than 'true' local self-help agencies."[50] LDA projects were at best tangential to and at worst diverted funds from national-level priorities. Fears among this modernist group were hardly allayed by the strong showing of the ultra-conservative Islamic Front in the 1982 elections,[51] but did abate considerably after the 1985/86 elections returned more regime-friendly faces.

Education

As always, one of the most contentious issues surrounded schools policy. About half of the approximately 3,000 schools in the country in 1982 were cooperatively built, and others partly maintained by localities. A national curriculum tried to promote a YAR civic culture by teaching the state anthem, flag, map, newspaper, and history, although the majority of teachers came from Egypt, the Sudan, or Palestine. Al-Ḥamdī's Ministry of Education commissioned and distributed a sixth-grade Yemeni history book designed for use in both North and South Yemen.

According to a very critical essay published in the *Kitāb al-Ta'āwun* series,[52] in the 1976–77 academic year all mosque schools or *kuttāb*, including ten higher-level academies, were closed to make room for a Ministry of Education (MoE) curriculum. Recalling the imamate's "exploitation of public ignorance" and "prohibition of knowledge" that left communities to rely on mosques and charitable donations for education, the author contended the republican MoE's policy was one of "Centralizing education ... in towns connected with paved roads, where cinemas were available, and modern buildings and homes, leaving the far distant rural areas in towns and villages far from education and educational renaissance, keeping the Kuttāb in their primitive state." Into this "great cavern" stepped cooperative solutions. Conceding that the self-help schools offered only rudimentary education, the author insists the stop-gap measures be maintained until the ministry can provide schools and teachers to localities currently relying on self-help. A case in point occurred in the town of Shahāra, where there was a fight between traditional Zaydī *'ulamā'* and more puritanical Islamists over control of the curriculum of a recently rejuvenated, historically renowned religious *ma'had*.[53]

The politics of education took on a new dimension in the early 1980s, about the time that "volunteers" helped the government defeat the popular insurgency in the southern uplands. Key commanders in these irregular militia had earlier been recruited to the Afghan jihad and became known as *Afghān al-'Arab*, the core of a militant Islamist faction then appearing in Yemen for the first time. To combat what they saw as Yemeni communism, and utilizing a technique used in Afghanistan to indoctrinate young men against the Soviets, the Saudi backers of the Afghan jihad made new money available for "scientific" schools. Unlike LDA schools which taught a Ministry of Education curriculum taught by state-employed teachers, the "scientific" institutes were independent parochial schools offering a curriculum Yemenis called Wahhabi. A couple dozen new *'Ilmī* institutes were built in the underpopulated northern and eastern frontier regions such as Ṣa'da, Ma'rib, and the Jawf and in the densely settled NDF strongholds of the southern uplands.[54]

Taxation

The major center–periphery conflict surrounded taxation. Having eliminated some of the pre-revolutionary tax-collection system's worst abuses, the republic found its *zakat* revenues plummeting. During the civil war, royalist enclaves, especially in Ḥajja and Ṣa'da provinces, held back their *zakat*, and a key Third Force demand had been freedom to expend the tithe on community services. Throughout its history, in fact, the YAR's taxation capability was very weak.[55]

One of DYLSA's first actions was release of a quarter of the *zakat* and municipality taxes for local "welfare." In the early 1970s, some communities engaged in tax resistance, diverting local taxes to local projects, and the right to do so was a demand of the first *ta'āwun* conference in 1973. Abū Shawārib and other popular leaders reputedly tripled or quadrupled *zakat* collections once it was clear funds went toward schools and water. When the proportion of *zakat* allocated to local projects was raised to half and then three-quarters, the center was merely recognizing the *de facto* situation. Elements of a center–periphery struggle were replicated in microcosm within provincial and regional LDAs over the allocation of resources to towns and districts, too, resulting in the fission of LDAs in Ḥajja, al-Maḥwīt, Zabīd, Zaydiyya, and elsewhere.

Yemenis also saw an element of class struggle in LDA conflicts, especially those in the southern uplands where village committees far predated any enabling legislation. An article in *al-Ghad* about Ḥujariyya suggested that the natural cooperation among farmers to build and maintain dams, wells, roads, mosques, and Quran schools, which gained a new momentum as migrants brought in cash and new technologies to construct schools and other services, ran afoul of the big *qaḍā' shaykhs* who saw their political and economic power eroding. Nonetheless, village and *'uzla* committees organized against tax-contracts and royal authorities, the *mashāyikh*. The Ḥujariyya Development Association, now officially the LDA of al-Shamāyitayn *qaḍā'*, attempted to mitigate these conflicts by publishing a plan featuring schools, clinics, and roads for every *'uzla;* while bringing several powerful traditional leaders, including the appointed *majlis al-shūrā* delegate, onto the LDA board. When the delegate and his cronies pilfered LDA funds, however, the founders resigned. Popular forces then organized *nāḥiyya-* level LDAs, and, encouraged by the glorious June 14 1974 corrective movement, supervised elections for new LDA boards that closed the books on their corrupt predecessors. The old board naturally fought to keep control of 2,000,000 riyāls in *zakat* collections in al-Shamāyitayn, but al-Ḥamdī's fellow Command Council member 'Abd Allāh 'Abd al-'Ālim got around all these squabbles by spearheading a new movement around "development welfare associations" (singular *jam'iyya khayriyya li-l-taṭwīr*) to combat the power of the bad old *shaykhs*.[56]

Subsequently, the Ḥujariyya LDA collapsed completely after 'Abd al-'Ālim led the military campaign of the NDF against the Ṣāliḥ administration. Now ten or more village committees claimed to be the rejuvenated successors to the earliest modern local betterment organizations. When the village committees neglected to play by the CYDA rules, they were banned by the government in 1982.

Registration and reporting

Although by 1980 "LDAs" theoretically covered three-quarters of the country, only a handful approximated the formal structure laid out in laws and CYDA guidelines. Moreover, some active LDAs nonetheless did not file accounts with CYDA. In the late 1970s the non-reporters included relatively active tribally organized LDAs in Sana'a and Ḥajja governorates, inactive ones in the frontier regions of Jawf, Ma'rib, and Ṣa'da, and dynamic but often oppositional groups in Ibb and Taiz governorates.[57] Of those that did report, perhaps a quarter maintained an ongoing institutional identity, while others collapsed after an initial project, became embroiled in debilitating disputes, or fell into the hands of reactionary elites.

For all this administrative and fiscal chaos, the LDAs and/or independent *ta'āwun* wielded considerable influence in a countryside where central institutions had little authority. With no constitution in effect, the state apparatus itself was not well institutionalized. Administrative decentralization undercut old bases of authority more easily than it established new. Few ministries were staffed at the district level, new provinces were still being created, few vehicles or drivers outside the cities were licensed, smugglers evaded customs posts. No political parties, parliamentary elections, or other channels helped mobilize or articulate local politics. Despite rapid GNP growth and rising expectations, financial and business institutions were similarly weak. The CPO's five-year plan, drafted with considerable input from World Bank experts, was little more than an exercise to satisfy donors: among other things, it consistently underestimated cooperative spending. Banks ranging from Citibank to the Cooperative Bank faltered. There were few corporations, no unions unless one counts a civil service buyers' club and the drivers' associations.

The nadir of central strength, 1976–79 – the era of two assassinations and widespread regional insurrection – was the zenith of *ta'āwun* power. This period of near-anarchy saw over 500 primary schools and some 8,000 kilometers of rough but jeepable track constructed, plus at least 100 water and/or electricity systems. In building public works, raising taxes and/or withholding them from the center, providing services, lobbying higher authorities, and coordinating with other communities, project implementors performed a range of state-like functions. Project-related disputes over rights of way, water rights, schools' locations, and the like were brought to cooperative fora for settlement, and these judiciary functions spilled into other areas. As the military governor of the new governorate of al-Maḥwīt admitted ruefully at the time, "there is no government here except *al-Ta'āwun.*"

Donor experiences

Overwhelmingly, projects were financed from non-central sources. Published CYDA records showed about 60 percent of financing from citizens, over 35 percent from LDAs, and 1–10 percent from the state, mostly for schools and miscellaneous projects.[58] The state contribution includes foreign aid. Moreover, two-thirds of LDA revenues came from non-central sources, while *zakat* and other official tax revenues amounted to one-third. These figures exclude unreported projects undertaken with no LDA funds. Central support came from the governors' funds, in the form of equipment passed on from donors to the CCs or LDAs, of projects in the Jawf and Ma'rib where Sana'a's control was so tenuous, and of teachers' and nurses' salaries. The government far underpaid its share of project costs under CYDA's accounting guidelines. Moreover, most of the "government" contribution recorded came through foreign donor projects.

Such complicated politics, combined with cultural misunderstandings, go a long way to explaining the admitted failures of a series of international donors' efforts to foster grassroots, participatory development through "the LDAs": USAID projects in al-Maḥwīt, Ḥajja, and Hodeida and a subsequent German project in al-Maḥwīt, all intended to help LDAs provide integrated rural services; Irish Concern preventative health care and agricultural cooperative projects in Wuṣāb al-A'lā and the northern Tihama; the British Volunteers project in Rayma, which ran a successful clinic but never engaged its envisioned participatory programs; the long-lived but problem-filled Netherlands integrated development program in Radā'; and a rural health project in the northern Tihama, technically under the Ministry of Health (MoH). The saga of these efforts is a separate inquiry; Morris captured their collective experience in the title of a book about the 'Abs basic health project, *The Despairing Developer.*[59] The reports written on the downstream and LDA institution-building projects were considerably less sanguine about "bottom-up" development than the project design documents.

Each of these technical assistance projects assumed expatriate technicians and trainers could help marshal local resources into well-planned and executed public services through the LDAs. They aimed to reach the "poorest of the poor," especially women, and to help them

Table 5.2. *Project funds from citizens, LDAs, and government, YAR, 1973–1981*

	1973–1976			1978/79–1980/81			1976–1981
	% from citizens	% from LDA	% from state	% from citizens	% from LDA	% from state	% from citizens
roads	72%	28%	–	62%	37%	1%	67%
schools	54%	45%	1%	39%	41%	18%	42%
water	32%	68%	–	52%	29%	10%	54%
health	31%	69%	–	32%	63%	5%	29%
misc.	17%	78%	5%	23%	63%	14%	41%
total	64%	35%	1%	52%	38%	8%	59%

Source: ʻUthmān and al-ʻAwdī, "al-Ḥaraka al-taʻāwiniyya al-Yamaniyya w'al-tanmiyya," table 1-5; Carapico, "Political Economy of Self-help," Table 8.6

Table 5.3. *Sources of LDA revenues*

	1976–1978	1978–1981	1976–1981
central incomes	9%	9%	9%
local revenues from *zakat*	18%	34%	28%
local revenues from citizens	73%	57%	63%

Source: ibid., Table 8.7

help themselves rather than provide help for them. Institution building was an explicit objective, and there were great plans for training road and water surveyors, generator-and-bulldozer-repairmen, and barefoot nurses and midwives. These rather altruistic objectives clashed head-on with the quick-fix, pay-as-you-go mentality of regional politicians, and conflicted with local expectations that foreigners would bring hard cash for physical construction.

For instance, the leaders and urban constituency of the al-Maḥwīt LDA wanted a water project like Ḥajja's, whose cost was beyond the LDA's means and also beyond the budget for individual capital improvements of the USAID-funded Save the Children (STC) project. Among other things, STC did, however, establish a primary mother–child health-care facility staffed by STC and the Peace Corps, whose focus on preventative care scrupulously avoided overlap with the mission of the Ministry of Health hospital. Some townspeople were suspicious of what unmarried Western women were teaching young Maḥwītī mothers, but the health center was well regarded in comparison with the hospital's uncaring, corrupt, inept, unloved Egyptian doctors. A crisis erupted when the distraught father of a badly burned infant burst into the STC clinic seeking emergency treatment and, when referred to the hospital, began brandishing a gun. Due in part to this incident, USAID canceled STC's contract.

More generally, the Western agencies hoping to extend technical assistance to the LDAs had trouble pinning them down. Where a board and its officers could be identified they met over qāt, and failed to keep minutes of meetings, receipts for expenditures, or records of who belonged to the general assembly that elected them. In addition, they were often unfamiliar with paradigms such as the germ theory of disease that underlay the logic of technical assistance to improve water supplies and health-care delivery, or with the reasons why engineers think mountain roads need culverts. In many ways that CYDA officials recognized only too well, their structure did not correspond to the functions they nonetheless performed, and the misplaced assumptions of legal rationality embedded in the construct of an LDA proved the undoing of most donor-funded "institution-building" projects.

Social services and societal transformation

Fraught with struggle and riddled by primordialism, the cooperative movement nonetheless had profound political, economic, and social implications. Cumulatively, roads, schools, water projects, electricity systems, and a range of miscellaneous projects revolutionized everyday life, facilitated market penetration of the hinterland, and, perhaps inadvertantly, extended the hegemony of the state to the countryside.

Even the roughest jeepable trails purvey commodities and commercialization, pave the way for other services, and link communities to a national polity. They realigned and rejuvenated the nationwide network of periodic markets, merged the formerly rigid distinction between community and market, redefined central places, commodified land and labor, increased travel and inter-community interaction, and enhanced central military and administrative control. Primary, middle, and especially secondary schools urbanized villages, markets, and towns with modern public spaces where boy and girl pupils dressed, acted, and talked differently. They disseminated a national consciousness not only through the curriculum but with flags, anthems, September 26 celebrations, and the like, and inculcated among students a sense of being Arab (through literature) and part of a modern world (through science and geography).[60] Improvements in water supply and the introduction of electricity added appreciably to people's sense of material well-being,[61] stimulated commercial and light industrial activity, and made it possible to run health clinics.

The cumulative effect of some 15,000 kilometers of tracks, 1,500 schools, several hundred water and electricity projects, and the other infrastructural projects is more than the sum of the effects of individual projects, however. Consistent with what geographers tell us about central place development in many societies, these effects radiated out from the main cities, along major transport arteries to secondary towns, and unevenly into rural communities.

North Yemen's five cities – Sana'a, Taiz, Hodeida, Ibb, and Dhamar, in descending order of size – metamorphosed from beautiful medieval towns into nascent third world cities. Of course the main reason for rapid urbanization in the five cities was the concentration of aid-financed public-sector airports, secondary and higher education, full-service hospitals, utilities, banks, and employment in the cities. Their rapid expansion was also financed by the LDAs in two ways, however. First, the urban LDAs were among the earliest, most active, and best-organized organizations, headed by merchants, intellectuals, and Free Officers. They built the earliest urban utilities and educational facilities, later providing secondary services and lobbying ministries for public–civic projects such as university campuses and waste collection. The combination of public and cooperative projects raised urban standards of living, attracting more investors and residents. Secondly, the network of rural roads and schools, in particular, made Sana'a, Taiz, and Hodeida central places as they had never been before, indirectly by creating more urban civil service jobs and directly by providing the transportation and education that brings rural people to the metropolis.

Cooperative-sector roads, utilities, schools, and other projects had a major impact on second-tier towns such as ʻAmrān, Khamir, Turba, al-Maḥwīt, Ḥajja, Jibla, and Zabīd which urbanized with secondary schools for boys and girls, full-service utilities, a hospital, and roads leading in several directions, drawing shoppers, students, patients, and, most importantly, investors from the immediate hinterland. Stores, restaurants, petrol-stations, light-industrial workshops lined roadheads as fields of grain gave way to suburban housing, ring-roads, and garbage dumps. Ashamed to face strangers in the market, freed from collecting water and fire-wood, and seduced by television, women secluded themselves inside their homes as never before.[62] Similar transformations occurred in some densely settled agricultural regions, especially where for qāt cultivation (in the upper elevations), irrigation from pump-equipped wells (in the plateau and the Tihama), or expansion of a major market (usually a Thursday market) offered business opportunities. By contrast, of course, areas too poor, dry, remote, or sparsely populated to accumulate capital for investment in new services mostly fell behind simply by staying where they were.

The ways *taʻāwun* straddled the line between public and private sectors is best illustrated by agricultural and fishing cooperatives, envisioned in the 1963 Egyptian-based enabling legislation, pursued by progressives in the early days of DYLSA and by several foreign donors, and promoted in the cooperative press as a means for generating income. Yet only a few productive-sector cooperatives had a period of successful operation, and even they were run like private businesses. One "agricultural" cooperative below Taiz began by buying a lime-mill to improve production of traditional whitewash, procured trucks to transport the whitewash to Taiz, and then upgraded the road – all amidst armed resistance from an old landlord faction. Just south of Hodeida, one of the best-publicized agricultural cooperatives ran a diesel-and-service station that required a generator that sold surplus capacity to the town. In a rich agricultural region near Sana'a, after the demise of the LDA an agricultural cooperative owned and rented out a drill-rig used for both private and public wells. All these, in other words, occupied the space between *taʻāwun* and the private sector. Many LDAs themselves operated bulldozers or other heavy equipment donated from Czechoslovakia or other countries through CYDA. Cooperatively owned earth-moving and well-drilling equipment affected private interests in various ways. Sometimes back-hoes fixed the LDA president's spate irrigation structures. In other cases, the LDA or the cooperative competed with private-sector contractors or with the military (which also owned a lot of heavy equipment). And so forth.

In short, the cumulative effect of cooperative projects was threefold: economic, political, and social. In economic terms projects represented a high level of capital formation in the non-governmental, not-for-profit sector and contributed to the rapid commercialization of small towns and farm districts. These economic effects intensified struggles between patrimonial and republican elites, but also paved the way for the state to extend its hegemony to the provincial centers and down to the district level through a myriad of physical, institutional, and budgetary connections. The impact of roads, schools, running water, electricity, and primary health care on the material and social content of everyday life was so profound it defies summary.

The centralization of cooperation

LDAs or *"al-ta'āwun al-ahlī"* incorporated many folk idioms and mechanisms, reflected profound societal struggles, and fell far short of what are sometimes seen as "pre-requisites" for civil society. The unit of action was the project rather than the institution. Those looking for ethnographic or photographic evidence of enduring primordialism could certainly find it, and one could also apply an NGO model or a state-first corporatist model. None of these models conveys the dynamism of a movement that consisted in large part of building services, however. Instead, these approaches tend to obfuscate the extent to which project activity at the interstices of state and society, public and private, national and local contributed to the power and hegemony of a central government. By the mid-1980s, Sana'a exercised unprecedented control over the countryside. Taxes and projects were more efficiently centralized than ever before. Military, judicial, administrative, and national security officers as well as teachers and nurses worked in every district center. Central appointees wielded increasing authority relative to customary leaders. What had begun as a series of conferences of regional republican elites ended giving legitimacy and top-down linkages to the regime. Civil society, itself very much a contested realm, nonetheless contributed to the very substance of state power.

The argument presented here has been that, however inadvertently, *ta'āwun* contributed directly to the empowerment of Sana'a. It was a Greek tragic hero of a movement, whose best virtues laid the groundwork for its own demise. It helped legitimize the government, create dependency-fostering technical and budgetary linkages, and extend the physical presence and ideological content of the republican state to the provinces. And it contributed to what amounted to a revolution in social relations as roads and other projects integrated the vestiges of a quasi-subsistence, semi-feudal agrarian economy into into global markets. If this was how people tried to preserve tradition or block market penetration, they must have been fools. All evidence is otherwise. People did not react to modernity writ large, but to specific circumstances and opportunities. While periodically resisting tyranny, many welcomed commerce. Furthermore, services were built, one step at a time, with nary an NGO in sight. Even if its roots were tribal, religious, or traditional, and its motif "*ahlī*," even if every step was fraught with conflict, even if projects were sometimes illegal or disorganized, the *effects* of cooperation modernized the polity and the economy. LDAs on the whole were a far cry from the formal, thoroughly secular criterion discussed in Cairo, but fitted many Europeanist or Africanist conceptions of civil society very well.

Postscript

Less than a year after unification, Law 52 of 1991 on local administration replaced both LCCDs and the PDRY's local popular councils with local councils defined as branches of a new Ministry of Local Administration. Executive councils of twenty-one to forty-one members in the newly established "administrative units" and thirty-one to fifty-one members at the provincial level were to be elected at some time in the future, and in the interim were comprised of existing councils plus some appointees. The old connection whereby LDA presidents served on the provincial CCs was abolished. Executive councils were to be chaired by appointed governors and district administrators. Governors' powers were restored to something like what they had been under the imamate: they held ministerial rank and were empowered to collect *zakat* and other taxes, appoint or demote officials including the executive councils, and issue security directives.[63] A partly new, partly old form of organization, the *jam'iyya khayriyya* (welfare association) took charge of a second tier of services – community centers, health clinics, returnee-camp services, and the like. While under terms of debt adjustment the government began privatizing its now run-down public services, welfare associations, many of them neo-Islamist but others secular, offered the cushion of charity.

The new system of local administration was now more centralized than it had ever been in either the YAR, where the reins had been tightening for several years, or the PDRY, where quasi-elected local governments had gradually been granted greater autonomy. This became a bone of contention in the Republic of Yemen during its "democratic experiment," when throughout the South, and especially in the Ḥaḍramawt with its long tradition of relative autonomy, and in many parts of the former YAR including Ḥujariyya, Ḥajja, the Tihama, and Bakīl territory, conferences of rural leaders called for greater local autonomy. Northern groups called specifically for revitalization of the LDAs, and a committee of the old CYDA activists fruitlessly lobbied parliament for revision of Law 52 in a way that could reenergize *ta'āwun*. "Decentralization" (*lā-markaziyya*) was a major demand of the many regional conferences of the early 1990s, and a key reform in the document hammered out by the National Dialogue Committee in early 1994. The Dialogue Committee itself was spearheaded by several old *ta'āwun* activists. As already noted, however, after the 1994 civil war decentralization was explicitly repudiated and the 1991 constitution was amended in 1994 to incorporate Law 52 binding local councils to implement the policy of the state.

6 Unity, pluralism, and political participation

Yemen's earlier civic openings, so different from one another in many respects, nonetheless followed a common fourfold outline. Each began with contingent liberalization[1] by a fledgling administration seeking to mobilize popular and investor participation in its governance project. Along with investment incentives, governments scheduled elections and allowed some autonomous organizing. In a second, simultaneous, process, civic activity transcended its rather narrow legal boundaries to challenge the regime: not by attempting to seize power but by demonstrating economic prowess, offering alternative constitutional visions, or conveying various social and economic interests. After failing to secure the hoped-for popular mandate, power-holders began amending the rules to increase control of elections, economic activity, and autonomous organizations. Amidst mounting elite and popular criticism, regimes then imposed higher penalties for transgressions, deployed troops to enforce compliance, and finally suspended the rules, resorting to arbitrary detentions, crude censorship, curfews, expulsions, and torture. Escalating violence and repression culminated in civil war and, eventually, an authoritarian triumph that crushed civic initiatives as well as armed resistance. In each case a new government issued edicts centralizing all significant political, civic, intellectual, and economic projects. Critics and alternative elites were banished.

Modern Yemeni governments have only intermittently subordinated civil society to a military or party apparatus, however. The authoritarian denouement to each of the earlier openings, one in the South and the other in the North, left both systems in crisis. Political and economic malaise provided the impetus for unity and, with unity, for liberalization. Aden and Sana'a each imagined a potential social base among the other's citizens, a groundswell of support among the other's dissidents, and a cozy relationship with Yemeni millionaires in the Gulf. Within each regime were factions advocating controlled liberalization as a means of maintaining power.

The unity accords ushered in Yemen's most liberal, most political civic opening. The relaxation of security, political, financial, and legal controls, the issuance of legal–constitutional guarantees to personal, press, and political freedom, and the unleashing of pent-up desires to travel within the country, publish, organize, and hold public debates were all unprecedented. Whereas labor issues dominated Aden's late colonial civic experience, and local services were the focus of the second opening, in the 1990s participation was overwhelmingly political, aimed at influencing the composition, policies, and constitution of government. Overnight, almost every partisan tendency from earlier times surfaced to run candidates, publish a newspaper, or issue resolutions and proposals.

The unique temporary balance of power between two former ruling parties was both the point of departure for the liberal experiment and the source of its demise. The initial power-sharing agreement divided posts in the five-man Presidential Council, the Council of Ministers, and the Parliament more or less equally between the General People's Congress (GPC) and the Yemeni Socialist Party (YSP), establishing a parity between them that left unusual scope for third parties and prominent individuals to campaign, publish, and organize, and for many others to be involved in public events. As the political–military rivalry between the GPC and the YSP intensified, and especially after elections failed to resolve the distribution of power, there were multiple efforts to revise and renegotiate the rules. In this process, civil society generated a counter-hegemonic vision that became intolerable to the respective military and security commanders. While skirmishes between two separate armies blasted holes in an already-tattered unity accord, however, autonomous groups sought to defend rights in court, force the intransigent leaderships to negotiate, and demonstrate mass support for far-reaching reform. Even in the final phase, amidst the defeat of the remainder of the PDRY army, wholesale revision of the rules, and lawless attacks on civilian institutions, compared to some other Arab countries a certain sphere for civic activity remained. As in the case of previous civic openings, the triumphant forces needed the popular legitimacy of autonomous initiatives to launch their own hegemonic project.

The analysis of the interplay between government and civil society since unification is divided here into two chapters. This chapter is devoted to the conditions of contingent liberalization and responses to the civic opening, or the first two processes. The evidence shows that the new government passed liberalizing legislation only to qualify legal freedoms, manipulate existing organizations, and attempt to incorporate autonomous initiatives. Nonetheless, an enthusiastic civic and political animation spanned both the political and the organizational spectrum. In addition to the wide range of parties, publications, political organizations, charitable associations, intellectual salons, and mass conferences opened new arenas for action and expression. Civic responses to the political crisis leading up to the civil war and to post-war contraction of autonomous space are the subject of chapter 8. In both chapters the lead actors are ruling and non-ruling parties, government-organized and autonomous formal organizations, and informal elite and mass conventions.

Liberalizing legislation

The liberalizing legislative package responsible for the post-unity political opening included the 1989 unity accords, the 1991 constitution, the 1990 press law, the 1991 political parties law, the 1992 elections law, and the announcement that the old national and central security forces would be disbanded. Inscribing rights and freedoms heretofore unknown, these documents also left large loopholes. The failure of the unity accords and the constitution to resolve many issues of executive, military, and local power was their ultimate undoing. The press, parties, elections, and security laws together created a legal framework for a relatively free and open public space, but also contained clauses restricting those freedoms.

The unity accords unveiled in November 1989 and signed on May 22 1990 provided for a complex transitional power-sharing arrangement that balanced GPC and YSP influence rather equally despite the fact that three-quarters of the population resided in the North. A five-man Presidential Council was divided 3:2, nearly forty ministerial positions were evenly distributed, and the unified transitional parliament contained 159 Northern parliamentarians, 111 from the PDRY, and 31 appointees rather well balanced. While the GPC got the presidency, the prime minister and speaker of parliament were both southern Socialists. With Sana'a the new capital of a unitary state, a whole class of Adeni civil servants were assigned to ministerial positions there. The removal of checkpoints from the former border and an exchange of battalions guarding Sana'a and Aden, respectively, were also part of the agreement. Until specifically superseded by new legislation, previous laws and budgets were to remain in effect. All of these items signified an intention of full and equal merger. With the exceptions of the family of the imam (deposed in 1962) and 'Alī Nāṣir Muḥammad (deposed in 1986), most former exiles were permitted to return, and the majority of all political prisoners were released. A planned, mixed economy with a free trade zone in Aden was to lure investments from Yemenis abroad. Businesses, parties, and organizations were allowed to establish at will, and newspapers permitted to use the government-owned presses.

The 1991 constitution described the rather complicated system for selecting the presidential and ministerial councils after parliamentary elections. It further granted many significant rights and freedoms to citizens of the republic, including voting and candidacy rights, liberty of expression, the right to a fair trial, judicial independence, and equal treatment under the law. Among the unresolved constitutional issues were the exercise of executive authority, command of the military, the character of local government, the design of the electoral system, and the organization of the judiciary. One quite controversial matter was resolved clearly in Article 3: Islamic law (Sharīʿa) is "the main source of legislation." On this issue Iṣlāḥ, representing the religious tendency, threatened to boycott the May 1991 referendum unless the word "main" was dropped. The contingent nature of the constitutional consensus was made explicit when the presidential council issued a communiqué on May 22, the day the constitution went into effect, specifying Sharīʿa as "the base and source of all legislation" and further rendering any previous or future legislation that "contradicts" the Quran and Sunna "null and void."

Law 25 of 1990 promised "freedom of knowledge, thought, the press, expression, communication, and access to information," press independence, and protection of journalists and authors, but also established barriers to the exercise of these freedoms by specifying journalists' qualifications, newspaper registration criteria, bookstore and publishing permits, conditions for press closures, and conditions for admitting or quoting foreign correspondents and publications. Article 113 is a list of prohibitions on anything prejudicial to Islam, national security, national unity, criminal investigations, high-level political deliberations, economic trends, or the person of the president. Article 114 gives the minister of information far-reaching authority. This was landmark legislation in its statement of basic press freedoms, and was accepted as such because it was issued amidst an atmosphere of extraordinary tolerance. In subsequent practice, it gave newspapers an opportunity to fight the Ministry of Information in court rather than face summary closure.

The parties and elections laws similarly open with guarantees of freedoms that are curtailed in subsequent sections. Law 66 of 1991 cites Article 39 of the constitution on political pluralism, and entitles citizens to form and affiliate with parties; but also cautions that "no party or political organization may misuse this right in contradiction with the national interest and in preserving sovereignty, security, stability, and national cohesion." Again there follows a lengthy enumeration of prohibitions, some vague and others specific. For instance, parties may not contradict either "Islamic precepts and values" or "international declarations on human rights"; cannot be tied to professional, tribal, foreign, or other discernible interests, or any exclusivist ideologies. Political parties or organizations must further meet organizational, membership, and leadership guidelines and submit petitions, accounts, and other materials as required to a ministerial-level committee. Here it was less the law itself that represented liberalization than the failure to implement the law. Instead, in the short term at least, people could form what parties and organizations they wished. As with publications, parties flooded the market.

The elections law, No. 41 of 1992, a far more technical piece of legislation, was likewise honored partly in the breach. It promised freedom of voter and candidate registration, observation of the counting process by candidates' representatives, and a fair winner-take-all contest in each of 301 district constituencies. These important provisions, often violated in Arab or African elections, were indeed observed, which is why so many candidates and observers experienced an open multi-party competition in the districts. On the other hand, whereas Article 20 specified a Supreme Elections Committee (SEC) comprised of five to seven independents (who must resign any party membership) selected from a list of fifteen names submitted by parliament to the presidential council, after political maneuvering the SEC actually consisted of seventeen persons carefully representing the various parties.[2] This was the first of several times when minor parties and independents were brought on to balance the tension between the GPC and the YSP. In this case, the law was circumvented in favor of a politically necessary compromise.

The decree dismantling the national security apparatus of the former YAR and the PDRY's central security establishment was especially disingenuous if not insignificant. It was disingenuous inasmuch as no one imagined the powerful, well-armed security forces could simply be dismissed, even if the political will had existed; and because some now-underemployed security officers were nominated to committees as "independents" or otherwise interfered in pluralist and civic experiences. It was nonetheless significant insofar as everyone from petty traders to foreign researchers noticed a short-term diminution of overt security surveillance. Illegal detentions and human rights abuses diminished. As constant security monitoring and occasional harassment had deprived citizens of various political rights and liberties in the past, this was a crucial element in the overall liberalization. The ongoing presence of two quasi-legal security organizations, on the other hand, and then the creation of a third force, the political security organization, helped make the liberalization contingent.

These documents were declarations of tolerance within rather wide parameters. Significant for the restrictions they lifted, liberalizing legislation cleared legal space for participation in political parties, the electoral process, non-governmental organizations, intellectual projects, and mass conferences. More independent political, charitable, social, and professional organizations were founded after 1990 than in the preceding eight decades, many of them loosely registered with the Ministries of Culture or Social Affairs. The hand-painted signs of NGO offices lined urban thoroughfares, kiosks overflowed with newspapers, and the calendar of public events was unprecedented.

As long as the bipartisan balance of power lasted, neither party was able to manipulate civil society as in the past, by issuing rules, appointing leaderships, and controlling bank accounts. Instead, former organizational monopolists were reduced to retail-level penetration or duplication of autonomous initiatives in order to dilute or displace their influence and criticisms. Notwithstanding these efforts in the short term, and more repressive legal and extra-legal measures as the balance of power collapsed, the opening gave ample evidence of the capacity of society to imagine an alternative to authoritarian dictatorship.

Party pluralism and electoral competition

In most liberalizing dictatorships a single ruling cadre faces a field of fledgling opposition parties. The uniqueness of Yemen's democratic interlude in the early 1990s was the presence of two former ruling parties each with its own organizational strengths, a third party with a significant social base, and a number of small but historically important opposition parties. About a dozen viable political organizations campaigned in the first-ever partisan elections, and angled for influence over public opinion and political outcomes. Indeed although the parties' electoral platforms tended toward generalities and did not clearly distinguish alternative policy positions, in the post-election period clear differences were articulated in alternative fora. Although democratization was contingent, political pluralism was vigorous.

The organization headed by ʿAlī ʿAbd Allāh Ṣāliḥ, the General People's Congress, calling itself an umbrella for all political tendencies rather than a party,[3] made no pretext of advancing a particular platform or ideology. Its leaders filled the top echelons of the YAR's government;

Table 6.1. *Major parties and party newspapers, 1990–1994*

English name(s)	Arabic name(s)	newspaper(s)	origins
General People's Congress (GPC)	al-Mu'tamar al-Sha'bī al-'Āmm	*al-Mīthāq* *22 May* *(26 September)* *(al-Thawra)*	'Alī 'Abd Allāh Ṣāliḥ administration, early 1980s
Yemeni Socialist Party (YSP)	al-Ḥizb al-Ishtirākī al-Yamanī	*al-Thawrī* *al-Mustaqbal* *(4 October)*	National Liberation Front, late 1960s–1970s
Yemeni Reform Gathering (Iṣlāḥ)	al-Tajammu' al-Yamanī li-l-Iṣlāḥ	*al-Ṣaḥwa* *al-Iṣlāḥ*	conservative movement in YAR, 1980s
Yemeni Arab Renaissance Socialist Party (Ba'th)	Ḥizb al-Ba'th al-'Arabī al-Ishtirākī (Quṭr al-Yaman)	*al-Jamāhīr* *'Ahd al-'Arab*	Arab nationalism movement, 1960s
The Truth Party (al-Ḥaqq)	Ḥizb al-Ḥaqq	*al-Umma*	Zaydī *sayyids*, 1990s
Yemeni Unificationist-Nasirite Organization (Waḥdawī-Nāṣirī)	al-Tanẓīm al-Waḥdawī al-Sha'bī al-Nāṣirī	*al-Waḥdawī*	founded *c.* 1990 from faction of 1960s movement
Yemeni Unity Gathering (Tajammu')	Ḥizb al-Tajammu' al-Waḥdawī al-Yamanī	*al-Tajammu'*	Adeni intellectuals, late 1980s
Yemeni Corrective Organization (Taṣḥīḥ)	Tanẓīm al-Taṣḥīḥ al-Sha'bī al-Nāṣirī	*al-Taṣḥīḥ*	al-Ḥamdī coup, 1974; insurrection vs. Ṣāliḥ, 1979
League of the Sons of Yemen (Rābiṭa, RAY)	Rābiṭat Abnā' al-Yaman (RAY)	*al-Ra'y* *al-Ḥaqq*	South Arabian League (SAL), late 1960s
Union of Popular Forces (UPF)	Ittiḥād al-Quwā al-Sha'biyya al-Yamaniyya	*al-Shūrā*	Zaydī *sayyid* constitutional movement, 1950s

its rank and file were the civil and armed services. Since GPC membership was a prerequisite for new political and civil service appointments in the 1980s, the Congress did encompass some diversity of opinion, ranging from liberals to Islamists to Arab nationalists. But it spoke with one voice. When for instance the Sana'a University branch of the party advanced a series of proposals for democratizing its structure, they were thanked politely and ignored.[4] Its newspapers and spokespersons identified the GPC with national security rather than with policy proposals.

The Mu'tamar's election-season media campaign rested on images of the president at ground-breaking and ribbon-cutting ceremonies for private and public construction projects or as military commander of the armed forces. Most of the 279 parliamentary candidates on the GPC ticket were incumbent deputies or local officials with strong local name recognition and access to public funds. *Shaykhs* – that is to say, leaders of extended families, villages, or tribes – figured prominently among them, as did army officers. Often they enjoyed the support of important local families, and they were positioned to promise projects or other payoffs. For all its lack of ideological appeal, the GPC carried 123 or nearly half of the constituencies in the former YAR, where 80 percent of the population resided. It garnered a third or more of the vote in Sana'a city, Hodeida, Dhamar, Ibb, Ḥajja, al-Maḥwīt, and Ma'rib. In former PDRY territory, however, the GPC had only its own reassigned troops as a natural voting constituency.

By contrast the YSP had a relatively more coherent ideology and wider popularity but a deeply fragmented leadership and constituency. Influenced by Gorbachev's late communism, the YSP presented itself as a social democratic party of the left, the party of law and order, and the custodian of women's rights.[5] In the context of unified Yemen, it stood for decentralization of authority. Yet within the YSP were several distinct groups. The party was formally in the hands of the survivors of the 1986 debacle, mostly *sayyids* from Ḥaḍramawt in the top political posts and military commanders from Radfān. Hardly ideologues, they concerned themselves mainly with the trappings of political power. Although 'Alī Nāṣir Muḥammad himself was more or less out of the picture in Damascus, the group associated with his name, some of whom had moved north in 1986 while others held out in Abyan, were a bitter, disenfranchised faction few of whom were nominated by the YSP to run for parliament. A third major faction comprised the northern supporters of the former National Democratic Front in the populous Taiz, Ibb, and al-Bayḍā' regions (the southern uplands or "middle" regions). This group, a numerically significant proportion of YSP membership, had strong local roots and a following among urban professionals. Whereas in the South the YSP constituted a ruling apparatus, in the North the YSP was a party of ideological opposition to the GPC.

YSP candidates were therefore of two sorts. In the fifty-seven constituencies of the southern and eastern governorates, they were not unlike the GPC candidates – well-networked, well-funded incumbents from the last PDRY regime. In the northern governorates, the YSP stood serious candidates in all the urban areas and many rural districts as well. The 217 YSP-backed candidates won most of the South and placed well in Taiz and al-Bayḍā' (but not Ibb), for a total of fifty-seven seats. The party leadership portrayed its near-sweep in the former PDRY as vindication of its rule and repudiation of GPC domination; Iṣlāḥ and some smaller parties that hoped to do well in the South claimed ballot-box tampering.

The fiercest electoral competition seemed to pit the Socialists against Iṣlāḥ. For the Social Reform Grouping, or Iṣlāḥ, presented itself as the conservative party of traditional values. In this way it is not unlike the American Republican party, encompassing a spectrum of social, political, and economic "conservatisms." Party head *Shaykh* 'Abd Allāh Ḥusayn al-Aḥmar, perennial power-broker in the YAR, was Reaganesque in his command of detail, his paternalistic charm, his moral certitude, and his appeal to homesteaders and gun owners. His cowboy conservatism contrasted sharply with the austere doctrinal puritanism preached by head of the party's consultative council, 'Abd al-Majīd al-Zindānī. For instance, al-Aḥmar's family is famous for its lavish tribal weddings, with generous bridal payments, opulent qāt-chews for men, and women's parties with henna and dancing – all sinful, according to al-Zindānī. From different perspectives, however, they shared a common antipathy to certain traditions associated with the imamate, particularly the privileges and religious interpretations of the prerevolutionary *sayyid* aristocracies. In promoting Wahhabi "scientific institutes," the neo-fundamentalist wing of Iṣlāḥ was countering tribal custom and much traditional religious scholarship as well as the secularism of socialist education. Al-Aḥmar and al-Zindānī had both long been identified as Saudi clients, both prospered under the Ṣāliḥ administration, and both despised communists and Westerners. The party or "grouping" was technically founded in 1990, after unification, but its roots in the Islamic Front of the 1980s were obvious, and one of its newspapers, *al-Ṣaḥwa*, had been allowed to publish since 1986 under an editor with known connections to Sana'a's security apparatus.

Iṣlāḥ also ran two sorts of candidates. Within Ḥāshid territory, mostly in and near Sana'a governorate, members of the al-Aḥmar family and its allies ran under the Iṣlāḥ banner. The *shaykh* and one of his elder sons won handily in home districts in and near Khamir, but another, younger, rather Americanized son, Ḥāmid ʻAbd Allāh al-Aḥmar, encountered stiffer competition in the district of al-Ḥabūr in Ḥajja governorate, where his rival was a local *shaykh* running on behalf of the YSP. Evidently fearful that loyalty to the Ḥāshid confederation alone would not necessarily carry this Ḥāshid district, his entourage attacked the local YSP office and later captured the ballot boxes. Iṣlāḥ's narrow victory in al-Ḥabūr notwithstanding, easily a score of Ḥāshid *shaykhs* running as such won seats for Iṣlāḥ.

Beyond the Ḥāshid homeland, Iṣlāḥ candidates broadly identified themselves as Islamist, glossing over the real differences within and beyond the party[6] among Wahhabis, Salafīs, the Muslim Brotherhood, and other tendencies, some close to the Saudi monarchy and others associates of its critics. Some Iṣlāḥ candidates were sage old *'ulamā'* in turbans, others recent graduates from al-Azhar in Cairo or schools in Saudi Arabia or Sudan. They made ample use of networks within mosques and the social centers run by the Iṣlāḥ Social Welfare Society (on which more below). The religious right, while condemning the YSP for running female candidates, made a special effort to register conservative women as voters especially where the YSP was strong. In the elections, out of nearly 200 Iṣlāḥ candidates, 62 won seats. Its best performance was in Ḥajja, where there are both Ḥāshid tribesmen and Islamists, but it garnered 20–25 percent of the popular vote in Sana'a city, Ibb, al-Bayḍā', Dhamar, and al-Jawf, and came in second (in terms of popular vote) in a majority of governorates.

Many of Yemen's leaders cut their political teeth in the Baʻth, the country's oldest proper party, now leaning towards Iraq. The 159 Baʻth candidates, mostly Northerners, included rural *shaykhs* and Iraqi-educated urbanites or officers. Among its top eight candidates featured on party posters, one was a female administrator at the Yemen Center for Research and Studies in Sana'a. The *shaykhs* were for the most part friends of Mujāḥid Abū Shawārib, a Ḥāshid *shaykh*, hero of the revolution and the cooperative movement, brother-in-law to *Shaykh* al-Aḥmar, and perennial deputy prime minister for interior affairs, who joined the Baʻth after quitting the GPC in 1990. Evidently thanks to his imprimatur, seven Baʻthīs were successful in the 1993 elections. Soon after the elections Abū Shawārib quit the party, however, and Qāsim Salām, a mercurial figure with strong ties to Baghdad, became its leader. Never far from power-holders in Sana'a, the Baʻth party would support the GPC–Iṣlāḥ axis during the 1994 civil war but fell in with the opposition after the war.

Among some forty other parties whose names and newspapers appeared in lists, a half-dozen played a serious role in domestic affairs. Limited in their power base, these parties nonetheless represented historically important political tendencies with legitimacy among the educated elite, and played a role in major negotiations such as the SEC and the National Dialogue Committee. Among them were two offering interpretations of Zaydī Islam, a couple of Nāṣirī organizations, and the heir to the protectorate-era South Arabian League.

Two Northern-based, avowedly Islamist parties antithetical to the neo-Islamists in Iṣlāḥ were the Ḥizb al-Ḥaqq (party of truth, or righteousness) and the Union of Popular Forces. Al-Ḥaqq's sixty-five candidates, most of them Sharī'a-educated Zaydī *sayyids* from prominent Hashemite families in Sana'a and Ṣa'da governorates, favored *shūrā* rule by Zaydī *'ulamā'*, and also articulated respect for the law. Reputedly getting some money from Shī'a Iran, but doctrinally rooted in Yemeni rather than Twelver Shī'aism, al-Ḥaqq presented itself as an alternative to Wahhabism.[7] Its slogan, *Hay'at al-Amr bi-l-Ma'rūf wa-l-Nahī 'An al-Munkar* (Enjoining Good and Forbidding Evil),[8] was employed earlier by both the imamate and the Muslim Brotherhood. Its leader, Aḥmad al-Shāmī, an aging, formally dressed Sharī'a judge from a famous family, was a forceful, humorous, non-dogmatic speaker, perhaps the most "traditional" of politicians, far more tolerant of women in public roles than al-Zindānī. Al-Ḥaqq's regional base was in Ṣa'da governorate in the far north, where it won two seats in a direct political contest between Zaydī *sayyids*, custodians of local religious tradition, and Sunnī–Wahhabi "converts" and managers of "scientific institutes" who allied with Iṣlāḥ. The Wahhabis, among them many youthful returnees from Saudi Arabia, advocate a more austere, puritanical Islam, in response to which al-Ḥaqq constituted one aspect of a sort of Zaydī revival.[9] On a national scale, al-Ḥaqq's newspaper, *al-Umma*, often took issue with the religious interpretations of *al-Ṣaḥwa* and of the "scientific institutes."

The other small party the Republican Palace labeled "royalist" was the Ittiḥād al-Quwā al-Sha'biyya. This party, the Union of Popular Forces (UPF), in effect returned from exile in 1990, although the party's official leader, Ibrāhīm al-Wazīr, stayed in Washington, D.C. Heir to the 1948 attempt to seize the imamate, Ibrāhīm 'Alī al-Wazīr had led the Union of Popular Forces, an element of the "third force" within the YAR in the 1960s. Long a potential rival of the royal family, in mid-century the al-Wazīr family was at the center of a group of Zaydī *sayyid 'ulamā'* who advocated a modern constitutional imamate or Hashemite kingdom. Later, from exile, they had bought advertisements in *The*

Washington Post denouncing the January 1990 visit of the "dictator of Yemen." In the 1990s, then, Popular Forces claimed two constitutional legacies, the Sacred National Pact and Khamir conference proposals, and tended to represent Jordan as a positive model. Its representative on the Dialogue Committee and in other venues, Zayd al-Wazīr, head of a small publishing house in London, has written widely on Yemeni and Islamic history and, recently, German federalism and unification. In its 1993 party platform and subsequent communiqués[10] the party advocated constitutionalism and "civil society." *Al-Shūrā,* its newspaper, editorially advocated separation of religion and politics. Garnering only several thousand votes mostly in Sana'a and nearby Banī Ḥushaysh for its two dozen candidates, the UPF nonetheless represented a threat in the form of what might be called an "alternative legitimacy." Although both al-Ḥaqq and UPF were based in the Zaydī north, in the competition between the YSP and the GPC they were fairly neutral; *al-Shūrā,* assuming the role of muckraker, criticized both and painted an especially unfavorable caricature of Iṣlāḥ's al-Zindānī.

A third small party that also identified with Islam, the Rābiṭat Abnā' al-Yaman (RAY) or League of Sons of Yemen, was the heir to the old South Arabian League (SAL) founded in the early 1950s, which had favored a separate South Yemeni federation of sultanates on a model something like the United Arab Emirates. The RAY announced itself in early 1990 in Sana'a and was able to run eighty-some candidates mostly in the areas of Shabwa (its "stronghold"), the Ḥaḍramawt, and Laḥj in the south, and in Ḥajja in the north. None of its candidates entered parliament, although among the smaller parties it was a leading vote-getter. Leader 'Abd al-Raḥmān al-Jufrī and many party members, *personae non gratae* in the PDRY, had spent over two decades in Saudi Arabia, where the al-Jufrīs had considerable assets and political connections. A fluent English speaker (with a penchant for bilingual acronyms such as RAY and TOM) and avid interview-giver, al-Jufrī's views on matters ranging from Yemeni unity to women's legal competence echoed Riyadh's.[11] He acknowledged Saudi financial support for the RAY. Given their history, coverage in RAY's newspapers, and al-Jufrī's public statements, there seemed to be no love lost between al-Rābiṭa and the YSP. Between 1990 and 1994, the RAY seemed equally antagonistic to the YSP and the GPC. When the war broke out, however, al-Jufrī joined the YSP leaders' bid to restore a separate South Yemeni state in 1994.

What had once been a significant Nāṣirite tendency in Yemen was fragmented into several different parties. Al-Tanẓīm al-Sha'bī al-Waḥdawī al-Nāṣirī (literally the popular unificationist Nāṣirite organization) was founded in Aden in February 1989 and organized in Sana'a a year later.[12] It ran ninety candidates, mostly educated urbanites and businessmen in the populous Ibb–Taiz region: several candidates ran well, but only one won. Labeled by Yemen's leading poet "the party of the laymen or the market-place,"[13] the Waḥdawī-Nāṣirī organization presented itself as liberal.[14] Two secretaries-general served during the political opening. On the eve of the civil war, then-secretary-general 'Abd al-Mālik al-Mikhlāfī said that though the party was once "whole-heartedly with the YSP," this support was all but gone: "The YSP cannot expect to become a hero for unifying the country and a hero for dismantling the unity."[15]

A second "Nāṣirī" party emphasized its identification with the corrective movement of the YAR's Ibrāhīm al-Ḥamdī. The Tanẓim al-Tasḥīḥ al-Sha'bī al-Nāṣirī, or simply al-Tasḥīḥ ("correction"), was formed from the 1991 merger of an offshoot of the National Democratic Front and the Nāṣirī Organization of Yemen. Al-Tasḥīḥ was headed by Mujāḥid al-Quhālī, a Bakīlī shaykh from the rebellious 'Iyāl Surayḥ. A former member of the al-Ḥamdī Command Council, he openly blamed President Ṣāliḥ for al-Ḥamdī's death, and was a military commander in the NDF insurrection against the president. At one time he was a frequent visitor to Libya. After a decade in exile in Aden, he was elected to parliament in April 1993 representing 'Iyāl Surayḥ. Given the personal antipathy between him and the president, al-Quhālī's election was rather remarkable.

The Yemeni al-Tajammu' al-Waḥdawī, or "Unificationist Gathering," founded in February 1990, was headed by Laḥj native and long-time Aden resident 'Umar al-Jāwī, a past president of the Writers' Guild, former YSP member, and human rights activist, who in public fora epitomized the pipe-smoking Arab intellectual. Ten party members who ran for election mostly in Aden, all technically as independents, won just a few thousand votes. If powerless in terms of numbers, the Tajammu' nonetheless articulated a sort of liberal–progressive social, economic, and political ideology that appealed to the most educated segment of society and won al-Jāwī a place on important committees. Like the Waḥdawī-Nāṣirī party, the Tajammu' tended toward a Southern-Socialist position during the first four years after 1990, but later rejected the separatist effort. Along with two primarily Northern-based or Zaydī parties, al-Ḥaqq and the UPF, they led the "opposition coalition" both before and after the civil war.

Other "parties" ran just one or two candidates as independents. Only one of these, the Liberal-Constitutional party, elected a well-known son of a famous Free Yemeni family, 'Abd al-Raḥmān Nu'mān, in his home district of Ḥujariyya where long before he had organized the LDA. The other minor parties were of two sorts. In the main, they were the project of individuals seeking a political following or role. For instance, Muḥammad 'Alī Abū Luḥūm, who attended college with George Bush's son, tried to recruit people to a Republican party. Several other individuals also founded microcosmic political parties. Secondly, there were several parties obviously backed by the highest circles in the GPC. One of these was a third Nāṣirite party. The Nāṣirī-Democratic party's legacy lay in the FLOSY wing of the anti-colonial movement and in the NDF. Soon after its official incarnation in 1990, the party was inundated by new members who said they were quitting the GPC and who managed to elect as party leaders persons known as security agents. The Nāṣirī-Democratic party won a seat in parliament and on every important multiparty committee, and joined the small-party opposition coalition. A similar more obscure party was called the NDF after the 1970s movement in the southern uplands. The third example seemed part individual initiative part GPC clientage, for Septembrist party head Aḥmad Qarḥash, also represented on some key committees, was a good spokesman of the Sana'a establishment.

Finally, several thousand independents, many of them active in the wider civic arena, campaigned for parliament. Among them were several distinct profiles. About a thousand foreign-educated intellectuals, some of them female, spent the winter and spring of 1992/93 formulating issues, platforms, and strategies. Some were GPC or YSP members not selected for the party slate, among them several appointees to the transition-period Parliament. Secondly, rural counter-elites mounted electoral campaigns around local issues such as services, especially education: this group included *shaykhs*, merchants, and activists from earlier times running against the party in power. Thirdly, in some districts the party in power floated additional independents to dilute the anti-incumbency vote. As the campaign progressed, some of each group dropped out.

The field was most crowded in the cities, where every party posted candidates and the educated elite ran as independents. Rural contests were played against rural issues. In Ma'rib or the Jawf one might find credible candidates from the Ba'th, al-Ḥaqq, the YSP, Iṣlāḥ, and the GPC; in Taiz, from all the main parties and well-known independents; in Laḥj, from the Rābiṭa, the Tajammu', Iṣlāḥ, and the YSP. In some constituencies each community ran a candidate and the largest village won; others were divided by controversies far removed from the national parties.

Fifty women, mostly independents but also some YSP members and

Table 6.2. *Results of parliamentary elections, 1993 and 1997*

Party name	% vote 1993	Seats 1993	% vote 1997	Seats 1997
General People's Congress	28	123	42	188
Yemeni Reform Gathering	17	62	23	53
Yemeni Socialist Party	18	56	0	0
Ba'th Arab Socialist Party	3	7	1	2
al-Ḥaqq	>1	2	>1	0
Waḥdawī-Naṣirī	1	1	2	3
Democratic-Naṣirī	>1	1	0	
al-Taṣḥīḥ	>1	1	0	
Independents	29	48	28	55
other parties	>2		>3	
		301		301

one official Ba'th candidate, campaigned for office. The majority were university-educated independents in Aden, Taiz, and Sana'a, where in a few constituencies several women ran. Campaigning was a novelty and a matter of principle in the North, where in 1988 women were legally authorized but actively discouraged from running for office. For Southern women the 1993 elections provided a different sort of challenge. The YSP had allowed women to hold office in the PDRY and was represented in the transition-period Parliament by ten women, but proved reluctant to put female names on its ticket in a more competitive contest. Only two women "supported" by the YSP, an Adeni Socialist and a young independent in al-Mukallā', won seats in the 1993/94 parliament. Like many male independents the women were campaigning to influence the discourse and the shape of the system.

In addition to the parties and candidates, other groups were involved in the campaign experience as well. During the registration period in early 1993, 2.7 million persons aged eighteen and over, including 77 percent of eligible (adult) males and 15 percent of eligible, mainly urban or southern, females,[16] signed up to vote. Although questions were raised about the system of recording the votes of illiterates, the process of registering and voting was freer than ever before, and attracted a sizable number of first-time voters. Thousands of men and dozens of women helped with the campaigns of some 4,800 declared candidates, or acted as observers on behalf of the SEC or the 3,200 election-day candidates. Hundreds more were recruited and/or trained by one of the two rival election-monitoring groups (on which more below).

Tables 6.2 and 6.3 show aggregate and provincial results of the 1993

Table 6.3. *Percentage votes by party and governorate, 1993 elections*

	# seats	GPC	YSP	Iṣlāḥ	Ba'th	Haqq	W-N	D-N	*Taṣḥīḥ*	UPF	YUG	RAY	Ind
Sana'a city	(18)	37	15	25	1	1	2	-	>1	>1	-	>1	10
Sana'a gov.	(36)	23	12	19	7	1	>1	-	2	>1	-	>1	12
Taiz	(43)	22	29	18	4	>1	9	1	-	-	-	>1	9
Ibb	(38)	32	14	21	2	>1	1	>1	>1	-	-	1	15
Hodeida	(33)	41	16	16	3	>1	2	>1	>1	>1	>1	-	7
Dhamar	(21)	32	12	22	3	>1	>1	>1	-	>1	-	>1	19
Ḥajja	(23)	38	11	32	10	>1	>1	>1	-	>1	2	-	10
al-Maḥwīt	(8)	43	2	15	6	>1	-	-	>1	-	-	>1	5
Ṣa'da	(9)	28	5	6	9	23	>1	-	-	-	-	-	11
al-Bayḍā'	(10)	25	25	23	7	>1	2	-	-	>1	>1	>1	7
Ma'rib	(3)	37	17	6	6	-	-	-	-	2	-	-	22
al-Jawf	(2)	23	17	23	2	7	>1	-	-	-	-	>1	25
Aden	(11)	7	59	7	-	-	1	>1	>1	-	>1	>1	17
Abyan	(8)	19	54	5	>1	-	2	-	-	>1	>1	>1	16
Shabwa	(6)	21	43	4	-	-	-	-	-	>1	-	6	12
Ḥaḍramawt	(17)	14	45	17	>1	-	>1	-	-	-	-	2	8
al-Mahra	(3)	20	61	-	-	-	-	-	-	-	-	-	4
Laḥj	(12)	4	80	1	>1	-	1	-	-	-	-	>1	7
Total	(301)	28	26	17	3	1	2	1	>1	>1	>1	5	11

Source: al-Ḥizb al-Ishtirākī al-Yamanī, "Natā'ij al-dawra l-intikhābiyya"

Parties in order listed: General People's Congress, Yemeni Socialist Party, Yemeni Reform Gathering, Ba'th Arab Socialist Party, al-Ḥaqq, Waḥdawī-Nāṣirī, Democratic-Nāṣirī, al-Taṣḥīḥ, Union of Popular Forces, al-Tajammu' al-Waḥdawī, Rābiṭa; Independents elections. Of 301 seats, the Congress won 123 constituencies; Iṣlāḥ came in second with 62 seats; the YSP took 57 constituencies; independents had 46; the Ba'th won seven; three Nāṣirī parties each gained one seat, and al-Ḥaqq took two constituencies.[17] The YSP took all but three seats in the former PDRY and a handful in the northern governorates. In terms of popular vote, according to the official estimate 28 percent went to the GPC; 18 percent to the Socialists, 17 percent to Iṣlāḥ candidates, 29 percent for independents, and the remainder for ten smaller parties led by the Ba'th with 3 percent.[18] The only province-by-province tally of the results came from a YSP politbureau report that circulated by photocopy. It gave the YSP 25 percent of the vote and also recorded for the small parties rather more votes than the official tally.[19]

Mass media and the press

The single most dramatic indicator of the opening that persisted until the eve of the 1994 war was the relative freedom of information via two competing broadcast companies, two national daily newspapers, a hundred new Yemeni periodicals, and satellite dish access to the London-based, Saudi-financed, Arabic-language Middle East Broadcasting Corporation (MBC, often characterized as the Arabic CNN) and broadcasts from Saudi Arabia, Egypt, and elsewhere. Newspaper consumption also reached beyond the literate quarter of the adult population as articles were read aloud or discussed with family and friends.

Whether because of competition or political directives, television and radio news coverage improved in 1990, featuring lengthy televised parliamentary debates, extended reporting on the Gulf Crisis of 1990/91, live video footage of street demonstrations in the fall of 1992, and initially unfettered call-in radio programs. In both Aden and Sana'a there was a perceptible shift away from the shallow laudatory accounts of domestic and foreign affairs to more serious reporting. Although their respective control of broadcast stations and daily papers gave the YSP and the GPC disproportionate access to state media, as in other arenas the competition between them was real. Indeed the widening disparities between the the two leaderships was manifested in increasingly divergent news accounts. From the electoral season through the onset of the civil war, the media constituted an arena for a "war of declarations" and for competition to influence public opinion. Whereas in the past political rivalries were secretive, now they played out in front of television audiences more aware of political events than at any time in their history.

The reading public could choose from a wider array of sources.[20] The two official daily newspapers, Sana'a's *al-Thawra* and Aden's *14 October*, the most widely available newspapers, each accustomed to a monopoly on the official line, became true competitors. The YSP's three weeklies, *al-Mustaqbal, al-Waḥda*, and *al-Thawrī* gave editorial space to its candidates, leaders, and ideologues. *Ṣawt al-'Ummāl* ("Voice of the Workers"), a professionally run Aden newspaper published in different forms since before the PDRY revolution, played a significant role in the post-1986 "*glasnost*" in South Yemen, and a wide readership in unified Yemen; technically independent from the Socialist party, and believed to reflect the views of its northern wing, it devoted special energy to reporting the perfidy of the GPC leadership. The paper of the Northern military, *26 September*, whose staff included some serious reporters, *22 May*, and the GPC's especially vituperative *al-Mīthāq* represented Sana'a's case against the YSP leadership. Southern provinces and the city of Taiz had their own semi-governmental local papers.

In addition, a number of opposition and independent weeklies and various tabloids were rather widely sold, purchased, read, and cited in a couple of dozen towns. The Iṣlāḥ published an official organ, *al-Iṣlāḥ*, created after the official founding of the party in 1990, and *al-Ṣaḥwa*, established in 1986, which called itself the voice of the Islamist current. Other party organs including *Ra'y* and *al-Ḥaqq* (both of the Rābiṭa), *al-Tashīḥ* (of the party by the same name), *al-Tajammu'* (also named for the party), *al-Waḥdawī* (of the Unity-Nāṣirī party), *al-Shūrā* (of the Union of Popular Forces), *al-Jamāhīr* (of the Ba'th) and *al-Umma* (of al-Ḥaqq) devoted most of their space to essays by party leaders and spokespersons, although *al-Shūrā*, like *Ṣawt al-'Ummāl* and sometimes *al-Jamāhīr*, did publish investigative stories. Independent, private papers, especially the reborn *al-Ayyām* and the *Yemen Times*, provided a mix of editorial and news content, with the *Yemen Times* serving Yemen's small international community with summaries of events and advertisements for franchises of international companies. A few papers such as *Ṣawt al-Jabha* (Voice of the Front, meaning the NDF) printed a straight GPC line. A couple of rags evidently rented out column space to any paying author. The Saudi-owned international Arabic daily *Al-Hayat*, whose coverage included major, especially military, events in Yemen, was widely read; *al-Sharq al-Awsaṭ*, which from the onset enthusiastically predicted the collapse of Yemeni unity, was banned (although articles of interest invariably circulated by fax).

Political differences were played out in the press, both between the GPC and the YSP and between and among other groups. Party organs reported events organized or dominated by their own leaderships and drew attention to their rivals' malfeasance. At the height of the mud-slinging in early 1994, for example, *Ṣawt al-'Ummāl* and two YSP organs published a list of the thirty-three top officers in Ṣāliḥ's army, all from his own tribe, Sanḥān, under the title "Yemen's new royal family." The GPC's *22 May* retaliated with names of Southern military officers from the districts of Radfān and Ḍāli'. Then *al-Shūrā* printed both lists side by side.[21] As the military situation deteriorated, Sana'a and Aden television and radio broadcast increasingly vociferous speeches and counter-speeches from Ṣāliḥ, al-Bīḍ, and their respective colleagues. GPC papers and Sana'a airwaves publicized Ṣāliḥ's long diatribe blaming the prime minister for the country's economic woes; al-'Aṭṭās counter-attacked with a letter published in at least two papers about billions of riyāls in unauthorized expenditures ordered by the president's office. In February and March, the organs of the two dueling parties accused each other of using the military to avoid implementation of the accords.[22]

Virtually all the Yemeni Arabic publications were printed on state-owned presses ultimately controlled by the two former ruling parties. The press law also countered the freedoms and autonomy guaranteed in some clauses with registration, licensing, and "truth" requirements interpreted by the Ministry of Information. According to many journalists, one indication of the reluctance of the regime to grant basic political liberties was the establishment in the spring of 1993 of a press prosecution office in Sana'a, with a mandate to monitor newspapers, editors, and reporters and bring suit against violators of the press law. At least twenty suits brought in Sana'a during the months following the elections for unauthorized reporting on public officials were defended by journalists and attorneys' syndicates on a *pro bono* basis. Most cases were ill founded, so the courts tended to either vindicate the newspapers or postpone the hearings. In a widely publicized case the *Yemen Times* was defended by private counsel and attorneys representing the Journalists' Syndicate, a human rights organization, and the faculty union.[23] *Al-Tasḥīḥ* was sued in August 1993 for its February publication of excerpts of an article from a Lebanese magazine where President Ṣāliḥ was quoted as saying he would change his stripes to support unity, socialism, tribalism, or any other cause in order to retain power.[24] The court and defense attorneys prolonged the case without resolution. The Ba'th's *al-Jamāhīr* was sued for a critical article about the Judicial Institute, even after publishing a rebuttal from one of its administrators.[25] A case against Iṣlāḥ's *al-Ṣaḥwa*, for revealing the contents of a letter from the Yemeni ambassador in Cairo to the Ministry of Foreign Affairs about the Gulf reactions to the Yemeni elections, ended in acquittal after the defense persuaded the court that the letter itself was based on materials already published in Egypt, thus already in the public domain.[26]

The relative tolerance of press freedom from 1990 through mid-1994, when efforts to bridle publication were pursued through the courts by lawyers and journalists eager to create court precedent, was put into stark relief when YSP presses were smashed, reporters or editors of most of the opposition press were detained, and new appointees staffed *14 October*. Yet in the meantime a virtually uncensored press gave ample space for reporters, professors, and others to contribute to the formulation of informed public opinion. Press conferences and press coverage of other conferences provided new sorts of material to an emerging "fourth estate." While many writers addressed political controversies in parables about pharaohs or villains from Islamic or Yemeni history, for the first time reporters also engaged in investigative reporting on prison conditions, electoral fraud, environmental degradation, and even military maneuvers.

Quasi-governmental and private voluntary associations

Non-profit voluntary associations were of three main types. First, well-established corporatist mass and professional associations affiliated with one or the other of the former regimes corresponded to what are sometimes referred to in the comparative literature as GO-NGOs. Secondly, in the 1990s charities proliferated in Yemen, as elsewhere in the Arab world. Thirdly, groups of urban professionals and intellectuals initiated a range of cultural, social, and civic associations. While many of these celebrated Yemeni culture in one way or another, they reflected contemporary state politics, economic conditions, and intellectual trends. In addition, a range of bilateral, multilateral, and non-profit development agencies made funds available for NGO, civil society, and democratization projects. As always, civil society was a zone where organization and social capital were contested.

Established formal associations

At the time of unification there were over two hundred and fifty agricultural societies and cooperatives, forty-eight consumers' associations, twenty-one craft societies, nineteen fishermen's associations, about a hundred housing cooperatives, a wide range of professional syndicates, the women's and youth organizations, and specialized societies such as the Red Crescent and chambers of commerce.[27] The YAR's LDAs had been brought into the state apparatus. The housing and agricultural cooperatives of the former PDRY's socialist system were scheduled for reorganization through real-estate privatization.[28] National women's and youth associations, professional syndicates, and the specialized institutions, scheduled for official merger, became microcosms of the partisan struggle for control of the state.

The merger of the two Yemeni women's unions, formalized around September 1991,[29] proved particularly difficult. The Northern union's founders, secular feminists many of whom ran for parliament in 1993, were outvoted in the Sana'a headquarters during the 1980s by emphatically veiled Islamists who insisted that Islam grants women the right to remain at home, rely on male relatives for financial support and legal representation, study in sex-segregated schools, and refrain from public life apart from charitable activities. Aden's women's union, one of the party-affiliated "mass organizations," had ministerial status and parliamentary representation in the PDRY, and held ten seats in the transition parliament. The Northern and Southern women's unions took opposite positions on the personal status law the GPC and Iṣlāḥ said promoted "family values" but Southerners saw as a revocation of the many rights to divorce, child custody, and housing enjoyed by women in the PDRY. Polarization around this issue (comparable to the debate over abortion in the US) in the antibellum period and its resolution in favor of conservative family values after 1994 help explain why many women participated in civil society through non-gender-oriented groups.

Some student and professional syndicates likewise encapsulated competition between the YSP and the GPC or Iṣlāḥ over leadership and agendas. In the Federation of Students, like the women's union, two quasi-governmental organizations, dominated respectively by Islamists and Socialists, clashed from the moment they first met in November 1989. In the case of teachers, not represented in the YAR, a new *Niqābat al-Mu'allimīn* was founded on the eve of unity to compete with the long-established Southern *Niqābat al-Miḥan al-Ta'līmiyya*, resulting in two national organizations competing to represent teachers. To avoid having the strong Aden-based Peasant's Federation swallow up its old Federation of Agricultural Cooperatives, the GPC promoted a new Confederation of Agricultural Cooperative Societies that elected a Nāṣirī-Democratic president, a Socialist vice-president, and a GPC secretary.

The professional syndicates of physicians and pharmacists, attorneys, journalists, and even judges consolidated more smoothly, and helped organize a politically conscious, educated, professional class with vested interests in political liberalization. Strikes and threats of strikes by educators, judges, bankers, oil workers, health professionals and others wrested concessions from government on several occasions.[30] The lawyers' and press syndicates defended journalists in court. Sana'a University faculty elected conservatives, while the YSP dominated on the Aden University campus; most professors set aside their differences, however, to lobby for pay raises in 1992, 1995, and 1996. Syndical delegations were prominent at public events such as the national conference of 1993. In early 1994 the lawyers, physicians, writers, and journalists syndicates announced a Syndicates' Coordinating Council for Human Rights intended to defend professional and personal rights of members, especially women.

Charities and welfare societies

By 1996 there were over three hundred community and religious charities in Yemen – more than the number in the rest of the Arabian Peninsula combined.[31] These contemporary welfare associations, while evoking the religious connotations of the traditional term *jam'iyya khayriyya*, were very much a 1990s phenomenon. As discussed in the last chapter, their appearance coincided with the demise of secular "development cooperatives," and with the rise of a neo-Islamist currency privy to public or private donations from the Gulf. The *jam'iyyat al-khayriyya* of the imamic and sultanic orders at the turn of the century provided some poor-relief, but in traditional Yemeni Islam private endowments or *waqf* supported mosques and quranic institutes. After that, states and civil society together constructed a basic modern infrastructure of transport, utilities, educational, and health services, subsequently nationalized and centralized. Local and regional groups that constituted powerful counter-hegemonic forces in the 1950s, 1960s, and 1970s had been co-opted. In the meantime, Sana'a, Aden, Taiz, and Hodeida had grown into third-world cities with burgeoning *barrio*-type neighborhoods of squalor and discontent to which half a million Gulf migrants "returned." Contemporary welfare associations thus differ from their traditional namesakes in their financing, their organization, and their services. In terms of ideological content, whereas some groups reflect traditional sectarian doctrine, the largest, best-known Islamist welfare society, *jam'iyya al-Iṣlāḥ al-khayriyya,* and some of its close rivals, preach decidedly neo-fundamentalist versions of Islam.

The Iṣlāḥ Social Welfare Society (ISWS), founded in Taiz 1990, is linked unofficially to both the political party and its namesakes in the Gulf. Relying heavily on business contributions that amounted to about $8 million a year before 1994,[32] it specializes in emergency (especially flood) relief and in social services for deprived urban communities, such as mother–child clinics, vocational training, religious education, needlework classes, summer camps, and group marriage ceremonies to discourage the poor from spending on traditional weddings.[33] In 1996 it was building a women's psychiatric hospital and a new university of science and technology.[34] Local branches, subsidized partly by local donations, run community centers where special attention is paid to training lower-class adolescent girls (who, as educational statistics show, typically leave school at the intermediate level) as frugal, obedient, modern homemakers. One of the messages is that traditional feminine pleasures such as bridal and post-natal parties ("showers") are sinfully frivolous. During the election season, ISWS installed water tanks in the "Madīnat Saddam" squatter settlement for tens of thousands of Gulf War migrant-refugees outside Hodeida; during the civil war it found shelter for refugees from the South in schools and other public buildings in Taiz. ISWS also raises donations for war victims in Bosnia, Palestine, and Lebanon.[35]

Among ISWS's competitors, especially in Taiz, was a rival al-Ḥikma Social Welfare Society purported to represent a purer *(salafī)* Islamic fundamentalism. Also based in Taiz, the leading merchant family, a past backer of the Iṣlāḥ Welfare society, founded the Hayel Sayeed Anam Group Charity Society with a proportion of corporate profits earmarked for mosques, schools, health centers, water-wells, and a productive families project.[36] Al-Ḥaḍārim Welfare Society, based in rural Taiz but led by urban intellectuals, secured Western and Japanese technical assistance. A new generation of Ḥujariyya social welfare associations founded regional coordinating councils, and undertook unfinished development projects such as electrification and roads. Sana'a, Taiz, Aden, and Hodeida neighborhood associations conducted sporadic garbage-removal campaigns, children's libraries, Ramaḍān meals for destitute families, or other projects. Two other self-declared Islamist parties, the Rābiṭa and al-Ḥaqq, had women's auxiliaries that held social and charitable events.

Some other welfare associations, including specialized medical services charities or associations serving occupational groups such as street-sweepers, were explicitly secular. Among these, a noteworthy physician-operated free clinic for artists in Sana'a later expanded its scope to include civic activists, too. The most prominent regional association, the Ḥaḍramawt Welfare Society, founded in Sana'a by merchants and professionals, and which hoped to raise an endowment for a Ḥaḍramawt university, was the venue for weekly *maqyal* where well-educated male professionals debated political and cultural issues and a women's section held some seminars and charity drives.

Literary societies and human rights groups

The third major category of activism involved educated elites and counter-elites in the most obviously civic types of associations, engaged by urban professionals: salons, human rights groups, environmental societies, foreign friendship associations, and the like. Explicitly engaged in the formation of public opinion, the protection of civic space, and the protection of legal rights, such organizations stand in a special relationship to the state not because of their mass following or their formal institutional presence but because of the ideas and discourses they articulate.

For the contemporary generation of intellectuals, the longest-lived, most important of these was the Writers' Guild. The *Ittiḥād al-Udabā',* established in Aden in 1972, played a singular role in intellectual civic life before unification. Responding to YAR–PDRY tensions that year, nationalist thinkers in the unified guild published a regular literary journal, met alternately in Sana'a and Aden, elected officers at triennial conventions, defied official bans on non-governmental conferences, formed a half-dozen or more provincial branches who held regional seminars, and sent joint delegations to Arab and international writers' meetings. Frequently banned in one capital or the other on account of political content, Writers' Guild journal *al-Ḥikma* remained the only regular independent scholarly publication prior to unification.

The guild's relationship to both governments was contradictory. Sana'a and Aden each courted the organ of a united intelligentsia, hoping to borrow its legitimacy. Their rivalry enabled the guild to evade domination. Failing outright control, both regimes censored, jailed, or banished writers to the other half of the country. In 1986 the guild published condemnations of the bloodshed in Aden and Abyan. In 1987 and 1988, as the political atmosphere in Aden relaxed, they called meetings of journalists, engineers, artists', and women's groups to encourage their unification. Ultimately, the guild exercised some pressure for unification, freedom of expression, pluralism, and political reconciliation. In the more open environment after May 1990, it voiced an intellectual conscience through its seminars, publications, and participation in the "peace movement." Prior presidency of the Writers' Guild conferred honor on the candidate who ran against al-Aḥmar as speaker of Parliament and 'Umar al-Jāwī of the Tajammu' party and the National Conference.

A few independent educational-cultural "think tank"-type organizations found private or international funding. The 'Afīf Foundation for Cultural Affairs founded in Sana'a by Aḥmad Jābir 'Afīf published a two-volume *Yemen Encyclopedia* with entries by an array of leading scholars, a booklet on women's rights, and linguistic, historical, and biographical studies.[37] 'Afīf, who had built a personal fortune in government service and banking (and was also active in some other associations including the Society to Eradicate the Effects of Qāt) established a formal trust. Others looked for foreign financing. An Iṣlāḥ-oriented professor hoped to establish an affiliate of the London-based, Sudan-leaning Islamic Future Studies Center. Exiled YSP member 'Alī Nāṣir Muḥammad had a Damascus institute for strategic studies funded as a "civil society project" by UNDP. Several Western-educated intellectuals looked for hard currency to support research, publications, conferences, or other activities in fields such as the environment.

Less formal groups did not need much money. The Academic Democratic Gathering, a collection of faculty and researchers, held its founders' conference in Sana'a in October 1993, and launched a political symposium within a month.[38] It was loosely and informally connected to the Yemen Center for Research and Studies (YCRS) in Sana'a, itself a semi-autonomous affiliate of Sana'a University where many leftists found themselves after al-Zindānī and his colleagues penetrated the university in the 1980s. After some criticisms that "Academic Democratic Gathering" sounded like a political party, that name was changed to the Academic Federation. The focus of weekly symposia turned to the accords of the National Dialogue Committee. Some of these were held in the seminar rooms at YCRS; in Ramaḍān 1994, they became night sessions over qāt that filled two large *dīwāns* (connected by intercom) at the Sana'a offices of the Writers' Guild. Each week there was a formal paper presentation on a specific topic, say judicial reform or local government, followed by remarks and general discussion. A range of positions was represented. Earnest discussants thought they might affect policy.

The experience of human rights and elections monitoring associations illuminate government efforts to offset autonomous initiatives by promoting substitutes with similar agendas. Between November 1989 and February 1990 activists in Sana'a and Aden exchanged drafts of a proposal for a Yemeni committee for the defense of democratic liberties.[39] When a couple hundred men and women gathered at the Sana'a Cultural Center to begin founding a human rights organization, they found that on the first day the electricity was cut and on the second day some 500 supporters of the Muslim Brotherhood and security officers constituted themselves as a voting majority. This broke up the effort. Two years later, in February 1992, an invitation-only founders' meeting of the Yemeni Organization for the Defense of Democratic Rights and

Liberties (ODDRL) convened at the Aden local people's council. Among those elected to the Supreme Council were members of the YSP, the GPC, the Tajammuʿ, and al-Ḥaqq, and the editors of *Ṣawt al-ʿUmmāl* and *Yemen Times*. In view of their earlier experience, they opted for relatively closed membership.[40] In addition to observing prison conditions and defending legal rights, ODDRL made it a policy to encourage other "institutions of civil society" including a society to combat unemployment and the National Committee for Free Elections. It also sought out Arab affiliates and Western donors.

In October 1992, a rival group calling itself the Yemeni Organization for Human Rights (YOHR) gathered about 1,200 persons at the Sana'a Police Academy. *Qāḍī* Ḥamūd al-Hitar, head of the Sana'a criminal court, was elected to head a thirty-five-member board of trustees comprising mainly members of the GPC, Iṣlāḥ, and the Baʿth. YOHR focused on application of existing protections of the rights of the accused and promoting the adoption of a proper penal code.[41] In late September 1993, President Ṣāliḥ urged the two legally registered human rights organizations to merge their activities in order to maximize their effectiveness in protecting human rights and particularly the rights of prisoners.[42] But rather than consolidating, human rights activities were proliferating. In 1994 Yemen had more Amnesty International groups than any other Arab country. One small informal effort worthy of mention was Sana'a University philosophy professor Abū Bakr al-Saqqāf's initiative to found an unregistered human rights association. And far from unifying, ODDRL and YOHR tended to compete for media coverage of certain issues, such as military checkpoints,[43] or to focus on contrary instances of human rights abuses.[44]

One of the organizations supported by ODDRL, called the National Committee for Free Elections (NCFE),[45] exemplifies what American consultants called "the government's hesitation about permitting completely autonomous groups to engage in political activism."[46] NCFE was founded in January 1993, after parliamentary elections had already been postponed, largely as result of contacts between ODDRL and the Washington-based National Democratic Institute (NDI), which hoped to train non-partisan Yemeni election monitors to complement the work of the multinational observer delegation sponsored by NDI's sister organization, the International Republican Institute. In February the Yemeni Supreme Election Committee granted permission to NCFE to train Yemeni elections monitors, and together NCFE and NDI began scheduling training sessions.

By March, however, as training was under way, GPC newspapers insinuated NCFE's "well-known partisan connections" (code for the

YSP, the only major group calling itself a party) and the government recommended a list of "genuine independents" for inclusion on the NCFE–NDI Advisory Council. When the ruling party's demands were not met, the SEC chairman, a GPC member of the Presidential Council, ruled that only international monitors (and candidates' representatives) could legally observe.[47] Moreover, when "NDI observers expressed consternation" to government officials over this decision, these sessions "were inaccurately portrayed on television as emphatic NDI endorsements of the SEC and its success in establishing foolproof mechanisms for free and fair elections."[48] A month before the elections were to be held, a newly founded Yemeni Committee for Free and Democratic Elections, also supposedly a non-partisan independent citizen action group,[49] approached NDI for financial support and training materials. In the end, both election-monitoring organizations collapsed.

The conference mode of participation

Alongside the "institutions" of civil society, seminars, round-tables and conferences constituted a space for elite and mass expression. One-time discussion sessions seemed especially suited to the garrulous, highly politicized, but still largely illiterate Yemeni culture; the diversity of political opinion and cross-cutting nature of political loyalties; the constraints on formal institutional political participation; and the fast-breaking pace of political events. Urban and rural traditions of scholarly salons and tribal convocations, respectively, fed into the elite and mass meetings that had marked the revolutionary era,[50] and authoritarian regimes subsequently sought to mobilize support through party conferences and by inviting key opinion leaders to meet with top officials. By the early 1980s the northern tribes were engaging in novel forms of political activism, holding conferences and even publishing a pamphlet calling for peaceful resolution of tribal disputes and meaningful "participation" in national politics – a noteworthy departure from their traditional *modus operandi*.[51] More than the party-platform-and-polling-booth or the file-cabinet-and-letterhead-civic-institutions, public events typified the mode of political participation in the post-unity opening.

Scholarly conventions

Autonomous academic symposia, outlawed in the YAR and the PDRY and convened only by the Writers' Guild, became routine in Sana'a, Aden, and other towns. Anticipating the parliamentary debate on the elections law, for instance, in February 1992, university and party representatives convened to debate the relative merits of proportional representation and winner-take-all electoral systems and to issue recommendations on the imperative of a Supreme Elections Committee to scrutinize the process, the participation of women and illiterates, an interdiction against using religious symbols in electoral propaganda, and a "code of political conduct" governing interactions among the political parties. The results were published by the Sana'a University GPC section, which sponsored the conference.[52] When, after the elections, the regime proposed a package of sweeping constitutional amendments to reconcentrate executive political authority, seminars and panels called attention to the issue. At one, hosted by the *Yemen Times* at the Sheraton, members of twelve parties, several newspapers, and a few academic departments rejected the idea of quick, wholesale amendments.[53] Symposia on human rights and civil society, culture and democracy, the constitution, and parties, syndicates, and press draft legislation were held by the Writers' Guild, other professional unions, and social clubs.

Another highly sensitive topic was the personal status law decreed by the Presidential Council in Ramaḍān 1992. This law retracting the generous protections granted to women in the PDRY in favor of paternalistic protections based on a conservative reading of Sharīʿa faced a series of panel discussions in various venues in Sana'a, including one in November 1993 with Dutch and United Nations funding.[54] At another, gender-mixed, session on women's rights at a human rights convention at YCRS, foreign Arab feminists debated veiled Sana'ani women who asserted that good Muslim men protect and provide for their daughters, sisters, and wives. At a smaller all-female round-table at the Ḥaḍramawt Welfare Society, a veiled teenager screamed down the Member of Parliament from al-Mukallā' with the words "You're a communist and I speak for God." Muslim feminists, as they called themselves, spoke from the podium in full black veil before Iṣlāḥ gatherings. In many civic fora in Sana'a, ironically, proponents of women's restriction to private spaces tended to dominate public discussion of the matter of women's rights.

Urban male intellectuals, politicians, and activists modified the most customary of Yemeni gatherings, the qāt-chewing session, now referred to as a "*maqyal*" or discussion circle. The customary "big man" weekly qāt parties certainly continued in the *dīwāns* of the president, Shaykh al-Aḥmar, candidates for office, and others. In many other venues, however, such as syndical offices, the offices of the Ḥaḍramawt Association, and some private homes, weekly or even daily "*maqyal*," over qāt in the afternoon (evening in Ramaḍān) adapted some of the mechanisms of Western committee meetings to the customary four-to-six-hour qāt-chew setting: they elected a chair, established an agenda, and agreed on rules of order (e.g. time limits; no cellular telephones). Remarkable for their candor as well as their scope, these sessions linked thousands of men in interlocking deliberations over the issues of the day. Such a traditionally sex-segregated venue as the qāt-session, though not technically closed to women (as my own experience and those of a handful of Western-educated Yemeni women attest), nonetheless constitutes a formidable social barrier to women's full civic participation, comparable to the smoke-filled men's clubs in an earlier era of Western politics.

For all the importance of the elite politics of parties, newspapers, formal associations, and intellectual salons, perhaps the single most widespread form of popular participation in the political opening that began with unification was the mass conference. Between unification and the 1993 elections a series of rural conferences culminating in a national conference became such a significant arena for mass expression that each of the three major parties orchestrated their own "non-partisan" mass meetings. After the first military skirmishes in early 1994, as discussed in the next chapter, a second round of conferences sought to resolve the deepening crisis.

In late 1989 and early 1990 several government-organized urban rallies in favor of unity drew unexpected numbers of youth enjoying their first opportunity to show support for a political project. Participation in the gala Unity Day (May 22 1990) celebrations was jubilant. By the fall of 1990 city-dwellers were given the opportunity to join anti-war demonstrations in protest against the build-up of foreign forces in the Peninsula. In January 1990, tens of thousands of Yemenis took to the streets to hear opinion leaders, including a couple of female faculty, denounce the US-led offensive against Iraq.[55] Although both the pro-unity and the anti-war marches and rallies in support of Yemeni government policies were encouraged by the country's leaders, crowds gathered in cities in numbers not seen since Aden's strike movement in the 1960s. People tasted the power of mass gatherings, developed a sense of the popular will.

Rural camp-outs

The unity opening was greeted by a round of tribal conferences, some of them huge. *Mu'tamar al-Taḍāmun li-l-qabā'il al-Yamaniyyīn*, the Solidarity Conference of the Tribes of the Yemenis, gathered thousands in October 1990; and by moving from one site to the next, the nine-day

Talāḥum (Cohesion) Conference of November 1991 was said to have drawn 10,000, and the Saba' gathering of September–October 1992 claimed 20,000 participants.[56] These events were tribal in several senses. The "summons" came to the 80–85 percent of the rural men in the northeast who belong to tribes, via their *shaykhs*, as an invitation to the "sons" of a given locality, mainly its small farmers. Traditional drummers (non-tribesmen attending in ceremonial capacity), distinctive tribal dances, and poetry readings lent a festive, folksy quality, much as kilts and bagpipes would in Scotland. Every tribesman carried his side-arms, typically, a dagger and an AK-47 kaliznikov semi-automatic rifle, occasionally an RPG grenade-launcher. They slept in tents. Women in surrounding villages baked mountains of bread from wheat donated by local *shaykhs*, who sometimes slaughtered lambs for a special lunch; pickup-truck-loads of qāt arrived every afternoon. While their representational motif was quintessentially tribal, however, non-Yemen specialists need to be aware of several caveats that complicate this characterization. First, although the largest conferences nominally identified with the Bakīl confederation, they met not in the name of Bakīl as such – leadership of which had been contested throughout the twentieth century, and was contested further in these gatherings – but of separate tribes variously affiliated with Bakīl, Ḥāshid, the resurgent Madhḥaj confederation, other prominent confederations, or no confederation beyond the tribal unit. Secondly, as regional mass meetings, these gatherings were by definition multiparty affairs expressing specifically rural concerns. Thirdly, then, they did not represent a cohesive "bloc," certainly not one led by urban politicians who claimed to represent "the tribes."

Finally, whereas tribalism was the one form of political organization tolerated in the North throughout the century, in the South tribal conferences of the early 1990s seemed part of a revival of this form of association. In Ḥaḍramawt in 1992, for example, federations virtually dormant for a generation, such as the Sayban, the Banī Zanna, and the Kathīrī, sent representatives of each subsection to a series of meetings that one anthropologist said were part exploration, where people learned anew about the members and leaders of local tribes; part celebration of folk holidays, dances, and poetry; and partly assertion of political support for unity. The seventeen tribes of the Sayban, who inhabit the area east of al-Mulkallā', formed a committee that drew up a set of resolutions signed by representatives of all eighty-eight branches of the Sayban tribes, and sent a delegation to Sana'a to convey them to state officials.[57]

The lengthy written resolutions (*bayān*) from tribal meetings did reflect tribal concerns. Both the 1990 Solidarity conference and the 1991 *Talāḥum* conference were concerned with truce-making in local disagreements over land or other matters, many of which involved tribes contractually. Among *Talāḥum's* thirty-three *bayān* were some explicitly tribal pleas directed to Sana'a. One was that government help reconcile tribal disputes. Others reflected allegations of tribal favoritism, and insisted that the government show equal dignity for all tribal leaders and peoples, end discrimination within the armed forces, review budgetary allocations for tribal affairs, and work to end tribal subsidies from foreign sources.[58] Most of the organizers, speakers, and elected officers were called *shaykh.*

The content of resolutions also reflected more broadly civic concerns, however. There was a call for revival of the local development cooperatives "as mini-parliaments." Corruption was the number one concern. There should be parliamentary elections as scheduled in the constitution; judicial independence and integrity; nationwide safety, security, and stability, including safety of road traffic; prison investigations by a parliamentary commission advised by popular organizations, unions, etc.; and evaluation of internal military camps. Special attention should be given to agricultural production and cooperatives, and to rural medical, health, and educational needs. There were calls for review of the official media, especially TV and radio; reduced dependence on foreign aid; and environmental and archaeological conservation. The Saba' conference in 1992 proposed a "dialogue with all forces (*ḥiwār ma'a kull al-quwā*)," an upper house of parliament or *Majlis al-Shūrā* with equal representation from all governorates, and enhanced powers for local government.[59] A half-dozen other tribe-based-but-civic-oriented mass conferences, including one in Ḥajja governorate calling for resolution of local disputes and a combination of "Sharī'a" and "human" rights,[60] punctuated the 1992 political calendar. Each issued written demands for the rule of law, pluralism, economic development, and a degree of local autonomy.

This series of tribally based conferences were not all of a seamless whole but themselves highly contested political spaces. The first conference, the *Taḍāmun*, convened as Yemenis expelled from Saudi Arabia were streaming across the border in punishment for Sana'a's stand on the Gulf Crisis. The pro-Saudi tone of some of its statements reflected a view characteristic of migrant-returnees. While those pronouncements implied criticisms of Sana'a, however, and the GPC contended that many tribal conferences reflected a "Socialist agenda," this was balanced by references to a well-known incident in 1972 when PDRY forces reportedly killed a group of Bakīl *shaykhs*. A different group organized the Cohesion conference under different circumstances:[61] the *Talāḥum* meeting originated in efforts by a Southern Socialist governor in Ṣa'da governorate to resolve a dispute over a *waqf* traditionally controlled by Zaydī *sayyids* but now challenged by Iṣlāḥ partisans. Party politics peculiar to Ṣa'da mobilized a much wider initiative that moved from the Jawf toward Sana'a in cumulative negotiations of local conflicts. Its resolutions freely mixed tribal with YAR nationalist and Socialist catch-phrases. The third major conference, the Saba', or Sheba, named for an ancient Yemeni empire, opened on the 1992 anniversary of the YAR's September 26 revolution, an unmistakable affront to Sana'a.

There was a partisan element to all of this, as the YSP tried to curry influence among dissident northern tribes, and the latter said they resisted YSP authorship of the *bayān* and consciously determined "to use rather than be used by" the YSP. These predominantly Bakīlī and/or Madhḥajī gatherings were countered by a conference claiming to represent "all tribes" headed by *Shaykh* al-Aḥmar with support from GPC member and Bakīlī *shaykh* Nājī 'Abd al-'Azīz al-Shāyif. What all this revealed was that parties did not represent tribes, nor did party loyalty rest on tribal affiliations. Rather, within each locality (and some families) were many parties, and within each party were people of different tribal (and non-tribal) origins.

Urban mass conferences

Public meetings in the cities had a different style and a somewhat different content from rural open-air gatherings. When they were held in convention halls with chairs and podiums, they included a small proportion of women as well as some men wearing business suits. The most important of these, the National Conference, met on the anniversary of the YAR revolution in September 1992, an official government holiday. Organized by urban professionals and chaired by the Adeni writer-politician 'Umar al-Jāwī, the National Conference (NC) drew together representatives of twenty-two non-ruling parties, forty-two political organizations and professional unions, and the leadership of the tribal conferences. Well publicized in the opposition and independent press, notably the *Yemen Times*, the NC published resolutions insisting on pluralism, separation of powers, public safety, union rights, and fair multiparty elections. It issued a code of political conduct calling for neutrality of military and security forces, restraint from the use of public money for political campaigns, a forbearing and interpretive view of

Islam, and "dialogue, respect and tolerance of the opposing viewpoint."[62] The NC documents defined "democracy" as "the real contribution and participation of individuals and groups in the dynamics of society to arrive at good solutions." Its protection, the argument continues, depends on either of two factors. It may be protected by a general social awareness that prevents competing forces from overstepping democratic channels, as in advanced democratic countries; or by a balance of power that prevents any faction from bypassing others and forces all of them to accept the rules of the game. Since in Yemen "institutions of civil society are not yet able to protect democracy if the balance is tipped among the political circles," the country must rely on "equilibrium and balance of power among the political forces running the country since the rise of Unified Yemen." Nonetheless, the conference recommended a series of legal and constitutional reforms, including neutrality of the armed forces and, most pressingly at that moment, free, fair, timely elections.[63]

Failing to delay, discourage, or co-opt the National Conference, the GPC scheduled an alternative event for the September 26 celebrations. This Conference of Parties and Popular Organizations issued a parallel set of resolutions including its own code of conduct based on the GPC's complaints against the YSP and numerous statements about the primacy of unity. Featured prominently in the Sana'a media, this gathering, co-sponsored by the GPC, Iṣlāḥ, the Ba'th, and the tiny Republican party, accused the NC of being "royalist," affirmed the neutrality of the media, equality of educational opportunity, reform against corruption, and the necessity of appropriate measures to arrest economic decline.[64]

Soon thereafter the government admitted that the elections, scheduled for that November, would be postponed. In the wake of this announcement and in view of deteriorating economic conditions, a group of the NC's "third" parties including al-Tajammu', al-Ḥaqq, al-Tashīḥ, the RAY, the Union of Popular Forces, the Constitutional-Liberal party, the Waḥdawī-Nāṣirī, and a small group called United Islamic Movement called, in a special one-issue newspaper (*al-Iḍrāb al-'Āmm*, copies of which were confiscated on the street), for a general strike in December 1993. Protest demonstrations were already in progress, but a widening strike by professional and labor unions was averted by eleventh-hour coordination between the YSP and the GPC.[65] On the night of December 20 on TV there was a joint YSP/GPC/Ba'th/Nāṣirī-Democratic party statement urging people to understand current difficulties, and not to go on strike.

For its part, the YSP managed to dominate what was originally planned as a non-partisan event in relatively cosmopolitan Taiz. The Taiz conference in November 1992 reflected the YSP line in its criticisms of the then-threatened postponement of parliamentary elections, the collapse of the riyāl against the dollar, political violence against Socialists, the president's dispute with the vice president, and the GPC governor of Taiz province.[66] Its slogan was "To bring popular efforts to bear in order to create a modern Yemen governed by justice, equality, and democracy,"[67] but in fact the Socialists' blatant manipulation alienated more Taizi activists than it persuaded.

Iṣlāḥ organized a huge "Unity and Peace Conference" at the military stadium in Sana'a in December 1992, under slogans including "The Quran and the Sunna Supersede the Constitution and Laws" and "Consolidate Unity and Affirm Islam." The "non-partisan" conference elected 'Abd al-Majīd al-Zindānī as chair, and 'Abd Allāh al-Aḥmar as vice chair.[68] Speeches and conference documents, combining Iṣlāḥ's own perspective with issues raised in the other conferences, blended ample references to Sharī'a with more mundane concerns over economic deterioration, corruption, the politicization of the military, and the government's inability to carry out its duties.[69] The YSP was singled out for criticism. At least twenty-nine unsigned working papers obviously prepared by different authors attempted to advance positions on a range of issues, especially social services. The most strident tone was struck in the papers on "what Muslims cannot differ on (*mā lā yajūz al-khilāf fīhi bayn al-Muslimīn*)" and "secularism and its danger to Islam"; and in two papers on external threats to Yemen, one of which, on the "new world order," took issue with the themes of American "imperialism": democracy, pluralism, human rights, and free markets.[70] The resolutions also demanded behavioral codes for women, including *ḥijāb*, separate educational facilities, and restrictions on travel without a male guardian, but at the same time offered to "give woman her rights fixed by God and which society has deprived her of, and to educate men on these rights." There was a call for an independent, Sharī'a-based judicial system, administered in strict accordance with codified law; and for law, order, public morality, and swift but fair trials for law-breakers. Statements on the economy valorized private economic initiative, restoration of nationalized property to former owners, and establishment of Islamic financial institutions.[71] Since by now the elections had been postponed to April 1992, the Unity and Peace Conference formed its own election protection committee which would later publish a list of infringements on the electoral law.[72]

Conclusion

The conclusion to this chapter is simply that civic spaces were hotly contested. Parties and individuals competed and campaigned for seats in the Chamber of Deputies, but political competition was by no means confined to legislative elections. Other spaces – the streets, the press, charitable endeavors, academic circles, tribes – were also politicized. At both the national and regional level, ruling parties recognized the potential power of civic spaces and of public opinion (heretofore hardly a meaningful construct in Yemeni politics), as their continued attempts to influence NGO and conference agendas demonstrated. Far from being either monolithic or predetermined by ascribed traits of gender, status, tribe, or region, public opinion was pluralistic, changing, and responsive. While folk and religious motifs were woven into the political fabric, people were equally cognizant of recent political history, current material circumstances, and, always, local social conditions. There was an expanded sense that public policy decisions should be subject to public, press, and scholarly debate, a widening sense of political efficacy, unprecedented if still not unmitigated eagerness for participation.

Aware that power would not simply be granted, many activists were skeptical about the commitment of either side to opening up the political process. Indeed, as explored in some detail in the next chapter, when the results of the electoral and expressive processes disappointed both Sana'a and Aden, they each took great liberties with the agreements they had signed. Rules were revised and manipulated, and there was an eventual resort to arms. Thousands of activists resisted these ominous developments using the mechanisms – meetings, publications, associations – of civil society. The next chapter looks at the third and fourth phases of the liberal interlude. As the constitutional consensus evaporated, civic leaders encouraged by mass conferences and autonomous associations attempted to generate an alternative model. Failing that, they nonetheless sought to preserve the liberties and freedoms tasted during the brief democratic opening.

7 Civic responses to political crisis

Thus unification brought with it a process of contingent legal liberalization that lifted restrictions on civic participation. Concomitant with these salutary processes, however, a political crisis was brewing that would culminate in the 1994 civil war. The supposedly co-equal parties to the unity coalition gradually but steadily retreated from the spirit and letter of the unity accords, the constitution, and democratizing legislation. Thus like earlier liberal experiments the civic opening rather quickly reached the limits of government tolerance, whereupon the space open to public activism contracted. Nonetheless, groups that emerged after unity sought by various means to forestall bloodshed and preserve constitutional liberties. The deeper the crisis within the state, the wider the civic pressure for reconciliation. Recalling earlier constitutional proposals emanating from non-ruling elites in times of acute state crisis, an independent committee backed by public rallies proposed a political compromise incorporating popular demands for personal liberty, freedom of information, local self-governance, limits on executive power, and less corruption. Although it failed to stop the war, the national dialogue – both within the committee and beyond – was a significant moment for civic involvement.

The rout of the more progressive of the ruling parties spelled a victory for conservative forces including the Islamist right, the political security organization, and a contorted private sector dominated by Sana'ani officer-*shaykhs*. In international and comparative terms, Yemen was one of many countries where formerly ruling socialist parties fell into defeat, disrepute, and despair in the 1990s. Nor was Yemen the first country where a combination of inflation, unemployment, and services deterioration have bolstered right-wing ideologies and social malaise. Economic recession, structural reform, and political intolerance created a new set of circumstances wherein voluntary energies would be channeled into two particular sorts of activities. First, the charitable and welfare societies became increasingly important after the incorporation of LDAs into the state, and more so with privatization of services and the worsening of standards of living in the mid-1990s. Secondly, a still small but growing urban, educated, increasingly independent and disillusioned professional class attempted to use formal and legal mechanisms to defend civil and legal rights such as due process, freedom of expression, and women's political participation. Once again, then, civic activism responds to specific political and economic. circumstances.

The material in this chapter divides naturally into the pre-war and post-war periods. The first two sections, respectively, document the demise of the unity coalition and non-governmental attempts to counteract praetorian impulses. Interestingly, whereas before the 1993 elections parties concerned themselves mainly with nominating and electing candidates, in the post-election crisis many groups issued policy platforms. The combative posture of the two leadership groups only intensified civic debate. Then, after collapse of the bipolar balance between two co-ruling parties undermined leeway for pluralist participation, a reinvigorated security establishment threatened to penetrate and overwhelm its critics; but with mixed success. While Yemen's civic space had contracted, it remained a contested rather than a closed space, an arena wherein some essayists and activists deliberately challenged arbitrary state repression. Thanks largely to its rather tenacious and resilient civil society, Yemen remains considerably more open and less repressive than most of its neighbors.

Governmental power struggles

For all the many positive developments between 1990 and 1994, processes of economic and political deterioration lurched the nation from one crisis to the next. In the economic sphere, instead of the anticipated benefits of unity and petroleum, Yemen faced the deleterious fallout from an initially popular but ultimately disastrous anti-Saudi, anti-Kuwaiti tilt in the Gulf War: loss of most foreign aid, and the return of more than half a million semi-skilled migrants who quickly spent their savings and entered the ranks of the unemployed. The results were catastrophic. The riyāl's dollar value in 1994 was approximately one-tenth of its 1990 value. The cost of living rose as earnings stagnated. Potential investors, especially Yemeni billionaires residing in Saudi Arabia, were politically and financially disinclined to back ventures in Yemen. In addition, after rapid growth in the late 1990s, exploration, investment, production, and revenues in the oil industry leveled off. Even this industry was plagued by banditry, Saudi warnings, corruption, and Southerners' complaints that Sana'a was profiting from

Shabwa and Ḥaḍramawt. All in all, revenues from oil were far short of covering the losses from aid and remittances, and the country slipped farther into debt and economic stagnation. By 1994, the government needed to reschedule foreign loan repayments.

Popular frustrations spilled onto the streets on several occasions. Middle-class consumers demonstrated for the first time in October 1991. In December 1992, outrage with the collapse of the value of the riyāl, inadequate services, mounting unemployment, government corruption, political assassinations, and postponement of the elections erupted in urban protests against government and merchants which resulted in sixty deaths, hundreds of injuries, and thousands of detentions by police. Demonstrations became riots when police fired on crowds in Sana'a.[1]

In retrospect the unity accords of May 1990 seemed to have been signed in haste, leaving many details to be resolved later on. After a rocky courtship and a brief honeymoon, ʿAlī and ʿAlī, as the two former presidents were known, quickly took to spatting. ʿAlī Sālim al-Bīḍ was twice "*ḥanīqa*" – the term used when a wife goes back to her father's house to get away from her husband. The YSP blamed Sana'a for the many attacks on prominent leftists, mostly Southern, among them a Tajammuʿ leader, Presidential Council member Sālim Ṣāliḥ Muḥammad, prime minister Ḥaydar al-ʿAṭṭās, then-speaker of Parliament Yāsīn Saʿīd Nuʿmān, and at least two other ministers. The two parties were each determined to maintain control of "their" budgets, civil service payrolls, media, and, especially, armed forces. After the old PDRY state and YAR national security organizations were formally disbanded, a new political security organization appeared. Having agreed to resolve outstanding issues in the power-sharing arrangement through parliamentary elections, the two sides locked horns over the design of the electoral system. A deal reached in the immediate wake of the December 1992 street disturbances brought the vice president back to Sana'a and allowed elections to be rescheduled for April 1993, but clearly many differences on political and security matters still festered. The respective official presses each accused the other side of reneging on the unity accords.

Unable to resolve their differences among themselves yet under public pressure to hold elections, the coalition government handed management of the elections over to the Supreme Elections Committee (SEC). Contrary to the 1992 Elections law, which called for a non-partisan SEC, the elections committee was given to a multiparty group of seventeen where the GPC and the YSP were equally represented but balanced by delegates from Iṣlāḥ, the Baʿth, the Waḥdawī-Nāṣirī,

Nāṣirī-Democratic, and Septembri parties, the Rābiṭa, al-Ḥaqq, the Union of Popular Forces, and a couple of independents including one woman. The Tajammu' declined to participate, cautioning against electoral irregularities, and the Waḥdawī-Nāṣirī representative resigned on election day because of what he called foul play. During the autumn of 1992, working with foreign technical experts, the SEC drew constituency lines and polling guidelines that became a key piece of the agreement signed by the president and the vice president in Hodeida in December 1992. Thus the first major dispute was resolved by multiparty negotiations, outside the letter of the law, in the face of mass demonstrations.

Although the elections themselves went smoothly enough, constitutional mechanisms for parliamentary selection of the Council of Ministers and especially the Presidential Council failed. Competition in district elections was fierce, with the three major parties, minor parties, and independents vying through various legal and clandestine means to win a plurality of votes. The one foregone conclusion, however, was that Northerners won in the North and Southerners in the South. While the Reform Grouping, other parties, and independents gained, the YSP's share of 301 Chamber of Deputy seats was reduced from nearly half to about one-fifth. Whereas Parliament and even the Council of Ministers were large enough to be broadly inclusive, the proximate focus of a political battle between Sana'a and Aden became the composition of the Presidential Council, and within that five-man executive body, designation of the chairman and deputy chairman (i.e. the president and the vice president). Although this fight centered publicly on the symbols of power, the real stakes were the budgetary and security controls that rested formally in the two former executives. Once the composition of the Presidential Council was thrown into question, a whole range of other constitutional issues was opened for public debate.

In the summer and fall of 1993 the contest played dramatically on the floor of the new *Majlis al-Nuwwāb*. By a three-quarters majority, the chamber elected as its speaker Iṣlāḥ's leader, the famous, powerful *Shaykh* al-Aḥmar, a key figure in the YAR revolution and the Sana'a establishment. One member each of the Congress, Socialist, and Ba'th parties were elected to join him on the chamber's leadership council. Outgoing prime minister Ḥaydar Abū Bakr al-'Aṭṭās, a Southern Socialist, formed a Cabinet of fifteen ministers from the Congress party, nine Socialists, Abū Shawārib, and, initially, four from Iṣlāḥ.[2] When Iṣlāḥ insisted on a share of Cabinet seats commensurate with its parliamentary representation,[3] the government was enlarged to give two more of its members posts. One of them, 'Abd al-Wahhāb al-Ānisī, had lost his campaign for Parliament. None of the other ministers came from Parliament. Only a third were new; twenty retained their posts; in the end, the new government looked much like the old – except that several seats had been transferred from the YSP to Iṣlāḥ. Still to be resolved was the very delicate question of how to divide the five seats on the Presidential Council, currently held by three members of the GPC and two from the YSP. Iṣlāḥ and the Socialists publicly threatened to withdraw from the coalition unless their respective demands were met.[4] Parliament postponed voting on this issue by extending the term of the transitional five-man executive.

Unable or unwilling to resolve the question within the parameters of the constitution, the GPC proposed wholesale amendments. Fifty revisions to the two-year-old constitution envisioned a more American system with a powerful president and weak vice president elected on the same ticket for no more than two terms, a bicameral legislature composed of the current chamber plus an upper house, a *Majlis al-Shūrā,* and elected local and provincial governments. The next proposal, Prime Minister al-ʻAṭṭās's eight-point government program, raising the sensitive, long-delayed merger of the two armies, was passed in Parliament then tabled pending constitutional amendments. Ironically, the only agreement Parliament's constitutional committees reached – a much-ballyhooed compromise between the YSP and Iṣlāḥ – concerned the wording of Article 3 of the constitution, on Sharīʻa, which would be "the basis of law in an interpretation consistent with the interests of the community and its development."[5] On less philosophical issues such as how to select a vice president or unify two armies, however, no compromise was forthcoming. Instead, Vice President al-Bīḍ issued "eighteen points" or demands. Several were familiar proposals with wide appeal – *Majlis al-Shūrā* and local council elections; extensive judicial, administrative, and budgetary reform; a national referendum on constitutional amendments drawn up by committees of specialists; and "general and comprehensive reconciliation." The YSP goaded the GPC by demanding immediate arrest of the perpetrators of what Socialists claimed were 150 attacks on leftists and southerners, the insinuation being that the villains were close to the Republican Palace. The vice president called for removal of security forces from the cities, and rapid development of the free trade zone in Aden. The most specific points proposed the election of two GPC, two YSP, and one Iṣlāḥ representative to the Presidential Council and then, contradictorily, called on them to resign their party memberships. There was a call for unification, restructuring, and depoliticization of the armed and security forces, and another for redrawing local administrative lines.

In response, the president's party issued its own nineteen points. Several were popular platitudes from the GPC's electoral platform: unity, parliamentary elections, constitutionalism, the rule of law, and human rights. One point condemned corruption. The others challenged the YSP implicitly or explicitly by emphasizing property rights and the return of confiscated buildings and land; calling for investigation into the demonstrations of December 9–10 1992, and the activities of arms and drug dealers, both of which the GPC blamed on the YSP. The GPC also called for complete merger of the armed forces and the "independence" of military and security forces from "political parties"; deplored any "regional basis" of political parties; and insisted that elected representatives pursue their responsibilities free of partisan pressures.[6]

This exchange of "points" was taken up by the leaders of five small parties holding among them only three parliamentary seats, who met in August 1993 to form a formal opposition coalition, al-Takattul al-Waṭanī li-l-Mu'ārada, deliberately given the nickname TOM. They were Aḥmad al-Shāmī of al-Ḥaqq, 'Abd al-Raḥmān al-Jufrī of the League of the Sons of Yemen; 'Umar al-Jāwī of the left-leaning Tajammu'; representatives of the Union of Popular Forces; and unnamed representatives of the GPC-fostered Nāṣirī-Democratic Party. Later, the TOM joined a group of 200 persons including Sinān Abū Luḥūm in forming something they called the Union of National Forces in allusion to the Third Force of the 1960s. This rather broad grouping issued "sixteen points" calling for parliamentary supervision of the executive, a new Council of Ministers, tight controls on government appropriations, judicial independence, a degree of local autonomy within new administrative divisions, civil service reform, military neutrality and reform, a committee to study constitutional amendments, a *Majlis al-Shūrā,* a National Security Council to review the competencies of the interior and defense ministries, a supervisory board for state media, a follow-up committee to pursue these resolutions, and a commitment by all political forces to the principle of dialogue.[7]

A last apparent effort to maintain the appearance of constitutionalism produced a further departure from the constitution. Just ahead of the October 15 deadline to elect a new Presidential Council, the GPC accepted the "2+2+1" formula for the Presidential Council, which (contrary to the rules) Speaker al-Aḥmar presented to the chamber as a slate: Ṣāliḥ and 'Abd al-'Azīz 'Abd al-Ghanī from the GPC, al-Bīḍ and Sālim Ṣāliḥ Muḥammad from the YSP, all holdovers; and Iṣlāḥ's puritanical *eminence grise* 'Abd al-Majīd al-Zindānī replacing the GPC's 'Abd al-Karīm al-'Arashī. When votes were tallied, the two Congress candidates took the lead, but al-Zindānī came in a few votes ahead of al-Bīḍ, and Sālim Ṣāliḥ Muḥammad failed to win the necessary majority. As Socialists and their allies stormed out of the chamber, the speaker called for voice acclamation for "our brother Sālim Ṣāliḥ." The next day President Ṣāliḥ offered to "nominate" al-Bīḍ as vice president. In response to these indications that the Socialists serve at the behest of al-Aḥmar and Ṣāliḥ, Al-Bīḍ again ensconced himself in Aden, boycotting the swearing-in ceremony for the Presidential Council. This left the country technically without a constitutional executive.

Nonetheless, a coalition negotiation committee hammered out an agreement which ʻAbd al-Karīm al-Iryānī of the GPC characterized as "submission" to YSP demands, calling for dilution of the preponderance of "certain tribes" in the army; gradual reduction of the military presence in the cities; phased financial and administrative decentralization, followed by local elections; new by-laws for amending the constitution; serious fiscal, monetary, and administrative reform; safety, security, and an end to banditry; and cessation of mud-slinging in newspapers of the coalition partners. The last point called vaguely for sorting out the separation of powers between the Presidential and Ministerial Councils.[8]

Snatching crisis from the jaws of compromise, someone shot al-Bīḍ's two sons and murdered his nephew before this agreement could be implemented.[9] A new wave of lawlessness ensued. Cars were hijacked even in cities. Five Southern villagers were killed by Northern troops; a security director in the northeastern province of al-Jawf was murdered; the Sana'a office of the labor union paper *Ṣawt al-ʻUmmāl* was firebombed; American diplomat Haynes Mahoney was taken hostage. Mahoney's kidnapping was "by the books," so to speak, for like other Western men held against their will by tribesmen negotiating with Sana'a he was treated to ample tribal hospitality. A good Arabist, Mahoney spent his captivity teaching English at a village school; when his host-captors went to pray, he said, they left him alone with their side-arms and vehicles. This sort of hostage taking, illegal in state terms, nonetheless observed customary law. Far more appalling to both Yemenis and expatriates was the kidnapping and murder of three French tourists, an elderly couple and their female companion, traveling north of Sana'a – an egregious breach of tribal convention. It was one symptom of the crisis that deepened by the week in the winter of 1993/94.

The national dialogue of political forces

The collapse of the unity coalition and renewed lawlessness spurred governmental, diplomatic, and civic responses. While the GPC and the

YSP continually reaffirmed their devotion to unity[10] and the Council of Ministers met for the first time in Aden,[11] Sālim Ṣāliḥ Muḥammad issued a proposal for a "federal" system that seemed to imply restored Southern autonomy.[12] All military forces were in a state of high alert, and security forces reasserted their prerogative to stop and search highway and urban traffic, especially at night. On the diplomatic level King Hussein of Jordan, Sultan Qābūs of Oman and the American and French embassies offered their good offices, and their military attachés later joined military negotiations. King Hussein sought to support the domestic dialogue by presiding at the signing of the accord document, later known as the Amman Pact. Sultan Qābūs later hosted a last-ditch effort to bring "the two 'Alīs" together. International mediation ended with a short visit by the US State Department's Middle East negotiator Robert Pelletreau on the very eve of the civil war, in early May 1994, when it was already too late. Concomitant with these diplomatic efforts, unfortunately, other Gulf states worked behind the scenes to deepen the rift between Sana'a and the Socialists. An increasingly obstreperous Sālim Ṣāliḥ Muḥammad toured Gulf capitals making statements the GPC easily reported as "separatist,"[13] and the vice president and other YSP leaders met "secretly" with potential backers of a reconstituted Southern polity.[14]

Unlike a virtually concurrent project in Egypt involving delegates hand picked by President Mubarak, the Yemeni National Dialogue of Political Forces originated in meetings beyond the ruling coalition. It was spearheaded by two famous, respected Northern *shaykhs*, both veterans of the YAR revolution and the cooperative movement, both part of the Northern establishment and yet widely regarded as "independent" and "neutral." One was Abū Shawārib, who for all his influence in Sana'a and past GPC and Ba'th memberships was consistently referred to in the whole press as an "independent social personality" and in conversation as "acceptable to all parties." Sinān Abū Luḥūm, the former Hodeida governor, most prominent of his confederation's *shaykhs*, co-founder of the United Bakīl Council and the Union of National Forces, was the other. Their specific identities were important because their tribal, republican, and Sana'a government connections were unassailably Northern and non-Socialist, the content of the document their initiative produced seemed to favor the YSP. Other very prominent personalities, including, from his death-bed, the first YAR president, 'Abd Allāh al-Sallāl, and, from exile in Damascus, deposed PDRY leader 'Alī Nāṣir Muḥammad, lent their approval.[15] Within the country a veritable who's who of political personalities, among them for instance the heads of the *'Ulamā'* Society, Aden

University and the Aden Welfare Society, and a range of failed parliamentary candidates and influential intellectuals publicly endorsed a national dialogue.

Faced with virtually unanimous pressure from non-ruling political elites, the three parties to the shaky tripartite ruling coalition agreed to send delegates to a meeting with the heads of the five TOM parties, Sinān Abū Luḥūm for the Union of National Forces, and Abū Shawārib for independents.[16] A subset of this gathering, headed by Abū Shawārib, Abū Luḥūm, and Aḥmad Jābir 'Afīf, agreed to form a committee to work out an accord the national leadership would sign onto later.[17] They nominated about twenty-seven nationally prominent men – three from each of the three ruling parties, another eight or nine heads of smaller parties, and a cross-section of independent and civic leaders – to the Dialogue Committee, or *Lajnat al-Ḥiwār*, whose mission was to work from the YSP's eighteen points, the GPC's nineteen points, the National Force's sixteen points, and solicit reports from scholars and experts to reach a national resolution to the political crisis.

The Dialogue Committee met in nearly continuous session from December through February, shuttling between Aden and Sana'a and occasionally abroad, seeking common ground between the two leaders. Even before issuing their final document, they had repeatedly appealed for restraint in both the media war and the several military incidents during late 1993 and early 1994.[18] The "*ḥiwār*" over meaty legal, military, and political issues finally did generate a consensus so powerful that the rival leaderships had no choice but to sign it. The document (or *Wathīqa*) unveiled on January 18 and signed a month later by the Sana'a and Aden regimes offered to end the political crisis by constructing a new constitutional order.[19]

The document opened with a set of proposals to deal with the immediate security crisis. Interior and Justice Ministries were promptly and fairly to investigate and prosecute political crime. Pending review of the competencies of the Ministries of Interior and Defense, security forces were to withdraw from the cities and military units to be redeployed from the former inter-Yemeni border to national borders. All extra-legal and paramilitary forces were to be dissolved. Neither the military police nor any other armed forces would interfere in civilian or private affairs. These immediate "law and order" concerns were reinforced institutionally through provisions for the independence of the judiciary, for separation of armed forces from criminal prosecution, and for ministerial, parliamentary, civilian control of the security establishment.

Three major modifications of the current constitutional order were called for: a bicameral legislature, a limited executive, and decentralization. The Chamber of Deputies was to remain "the legislative body of the Republic." A *Majlis al-Shūrā* elected by regional councils with equal representation for each governorate would be empowered to comment on drafts of basic laws and government budgets, help elect the Presidential Council, and elect the Supreme Court (heretofore appointed), the Information Council (replacing the Ministry of Information), and the civil service authority council (charged with curbing corruption). The courts, the press, and financial auditors would all be institutionally protected from political or security interference.

The 1994 accord limited the powers of the Presidential Council (PC), defined as the "sovereign head of state." The PC was to be popularly elected for no more than two terms. Whereas the constitution allowed wide unspecified powers to the PC and its chairman, the 1994 document restricted the executive's functions to representing the state abroad, calling for elections and referenda, nominating the prime minister, discussing government programs, enacting laws approved by Parliament, and signing the Cabinet's military appointments. PC powers to create law through executive order and to declare states of emergency were specifically curtailed.The duties of the chairperson – the president – were limited mainly to chairing PC meetings and (in wartime) meetings of the National Security Council, representing the nation abroad, and signing laws. Unlike the constitution, the *Wathīqa* also defined the responsibilities of the vice chair of the council, to assist and if necessary serve in the place of the chair. All in all, presidential constitutional and extra-constitutional powers would be reduced.

The third major set of reforms concerned local government "based on administrative and financial decentralization." Governorate and local administrative boundaries would be redrawn by technical experts, to eliminate vestiges of the former division and maximize regional economic potential "within the tenet of free market economics." A thoroughgoing reconstruction of local and provincial government would permit, as in the German and American federal systems, some regional variation within a national system. Elected district and provincial governments would enjoy a high degree of budgetary and administrative discretion in a radically decentralized system of local governance within redrawn administrative units.

In addition to these three major areas of reform – merger, restructuring, and depoliticization of the armed and security forces; devolution of power from the executive to strengthened, reconstituted legislative and judicial authorities; and decentralization of a wide range of government powers and responsibilities to local government – the document also nonetheless specified a more rigorous, consultative amendment process than the easily revised 1991 constitution.

The *Lajnat al-Ḥiwār* appointed its own heavyweights to a military committee assigned to work with the official "joint military committee" headed by the president's powerful cousin 'Alī Muḥammad Ṣālaḥ[20] and advised by American, French, Jordanian, and Omani advisors. In April after talking to the president and vice president, the Dialogue Committee convinced the Cabinet to create a new Cabinet-level military committee to implement its military and security provisions.[21] Finally, the Dialogue Committee reached beyond its own numbers to constitute ten national committees that would reflect its vision of balancing political representation with technical expertise. Over half the committees dealt with checkpoints, political violence, tribal feuds, the stationing of military units, and security violations.

Every party, public personality, newspaper, and civic association came out in favor of the accord. The GPC and Iṣlāḥ leadership sometimes dismissed it as extra-institutional, thus unconstitutional, and suddenly began citing the constitution as the basis of public decision making. But even in the GPC and Iṣlāḥ, and especially within the YSP, the rank and file waxed rhapsodic about the document. After the televised reading and wide publication of the text, virtually everyone officially endorsed the reform proposals. Subsequently all three major parties took pains to look as though they intended to implement what they had signed.

The expression of public opinion

The Dialogue Committee finished its work on January 18. Normal television programming was interrupted for Aḥmad Jābir 'Afīf to read the dialogue proposal that its twenty-seven authors then signed. Despite a jubilant reaction among opinion leaders and the mass public, the leadership dallied for more than a month, until February 20 1994, before signing the accord in a ceremony in Amman, Jordan, where King Hussein was seen on television physically forcing two unwilling former dictators to shake hands. *Shaykh* al-Aḥmar scribbled beneath his signature the words "conditional on the return of the vice president to Sana'a." That very evening the first military skirmish of the civil war occurred in Abyan. Abyan, a site of fighting in 1986, widely considered an 'Alī Nāṣir Muḥammad stronghold, is a militarily significant location because it separates Aden from the eastern portions of what was the PDRY. Both former PDRY and former YAR forces were stationed there, and a disagreement over the appointment of a military governor was in progress. The military events of the night of February 20 also involved a so-called "Jihad" camp evidently founded by the son of the former sultan of Zinjibār (the capital of Abyan), a long-time resident of Saudi Arabia and commander of Arab volunteers in the Afghan jihad.[22] It was not clear at the time what maneuvers sparked gunfire.

This would also be true of subsequent military events. Skirmishes in 'Amrān, Dhamar, Harf Sifyan, Khawlān, and Shabwa had an almost slapstick quality inasmuch as rounds of artillery exchanged between Northern and Southern troops stationed in close proximity caused few casualties. At one point the Aden utilities companies cut off the power and water to the 1,500-man Northern security base in the port city. A military checkpoint halted the prime minister's convoy outside Sana'a. Everyone in the country was aware that the militaries were squaring off, but there seemed to be hope of averting a military confrontation. When, as increasingly, conversation in qāt circles turned to war, the models advanced were Lebanon, Somalia, Yugoslavia, and finally Rwanda, all examples of mass mayhem among rival armies and armed gangs. It was certainly a consummation to be avoided.

The crisis mobilized unprecedented expression of public opinion. With information spread in the press and by word of mouth, the dialogue process, having drawn heavily on proposals from pre-election seminars and conferences, was now replicated in these same arenas. Groups from the professional syndicates to the Academic Federation to the *'Ulamā'* Society conferred over the accord, while in every province nationwide more mass conferences, mostly organized by regional committees mirroring the multiparty composition of the Dialogue Committee itself, issued supportive resolutions. Finally, members and supporters of the Dialogue Committee helped organize numerous if small peace demonstrations. One indicator of widespread popular support for the accord was how every party and newspaper tried to claim ownership of these demonstrations.

The salons established in the pre-election period held weekly and even daily round-tables or qāt-chews in the first months of 1994. The Academic Federation, the Writers' Guild, professional syndicates, the semi-governmental Yemeni Center for Research and Studies (YCRS), academic departments on the various university campuses, the Ḥaḍramawt Welfare Society, some political parties, the newly created United Bakīl Council, and other groups invited specialists in various public policy spheres to present their research. Many intellectuals, community activists, tribal conference leaders, and politicians were especially concerned with local elections and authority.[23] After a series of small independent seminars on this topic at welfare societies, the

Writers' Guild, and professional syndicates, including several where a Northern Socialist presented a detailed plan for decentralization, the GPC funded a two-day session entitled "The Future of Local Government" in late March 1994. The group of liberal intellectuals who had been meeting to discuss founding a "Yemeni institute for democratic development" approached Western embassies for funding. An 18 January Committee constituted itself in Taiz to canvass for the accord signed on that day, and the GPC backed a rival 10 Ramaḍān (the same date) Committee.

The *'Ulamā'* Society, among others, attempted to take matters in hand. The several hundred religious scholars, many of them Sharī'a judges, although tending towards the Iṣlāḥ and/or the GPC position, were not necessarily single-minded, for they included scholars of both *sayyid* status and *qāḍī* education, Zaydīs as well as Shāfi'īs, associates of the Muslim Brotherhood, and neo-fundamentalist Wahhabi or Salafī zealots. They invited the president and vice president to meet together at al-Janad, half-way between Sana'a and Aden, to discuss scholars' proposals for better economic policy, proactive parliamentary crisis resolution, preservation of unity, and stronger local government. Islamic scholars argued among themselves over how to orchestrate the proposed Ṣāliḥ-al-Bīḍ meeting, and a minority of about seventeen left for Aden to visit the vice president and issue their own resolutions.[24]

From Ḥaḍramawt in the distant southeast to Ḥajja in the northwest, multiparty committees issued their own lists of policy positions. One of the more controversial meetings, in December 1993, when the "Sons of Ḥaḍramawt" threatened to hold separate local elections,[25] was mobilized by the active Ḥaḍramī branch of the Writers' Guild. Although clearly emphasizing local identity, this conference and the related meetings made a point of identifying its multiparty support from the Tajammu', RAY, Iṣlāḥ, YSP, and GPC; conference leaders meeting in follow-on committees later issued statements endorsing the Dialogue Committee's accord.[26]

Support for the accord was widely expressed. In the last week of 1993, a Taiz conference reportedly convened some 1,700 representatives of parties, political organizations, syndicates, the *'ulamā'*, and professional associations. Its resolutions endorsed unity, urged removal of troops from populated areas, demanded constitutional rule, specified the "necessity of democratically elected local government," and insisted on administrative, fiscal, and civil service reform. If the two sides decided to fight it out, they declared, they would "have no part of it."[27] Co-sponsors of the Ibb Popular Meeting included the Waḥdawī-Nāṣirī, Ba'th, National Democratic Front, al-Taṣḥīḥ, RAY, al-Tajammu', al-Ḥaqq, the Writers' Guild, ODDRL, the farmers', teachers', lawyers', and physicians' syndicates, and youth and women's federations.[28] The Waḥdawī-Nāṣirī, RAY, Liberal-Constitutional, Ba'th, Socialist, and Iṣlāḥ parties, and the teachers', stevedores', oil workers, civil service, fish wealth workers, and agricultural professional unions and syndicates, plus *'ulamā'* and "social personalities," helped plan an autonomous Hodeida Popular Conference in early 1994.[29] The Ḥajja meeting brought together local representatives of the GPC, YSP, Iṣlāḥ, NDF, Ba'th, and the Union of Popular Forces as well as syndicates and political organizations[30] and defied Sana'a by sending a delegation to Aden.[31]

As before, the GPC and/or the YSP attempted to co-opt or control these mass conferences, ordering that they be called "meetings" rather than "conferences," offering to participate only under conditions, submitting or publishing their own versions of conference resolutions, etc. The GPC's interference delayed the Ibb conference.[32] The YSP tried to orchestrate a meeting in Aden widely reported as a failure: the RAY said the YSP issued *bayān* before the conference even met, and even the YSP's own press reported only bare-bones resolutions.[33] In mid-March Sana'a television and *al-Thawra* reported a popular meeting of Hodeida governorate, a rival to the autonomous meeting; it claimed to be organized by a new association impressively entitled *al-Hay'a al-Sha'biyya li-l-Difā' 'an al-Waḥda wa-l-Ḍīmuqrāṭiyya wa-Man' al-Infiṣāl* (Popular Body to Defend Unity and Democracy and Resist Partition) with an exceptionally long list of participating organizations, all pro-Sana'a: the GPC, Iṣlāḥ, the NDF, the Nāṣirī-Democratic Party, and several little-known parties, plus the Hodeida branch of the *'Ulamā'* Society, the Federation of Workers, several youth federations, the Women's Union, the Scouts' Associations, the Children's Rights Organization, the Chamber of Commerce, and twenty unions including engineers and the Northern-based teachers' union (but none of the other professional syndicates).[34]

By the spring of 1994 it was possible to tell from press coverage, lists of participating organizations, and catch phrases in the resolutions whether gatherings supported one side or another. The majority of them did not blindly follow either Sana'a or Aden. Their resolutions reflected a set of common themes: public safety; removal of the security forces from population centers; elections for local administration; a serious plan to limit government corruption; and the building of modern judicial, legislative, and executive institutions with clearly delineated responsibilities. While there were notable differences between the grammatical correctness and political sophistication of the resolutions of urban conferences such as Ibb's [35] and those of some rural tribal conferences,[36] they reflected many common concerns. And once the accord incorporating the major conference demands had been signed by the Dialogue Committee and the then top leadership, conferences and follow-up committees in Ibb, Taiz, al-Jawf, Ma'rib, Ḥajja, Shabwa, al-Bayḍā', Ṣa'da, Laḥj, Sana'a, and Aden governorates bombarded the press, the public, and the government with statements of support.

At the beginning of March 1994, the National Dialogue Committee itself disintegrated when Abū Luḥūm and Abū Shawārib left the country after publicly accusing the two leaderships of duplicity in their negotiations. At this crucial juncture, an even less formal type of expression swung into action. Remaining "members of the Dialogue Committee outside the ruling coalition" issued a statement, [37] vowing to organize sit-ins until the accord was implemented. They circulated among the politically active public calling for a mass protest movement. Flanked by the 18 January Committee, ODDRL, the Academic Federation, the Writers' Guild, and the lawyers, faculty, and physicians' syndicates, they arranged "protests" on university campuses in Sana'a, Aden, and Taiz. In Aden, for instance, several Dialoguers attended a packed Ramaḍān *maqyal* at the ODDRL offices where other associations' and syndicates' representatives promised to call special meetings to pass the word. The following morning there was a planning session at an Aden University auditorium. The press reported meetings in Hodeida, Ibb, Dhamar, Radā', Ḥajja, Ḥaḍramawt, Ma'rib, al-Bayḍā', Laḥj, Shabwa, Bayt al-Faqīh, some rural areas, and the Yemeni community in Cairo. At Sana'a University small but different groups of men, women, and children turned up every day for a month to demonstrate for peace and democracy.

These protests were known as *i'taṣim,* from a quranic verse not heretofore invoked in public discourse in Yemen (Quran 3:103): "*I'taṣimū bi-ḥabl Allāh jamī'an wa-lā tafarraqū,*" a call for collective political action. This was one among many cases when civic organizers invoked religion to mobilize support for a modern project. The other basic slogan for these demonstrations was very specific to the crisis: "No to War, No to Separation, Yes to the Accord." There was debate at the initial meetings over the order of these priorities, and in different places they were ranked differently: in Sana'a, "No to Separation, No to War, Yes to Accord;" in Aden, "No to War, Yes to Document, No to Separation"; in Taiz, "Yes to the Document, No to Separation, No to War";[38] in Ḥaḍramawt and al-Ḍāli', "No to Separation, No to Killing, Yes to Implementing the Document";[39] and in the tribal area of Nihm, "Yes to Unity, Yes to Democracy, Yes to Security and Stability, No to War and Destruction."[40]

One of the unique aspects of this "protest" or "peace" movement was unprecedented coverage of the *i'taṣim* across the media spectrum, as each party endeavored to call the movement its own. Channel 1 (Sana'a) and Channel 2 (Aden), Sana'a's *al-Thawra,* Aden's *14 October, Ṣawt al-'Ummāl, al-Shūrā* and *al-Taṣḥīḥ*, and the independent *al-Ayyām* and the *Yemen Times* ran long and/or frequent accounts.[41] Ibb's meetings, for instance, were covered by the GPC's *al-Mīthāq*, the pro-GPC *Ṣawt al-Jabha,* the pro-YSP labor rag *Ṣawt al-'Ummāl*, the YSP paper said to represent its Northern faction *al-Mustaqbal*, and small party organs including *al-Shūrā* and *al-Waḥdawī*. Predictable differences in the emphasis of accounts in the Sana'a and Aden press notwithstanding, all sides tried to claim leadership of what was indisputably majority popular sentiment.

In the final days before the war two contrasting public events, one on a barren hilltop and the other in a campus auditorium, reflected the different forms of popular meetings. In the tribal arena, thousands of men from tribes in the Bakīl confederation camped out for over a week in the territory of 'Iyāl Surayḥ/Jabal 'Iyāl Yazīd, gathering in the mornings to receive newcomers with folk music, dancing, poetry, and speeches, and after lunch to chew qāt with their *shaykhs*. One of the chief organizers was Taṣḥīḥ member of parliament and NDF veteran Mujāhid al-Quhālī, longtime foe of the president. The formal sponsor of the gathering was the recently formed United Bakīl Council, headed by young Muḥammad 'Alī Abū Luḥūm, holder of an American master's degree in economics, who used his family name in a tribal sphere after his effort to found a political party faltered. The United Bakīl Council had already held a convention at Ānis earlier in the year, published a booklet about the council, the conference, and its resolutions,[42] and sponsored seminars where college professors and tribesmen discussed the events of the day. The demands of the 'Iyāl Surayḥ "sit-in" were implementation of the accord; completion of a delayed and diverted road project and provision of local services in 'Iyāl Yazīd/'Iyāl Surayḥ; and compensation to victims of a scam by a merchant named 'Aqlān al-Rāshidī, who had purchased thousands of vehicles, plus gold and weapons, with counterfeit Saudi or Yemeni bills and false checks. Of these, only the road issue was partly "tribal," for participants claimed that al-Aḥmar diverted the planned Ahnūm road from this area to serve his own constituents.

If there was any group poised to fulfill the Somali scenario when war broke out, it was this one, heavily armed and subsidized by the YSP, which helped cover the retreat of Southern troops defeated in a battle at 'Amrān on April 27. After tribal-style negotiations with Speaker-*Shaykh* al-Aḥmar failed to satisfy their demands, moreover, the Bakīl group "cut the roads" into Sana'a to what they identified as "Ḥāshid vehicles" – mainly, the petrol trucks owned by al-Aḥmar's family business. This familiar tactic, quintessentially tribal but also a mimicry of the army's checkpoints, caused a short-term petrol shortage in Sana'a that exacerbated political tensions in and around the capital on the eve of the war. Despite all these factors, when the war spread from the 'Amrān camp down the center of the country, a significant oppositional force of armed, angry tribesmen took their rifles home.

The second meeting, hosted by political scientists at Sana'a University, invited several members of the Dialogue Committee, spokesmen for at least a dozen parties, journalists and faculty, some foreigners, and several hundred students to panel discussions on the political crisis. There was a palpable tension in the packed auditorium as faculty laid out best- and worst-case scenarios. An Egyptian senior member of the faculty compared the accord to the Magna Carta. Five members of the Dialogue Committee insisted the accord could preserve unity and peace. An Iṣlāḥ spokesperson said his party and the GPC began the *i'taṣim* movement and the other parties followed the bandwagon, and the head of al-Ḥaqq knocked his own *qāḍī*-cap off in enthusiastic gesticulation of the *Wathīqa* as the culmination of a decades-long constitutional struggle. There were many calls for reason and rationality. On the floor, however, tempers boiled. Someone in the back accused the RAY of taking Saudi money to foment dissent. Qāsim Salām of the Ba'th called openly for a war on those who threatened separatism. Although faculty restored scholarly decorum at the end, the angry exchanges foreshadowed events to come. After this meeting, political science faculty were specifically forbidden from organizing seminars.

The civil war and its aftermath

The war began in earnest between April 27, when the 'Amrān tank battle provoked a declaration of war from the president, and May 4, when renewed fighting at Dhamar sparked a full-scale nationwide army-to-army confrontation. Within a week Southern battalions in the North were surrounded or scattered. What had been the YAR army entered what had been the PDRY. On May 21 a group of sixteen top Socialists and some new-found allies declared a Yemeni Democratic Republic (YDR) in the southern governorates. The major battles between the army of Yemen and the separatist forces were fought in Laḥj, above Aden, and in Abyan, east of the port city.[43] When Ṣāliḥ's forces reached the outskirts of Aden in early July, the leadership of the short-lived rebel government, disappointed by their failure to gain either domestic support or international recognition, boarded ships to al-Mukallā'. Soon thereafter they fled to Oman.

The sixteen ministers of the irredentist Cabinet were mostly the top post-1986 leaders of the YSP, including 'Alī Sālim al-Bīḍ, Sālim Ṣāliḥ Muḥammad, and Ḥaydar Abū Bakr al-'Aṭṭās. The two non-Socialist members of the YDR Cabinet whose support for the YSP was not necessarily predicted by their pre-war behavior were 'Abd al-Raḥmān al-Jufrī of the RAY, one of the most vocal opponents of the former PDRY; and a leftist Sana'a University philosophy professor Abū Bakr al-Saqqāf, appointed minister of education. Some other Southerners, Socialists, and former YAR dissidents joined them in Aden before the war broke out but did not declare for the breakaway republic. The YDR obviously had the support of some army commanders and public-sector managers who fled with the leadership; but it lacked either a mass following or the support of the so-called Democratic Front and 'Alī Nāṣir wings of the YSP; indeed members of the latter faction, disenfranchised in 1986, joined the looting and occupation of Aden.[44] Al-Jufrī's collaboration seemed to represent Saudi-based, dispossessed South Yemeni sultans and merchants, a group that opposed unity even more fervently than it despised the Socialists. Others whose backing al-Bīḍ and his colleagues must have been counting on, including some YSP members, smaller parties, and dissident northern tribes, stood on the sidelines.[45]

With the notable exception of the philosophy professor, supporters of the rebel government fled to the Gulf where they constituted yet another opposition-in-exile. With some Saudi funds and some support among the political community in exile including the old Adeni elite, al-Jufrī and the 1986–94 leadership of the YSP founded an "opposition" movement identified in both English and Arabic by the acronym MAWJ (possibly for al-Jabha al-Waṭaniyya li-l-Mu'āraḍa). Sana'a hoped that the February 1996 memorandum of understanding with Saudi Arabia on their common border – in which Yemen promised, among other things, not to ban Saudi newspapers – would reduce Riyadh's support for MAWJ. Within Yemen, thousands of Socialists, some prominent and others not, disavowed association either with the separatist government or with the opposition in exile. In keeping a token few YSP members in the government, declaring a general amnesty for all except sixteen rebel leaders who remained abroad and scheduling only four, al-Bīḍ, al-Jufrī, al-'Aṭṭās, and the former governor of Aden (believed to have died in the war), for mutiny trials, the administration itself contended that there was little or no domestic support for the insurrection.

Nonetheless, during and after the war-time state of emergency hundreds of people were accused of sympathy with the rebels. The war was an occasion to ransack public and private property associated with the YSP, its cadre, and friends. At dawn on May 5 Sana'a declared martial law, firebombed and looted the YSP's offices in Northern cities, raided selected private homes and other party and newspaper offices, and detained hundreds of people. The truncated Presidential Council declared a state of emergency pursuant to an obscure 1963 YAR law, approved and extended by a pliant parliamentary quorum for three thirty-day periods. The political security organization seized establishments and detained individuals with impunity.

When the "legitimate forces" entered Aden, joined at the very end by Afghan-jihad zealots and some booty-hunters, there was extensive looting and pillage of physical property. Adenis had been terrorized by bombardment and deprived of water during the war but were spared close-range personal violence in a rampage aimed not at citizens but at economic infrastructure. Water stations outside the city were deliberately disabled by close-range gunfire. Establishments from the infamous Ṣīra Beer factory to the nationalized colonial-legacy domestic trading corporation were torched. Files from the former PDRY ministries of planning, housing, and justice, the YSP, and dozens of other agencies were deliberately destroyed. Employment rolls were shredded. Foreign consulates, UN and Red Cross facilities, oil company offices, hotels, museums, prisons, factories, port warehouses, NGO offices, and selected private homes were looted extensively and then occupied by the Northern army and its allies, including the faction of the YSP ousted in 1986. In one swoop, vestiges of the old PDRY's institutions were obliterated. Troops were stationed throughout the South. Later, despite the massive security and police presence, Afghan-jihad factions identifying themselves as Salafis or "puritans" smashed mosques they said were idolatrous Shāfi'ī shrines.

Unlike many Arab leaders who declare martial law, Ṣāliḥ lifted the state of emergency on July 27 1994. A general amnesty was also declared. Nevertheless, even in the absence of any military resistance from within or beyond Yemen's borders, there was no restoration of the privileges and tolerance established during the four-year liberal interlude. Instead, legal and extra-judicial measures retracted the leeway briefly granted to parties, the press, intellectuals, and autonomous groups. Whereas before the war civil society stretched the boundaries of the space of mass expression, it now represented a fragile but still meaningful defense against extra-legal harassment by security personnel and public prosecutors. Activists now attempted to use the courts and authorized channels within syndicates, universities, and other settings to protect constitutional rights. Indeed independent professionals, papers, and parties wielded legal mechanisms successfully enough that the regime resorted to criminal activities and tribal law. Government attempted to evade its own laws to escape the legal-constitutional pressures of civil society.

With Parliament purged of die-hard Socialists, Southerners and a few others, the GPC and Iṣlāḥ easily railroaded through exhaustive constitutional amendments granting a long list of powers to the president, incorporating neo-conservative interpretations of Islamic law, and mandating central control of regional and local affairs. The Cabinet was reconstructed with Iṣlāḥ filling most of the posts formerly held by the YSP including not only the obvious ideological portfolios such as justice and education but also supply, linchpin of the kleptocracy. The new unity government, requesting hundreds of millions of dollars in new international loans to cover reconstruction even as the value of the riyāl dipped to a new all-time low of 175 to the dollar, promised to comply with IMF and the World Bank structural adjustment proposals. They embraced privatization, selling what remained of the PDRY's assets to regime supporters; and streamlined the civil service by dismissing thousands of suspected critics. The center of political gravity shifted rightward, with lingering progressive tendencies purged in favor of social conservatives and the military establishment.

Some in Iṣlāḥ now cast their party as "the opposition within the ruling coalition." The Yemeni Reform Grouping issued a party platform in July 1995.[46] Its opening sections defined the individual, the family, justice, freedom, society, and culture in conservative neo-Islamist terms, identifying "consultation" with democracy and republicanism. The commitment to Yemeni unity reflects a pan-Yemeni nationalism then more popular among Northerners than Southerners; there is no question that it is an anti-Socialist manifesto, albeit one calling for some state economic management and social spending. It further contains a chapter on civil society, however, in which there is a call for revival and independence of unions, development cooperatives, *waqf*, and mosques, listed in that order. Several sections emphasize the autonomy of "scientific institutes" from the state curriculum. The section on the judiciary begins with a strong statement of judicial independence. There is an explicit call for an expansion of the jurisdiction of elected local governments. The platform calls for extensive reforms, for instance in the media and the security forces. Finally, there is a statement of concern for the security of the neighboring monarchies. It is then, a conservative platform, distinct from that of the GPC, and one that

Table 7.1. *Major Cabinet changes, Republic of Yemen, 1990–1997, by Party*

Post	1990	1993	1994	1997
prime minister	YSP	YSP	GPC	Independent
deputy PM	GPC	GPC	Islah	
deputy PM	GPC	Ba'th		
deputy PM	YSP	YSP		
cabinet affairs	GPC			GPC
foreign minister	GPC	GPC	GPC	GPC
minister of state, foreign affairs	YSP			
oil	YSP	YSP	GPC	GPC
planning	Independent	GPC	GPC	GPC
administrative reform	YSP	Iṣlāḥ		GPC
agriculture	GPC	GPC	GPC	GPC
Awqaf	GPC	Iṣlāḥ	Iṣlāḥ	al-Haqq
civil service	GPC	GPC	GPC	GPC
construction	GPC	GPC	GPC	GPC
communications	GPC	GPC	GPC	GPC
culture	GPC	YSP	GPC	GPC
defense	YSP	YSP	GPC	GPC
education	GPC	GPC	Iṣlāḥ	GPC
electricity and water	GPC		Iṣlāḥ	GPC
finance	GPC	GPC	GPC	GPC
fisheries	YSP	YSP	Iṣlāḥ	GPC
health	GPC	Iṣlāḥ	Iṣlāḥ	Independent
higher education	Independent			
housing	YSP	YSP	GPC	
industry	GPC	GPC	GPC	GPC
information	YSP	GPC	GPC	GPC
interior	GPC	GPC	GPC	GPC
justice	YSP	GPC	Iṣlāḥ	GPC
legal affairs	GPC		GPC	GPC
local administration	YSP	Iṣlāḥ	Iṣlāḥ	GPC
labor	YSP			GPC
migrant affairs	YSP			Independent
parliamentary affairs	GPC?			Iṣlāḥ
social affairs	GPC	GPC	GPC	GPC
supply	YSP	Iṣlāḥ	Iṣlāḥ	GPC
tourism	GPC			
transport	YSP	YSP	GPC	GPC
youth	GPC	GPC	GPC	GPC
without portfolio	GPC	Iṣlāḥ		

envisions some protection of some popular civic spaces from state interference.

Narrowing the field

The post-war regime resorted to both legal and illegal tactics to neutralize the opposition. The parties law was revised to require registration and allow the Supreme Parties Commission to intervene in internal affairs. The several remaining opposition parties were also each subject to an influx of former GPC supporters demanding to influence the choice of party leadership. Under the revised rules for parties, internal crises precipitated by security operatives posing as new members allowed the government to contest opposition parties' leadership or newspapers in court. Still, as the polity geared up for a project funded by Western donors, the 1997 elections, democratization consultants found a much more varied and influential legal opposition than in most Arab countries.

The Yemeni Socialist party, already fragmented before the war, was now further divided. After the flight of the irredentist faction of its top leadership, a few members of its parliamentary delegation defected to the General People's Congress, and several others sought asylum abroad. Besieged from without and beset by internal disagreements, the rejuvenated YSP elected a new central committee of forty-some members primarily from the faction defeated in 1986 (the so-called Abyan or 'Ali Naṣīr group) who for a decade had tended to side with Sana'a in its quarrel with Aden. Having lost many of its top cadre in several generations of purges and some defections, the weakened Socialist party still included prominent individuals, thousands of sympathizers among the professional class, a parliamentary delegation, a newspaper (*al-Thawrī*), and several hundred thousand adult members. Among resentful Southerners, however, voter-registration rates for the 1997 parliamentary elections were noticeably lower than the enthusiastic participation of 1993. In the run-up to the April 27 polling date, amidst rumours of a preelection agreement between the GPC and its ally the Reform Grouping to split the majority of seats between themselves (leaving only 61 constituencies to be genuinely contested among all other candidates), the demoralized leadership of the party decided to boycott the elections.

The destruction of the YSP's printing presses and arrests of a handful of journalists during the war put *al-Mustaqbal*, *Ṣawt al-'Ummāl*, *al-Umma*, *al-Shūrā*, *al-Tajammu'*, and *al-Ayyām*, among others, temporarily or permanently out of business. GPC-controlled papers began emphasizing "responsibility" of the press over "freedom" of the press.[47] Critics were dubbed "separatist." When the Aden press agency was reestablished under GPC control, a couple of Aden papers, most notably the YSP daily *14 October*, appeared under new editorship; *Ṣawt al-'Ummāl* became simply *al-'Ummāl*, or as cynics quipped, "labor without voice." *Al-Umma*, of Ḥizb al-Ḥaqq, could no longer afford the high state-controlled price of paper and printing facilities by 1996, and *al-Tajammu'* was reduced to a mere eight pages a week. Some new newspapers including one called *al-Tayyār al-Waḥdawī* filled in the gaps in the newsstand displays, along with foreign Arab publications including, after the February 1996 memorandum of understanding, the Saudi paper *al-Sharq al-Awsaṭ*.

Other parties were harassed, penetrated, or curtailed in various ways, as illustrated by the experience of the Union of Popular Forces (UPF) and its newspaper. *Al-Shūrā*, noted for its critical pre-war coverage of all three major parties, ran afoul of the authorities in the summer of 1994, when the editor and a reporter were briefly detained by security forces. Nonetheless, with the financial resources of the al-Wazīr family at its disposal, like the privately operated *al-Ayyām* and *Yemen Times*, *al-Shūrā* was able to resume publication after the war. By October, the paper was accused of fomenting "*tā'ifiyya*" (sectarianism), slandering the president, and employing an unqualified editor. Thanks in part to the efforts of a team of twenty lawyers, Judge Ḥamūd al-Hitar (of the pro-government human rights group YOHR) acquitted the paper of the charges. Subsequently, 'Abd al-Majīd al-Zindānī filed charges against *al-Shūrā* for unauthorized publication of some of his writings. Then, in July 1995, the UPF held a well-publicized conference of 260 party delegates and some invited government observers. When an unruly dissident former UPF member challenged the reelection of Ibrāhīm al-Wazīr as party leader *in absentia*, police drove the hecklers away and promised round-the-clock guards for the UPF premises. A day or two later the party offices were attacked with grenades. On account of this altercation, the Ministry of Legal Affairs issued a decree closing the party offices, freezing its financial accounts, and prohibiting publication of *al-Shūrā*. The Ministry of Information concurred that the paper must not publish because the party's activities were "disputed."[48] In addition, at least one UPF member was arrested amidst a group of mostly Adeni students accused of collaboration with the MAWJ.[49]

Other parties had similar experiences. Ironically, perhaps because of his strident anti-Saudi rhetoric, Qāsim Salām of the Ba'th, cheerleader for Sana'a in 1994, was among the politicians subsequently beaten up by unapprehended criminals. Later, a complicated, debilitating dispute developed between Salām's supporters and a rival for the party's leadership, resulting in two court cases: one by the government against the Ba'th, and the other by the party against the government. United by their common straits, nine parties callling themselves "the opposition parties" and waving copies of the 1990 political parties law staged a protest against the closing of the UPF offices and *al-Shūrā*: The Yemeni Socialist party, the Waḥdawī-Nāṣirī organization, al-Ḥaqq, the Tajammu', Popular Forces, the Ba'th, the conglomerate Union of National Forces, and the Liberal-Constitutional party.[50] In response, in 1996 the new Supreme Elections Committee suggested that they might run on a common opposition slate in the next elections. Court cases, leadership disputes, debates on whether to unite the opposition, and the YSP's decision to boycott the elections consumed all nine opposition parties in the lead-up to the polling season.

Professional syndicates and independent organizations were also the target of penetration. Two thousand attorneys, convening in Aden in April 1996, said the government was playing "Trojan horse."[51] At the journalists' syndicate meeting, about a hundred representatives of independent publishing were outvoted by 850 employees of the government, many of them recently credentialed.[52] The exodus of many Western-educated faculty from Sana'a University gave a majority in the campus unions to social conservatives, and new appointments to Aden University represented the neo-conservative bloc. In the case of human rights organizations, the independent ODDRL published detailed reports of wartime detentions and post-war dismissals,[53] and the founding of branches in the Ḥaḍramawt and Shabwa, together with contacts with Arab and international human rights groups, helped sustain the energies of a small group of volunteers. YOHR, on the other hand, issued a bilingual booklet of its own by-laws together with the amended constitution,[54] but after its leader criticized the government in interviews with foreign human rights monitors and handed down controversial court decisions volunteers who showed up at the office found its doors consistently locked.

Intellectuals became targets of an intimidation campaign utilizing extra-legal methods during the wartime state of emergency and beyond. A dozen participants in a *Yemen Times* seminar at the Sana'a Sheraton right after the war, including editors or writers for *al-Shūrā*, the YSP's *al-Mustaqbal*, and the magazine *al-Waṭan*, the head of the nascent Yemeni Institute for the Development of Democracy, and a legal scholar at the Yemen Center for Research and Studies, were removed from their homes, held incommunicado for several days, beaten, and released.[55] Perhaps the most audacious of the regime's intellectual critics, philosophy professor Abū Bakr al-Saqqāf, returned to his Sana'a University post after having served in the ill-fated DRY government, and subsequently published essays in the privately owned weekly *al-Ayyām* referring to the "colonial occupation" of Southern provinces. During a year-long dispute of his dismissal from a tenured faculty position, he was vilified in the GPC press and mugged twice by plainclothes security teams. Other faculty who also attended a well-publicized academic conference at the School of Oriental and African Studies of the University of London hosted by RAY–DRY–MAWJ leader al-Jufrī were harassed by Sana'a airport security officials upon their return.

The 1997 elections

The same year that President Ṣāliḥ celebrated his twentieth anniversary in office, the Republic of Yemen's second nationwide parliamentary elections enabled him to consolidate the General People's Congress's legislative control while obtaining a stamp of approval from international election monitors. At about the same time, a new parliamentary institution, the Consultative Council, was constituted by presidential appointment. These developments, resonant with echoes of past episodes, furthered the process of constitutional and even democratic development, but at the same time offered further evidence of the incomplete, ongoing process of state construction.

The wartime alliance between the GPC and the political Islamists proved short lived. Amidst preparations for combat and then the sacking of Aden, Afghan-jihad zealots had delivered religious motivation and justification. They were rewarded with plum ministerial posts, and Iṣlāḥ returned the favor by mediating bilateral negotiations with Saudi Arabia. Opposition parties apparently thought the alliance firm when rumors circulated that the two post-war ruling parties had agreed between them that the GPC would take 160 seats and Iṣlāḥ 80, for this was the reason given by the YSP for its boycott of the 1997 elections. Whatever agreement existed had collapsed by April, however, to the extent that competition in the 301 constituencies was primarily between the two erstwhile partners. The GPC won this competition, picking up 188 seats while Iṣlāḥ managed to win only 56, fewer than in the 1993 elections. The GPC's majority in the Chamber of Deputies enabled it to form a government without coalition partners. Instead, a couple of independents were given ministerial posts, and in a particular affront to the neo-Islamists, the head of the Zaydī-traditionalist party al-Ḥaqq gained the *awqaf* portfolio (see table 7.1). The Reform Grouping, then, was the big loser in these elections, and joined the Socialist party in condemning the polling as rigged and unfair.

International observers on hand between April 25 and May 1 were relatively pleased with the experience, however. As in 1993, reports of irregularities in several constituencies, complaints by the losers, a fair enthusiasm among ordinary voters and poll-workers, and an element of surprise at the outcome all seemed to indicate that the overall process was relatively free and fair. Monitors and reporters believed the GPC won in a majority of districts because of its superior candidates and/or campaign organization and congratulated the president for both the success of the experience and his party's victory. These positive assessments were influenced by a range of factors: Yemen's cooperation with its creditors and neighbors; the strong showing for business interests; outsiders' antipathy toward opposition parties labeled variously communist, pro-Iraqi, pro-Iranian, or Islamist: the nature of "elections tourism" featuring the polling process detached from the larger political context described above; the field of comparison which for journalists and monitors included Liberia, Serbia, Algeria, and other unsavory examples; and the fact that, as always, Yemen is great fun to visit.

Establishment of *al-Majlis al-Shūrā* was significant in several ways. First, creation of a consultative council had been a common element in constitutional proposals from the 1950s through the 1990s, and thus represented a clear response to popular demand and judicial recommendations. In addition, the structure of the Yemeni government, though still technically a parliamentary system, now increasingly resembled the American structure, with a strong president, a parliament comprising a senate and a house of representatives, and some local autonomy along the lines of a relationship Americans call federal. If, as promised, elections are held for both the consultative council and provincial governments by the year 2000, then both the congressional and federal elements of the system-in-the-making will be democratized. In the interim, however, the fifty-nine senators were appointed. The pattern of appointments strengthened the hand of the executive, but also showed its need for support from civil society. For they included the two initiators and several other members of the pre-war Dialogue Committee, two former ambassadors to the US, several prominent former ministers, al-Zindānī, the editor of the *Yemen Times*, and, more generally, a wide spectrum from progressive social democrats to Arab nationalists to neo-Islamists, some of them defeated or demoted in the 1997 elections and others prominent in national affairs since the early republican movement.

Contests over public space

Beyond the politics of national appointments and offices, at and beyond the frontiers of state and civil society, activists still worked with the tools at hand to clear space for civic expression. An especially noteworthy development in the mid-1990s was the appearance of at least a dozen private universities: one a Wahhabi institution, another a technical college in the Ḥaḍramawt, a third a moonlight operation by Sana'a University faculty. Private education opened another significant extra-governmental space for intellectual activity, one destined to be internally competitive but also already recognizing common interests vis-à-vis taxation, the Ministry of Education, and independent academic standards. For the first time in a long time, scholars could seek employment beyond the public sector. At the same time, in many localities the long-term issue of control of parochial education, and especially of *waqf* endowments, persisted. Privatization of health care and growth of private legal practice also contributed to the autonomy of professional classes from civil service. Individuals, parties, and organizations increasingly petitioned the courts for legal protection against closure, censorship, and manipulation, and judge proved increasingly responsive to such appeals. Three anecdotal cases characterize the complex contestation of civic space and legal rights in the post-war period.

The first example is a sequel to the discussion in the previous chapter of rivalry between competing human rights and election-monitoring groups. Before the 1994 war, a group of liberal and socialist intellectuals began meeting with ministers and foreigners to gain support for a Yemeni Institute for Democratic Development, or YIDD (an acronym meaning "hand" in Arabic). This project got off the ground after the war with donor funds under their "civil society projects," although it needs mentioning that Western sponsors were apparently dissatisfied with YIDD's money management. Soon a second group with much stronger government support, initially called the Arab Institute for Democracy (AID), began competing for these funds. AID proposed projects with a focus on women, including seminars for past and future female candidates and a campaign to increase women's voter registration in northern constituencies (the eighty-three districts of lowest female voter registration). Thanks largely to the leadership of Sana'a's most prominent Western-educated feminist, Professor Raufa Hassan, an experienced organizer, campaigner, and spokesperson, the institute opened in the summer of 1996 with considerable government fanfare and won a hefty share of the millions of dollars in international support for the 1997 elections. Rumors spread that the GPC would run female candidates in the 1997 elections. In this case, then, a contest for control of donor "civil society project" funding rebounded in favor of women's inclusion in the political process. Twenty-three women ran for election in 1997, fewer than before; again, two won seats, both in Southern constituencies.

The second case is but a glimpse of the nuanced, perhaps contradictory developments within the judiciary in the post-war period. Under a right-wing justice minister a contest between judges asserting a degree of judicial autonomy and public prosecutors beholden to the executive challenged some judges to risk their appointments by protecting individuals, publications, and organizations from unlawful harassment. In 1996, the 1,100-member judiciary prepared for a major conference of the *Munṭaḍa al-Qaḍai* (judges' association), founded in 1991, and headed by the leader of the now semi-dormant YOHR. An equal or greater number of prosecutors sought membership in the *Munṭaḍa* and the right to vote on agendas and officers. Moreover, despite what might be predicted from the misogynist rhetoric of the minister, in Aden and other parts of the South about a dozen female judges, many but not all of them in family or juvenile court, remained on the bench in mid-1996. One of them, Ruqayya Humaydān, wrested a public acknowledgment of the legality of female justices from the president. In a separate process that nonetheless also fortified the court system as a whole, international creditors pushed for rapid strengthening of commercial courts. This in turn stimulated demand for private-sector attorneys, a newly visible professional lobby for legal practice. Although far from internally monolithic, a discernible professional legal community nonetheless developed a more self-conscious sense of themselves as defenders of the law and citizen rights.

All three cases engage gender issues obliquely, as a subset of broader civic struggles. The third anecdote begins when two Ḥaḍramī women from the village of Shiḥr were detained by a Northern police chief in al-Mukallā' on "morals" charges in late spring 1996. After their release they filed charges against the police for sexual molestation and monetary extortion. In June the reported comment by a Northern prosecutor in a Mukallā' court to the effect that "all Ḥaḍramī women are whores" touched off three days of demonstrations that turned violent when police opened fire. While these protests obviously reflected generalized animosity toward "occupying" forces, in the event they became demonstrations not just for the traditional "honor" of women but for protection of legal and civil rights. The president, several ministers, and the human rights committee of the Chamber of Deputies all rushed to the Ḥaḍramawt to assure a disgruntled population that their concerns were being heard. As Aden attorneys affiliated with ODDRL went to al-Mukallā' to defend the women, one immediate outgrowth of the incident was formation of a new Ḥaḍramī branch of the human rights group.[56]

Contending forces

The causes of the collapse of the post-unity coalition government were complex. Defeat of the Yemeni Socialist party and renunciation of its policies conformed to the global dismantlement of socialist governments in other countries including Nicaragua, Vietnam, Angola, and Albania. Within the region, Gulf antipathy toward Yemeni unity, Yemeni ambivalence about the Iraqi invasion of Kuwait, Yemen's resulting isolation, and a general repudiation of progressive ideologies were all surely at work. At the level of the newborn Yemeni state the crux of the problem was that an agreement to share power equally between what proved to be unequal armies defied the principles of realism, as did the idea that Aden would voluntarily relinquish its commands. Certainly neither group of incumbents showed a philosophical disposition toward genuine power sharing. All the while the economy, racked by the Gulf War, burdened by the financial costs of unification, and cannibalized by kleptocracy, experienced negative growth for six straight years during which economic policy making was abdicated to foreign donors. Both sides in the leadership equation raided public coffers. All these circumstances ate away at social services to one of the world's most rapidly growing populations (nearly 4 percent natural increase plus immigration from Saudi Arabia and Somalia). Living standards depreciated in Sana'a, Taiz, Hodeida, and Aden, all growing far too fast for their water supplies, electrical plants, schools, health care, streets, public spaces, and waste-removal systems.

Any government might collapse under such conditions. This chapter has shown how incumbents twisted the rules but faced considerable pressure from the press, mass conferences, and non-ruling political elites to hold to some semblance of civility. Tendencies identified in past civic openings were repeated: the coincidence of closure with economic recession, the semi-voluntary exile of a significant dissident force, the efforts to build legitimacy on co-opted autonomous projects, the resort to legalistic rhetoric confounded by simultaneous tightening and circumvention of law.

Above all, this chapter demonstrates the symbiotic relationship between a state-in-the-making and an emerging civil society. The Yemeni state is as new as the Eritrean state or the Palestinian Authority, yet unlike them does not enjoy the residual legitimacy of a successful national liberation struggle. Fiscally insolvent and lacking many of the basic prerequisites of statehood – defined borders, a monopoly over violence, a constitutional order – the Republic of Yemen may be unique in its craving for civic institutions on which to build the foundations of a state capable of either democracy or full-fledged dictatorship. Even with some 30 percent of the post-war government budget Western embassies say goes directly to perks and payoffs, the state cannot simply buy loyalty from elites, social groups, or the population at large. Scarcely able to meet payroll for engorged armed forces, the government cannot militarily control even the Northern highlands where its base of support is said to lie. Faced with a neighbor capable of distributing services and passports to communities along an unpatrolled frontier, Sana'a cannot afford to alienate the Ḥaḍramawt, Ma'rib, the Jawf, or Ṣa'da. However many judges or intellectuals flee or accept payoffs, a military regime lacking either coercive or ideological hegemony remains sensitive to scholarly and legal opinion. A regime that devours its own budget and flouts its own criminal codes soon runs short of resources. Unlike post-colonial states that come with a governmental apparatus, post-revolutionary states that come to power on a wave of popular enthusiasm, or some third world governments with great-power support, Yemen has to construct a state. Such a project may require the consent of the governed.

The position of women is a case in point. From their narrow but protected spaces within the primordial private realm women have hardly clamored for individual political rights in an environment where even male rights have yet to be established. The illiterate female majority know well enough what they want – welfare, services, and non-violence – but are not necessarily more trustful of government, often seen as violent and capricious, than of patriarchal authorities, who at least make the case for a moral economy. The small educated female elite participates in the public sphere not as a special interest group but as a minority among philanthropists, writers, jurists, volunteers, parliamentary candidates, or entrepreneurs. The assertion of their rights is non-linear, part of the paradoxical contests in the sphere between households and regimes. With more citizen rights than their sisters in neighboring monarchies, Yemeni women have nonetheless suffered setbacks under an increasingly powerful neo-Islamist current and deepening economic recession. At the same time, Yemen's political leaders have historically recognized that any broadly transformative socio-political project needs the support of women. This is why Southern revolutionaries adopted feminism as state policy, the Islamist wing of

Iṣlāḥ launched the first post-unity women's voter-registration drive, and the GPC has promoted several token women to visible positions. The post-civil-war environment produced contradictions between the deliberate repudiation of the PDRY's feminism and women's consummate capacity to withdraw from the public realm; and between the two contrary results of recession and unemployment: the sexism of unemployed alienated men, on the one hand, and pressures on women to be wage-earners, on the other. Thus as revisions in criminal and personal status codes reduced women's legal capacity, on the other hand there were incongruous public affirmations of women's suitability to serve in parliament and the judiciary. Although Western "democratization projects" were one factor in the inclusion of women in formal politics, ordinary events threatening women's customary protection from violence created domestic pressure for their protection in the public realm. While ideologically determined personal status laws gave men disproportionate power over women, the regime's state-building interests favored inclusion of the unarmed half of the electorate.

8 Political movements, cultural trends, and civic potential

The two-part hypothesis with which this study began was that civic spaces are defined by political, economic, and cultural factors, and in turn civic activism has discernible (though certainly not determinant) effects on states, material conditions, and popular culture. A particular effort has been made to demonstrate the dynamic, contested, even contradictory elements of this process. The task of this conclusion is to summarize the generalizations that can and cannot be drawn from this study of Yemen about Arab culture, political economy, and civic potential.

Yemen is so far off the beaten path that even Arab or Western Middle East specialists often neglect to visit. To the extent that a conventional wisdom exists about Yemen, however, it is that a combination of Islam and tribalism explains everything. Journalists infer from outward appearances (men wearing skirts and daggers, women in all-encompassing black, aesthetic preferences for indigenous architecture, and the folksy exoticism of the scenery) that something along the lines of the "Islamic conservatism of the traditional tribes of the north" accounts for political outcomes. Conveniently unencumbered by facts about recent history, this shallow cultural determinism does not hold up to close scrutiny. Islamic and tribal law have been used as the antonym for ideal-typical Western modernism by writers from Weber to Huntington, but in an era of post-modern scholarship no serious analysis can result from laying a traditional–modern/primordial–civic heuristic foil sidewise across geography, as though some places are frozen in time while others have history.

Culture is certainly important to understanding the civic life of any polity. In Yemen culture plays a salient role in the sorts of social, intellectual, political, and voluntary activities covered in this study. Customary and religious rhythms of the day, the week, the month, and the year strongly affect who meets where, when, and why. The Arabic language and literature, the way they are taught and written, cultural forms of poetry and rhetoric – all these naturally permeate public discourse. Gender segregation in spaces between the family and the government is a barely modified cultural given. Educational differences and status consciousness perpetuate the *sayyid*–tribe–subaltern division. Features of material culture including water scarcity, topography, cereal and ruminant production, and qāt-chewing substantially affect economic, civic, and political behavior. Yemen's relative ethnic homogeneity, on the one hand, but on the other hand a strong regionalism often expressed in tribal and/or sectarian terms as well as in dialect, dress, and mannerisms, do bear directly on national public life. Most of the relevant dimensions of culture are not general for all of Yemen but represent a crazy-quilt of local variations, with noteworthy differences among the distinct regions, between towns and farm communities, and among social groups and classes. Overarching these are a common reverence for the Quran, and to a lesser but still significant extent, for Yemeni historical legends – among whose leading figures, it should be said, two Yemeni queens, Queen Bilqīs of the ancient Sheba empire Yemenis say was based at Ma'rib and Queen Arwa of the Islamic capital at Jibla, figure most prominently.

Yet the appeal of tribalism and religion are not only ideological, for each is also a system of law capable of functioning in the absence of a state, and each contains customary mechanisms for creating public social capital. Although an incomplete account of either the complex evolution of the Yemeni legal system or the full range of water, education, and other services, this study shows how the contractual and material dimensions of state-like mechanisms operating on a local level affect the creation and control of public spaces. Anecdotes and case studies have demonstrated that mechanisms inherited from religious or tribal practice could be applied to either progressive or reactionary political purposes.

All regimes in twentieth-century Yemen have grappled with tribes. Tribalism was the bugaboo of imams, colonial authorities, and Socialists, all seeking to replace common law with a centralized judicial system. Yet the British and the imams made treaties with tribes as such, and the Mutawakkilite, colonial, and Socialist governments all pursued the contradictory policy of supplanting *'urf* with their own judiciaries and using tribes as the basis of military recruitment, thus exaggerating military tribalism and tribal militarism while undermining tribal legal order. In their various efforts to influence military outcomes the British, Egyptian, and Saudi governments have distributed millions of rifles to Yemeni tribesmen through their *shaykhs*. Republican military regimes in Sana'a have also used tribalism as a basis for military recruitment, command, and organization. Beyond government, tribal symbols and mechanisms were mobilized for causes radical and counter-revolutionary, for and against states and armies, in celebration of modernity as well as of custom.

In recent times a two-pronged process of "retribalization" is apparent. The counter-intuitive prong of this process is governmental advocacy of tribal law as an alternative to codified civil law, accompanied by official resort to tribal explanations and solutions to political crimes. For instance, one of the improbable events marking the outbreak of the 1994 war was the shooting of then acting prime minister Ḥasan Makkī, a respected Northern elder statesman and GPC member, three of whose bodyguards died in the attack. Subsequently Nājī al-Shāyif, a GPC member close to *Shaykh* 'Abd Allāh Ḥusayn al-Aḥmar whom the Saudi press usually identify as paramount *shaykh* of Bakīl, publicly claimed responsibility, saying he ordered his men to arrest Makkī for his opposition to a war against the YSP. According to a front-page spread in the official daily *al-Thawra*, al-Aḥmar accompanied al-Shāyif to Makkī's house where al-Shāyif had oxen slaughtered in a process the paper called the tribal custom of "*hajar*."[1] The family of the tribesman who firebombed the office of the Union of Popular Forces also killed a bull on the steps of the offices "according to custom." In a sense killing bulls is a customary gesture in lieu of retaliation by a victim's family, and in the 1970s bulls were sometimes slain on the steps of the Sana'a Ministry of Public Works as a demonstration for services, but in the recent, well-publicized cases, government spokespersons deliberately advanced the ritual public slaughter of livestock as a viable alternative to criminal investigation and trial. Public prosecutors have declined to investigate some assassinations, hijackings, and other crimes it classifies as "tribal."

In tribalizing criminal law and social services provision, Sana'a was attempting simultaneously to counteract the PDRY legacy of "law and order," the relative autonomy of its own judiciary, and an autonomous process of oppositional rural retribalization. To the rather considerable extent that the military was tribally organized, the top military commands held by Sanḥānī tribesmen, the president and the speaker of parliament shared both Ḥāshid membership and (coincidentally) the family name al-Aḥmar, the speaker's political style was that of *shaykh*, and the two families controlled so much semi-public private wealth, the promotion of tribalism by the state encouraged rural opponents to identify the government, and especially the army, as Sanḥān/Ḥāshid. This was one stimulus for resurgent Bakīlī consciousness and, more surprising, tribal stirrings in the middle and southern regions where for the past couple of generations tribalism was a status-marker rather than the basis of either ideology or social organization. The revival of tribal federations such as al-Madhḥaj in the largely Shāfiʿī regions south of the Ḥāshid–Bakīl heartland followed the demobilization of formerly active community development cooperatives and of the Socialist party in the Southern uplands. In a related development, some of the Saba' conference follow-up committees named five Madhḥaj and twelve Bakīl tribes they said were prepared to join a Saba' political party, then met abroad with representatives of the purportedly *sayyid* Union of Popular Forces. Expressions of tribal identity became more visible throughout the South than they had been for many years. Not a viable alternative to political parties, as a way of holding a predatory state at bay or at least bargaining for a good deal, tribalism seemed more efficacious in the post-war environment than partisanship.

Even more dramatic was the reinvention of Islam in the 1980s and 1990s in a variety of forms. Some of these are indigenous, but the most radical self-identified fundamentalists spurn traditional Yemeni Zaydī, Shāfiʿī, or Ismāʿīlī political thought in favor of imported, modern Wahhabi and Salafī puritanism. Even these "converts" are not of a single mind, however. Some former migrants identify with an official Saudi version of Wahhabism, while other Wahhabis defile the Saudi monarchy. In northernmost Yemen Wahhabis have come into conflict with a Zaydī revival represented in part by Ḥizb al-Ḥaqq but also manifested in recreation of Zaydī rituals. Born-again Salafīs, purportedly Sunnī Muslims, have inflicted serious physical damage on historic Shāfiʿī mosques and shrines in Jibla, Aden, and the Ḥaḍramawt. As in the Zaydī areas, Shāfiʿīs respond by rediscovering half-forgotten saints' days and religious practices.

The re-Islamicization of a deeply religious, homogeneously Muslim culture is also government policy. As elsewhere in the region, Yemen's neo-fundamentalists were encouraged by regimes preoccupied with a challenge from the left. Iṣlāḥ's religious spokespersons boasted that it was the first Islamist party to come to power through the ballot-box, but in fact zealots had been recruited over the previous decade by a regime lacking a distinct ideology but facing widespread domestic disaffection, a meaningful challenge from the left, and an ultra-conservative, meddlesome northern neighbor. Like Riyadh, Sana'a uses religion to justify political repression, arbitrary justice, and summary executions. It is certainly true that there is precedent for beheadings of political opponents in the name of Sharīʿa – for instance, the father and brother of *Shaykh* al-Aḥmar were beheaded by order of the imam – but at least two generations of Yemeni religious scholars and tribal leaders railed against such "traditions."

Historically, aristocracies interpreted Sharīʿa in self-serving, political ways, seeking always a legitimizing cadre of loyal *'ulamā'*. In historic towns, Islamic endowments guaranteed the intellectual autonomy of independent academic institutions and some legal autonomy to Islamic judges. The first waves of what is now called the Islamist current embodied a radical egalitarianism opposed to monarchy and aristocracy: fundamentalism as protest movement, Islamic constitutionalism, bourgeois enlightenment. As such it appealed to the non-*sayyid*, primarily tribal majority, by promising improved social conditions. In those days, however, political Islam was overshadowed by Arab nationalism, bourgeois liberalism, and radical socialism. Nonetheless, otherwise secular fund-raising drives for water and school projects naturally invoked Islamic piety, charity, and community. In other words, the fact that cultural material may be manipulated symbolically does not establish an axiomatic predisposition to any particular ideological orientation. The careful selection of particular traditions (capital punishment; female subordination) over others (exacting standards of judicial evidence; intellectual freedom) is a political act that can only be explained in concrete socio-economic terms.

The reaccentuation of tribal and religious "traditions" has direct and indirect material underpinnings as well. Broadly speaking, socio-economic conditions – high inflation and unemployment, rapid urbanization, and the deterioration of public services – are conducive to right-wing politics, what Erich Fromm, writing about Nazism, called an "escape from freedom." There are also much more specific economic reasons for 1990s tribalism and fundamentalism. First, although the Yemeni state has been weaned from Gulf clientage, money is still available to tribal and religious *shaykhs*. The flow of petro-dollar donations into religious seminaries and charities goes a long way toward explaining the neo-Islamist movement, now the most significant locus of new social capital formation. Increasingly important during a decade of worsening economic conditions, religious establishments offered a modicum of welfare to women and children and relief from disasters such as war and floods. In cushioning society from the ravages of corrupt economics they also helped cushion the government from popular discontent. The very recent emergence in Yemen of Islamic banks signals a new source of capital formation in the name of religion.

Since intervening in commercial markets in the mid-1980s, Sana'a systematically redirected import licenses, monopoly contracts, credit packages, and other state-controlled financial opportunities to urban-based officer-*shaykhs* whose national prominence was enhanced by their increasing wealth but who, by and large, lost touch with their agrarian roots. At the same time, the constriction of legitimate entrepreneurship led directly to an increase in illegal commerce, especially the smuggling of narcotics, currencies, and weapons across the border into Saudi Arabia, and kidnappings and hijackings for ransom: all activities well suited to the highly mobile, interlocking, heavily armed tribes of the northern and eastern frontiers, organized through rural chiefs and utilizing certain customs regarding safe passage and the treatment of hostages. Through their tribes and chiefs, ranchers and farmers supplemented stagnant incomes with political payoffs from Sana'a, Riyadh, Aden, Kuwait, Baghdad, Tehran, and Tripoli; and from activities that the government was pressured by international creditors (anxious to create a safer environment for foreign investors) to prosecute as criminal. Religious charities and macho tribesmanship each constituted, and to some degree circulated, wealth.

Evidence throughout this work shows, then, that state politics and policies are highly salient. Governments deal with the outside world, print currency, and possess substantial capital. These advantages alone usually enable administrations to manage international trade and domestic capital formation to the advantage of their friends. Executive directives move tax collectors, police, and investments, courts resolve disputes and punish criminals, and "employment" (*waẓīfa*) is synonymous with "civil service." All citizens came to depend on government roads, schools, hospitals, and utilities, and even in an era of privatization of health care, power, water, and education these services remain physical conduits of a national system whose hub is Sana'a. Most importantly for purposes of this study, imams, governors, and command councils regulated the scope for autonomous projects in either the private or the public sphere. Normally, they have used state authority to monopolize entrepreneurial and civic ventures by driving competitors abroad or underground. When opportunities for autonomous initiatives are expanded, it is at the discretion of leaders of the state.

Nevertheless, the fragility of state institutions is obvious. The Republic of Yemen is unlike other Arab states built on either colonial institutions or oil wealth. However much unity fulfilled nationalist aspirations, the current state is a toddler, unsteady on its feet. Its predecessors proved incapable of reproducing themselves, advancing a persuasive value package, or exercising stable hegemony. Regimes have shown predatory tendencies, devouring the public-sector wealth and even the legal basis of their own power. Periodic liberalizations have never been inspired by enlightened leaders voluntarily ceding powers but by governments with shallow historical, constitutional, social, and material foundations seeking to draw strength from civil society and investments from the private sector. The state disaggregates as a well-entrenched but little-professionalized national security apparatus with soft legislative, judicial, and infrastructural institutions. Limited by its position in regional and global systems as well as its own incapacity to implement a developmental program, Sana'a has demonstrated an ability to release or suppress autonomous economic or civic entrepreneurship but not to channel popular and elite energies to its own purposes. In this study, therefore, the state is both an independent and a dependent variable.

This inquiry has focused on three periods of relative economic and political liberalization that gave greater scope to activity in the non-profit non-state sector. In each case a fledgling administration tried to rally opinion and investment around its governance project by relaxing legal restrictions on autonomous projects. The main findings have been, first, that civic participation quickly fills any space ceded to it by the state; second, that this participation takes different forms depending on economic and political circumstances; and third, that activism materially affects broad trends in political and economic development. In the colonial port city labor and merchant interests organized syndicates, clubs, and political parties. In the second opening, and indeed for much of the twentieth century, voluntary energies and donations supported projects rather than organizations. The third opening, Yemen's most democratic experience, saw more specifically political participation in parties, intellectual seminars, conventions, and lawsuits as well as a surge of charitable activity.

If it is true that formal autonomous activity in the public civic realm requires protection rather than harassment by the police, it is equally true that legal protections require civic monitoring. Above all, this study has documented the myriad, complex, specific, and meaningful ways civic activism furthered the constitutional, electoral, legal, infrastructural, institutional, and ideological dimensions of state power. State structures situated in the international community of nations do not rule without legal and institutional connections to their own societies. Even while revising, suppressing, and negating the demands of counter-elites and public opinion, governments have historically tried to draw legitimacy from constitutional, electoral, and services projects advanced by *'ulamā'*, *shaykhs*, and the ever-expanding cadre of university and graduate degree-holders. The PDRY's valorization of mass organizations, the GPC's co-optation of the cooperative movement, and the grudging post-1994 legal tolerance of token opposition are all instances of state-building on institutions rooted in the civic sphere. Given first the extraordinary diversity and unevenness of "state" history in the twentieth century and secondly social access to hard cash in the form of remittances, a high proportion of social capital and services have been constructed under the auspices of religious foundations, community betterment initiatives, urban development associations, or other non-governmental projects. Nationalization of these projects is an important feature of state building, especially to governments in severe fiscal crisis.

The economics of investment and ownership influence civic activism in a triangulated relationship among state, private, and civic sectors. In twentieth-century Yemen a strong correlation exists between economic growth and liberalization, such that the investment of overseas capital – in the Aden trade and military sectors, during the second-hand oil boom, and during the initial development of the petroleum sector – seems to encourage regimes to loosen restrictions on everything from currency exchange to newspaper publishing. More broadly, however, a range of very different regimes – theocratic, colonial, socialist, and military-republican – have all maintained a majority interest in the economy, wielded economic policy as a political tool, and struggled to capture the domestic formation and disposition of financial and social capital. Such policies have stunted both economic and civic participation. On the other hand, a highly mobile commercial class and migratory labor force offer communities access to hard currency that has financed projects from the Ḥaḍramī institutes of the 1920s to the new private universities of the 1990s. Remittances and donations from abroad have given non-state projects relative autonomy vis-à-vis a state itself heavily dependent on foreign financing.

Although denationalization of socialist enterprises is crony capitalism at its best, putting public property in the private hands of the political elite, the current wave of privatization of health care, utilities, and education will affect the civic realm in several ways. First, it will presumably increase the private wealth and autonomy from the state of professionals, the class with the greatest interest in bourgeois liberties and the greatest propensity for straightforwardly civic involvement. Secondly, it will almost certainly thrust charitable programs to the fore of social services provision, as it has elsewhere. In addition to funding from abroad, welfare societies can only appeal to the sorts of moral appeals that mobilize donations: mainly, religion, family values, and localism. Thirdly, the alienation of public services from the state even as it subsidizes the lifestyles of the rich and famous may further alienate people from a polity whose legitimacy rested tenuously on its material relevance to everyday life.

It is not difficult to spin disaster scenarios for Yemen in the late 1990s. Already economic, social, political, and military circumstances are conducive to instability. Structural adjustment in the externally financed state sector, porous borders, continued Saudi antipathy, and a well-armed population spread out over a wide, rugged terrain all contain possibilities for upheaval. The ruling coalition now comprising social conservatives, technocrats, and the security establishment is haunted by many ghosts. Based on the record of the past half-century, the possibility that factions within this coalition will fight over the spoils of state cannot be ruled out. The most obvious of several fault lines just below the surface is the interface between the secular pragmatists and the religious ideologues within the ruling coalition. On the other hand, the military-commercial elite might cloak itself with religious piety. If the economy continues to contract, a clear potential exists for eruptions of frustration among urban youth and an escalation of ordinary as well as political criminality. Unfortunately, the combination of painful economic reforms, sagging world prices for oil and gas, and one of the world's highest population growth rates do not bode well for the economy. Whereas past liberalizations have coincided with economic optimism, recessions have tended to bring repression. Moreover, the potential for upheavals elsewhere in the Peninsula affecting internal affairs in Yemen is greater than at any time in this century. Finally, given their sixty-some-year history, the possibilities for an entanglement between Yemen and Saudi Arabia are too complex and numerous to list in the conclusion to this book.

Yet a potential does exist for society to help civilize the state. In the realm of ideas, scores of twentieth-century Yemeni writers have addressed the potential for representative, fair, constitutional governance in their country. Sometimes polemical, often allegorical, revolutionary and post-revolutionary nationalist political prose and poetry are rich with ruminations on problems of democratization. Serious students of Islamic and Latin legal systems, Arab and Yemeni historiography, Greek philosophy, Western literature, Marxist social theory, and third world revolutionary movements have generated a significant body of political literature where, at the very least, liberty, equality, and justice are recurrent themes. In the literary imagination, if not in reality, these ideas are alive. For many people the important concepts from Islamic and/or tribal practice have to do with constitutionalism, dignity, non-violence, civic conscience, justice, and judicial and scholarly independence. Some "foreign" ideas such as peaceful transfer of power and rights of legal representation are well on their way to being internalized as ideals.

Institutionally, politically, and materially, past civic projects have left their legacies. Private schools and other services have played an important role in every political era, and the struggle for political control of education continues. Though elections themselves do not necessarily mean democratic practice, and may only serve to legitimize military rule, the holding of parliamentary elections seems reasonably well routinized, and rights of adult men and women to vote and campaign have been recognized. Whereas previous Sana'a administrations have casually dismissed constitutions, now much ado is made of constitutional governance. There are several legal, historically rooted, autonomous opposition parties and newspapers. None of these conditions obtains elsewhere in the Peninsula. Attorneys, male and female, are practicing law, and greater recourse is made to the courts than previously. Legal scholarship is directed toward codification and procedure. Some professional syndicates have stood the test of time, yet will play an increasing role as legal, medical, and engineering practices are privatized. A tenacious press and a nascent human rights movement attempt to define and defend basic rights and liberties. These may be weak defenses against more powerful states, but bankrupt regimes without substantial foreign support sometimes have to make concessions to domestic constituencies. The administration of a debt-ridden, unstable, recently created nation-state can ill afford permanently to alienate private investors and liberal intellectuals, not to mention women, Socialists, independents, Southerners, Bakīl, *sayyids*, Shāfiʿīs, Afro-Yemenis, and the large restive group of semi-employed migrant-returnees: for these are the overwhelming majority. A stable state will have to expand its social base and create an attractive climate for investment. To the extent that they constitute themselves within the body politic, the government may well be forced to negotiate with investors, localities, professionals, exiles, civic and political groups, and the public at large.

Indeed, the fact is that for all its troubles Yemen is today relatively open by Arab, especially Arabian Peninsula, standards. Most neighboring countries muzzle unofficial parties and publications; many prolong martial law for years; some torture and murder large numbers of citizens; some prohibit women from driving, voting, or practicing law; several have never held elections. Yemen has a constitution that enunciates some basic rights and freedoms, an elected legislature, a certain degree of political and civic pluralism, courts that tend to protect the law. Foreign and native researchers and human rights investigators are given greater latitude than in most countries of the region, and Yemenis are remarkably candid in conversation. American and Dutch diplomats judge the human rights abuses to be petty and trivial rather than massive and brutal. Among Arab countries it offers greater hope for democratization in the medium term than most.

Over the past couple of generations there has been a certain uneven, incomplete, even stunted progress toward constitutional, representative government, and it has been generated for the most part internally, from civil society. Foreign influence has hardly promoted democratization: the British did not do so in Aden or the protectorates; the USSR and other donors did not do so during the cold war; regional donors are explicitly anti-republican and anti-democratic; and since the Gulf War Western donors have pressed for normalization of relations with repressive monarchies and rescheduling of debt more assiduously than they have clamored for elections or human rights. Moreover, progressive or populist moments notwithstanding, regimes have never articulated a vision, advanced a program, or evidenced a commitment for genuine democratization, liberalization, or even consultation. If neither foreign pressure nor enlightened leadership explain the relative pluralism and tolerance of the Yemeni polity in the mid-1990s, then the logical deduction is that civic pressures, although cumulative rather than momentous, are responsible.

Even if, in the coming decade, a regime continues to squander public resources, manages to assert totalitarian control, or brings the country to war, these conditions would not in themselves disprove the theoretical point of this study about the adaptability and resiliency of Yemeni civil society. Although German, Italian, Irish, American, Argentine, and South African social theorists certainly grapple with the systemic conditions that have engendered political extremism and societal violence, they do so in the hope of discovering both the causes of brutality and the possibility of tolerance. Like citizens of other parts of the world, Yemenis will have learned that legal rights and democratic liberties are won, not granted. If as outsiders we corroborate the contention of Arab dictators that violence, misogyny, and repression are "customary" then we collaborate in their project to suppress democratic impulses. My own close personal observation of twenty years of events in Yemen testifies that to the contrary people are always working toward something better. While nothing documented in this book by any means guarantees a future more democratic, rule-bound, open polity in Yemen, neither should we underestimate the dialectical potential for society to "invent democracy" and eventually bridge "epistemic gulfs."

Endnotes

1 CIVIL SOCIETY IN COMPARATIVE PERSPECTIVE

1 For a review of the debates and the issues, see Augustus Richard Norton, "Introduction," in Augustus Richard Norton (ed.), *Civil Society in the Middle East*, vol. I, Leiden: E. J. Brill, 1995, pp. 1–25; and Saad Eddin Ibrahim, "Civil Society and Prospects of Democratization in the Arab World," in ibid., vol. I, pp. 27–54.

2 See Edward N. Muller and Mitchell A. Seligson, "Civic Culture and Democracy: The Question of Casual Relationships," *American Political Science Review*, 88, 3, September 1994, 635–52.

3 Ernest Gellner, "From the Ruins of the Great Contest: Civil Society, Nationalism, and Islam," *Times Literary Supplement*, March 13 1992, 15, reprinted in *Civil Society*, 7, July 1992, 12–16.

4 Samuel P. Huntington, "The Clash of Civilizations," *Foreign Affairs*, 72, 3, Summer 1993, 22–49.

5 For a critical review, see Yahya Sadowski, "The New Orientalism and the Democracy Debate," *Middle East Report*, 183, July–August 1993, 14–21, 40.

6 See esp. Robert Bianchi, *Unruly Corporatism: Associational Life in Twentieth-Century Egypt*, New York: Oxford University Press, 1989; and Nazih N. Ayubi, "Withered Socialism or Whither Socialism The Radical Arab States as Populist–Corporatist Regimes," *Third World Quarterly*, 13, 1, 1992, 89–105. This is quite different from the way anthropologists use the notion of "corporate" groups to describe the unit of cohesion in the moral economy. The political scientists' use of the term is borrowed from Latin American politics, where it generally refers to right-wing authoritarian regimes allied with business interests.

7 Mohamed Said El-Ashmawy, "Islamic Government and Civil Society," *Al-Ahram Weekly*, October 29–November 4 1992, Cairo.

8 Mustapha K. al-Sayyid, "A Civil Society in Egypt" *The Middle East Journal*, 47, 2, Spring 1993, 228–216.

9 Sa'ad al-Dīn Ibrāhīm,"al-Mujtama' al-Madanī wa-l-taḥawwul al-dīmuqrāṭī fī-al-waṭan al-'Arabī," *al-Ḍīmuqrāṭīyya*, 1, December 1991, 8–17 contrasts these formal associations with either state or "*ahlī*" institutions. See also Sami Zubaida, "Islam, the State and Democracy: Contrasting Conceptions of Society in Egypt," *Middle East Report*, 179, November–December 1992, 2–10.

10 Amānī Qindīl, "al-Jam'iyyāt al-ahliyya wa-l-mujtama' al-madanī," *al-Dīmuqrāṭiyya*, 2, February 1992, 51.

11 Munā Makram 'Ubayd, "Kayf yu'addī al-mujtama' al-madanī dawran fī-l-tanmiya." *al-Mujtama' al-madanī*, May 1992, 12–13.

12 Ḥilmī Sha'rāwī, "Mulāḥaẓāt ḥawl ḥuqūq al-insān al-jamā'iyya wa-l-ijtimā'iyya," *Ḥuqūq al-insān wa-ta'khīr Miṣr*, Cairo: Legal Research and Resources Center for Human Rights, n.d., esp. 199–200, 218–20.

13 Mustafa Kamil al-Sayyid, "Non-Governmental Organizations, Political Development and the State with a Special Reference to Egypt," paper presented to the Conference on the Role of Arab and Middle East Non-Governmental Organizations in National Development Strategy, Cairo, April 1–3 1993.

14 Giuseppe Di Palma, "Why Democracy Can Work in Eastern Europe," in Larry Diamond and Marc F. Plattner (eds.), *The Global Resurgence of Democracy*, Baltimore: Johns Hopkins University Press, 1993, pp. 257–67 criticizes what he calls the "language of prerequisites," the naive view that political will is necessary and sufficient for political liberalization.

15 Goran Hyden, *Beyond Ujamaa in Tanzania: Underdevelopment and an Uncaptured Peasantry*, Berkeley: University of California Press, 1980; Suzanne Berger, *Peasants against Politics: Rural Organizations in Brittany, 1911–1967*, Cambridge, Mass.: Harvard University Press, 1972.

16 Jean Francois Bayart, "Civil Society in Africa," in Patrick Chabal (ed.), *Political Domination in Africa: Reflections on the Units of Power*, trans. P. Chabal, Cambridge: Cambridge University Press, 1986, pp. 111–12.

17 Ibid., pp. 118, 124.

18 Naomi Chazan, "Africa's Democratic Challenge: Strengthening Civil Society and the State," *World Policy Journal*, 9, 2, 1992, 281–82.

19 Mahmood Mamdani, "Africa: Democratic Theory and Democratic Struggles – Clash between Ideas and Realitiesṭ" *Dissent*, Summer 1992, 312–18.

20 Donal B. Cruise O'Brien, "Wails and Whispers: The People's Voice in West African Muslim Politics," in Chabal (ed). *Political Domination in Africa*, pp. 71–83.

21 Richard Joseph, "Africa: The Rebirth of Political Freedom," in Diamond and Plattner (eds.), *The Global Resurgence of Democracy*, p. 314.

2 TWENTIETH-CENTURY STATES AND ECONOMIES

1 Fred Halliday, *Arabia without Sultans*, London: Penguin, 1974.

2 R. J. Gavin, *Aden under British Rule, 1839–1967*, London: C. Hurst, 1975, pp. 101–02.

3 Tom Little, *South Arabia: Arena of Conflict*, London: Praeger, 1968, p. 124. See also Stanford Research Institute, *Area Handbook for the Peripheral States of the Arabian Peninsula*, Washington, D.C.: US Government Printing Office, 1971, pp. 75–76.

4 Gavin, *Aden under British Rule*, p. 322.

5 Tareq Y. Ismael and Jacqueline S. Ismail, *PDR Yemen: Politics, Economics and Society*, London: Frances Pinter, 1986, pp. 79–80.

6 See *Aden: Report for the years 1957 and 1958*, London: Her Majesty's Stationery Office, 1961, pp. 56–61.
7 Little, *South Arabia*, pp. 15–16, 29.
8 International Fund of Agricultural Development, *Report of the Special Programming Mission to People's Democratic Republic of Yemen* (Rome, IFAD: June 1985), p. 67.
9 *Aden: Report for the Years 1957 and 1958*, pp. 129–30; see also Robin Bidwell, *The Two Yemens*, Boulder: Longman, Westview Press, 1983, pp. 90–91.
10 Little, *South Arabia*, p. 128.
11 *Aden: Report for the Years 1957 and 1958*, pp. 120–23.
12 For further analysis, see Muhammad Ahmad Zabarah, *Yemen: Tradition vs. Modernity*, New York: Praeger, 1982.
13 Sheila Carapico and Richard Tutwiler, *Yemeni Agriculture and Economic Change*, Milwaukee: American Institute for Yemeni Studies, 1981, pp. 31–42. See also Sheila Carapico, "Yemeni Agriculture in Transition," in Keith McLachlan and Peter Beaumont (eds.), *The Agricultural Development of the Middle East*, London: Wiley Press, 1986.
14 Hans Steffen et al., *Final Report of the Airphoto Interpretation Team of the Swiss Technical Cooperation Service*, Zurich, 1978, pp. I/109–I/110; Mohamed Said El Attar, *Le sous-développement économique et social du Yémen: perspectives de la révolution yéménite*, Algiers: Editions Tiers-Monde, 1964, pp. 89–99.
15 See John Baldry, "The Anglo-Italian Rivalry in Yemen and 'Asir, 1900–1934," *Die Weld des Islams*, 17, 1-4, 1977, 155–93; Ibrahim al-Rashid, *Yemen under the Rule of Imam Ahmad*, Chapel Hill: Documentary Publications, 1985, pp. 115–16.
16 For further discussion, see Sheila Carapico, "Autonomy and Secondhand Oil Dependency of the Yemen Arab Republic," *Arab Studies Quarterly*, 10, 2, Spring 1988, 193–213.
17 Nadav Safran, *Saudi Arabia: The Ceaseless Quest for Security*, Ithaca: Cornell University Press, 1988, pp. 282, 284.
18 Joe Stork, "Socialist Revolution in Arabia: A Report from the People's Democratic Republic of Yemen," *MERIP*, 15, March 1973, 1–25.
19 *Aden: Report for the Years 1957 and 1958*, pp. 35–40.
20 See Robert W. Stookey, *South Yemen: A Marxist Republic in Arabia*, Boulder: Westview, 1982, pp. 69–70; Fred Halliday, "Yemen's Unfinished Revolution: Socialism in the South," *MERIP*, 181, October 1979, 3–20.
21 Naguib A. R. Shamiry, "The Judicial System in Democratic Yemen," in B. R. Pridham (ed.), *Contemporary Yemen: Politics and Historical Background*, London: Croom Helm, 1984, pp. 175–94.
22 Maxine Molyneux, "Legal Reform and Socialist Revolution in Democratic Yemen: Women and the Family," *International Journal of the Sociology of Law*, 13, 1985, 147–72; Maxine Molyneux, "The Law, the State and Socialist Policies with Regard to Women: The Case of the People's Democratic Republic of Yemen, 1967–1990," in Deniz Kandiyoti (ed.), *Women, Islam, and the State*, Philadelphia: Temple University Press, 1991, pp. 237–71.
23 See Brinkley Messick, "Prosecution in Yemen: the Introduction of the *Niyaba*," *IJMES*, 15, 1983, 507–18.

24 See Isam Ghanem, *Yemen: Political History, Social Structure and Legal System*, London: Arthur Brobsthain, 1981, esp. pp. 14–19.

25 Both figures from International Fund for Agricultural Development, *Report of the Special Programming Mission to People's Democratic Republic of Yemen*, Rome: IFAD, June 1985, p. 8, where import and remittance figures are cited as evidence of the unexpected "openness" of the PDRY economy.

26 John M. Cohen and David B. Lewis, "Capital Surplus, Labor Short Economies: Yemen as a Challenge to Rural Development Strategies," *American Journal of Agricultural Economics*, 1979, 523–28. See also Jon Swanson, "Some Consequences of Migration for Rural Economic Development in the Yemen Arab Republic," *Middle East Journal*, 33, 1, 1979, 34–45, and his "Emigrant Remittances and Local Development: Cooperatives in the Yemen Arab Republic," in B. R. Pridham (ed.), *Economy, Society, and Culture in Contemporary Yemen*, London: Croom Helm, 1985, pp. 132–46.

27 On these issues, see J. S. Birks, C. H. Sinclair, and D. A. Socknat, "Aspects of Labor Migration from North Yemen," *Middle Eastern Studies*, 17, 1, 1981, 49–63; and their *Arab Manpower*, New York: St. Martin's Press, 1980; Fred Halliday, *Arabs in Exile: Yemeni Migrants in Urban Britain*, London: I. B. Tauris, 1992.

28 See Shelagh Weir, *Qat in Yemen: Consumption and Social Change*, London: British Museum Publications, 1985.

29 Ilhām Muḥammad Māni', *al-Aḥzāb wa-l-tanẓīmāt al-siyāsiyya fi-al-Yaman (1948-1993): dirāsa taḥlīliyya*, Silsilat Kitāb al-Thawābit, al-Thawābit, 1994, pp. 176–79.

30 Ibid., p. 182.

31 See Fred Halliday, "Catastrophe in South Yemen: A Preliminary Assessment," *Middle East Report*, 16, 2, March–April 1986, 37–39; Jean Gueyras, "The Last Days of 'Ali Nasir," *Middle East Report*, 16, 4, July–August 1986, 37–40.

32 For further background and details, see Robert D. Burrowes, "Prelude to Unification: The Yemen Arab Republic, 1962-1990," *International Journal of Middle East Studies*, 23, 1991, 483–506, and his "Oil Strike and Leadership Struggle in South Yemen: 1986 and Beyond," *The Middle East Journal*, 43, 3, 1989, 437–54.

33 Amnesty International, "Yemen: Unlawful Detention and Unfair Trials of Members of the Former National Democratic Front," 26 August 1993.

34 Ismael and Ismail, *PDR Yemen*, p. 65.

35 Sheila Carapico, "The Economic Dimension of Yemen Unity," *Middle East Report*, 184, September/October 1993, 9–14.

36 Saeed Abdul Khair Al-Noban, "Education for Nation-Building – Experience of the People's Democratic Republic of Yemen," in Pridham (ed.), *Contemporary Yemen*, pp. 102–23.

37 World Bank, *Yemen Arab Republic, Current Position and Prospects*, Washington, D.C.: Country Economic Memorandum, Report No. 5621-YAR, 1984.

38 Gerd Nonneman, *Development, Administration, and Aid in the Middle East*, New York: Routledge, 1988, p. 103; "Merger Proves an Attractive Option," *MEED*, January 19 1990.

39 See Fred Halliday, "Moscow's Crisis Management: The Case of South

Yemen," *Middle East Report*, 151, 18, 2, March–April 1988, 18–22; Norman Cigar, "Soviet–South Yemeni Relations: The Gorbachev Years," *Journal of South Asian and Middle Eastern Studies*, 12, 4, Summer 1989, 3–38.

40 Data on "Percentage of External Public Loans from Major Donors" released by the Bank of Yemen, Aden, December 12 1983; and the Central Yemen Bank, Sana'a, June 30 1987, YAR, are several years apart, but this makes little difference in the long time frame for accumulated debt. The data is consistent with the report of the World Bank, *World Debt Tables 1986–87 Edition*, Washington, D.C., 1987, pp. 410, 414, which also shows nearly identical official credits of about $2.5 billion owed by both countries, with the YAR owing more to the multilaterals and the PDRY owning more to other governments, the YAR only resorting to private creditors (for $13 million), and only limited ($10–14 million) resort to IMF credits.

41 Arthur S. Banks, "People's Democratic Republic of Yemen," *Economic Handbook of the World 1981*, New York: McGraw Hill, 1981.

42 International Fund for Agricultural Development, *Report of the Special Programming Mission to PDRY*, pp. 15, 142.

43 International Labor Organization, Economic Commission for Western Asia, *Employment Problems and Policies in the Least Developed Countries (PDRY, Oman, ARY)*, Report 75-389, Beirut, May 12–24 1975.

44 Shahid A. Chaudhry, Abdallah Bouhabib, Michel Cretin, and Elco Greenshields, *People's Democratic Republic of Yemen: A Review of Economic and Social Development*, Washington, D.C.:World Bank, based on a field trip February/March 1978, pp. 9–18.

45 Helen Lackner, *PDR Yemen: Outpost of Socialist Development in Arabia*, London: Ithaca Press, 1985, p. 157, citing Ministry of Planning, Aden, PDRY.

46 International Fund for Agricultural Development, *Report of the Special Programming Mission to PDRY*, p. 139.

47 World Bank, *People's Democratic Republic of Yemen, Special Economic Report: Mid-Term Review of the Second Five-Year Plan, 1981-85*, Washington, D.C.: Report No. 4726-YDR, June 4 1984, pp. 19–32 on agriculture, p. 56 on construction.

48 A. A. El-Sherbini, "An Analysis of Public Sector Management Development in the People's Democratic Republic of Yemen," desk study for UNDP, December 1989.

49 Arab–British Chamber of Commerce, *Focus on Yemen Arab Republic*, conference proceedings, London, November 4 1982.

50 Central Planning Organization (CPO), "Evaluation of the Second Five-Year Plan, April 1987," Sana'a: CPO, 1987, pp. 33–37.

51 Ibid.

52 Kiren Chaudhry, "The Price of Wealth: Business and State in Labor Remittance and Oil Economies," *International Organization*, 43, 1, Winter 1989, 101–45, at 141. A thorough, nuanced analyis of the YAR's financial policies is Kiren Chaudhry, *The Price of Wealth:Oil and Labor Exporters in the International Economy*, Ithaca: Cornell University Press, 1997: see esp. pp. 397–98.

53 Chaudhry, *The Price of Wealth*, pp. 411–15 details both the policies and the effects.

54 Burrowes, "Oil Strike and Leadership Struggle."

55 "CIOMR Signs Production-Sharing Agreement for Joint Yemen Acreage," *Middle East Economic Survey*, March 19 1990; "North, South Yemen Sign Oil Exploration Deal with 5 Foreign Companies," *Gulf News*, March 15 1990. Later, the Soviet firms withdrew and other US and international private corporations bid for rights in their blocks. For details on oil concessions, see Ahmed Noman Kassim Almadhagi, *Yemen and the United States: A Study of a Small Power and Super-State Relationship, 1962–1994*, London: I. B. Tauris, 1996.

56 See Fred Halliday, *Revolution and Foreign Policy: The Case of South Yemen 1967–1987*, Cambridge: Cambridge University Press, 1990; Cigar, "Soviet–South Yemeni Relations."

57 Petroleum Finance Market Intelligence Service, *Yemen: Border Disputes and Relations with Saudi Arabia*, Washington, D.C.: The Petroleum Finance Company, May 1992.

58 Abdu Al-Sharif, "Yemen and Arabian Peninsula Security: Quest for Inclusion, Consequences of Exclusion," paper presented at the 1994 annual meeting of the American Political Science Association, New York, September 1–4 1994; Ahmed Noman Almadhagi, "Yemeni–Saudi Relations in an Era of Democratization," paper presented at the Middle East Studies Association, Washington, D.C., December 6–10 1995.

59 Jār Allāh 'Umar, "*Fī jadaliyyat al-waḥda wa-l-dīmuqrāṭiyya*," mimeo, Aden, n.d.

60 Khālid (Jār Allāh 'Umar), "*Ahamiyyat wa-mawqi' al-ta'addudiyya al-siyāsiyya fī iṭār al-iṣlāḥ al-siyāsiyya*," mimeo, April 1 1989.

61 Qā'id Muḥammad Ṭarbūsh, *Taṭawwur al-niẓām al-intikhābī fī al-Jumhūriyya al-Yamaniyya 1948–1992*, Manshūrāt 26 Sabtambar, 1992, pp. 63–80.

62 Charles Dunbar, "The Unification of Yemen: Process, Politics, and Prospects," *Middle East Journal*, 46, 3, Summer 1992, 456–76, at 465. The PDRY was then still on the US list of terrorist states.

63 F. Gregory Gause III, *Yemeni–Saudi Relations: Domestic Structures and Foreign Influences*, New York: Columbia University Press, 1990, pp. 16–53.

64 In Michael Hudson's terms, the YAR lacked a strategy for legitimization capable of replacing "tribalism and religiosity" with "a civic culture and loyalty to a modernizing central government." Michael C. Hudson, *Arab Politics: The Search for Legitimacy*, New Haven: Yale University Press, 1977, p. 344.

65 F. Gregory Gause III, "Yemeni Unity: Past and Future, *Middle East Journal*, 42, 1, Winter 1988, 33–47; and his "The Idea of Yemeni Unity," *Journal of Arab Affairs*, 6, 1, Spring 1987, 55–81; Mark N. Katz, "Yemeni Unity and Saudi Security," *Middle East Policy*, 1, 1, 1992, 117–35.

66 David Warburton, "The Conventional War in Yemen," *Arab Studies Journal*, 3, 1, 1995, 20–44.

67 International Monetary Fund, "Republic of Yemen 1993 Article IV Consultation," Sana'a, September 18 1993.

68 Chaudhry, "The Price of Wealth," 142, citing an internal memorandum from the Grain Corporation of the Yemen Arab Republic, Sana'a, 1986.

69 *Yemen Times* (*YT*), October 23 1991, pp. 1, 8, 9.

70 *YT*, September 12 1994, p. 7.

71 Jemera Rone and Sheila Carapico for Human Rights Watch, "Yemen: Human Rights in Yemen During and After the 1994 War," 6, 1, New York, October 1994.

72 Previously there had been three rates: an "official" rate of eighteen to the dollar given at the bank or salaries financed in dollars but paid in riyāls, a "diplomatic" rate of twenty-five to the dollar for imports by development agencies and diplomats, and the freely floating rate. See International Monetary Fund, "Republic of Yemen 1993."

3 ISLAM, TRIBES, AND SOCIAL SERVICES

1 For a discussion of the historical development of the sectarian interpretations of Islam in Yemen, see Joseph Chelhod, "L'Islam en Arabie du Sud," in Joseph Chelhod (ed.), *L'Arabie du Sud, histoire et civilisation*, vol. II, *La société yéménite de l'hégire aux idéologies modernes*, Paris: Maisonneuve & Larose: 1984, pp. 13–55; and Etienne Renaud, "Histoire de la pensée religieuse au Yémen," in ibid., pp. 57–68.

2 Patricia Springborg, "Politics, Primordialism, and Orientalism: Marx, Aristotle, and the Myth of Gemeinschaft," *American Political Science Review*, 80, 1, March 1986, 204.

3 Janet L. Abu-Lughod, "The Islamic City – Historic Myth, Islamic Essence, and Contemporary Relevance," *IJMES*, 19, 2, November 1987, 155–76. Passages cited, 162–63 and 169, respectively.

4 Carapico and Tutwiler, *Yemeni Agriculture and Economic Change*.

5 See R. B. Serjeant, "Some Irrigation Systems in Hadramawt," *BSOAS*, 27, 1964, 33–76.

6 Shelagh Weir, "Trade and Tribal Structures in North West Yemen," *Arabie du Sud: Cahiers du Gremano*, 10, 1991, 87–101.

7 'Abd al-Raḥmān al-Bayḍānī, *Asrār al-Yaman,* Sana'a: Kitāb al-Qawmiyya, n.d., pp. 89–103.

8 Manfred W. Wenner, *Modern Yemen 1918–1966*, Baltimore: Johns Hopkins Press, 1967, p. 159.

9 Joseph Chelhod, "Le système juridique traditionnel," in Chelhod (ed.), *L'Arabie du Sud*, vol. III, *Culture et institutions du Yémen*, Paris: Maisonneuve & Larose, 1984, pp. 127–81.

10 The text of the Sacred National Pact, originally published in Cairo, February 20 1948, appears in Ibrahim al-Rashid, *Yemen Enters the Modern World*, Chapel Hill: Documentary Publications, 1984, pp. 152–58.

11 Muhammad Muhsin Khan, *Translation of the Meanings of Sahih al-Bukari*, Gujranwala: Sethi Straw Mills (Conversion), Ltd., n.d., vol II, pp. 302–10, 327, 333–42.

12 al-Attar, *Le sou-développement*, pp. 109–12 on land ownership and pp. 202–03 on commerce. For comparative land ownership data, see Carapico and Tutwiler, *Yemeni Agriculture and Economic Change.*

13 Joseph Kostiner, *The Struggle for South Yemen*, London: Croom Helm, 1984, p. 22.
14 On the local rebellions during this period, see Abdulaziz Kaid al-Msaodi, "The Yemeni Opposition Movement, 1918–1948," PhD dissertation, Georgetown University, 1987, pp. 121–41.
15 al-Tayib Zein Al-Abdin, "The Role of Islam in the State, Yemen Arab Republic (1940–1972)," PhD dissertation, Cambridge University, 1975, esp. pp. 42, 205.
16 See, for a comparative perspective, Juan R. I. Cole, "Rival Empires of Trade and Imami Shi'ism in Eastern Arabia, 1300–1800," *IJMES*, 19, 2, May 1987, 177–204.
17 Brinkley Messick, "Transactions in Ibb: Society and Economy in a Yemeni Highlands Town," PhD dissertation, Princeton University, 1978, pp. 247–48.
18 R. B. Serjeant and Ronald Lewcock, *Sana'a: An Arabian Islamic City*, London: The World of Islam Festival Trust, 1983, pp. 154–59, 293–302.
19 Tomas Gerholm, *Mosque, Market, and Mufraj: Social Inequality in a Yemeni Town*, Stockholm: University of Stockholm Press, 1977, pp. 59–60, 45; Daniel Varisco, "The Adaptive Dynamics of Water Allocation in Al-Ahjur, Yemen Arab Republic," PhD dissertation, University of Pennsylvania, 1982, p. 208.
20 Shelagh Weir, "Tribe, Hijrah and Madinah in North-West Yemen," in Kenneth Brown, Michele Jole, Peter Sluglett, and Sami Zubaida (eds.), *Middle Eastern Cities in Comparative Perspective*, London: Ithaca Press, 1986, pp. 225–39.
21 Hamid al-Iryani, "School and Education – Formation and Development," in Werner Daum (ed.), *Yemen: 300 Years of Art and Civilization in Arabia Felix*, Innnsbruck: Penguin, 1988 pp. 375–85; Wolfgang von Weisel, "Theocracy in the Yaman: Mussolini's Arab Ally," reprinted from *The Near East and India*, March 31 1927, in Reginald Sinclair (ed.), *Documents on the History of Southwest Arabia*, Salisbury, N.C.: Documentary Publications, 1976, pp. 290–94.
22 Martha Mundy, *Domestic Government: Kinship, Community, and Polity in North Yemen*, London: I. B. Tauris, 1995, pp. 26, 44 .
23 Bilfaqīh 'Abdillāh Ḥasan, *Tadhkirat al-bāḥith al-muḥtāṭ fī shu'ūn wa-ta'rīkh al-Ribāṭ*, Maṭba'at al-Fajjāla al-Jadīda, n.d.
24 Messick, *Transactions in Ibb*, p. 336.
25 Timothy Christopher John Morris, "Adapting to Wealth: Social Change in a Yemeni Highland Community," PhD dissertation, University of London, 1985, p. 105.
26 See Hugh Scott, *In the High Yemen*, London: Macmillan, 1942, pp. 83–85, 99, 113, 155, 161; Harold Ingrams, *Arabia and the Isles*, London: John Murray, 1966, pp. 137, 145–46, 167.
27 'Abduh 'Alī 'Uthmān, Ismā'īl Muḥammad al-Faḍlī and 'Abd Allāh al-Wasamī, "al-Ḥaraka al-ta'āwuniyya al-Yamaniyya wa-mashākilhā," study presented to the Sixth Conference of Arab Co-operative Specialists, mimeo, Sana'a, 1975.
28 Aḥmad Muḥammad al-Ḥarbī, "Ẓāhirat al-Ta'āwun al-Ahlī li-l-Taṭwīr wa-

atharhā fi-al-tanmiya al-iqtiṣādiyya wa-l-ijtimā'iyya," *al-Ghad*, 10, 1978, 6–31.

29 Ḥamūd al-'Awdī, *al-Tanmiyya wa-tajribat al-'amal al-ta'āwunī fi-al-Yaman*, Kitāb al-Ghad (2), al-Ghad, n.d. (*c.* 1977), pp. 60–75.

30 Walter Dostal, "Traditional Economy and Society," in Daum (ed.), *Yemen*, pp. 336–66, esp. pp. 336–49.

31 Ibid., esp. pp. 362–63.

32 Ibid., p.365.

33 Paul Dresch, "The Significance of the Course Events Take in Segmentary Systems," *American Ethnologist*, 13, 2, 1986, 310–11.

34 On the role of tribal verse, see Steven C. Caton, *"Peaks of Yemen I Summon": Poetry as Cultural Practice in a North Yemeni Tribe*, Berkeley: University of California Press, 1990. On tribal dance, see Najwa Adra, "Qabyallah: The Tribal Concept in the Central Highlands of the Yemen Arab Republic," PhD dissertation, Temple University, 1982.

35 Yosef Tobi, "Histoire de la communauté juive du Yémen aux XIX et XX siècles," in Chelhod (ed.), *L'Arabie du Sud*, vol. II, pp. 119–37, esp. p.128. See also Yehuda Nini, *The Jews of the Yemen, 1800–1914*, Chur: Harwood, 1991, pp. 89–135.

36 Liliane Kuczynski, "Les juifs du Yémen: approche ethnologique," in Chelhod (ed.), *L'Arabie du Sud*, vol. III, pp.295–301.

37 Shelomo Dov Goitein, "Portrait of a Yemenite Weavers' Village," *Jewish Social Studies*, 17, 1, 1955, 1–16.

38 Thomas B. Stevenson, *Social Change in a Yemeni Highlands Town*, Salt Lake City: University of Utah Press, 1985, pp. 47–49, 53–54.

39 al-Bayḍānī, *Asrār al-Yaman*, p. 100.

40 A. S. Bujra, "Political Conflict and Stratification in Hadramaut," *Middle Eastern Studies*, 4, 3, July 1967, 355–75.

41 R. B. Serjeant, "Historians and Historiography of Hadramawt," *BSOAS*, 1962, 239–61, at 249.

42 Nājī, Sulṭān, "Dawr al-jam'iyyāt al-iṣlāḥiyya wa-l-nawādī fī-al-mujābaha al-siyāsiyya al-ta'līmiyya fī 'Adan khilāl fatrat tab'iyyathā li-l-Hind (1939–1937)," *al-Tarbiya al-Jadīda*, September/December 1982, 3–15; and chap. 4 of this volume.

43 al-Msaodi, "The Yemeni Opposition Movement," 165–73.

44 J. Leigh Douglas, *The Free Yemeni Movement 1935–1962*, Beirut: The American University in Beirut, 1987, pp. 75–76; see also pp. 99–100.

45 Sālim 'Abd Allāh 'Abd Rabbih and Mund'ī Dayān, *Jabhat al-Iṣlāḥ al-Yāfi'iyya 13 Abrīl 1963–31 Yūlyū 1967 (wa-naẓra fi-al-niẓām al-qabalī al-ladhī sād qadīman fi-al-minṭaqa*, Aden: Mu'assasat 14 Uktūbir, 1992., p. 63.

46 al-Ḥarbī, "Ẓāhirat al-Ta'āwun al-Ahlī li-l-Taṭwīr."

47 Hay'at Taṭwīr al-Ḥujariyya, *Hay'at Taṭwīr al-Ḥujariyya: Thalāth sanawāt min al-binā'*, n.p., 1976.

48 al-Msaodi, "The Yemeni Opposition Movement," 201–03.

49 al-Ḥarbī, "Ẓāhirat al-Ta'āwun al-Ahlī li-l-Taṭwīr."

50 Douglas, *The Free Yemeni Movement*, pp. 167–68.

51 These documents, including plans, receipts, by-laws, and correspondence of the association, were still in a file folder kept at the Hodeida Civil

Employees' Union office in 1979/80. I inspected them and took extensive notes then.

4 COLONIALISM, ACTIVISM, AND RESISTANCE

1 These categories are offered by Muḥammad 'Umar al-Ḥabshī, *al-Yaman al-Janūbī siyāsiyyan wa-iqtiṣādiyyan wa-ijtimā'iyyan*, Beirut: Dār al-Ṭalī'a, 1968, pp. 106–07. For another Yemeni view see Salem Omar Bukair, "The PDRY: Three Designs for Independence," in Pridham (ed.), *Contemporary Yemen*, pp. 63–75.

2 Māni', *al-Aḥzāb wa-l-tanẓīmāt al-siyāsiyya*, pp. 46, 120–25.

3 On colonial policy making, see Karl Pieragostini, *Britain, Aden, and South Arabia: Abandoning Empire*, New York: St. Martin's Press, 1991; Michael Crouch, *An Element of Luck: To South Arabia and Beyond*, London: Radcliffe Press, 1993; Z. H. Kour, *The History of Aden 1839–1872*, London: Frank Cass, 1981.

4 Gavin, *Aden under British* Rule, p. 323. See also pp. 329–31.

5 *Aden: Report for the Years 1957 and 1958*, pp. 86–88.

6 Halliday, *Arabia without Sultans*, pp. 172–73.

7 Pieragostini, *Britain, Aden, and South Arabia*, p. 38.

8 Ibid., p. 62.

9 A. S. Bujra, "Urban Elites and Colonialism: The Nationalist Elites of Aden and South Arabia," *Middle Eastern Studies*, 6, 2, May 1970, 189–210, at 210.

10 Pieragostini, *Britain, Aden, and South Arabia*, p. 68.

11 Ibid., pp. 92–100.

12 On the development of the revolutionary movement, see Halliday, *Arabia without Sultans*; Lackner, *PDR Yemen*.

13 *Laws of Aden*, 1955, vol. I, p. 326. A registration form is provided in the law.

14 *Aden: Report for the Years 1957 and 1958*, pp. 23, 50–53.

15 'Alwī 'Abd Allāh Ṭāhir, "al-Nawādī wa-l-jam'iyyāt fī 'Adan," in Aḥmad Jābir 'Afīf et al. (eds.), *al-Mawsū'a al-Yamaniyya* (*EY*), Sana'a: Mu'assasat al-'Afīf al-Thaqāfiyya, 1992, pp. 970–73.

16 For an analysis in English of al-Shawkānī's work, see Bernard Haykel, "Al-Shawkani and the Jurisprudential Unity of Yemen," *Revue du monde musulman et de la Mediterranée*, 67, 1994, 53–65.

17 Ṭāhir, "al-Nawādī wa-l-jam'iyyāt fī 'Adan."

18 Among the accounts of these activities are Sultan Naji, "The Genesis of the Call for Yemeni Unity," in Pridham (ed.), *Contemporary Yemen*, pp. 240–60, at p. 244; Zaid Mahmoud Abu-Amr, "The People's Democratic Republic of Yemen: The Transformation of Society," PhD dissertation, Georgetown University, 1986, p. 215.

19 Bujra, "Urban Elites and Colonialism."

20 Aḥmad Qā'id al-ṣā'idī, "al-Jam'iyya al-Islāmiyya al-Kubrā," *EY*, p. 324.

21 'Alī Qāsim 'Aqlān, "al-Jabha al-Waṭaniyya al-Mutaḥḥida," *EY*, pp. 317–18.

22 'Alī Qāsim 'Aqlān, "al-Jam'iyya al-'Adaniyya," *EY*, pp. 324–25; Māni', *al-Aḥzāb wa-l-tanẓīmāt al-siyāsiyya*, pp. 48–51.

23 Muḥammad Sālmīn Aḥmad Barqa, "al-Niqābāt," *EY*, pp. 962–63; *Aden: Report for the Years 1957 and 1958*, p. 14.

24 See Halliday, *Arabia without Sultans*, esp. pp. 182–83; Kostiner, *The Struggle for South Yemen*, pp. 43–45.
25 *Aden: Report for the Years 1957 and 1958*, pp. 8–14.
26 Muḥammad Sālmīn Aḥmad Barqa, "al-Mu'tamar al-'Ummālī," *EY*, pp. 932–33.
27 Muḥammad Sālmīn Aḥmad Barqa, "al-Niqābāt al-Sitt (ta'rīf)," *EY*, pp. 962–63.
28 'Umar al-Jāwī, *al-Ṣiḥāfa al-Niqābiyya fī 'Adan, 1958–1967*, Aden: Mu'assasat 14 Uktūbir, n.d., pp. 16–18.
29 Little, *South Arabia*, p. 70.
30 'Alī Qāsim 'Aqlān, "al-Jabha al-Waṭaniyya al-Mutaḥḥida," *EY*, pp. 317–18.
31 Aḥmad Qā'id al-Ṣā'idī, "al-Ittiḥād al-Sha'bī al-Dīmuqrāṭī," *EY*, p. 45.
32 Stork, "Socialist Revolution in Arabia," is the only account that mentions a women's association, in Aden.
33 *Aden: Report for the Years 1957 and 1958*, p. 128.
34 al-Msaodi, "The Yemeni Opposition Movement," pp. 199–201.
35 Robin Bidwell (ed.), *Arabian Personalities of the Early Twentieth Century*, Cambridge: Oleander Press, 1986, pp. 271–73; Gavin, *Aden under British Rule*, p. 225.
36 'Abd Rabbih, *Jabhat al-Iṣlāḥ al-Yāfi'iyya*, pp. 61–67.
37 Ibid., pp.94–101. Note that the author was a leader of the organization.
38 Kostiner, *The Struggle for South Yemen*, p. 27.
39 Bujra, "Political Conflict and Stratification," esp. 360–63.
40 Halliday, *Arabia without Sultans*, p. 179.
41 Kostiner, *The Struggle for South Yemen*, pp. 40–41.
42 Māni', *al-Aḥzāb wa-l-tanẓīmāt al-siyāsiyya*, p. 47; Bidwell, *The Two Yemens*, p. 92.
43 Little, *South Arabia*, p.109.
44 Ṣāliḥ 'Alī Bā Ṣurra, "Intifāḍat talāmīdh wa-ṭullāb madāris madīnat Ghayl Bā Wazīr fī Ḥaḍramawt 1958," *Saba'*, 4, October 1988, 142–53. See also Crouch, *An Element of Luck*, p. 163.
45 A. S. Bujra, "Political Conflict and Stratification in Hadramaut II – Nationalism and the Yemeni Revolution: their effects on the Hadramaut," *Middle Eastern Studies*, 4, 4, October 1967, 1–28.
46 Aḥmad Qā'id al-Ṣā'idī, "Jam'iyyat al-Iṣlāḥ," *EY*, p. 324.
47 Douglas, *The Free Yemeni Movement*, pp. 33–43.
48 Khālid 'Abd al-Jalīl Shahīr, "al-Jam'iyyāt al-Yamaniyya al-Kubrā," *EY*, p. 325; al-Msaodi, "The Yemeni Opposition Movement,", pp. 181–83.
49 See a memorandum from S. Pickney Tuck of the US embassy in Cairo (al-Rashid, *Yemen Enters the Modern World*, pp. 170–74).
50 Ahmad Muhammad al-Shami, "Yemeni Literature in Hajjah Prisons 1367/1948–1374/1955," in R. B. Serjeant and R. C. Bidwell (eds.), *Arabian Studies*, vol. II, London: C. Hurst, 1975, pp. 43–59; see also R. B. Serjeant, "The Yemeni Poet al-Zubayri and his Polemic against the Zaydi Imams," in ibid., vol. V, 1979, pp. 87–130.
51 Khālid 'Abd al-Jalīl Shahīr, "al-Ittiḥād al-Yamanī," *EY*, pp.45–46.
52 Māni', *al-Aḥzāb wa-l-tanẓīmāt al-siyāsiyya*, pp. 52–55. Al-Ḥabshī, *al-Yaman*

al-Janūbī, pp. 113–17 and 132–33, identifies it as part of the "Islamic/reformist current." See also Lackner, *PDR Yemen*, pp. 46–47.

53 Lackner, *PDR Yemen*, p. 36.

54 For a comparison of South Yemen with other Arab countries, see William A. Rugh, *The Arab Press*, Syracuse: Syracuse University Press, 1979.

55 Muḥammad 'Abd al-Malik al-Mutawakkil, "al-Ṣiḥāfa," *EY*, pp. 560–65; 'Ali Mohammad Luqman, "Education and the Press in South Arabia," in Derik Hopwood (ed.), *The Arabian Peninsula: Society and Politics*, London: George Allen & Unwin Ltd., 1972, pp. 255–68.

56 'Umar al-Jāwī, *al-Ṣiḥāfa al-Niqābiyya fī 'Adan*, pp. 18–21, quoting from an interview with ATUC leader 'Abd Allāh al-Aṣnaj. See also Lackner, *PDR Yemen*, pp. 33–34.

57 Halliday, *Arabia without Sultans*, pp. 203–205. See also Crouch, *An Element of Luck*, pp. 193–203.

58 Pieragostini, *Britain, Aden, and South Arabia*, pp. 146–48, 153–57 describes one such occasion, in 1965, when eight Aden labor leaders were arrested; the next time, police rounded up 760 people, 300 of whom were deported and 80 charged with criminal offenses.

59 Ṭāhir, "al-Nawādī wa-l-jam'iyyāt fī 'Adan."

5 SELF-HELP, SOCIAL CAPITAL, AND STATE POWER

1 World Bank, *Yemen Arab Republic Local Development Associations: A New Approach to Rural Development*, Washington, D.C.: March 1981, p. 1.

2 James Wyche Green, *Local Initiative in Yemen: Exploratory Studies of Four Local Development Associations*, report to the US Agency for International Development, Washington, D.C., October 1975, p. 14.

3 David Gow et al., *Local Organizations and Rural Development: A Comparative Reappraisal*, Washington, D.C.: Development Alternatives, Inc., 1979, vol. I, pp. 70–74. The other six countries were Cameroon, Guatemala, Jamaica, Philippines, Peru, and Upper Volta.

4 Among the other reports are Peter G. L. Wass, "The Role of Local Development Associations and the Confederation of Yemeni Development Associations, Yemen Arab Republic," Amman: Middle East Developent Division, Ministry of Overseas Development, August 1976; R. A. Blackmore, "Report on the Establishment of an Agricultural Distribution Cooperative in Sanhan, Sana'a Governorate, YAR," report to CYDA and Irish Concern, Sana'a, November 1976.

5 John M. Cohen, David B. Lewis, Mary Hebert, and Jon C. Swanson, "Development from Below: Local Development Associations in the Yemen Arab Republic," *World Development*, 11–12, 9, 1981, 1039–61. See also David B. Lewis, "Local Development Associations in the Yemen Arab Republic," *Rural Development Participation Review*, 1, 2, 1980, 1–2.

6 Swanson, "Emigrant Remittances," p. 137.

7 Jon C. Swanson and Mary Hebert, *Rural Society and Participatory Development: Case Studies of Two Villages in the Yemen Arab Republic*, Ithaca: Cornell University Rural Development Committee, Yemen Research Program, September 1981, p. 95.

8 Daniel Martin Varisco and Najwa Adra, "Affluence and the Concept of the Tribe in the Central Highlands of the Yemen Arab Republic," in F. Salisbury and E. Tooker (eds.), *Affluence and Cultural Survival*, Washington, D.C.: American Ethnological Society, 1984, pp. 134–49. A direct quote on *jayyish* appears on p. 140.

9 Varisco, "The Adaptive Dynamics of Water Allocation," pp. 344–47.

10 Paul Dresch, "The Northern Tribes of Yemen," PhD dissertation, Oxford University, 1981, p. 203.

11 Dresch, "The Significance of the Course Events Take," 310–11.

12 Mary Herbert, "Interim Field Report: Local Organization and Development in Maghlaf, Hodeidah Governorate," Working Note No. 10, Ithaca: Cornell University Center for International Studies, Yemen Research Program, June 1981.

13 Weir, "Tribe, Hijrah and Madinah," p. 231.

14 Charles Swagman, *Development and Change in Highland Yemen*, Salt Lake City: University of Utah Press, 1988, p. 127. See also his "Tribal Organization, Corporate Groups and Development: Contrasting Examples from the Yemen Arab Republic," paper presented at the Middle East Studies Association Meeting, New Orleans, 1985.

15 Weir, *Qat in Yemen*, pp. 20, 87, 122–23.

16 Stevenson, *Social Change in a Yemeni Highlands Town.*

17 Morris, "Adapting to Wealth."

18 Richard Tutwiler, "Ta'awun Mahwit: A Case Study of a Local Development Association in Highland Yemen," in Louis J. Cantori and Iliya Harik (eds.), *Local Politics and Development in the Middle East*, Boulder: Westview, 1984, pp. 166–92.

19 Richard Tutwiler, "Tribe, Tribute, and Trade: Social Class Formation in Highland Yemen," PhD dissertation, State University of New York at Binghamton, 1987.

20 S. Tjip Walker, Sheila Carapico, and John Cohen, "Emerging Rural Patterns in the Yemen Arab Republic: Results of a 21-Community Cross Sectional Study," Ithaca, Cornell University Center for International Studies, Yemen Research Program, March 1983; Sheila Carapico, "The Political Economy of Self-help: Development Cooperatives in the Yemen Arab Republic," PhD dissertation, State University of New York at Binghamton, 1984.

21 CYDA (al-Ittiḥād al-'Āmm li-Hay'āt al-Ta'āwun al-Ahlī li-l-Taṭwīr), published the early legislation in *Kitāb al-ta'āwun: Tashrī'āt wa-maujazāt wa-ṭumūḥat al-'amal al-ta'āwunī fi-al-Jumhūriyya al-'Arabiyya al-Yamaniyya*, CYDA, 1977. See also CYDA, *Hay'āt al-Ta'āwun al-Ahlī li-al-Taṭwīr fi-al-Jumhūriyya al-Yamaniyya,* Silsila ta'kis nashāṭ Hay'āt al-Ta'āwun al-Ahlī li-l-Taṭwīr al-Yamaniyya (2), CYDA,1975; Aḥmad Muḥammad al-Ḥarbī, "Ẓāhirat al-Ta'āwun al-Ahlī li-l-Taṭwīr"; Aḥmad Muḥammad al-'Alīmī, "al-Ta'āwun qadr wa-maṣīr: dirāsa ḥawl ẓāhirat al-Ta'āwun al-Ahlī li-l-Taṭwīr," *al-Ghad*, 11, 1978, 7–31; 'Abd al-Ḥāfiẓ Baḥrān, *Wathīqat al-'amal al-ta'āwunī*, Kitāb al-Ghad (3), Sana'a: CYDA, n.d.

22 'Uthmān, al-Faḍlī, and al-Wasamī, "al-Ḥaraka al-ta'āwuniyya."

23 'Abd al-Wahhāb al-Mu'ayyad, "Fī al-dhikra al-sādisa li-ta'sīs al-Ittiḥād,"

Ittiḥād al-Ta'āwun al-Yamanī, 2, year 1, July 1979; *al-Ta'āwun* newspaper, January 22 1979.

24 See Dirar Abduldaim, "The Cooperative Movement in North Yemen: Beginnings and Development," in al-Saidi (ed.), *The Cooperative Movement in Yemen*, pp. 22–39.

25 Muḥammad al-'Izāzī, "al-Maṣādir al-māliyya li-Hay'āt al-Ta'āwun al-Ahlī", *al-Ghad*, 4, 1977, 45–52 ("The Financial Resources of the LDAs and Some Possibilities for their Development").

26 'Uthmān, al-Faḍlī, and al-Wasamī, "al-Ḥaraka al-ta'āwuniyya," p. 6; Richard Verdery, "Local Development Association Finances and their Borrowing Potential," Washington, D.C.: Institutional Report No. 2, Chemonics, Inc., June 1982.

27 *al-Thawra*, November 27 1978.

28 *al-Thawra*, January 24 1979.

29 Lead story in *al-Thawra*, January 27 1979; text of presidential speech, in *al-Ta'āwun* magazine, October 1979, pp. 20–26. The report on the entire election season was published: CYDA, *al-Ta'āwun: Wathā'iq al-mawsim al-thānī li-l-intikhābāt al-ta'āwuniyya wa-l-mu'tamar al-'āmm al-rābi'*, Silsila ta'kis nashāṭ Hay'āt al-Ta'āwun al-Ahlī li-l-Taṭwīr al-Yamaniyya (7), CYDA, 1979.

30 Law 41 of 1981, in CYDA, *al-Ta'āwun: al-Tashrī'āt al-ta'āwuniyya, al-juz' al-awwal*, CYDA, n.d., pp. 37–44; CYDA bylaws, pp. 45–76, 77–87.

31 *al-Ta'āwun* magazine editorial, no. 174–75, May–June 1982, p. 19.

32 CYDA, *Taqrīr al-amāna al-'āmma li-l-Ittiḥād al-'Āmm 'an a'māl wa-anshiṭat al-Ittiḥād al-'Āmm wa-l-Hay'āt al-Ta'āwuniyya wa-l-jam'iyyāt al-naw'iyya khilāl al-fatra al-intikhābiyya min Yanāyir 1982 ḥattā Yūnyū 1985*, CYDA, 1986.

33 Fritz Peipenberg, "The Cooperative Movement of Yemen: Developments after 1985," in al-Saidi (ed.), *The Cooperative Movement in Yemen*, pp. 55–66.

34 *Wathā'iq al-dawra al-intikhābiyya al-thāniyya li-l-hay'a al-idāriyya li-l-majālis al-maḥaliyya li-l-taṭwīr al-ta'āwunī*, Sana'a: al-Amāna al-'āmma li-l-majālis al-maḥaliyya li-l-taṭwīr al-ta'āwunī, 1989.

35 Aḥmad Muḥammad al-Ḥarbī, *25 'āman min al-'aṭā' al-ta'āwunī fī ẓill Thawrat 26 Sabtambar 1962–1987'*, al-Ittiḥād al-'Āmm li-l-Majālis al-Maḥaliyya li-l-Taṭwīr al-Ta'āwunī, n.d.

36 'Abd Allāh al-Shayba, "al-Taṭawwur al-tashrī'ī li-ḥarakatnā al-ta'āwuniyya," *al-Ghad*, 12, 1978, 77–86; 'Abd Allāh Qāḍī, "al-Waṭan wa-l-ta'āwun," *al-Waṭan*, 3, 4, June 1980, 46–47.

37 al-Shayba, "al-Taṭawwur al-tashrī'ī," 79.

38 'Abd al-Wahhāb al-Mu'ayyad, *al-Ta'awon: Cooperative Work and Its Role in General Education*, Kitāb al-Ta'āwun (8), Sana'a: CYDA, n.d. (in English and Arabic), English p. 12.

39 These early documents were kept on file in the LDA office.

40 "Ānis," in Ittiḥad al-Ta'āwun al-Yamanī, *Ittiḥād al-Ta'āwun al-Yamani*, June 1979.

41 CYDA, *Hay'at al-Ta'āwun al-Ahlī li-l-Taṭwīr*, Kitāb al-Ta'āwun (2), Sana'a: CYDA, 1975, pp. 39–40; 45, 106–07.

42 Khālid ʻAbd al-Raḥmān al-Yūsufī, "al-Taʻāwun fī minṭaqat al-Ḥujariyya," *al-Ghad*, 1, year 2, 1976, 78–86.
43 Hay'at Taṭwīr al-Ḥujariyya, *Hay'at Taṭwīr al-Ḥujariyya*, p. 5.
44 Ibid., pp. 42–44.
45 ʻAlī Ḥamūd ʻAfīf, *Muʻjiza ʻalā jibāl Ḥajja*, al-Sharika al-Yamaniyya li-l-Tibāʻa wa-l-Nashr, 1974.
46 J. E. Peterson, *Yemen: The Search for a Modern State*, Baltimore: Johns Hopkins University Press, 1982, p. 119.
47 Robert D. Burrowes, *The YAR: The Politics of Development 1962–1986*, Boulder: Westview, 1987, pp. 69–70.
48 Peterson, *Yemen: The Search for a Modern State*, p. 50.
49 Burrowes, *The YAR*, p. 71.
50 Ibid., p.72.
51 Ibid., p. 132.
52 ʻAbd al-Wahhāb al-Mu'ayyad, *al-Taʻāwun: al-ʻamal al-taʻāwunī wa-dawrhu fi-al-taʻlī* m *al-ʻāmm*, Silsila taʻkis nashāṭ Hay'āt al-Taʻāwun al-Ahlī li-l-Taṭwīr al-Yamaniyya (8), CYDA, 1979; al-Mu'ayyad, *al-Taʻawon: Co-operative Work*.
53 *al-Thawra*, February 11 1979.
54 Anthony Cordesman, *The Gulf and the Search for Strategic Stability: Saudi Arabia, the Military Balance in the Gulf, and Trends in the Arab–Israeli Military Balance*, Boulder: Westview, 1984, p. 473 says that in 1982 Saudi Arabia increased financial and weapons transfers (automatic rifles and SA-7 missile launchers) to the Zaydī tribes, the Muslim Brotherhood, and the Taʻāwun movement.
55 Gause, *Yemeni–Saudi Relations*, pp. 53–56. See also the UN Economic and Social Council report, ECOSOC/Beirut, "Tax Structure, Government Savings, and Tax Problems: A Case Study of Yemen," New York, United Nations Studies on Development Problems in Selected Countries of the Middle East, 1974.
56 al-Yūsufī, "al-Taʻāwun fī minṭaqat al-Ḥujariyya."
57 "al-Taqrīr al-mālī li-Hay'at al-Taʻāwun li-l-ʻām al-mālī 1977–78," mimeo, CYDA lists the names of twenty-nine non-reporting districts and some reasons for non-reporting, including reluctance to work with the center as well as administrative and accounting problems. In *al-Taʻāwun* newspaper on August 18 1977, a reporter recognized that some non-reporters were inactive, but that others worked outside the formal structure. The account is also based on personal observation.
58 ʻUthmān and al-ʻAwdī, "al-Ḥaraka al-taʻāwuniyya al-Yamaniyya wa-l-Tanmiya."
59 Timothy Christopher John Morris, *The Despairing Developer: Diary of an Aid Worker in the Middle East*, London: I. B. Tauris, 1991.
60 See Horia Mohammad al-Iryani, "The Development of Primary Education and its Problems in the Yemen Arab Republic," in Pridham (ed.), *Economy, Society, and Culture*, pp. 178–89; Peter Clark, "Aspects of Education in the Yemen Arab Republic," in ibid.; pp. 172–77 and Mohamed A. Alkhader, "Low Enrollment of Students at the Faculty of Education and its Effects on the Second Five-Year Plan," in ibid., pp. 190–99.

61 See Zohra Merabet, "A Survey on Development and Management of Water Resources in the Yemen Arab Republic," report to USAID, Sana'a, May 1980; Zohra Merabet, "A Survey of Water Activities under Foreign Assistance in the Yemen Arab Republic," report to USAID, Sana'a, October 1980; Christine Ansell, "The Benefits of Rural Water Projects: An Impact Survey of 5 Villages," report to Transcentury Corporation, Sana'a, October 1981.

62 See Cynthia Myntti, *Women and Development in Yemen Arab Republic*, Eschborn: German Agency for Technical Cooperation (GTZ), 1979; Sheila Carapico and Cynthia Myntti, "A Tale of Two Families: Change in North Yemen 1977–1989," *Middle East Report*, 170, 21, 3, May/June 1991, 24–29.

63 "Qānūn al-idāra al-maḥaliyyah," *al-Jarīda al-rasmiyya*, 8, April 30 1991. See also Peipenberg, "The Cooperative Movement of Yemen."

6 UNITY, PLURALISM, AND POLITICAL PARTICIPATION

1 John P. Entelis, "Civil Society and the Authoritarian Impulse in Algerian Politics: Islamic Democracy vs. The Centralized State," in Norton (ed.), *Civil Society in the Middle East*, vol.II, pp. 45–86 compares events in Algeria to those in Eastern Europe as analyzed by Marcia A.Weigle and Jim Butterfield, "Civil Society in Reforming Communist Regimes: The Logic of Emergence," *Comparative Politics* 25, 1, October 1992.

2 As analyzed by Iris Glosemeyer, "The First Yemeni Parliamentary Elections in 1993: Practicing Democracy," *Orient*, 34, 3, 1995, 439–51.

3 al-Mu'tamar al-Sha'bī al-'Āmm (GPC), *al-Barnāmaj al-intikhābī li-l-Mu'tamar al-Sha'bī al-'Āmm*, al-Mu'tamar al-Sha'bī al-'Āmm, n.d., *c.* 1991. See also Rashād Muḥammad al-'Alīmī and Aḥmad 'Alī al-Bishārī, *al-Barāmij al-intikhābiyya li-l-aḥzāb wa-l-tanẓīmāt al-siyāsiyya fi-al-Jumhūriyya al-Yamaniyya: dirāsa muqārana*, Silsilat Kitāb al-Thawābit, al-Mu'tamar al-Sha'bī al-'Āmm, 1993.

4 al-Janāḥ al-Dīmuqrāṭī li-l-Mu'tamar al-Sha'bī, *Taṣawwurāt ḥawl taf'īl al-Mu'tamar al-Sha'bī*, Abū Ayman, 1992.

5 al-Ḥizb al-Ishtirākī al-Yamanī (YSP), Sikritāriyyat al-Lajna al-Markaziyya, *Mashrū' al-barnāmaj al-siyāsī li-l-Ḥizb al-Ishtirākī al-Yamanī*, Mu'assasat 14 Uktūbir, 1991; and YSP, *al-Barnāmaj al-intikhābī li-l-Ḥizb al-Ishtirākī al-Yamanī*, n.p., n.d.

6 See Paul Dresch and Bernard Haykel, "Stereotypes and Political Styles: Islamists and Tribesfolk in Yemen," *IJMES*, 27, 4, November 1995, 405–31.

7 See interview with Ahmad Muhammad Bin Ali al-Shami (sic), *YT*, July 1 1992, p. 3; party profile, *YT*, April 10 1991; Bernard Haykel, "Hizb al-Haqq and the Doctrine of the Imamate," paper presented to the Middle East Studies Association annual meeting, Washington, D.C., November 1996.

8 al-'Alīmī and al-Bishārī, *al-Barāmij al-intikhābiyya li-l-aḥzāb*, p. 12.

9 Shelagh Weir, "Religious Conflict in the Yemeni Highlands," paper presented to the Middle East Studies Association annual meeting, Washington, D.C., December 1995.

10 The platform is in al-'Alīmī and al-Bishārī, *al-Barāmij al-intikhābiyya li-l-*

aḥzāb, pp. 169–72; text of the communiqué, *al-Shūrā*, March 6 1994, p. 2. Note that there is another very small Islamist party also headed by members of the al-Wazīr family.

11 For the party platform, see Ḥizb Rābiṭat Abnā' al-Yaman (RAY), *al-Khuṭūṭ al-'Arīḍa li-manhaj wa-barnāmaj Ḥizb Rābiṭat Abnā' al-Yaman*, Dār al-Muhājir, 1992.

12 Māni', *al-Aḥzāb wa-l-tanẓīmāt al-siyāsiyya*, p. 226.

13 Interview with Abdullah al-Baraddoni, *YT*, February 19 1992, p. 3. See also interview with Abdulghani Thabit, Secretary-general of Tanzim al-Sha'abi al-Wahdawi al-Nasiri, *YT*, May 13 1992, p. 3.

14 See the profile of the party, *YT*, February 27 1991, p. 2; and the party platform, in al-'Alīmī and al-Bishārī, *al-Barāmij al-intikhābiyya li-l-aḥzāb*, pp. 151–59.

15 *YT*, April 17 1994, p. 3.

16 SEC Information Committee, "Parliamentary Elections 27th April, 1993," pamphlet, Sana'a, n.d. (in English).

17 By May 1, when official results were announced by the SEC, two constituencies remained to be decided.

18 *al-Thawra*, May 3 1993, p. 1. Slightly different figures were published in *al-Quds* (of Jerusalem), May 13 1993, p. 1.

19 al-Ḥizb al-Ishtirākī al-Yamanī, "Natā'ij al-dawra al-intikhābiyya al-barlamāniyya fī 27 Abrīl 1993," Sana'a, n.d.

20 Ḥusayn 'Umar Bā Salīm, *Dalīl al-ṣiḥāfa al-Yamaniyya*, Wizārat al-I'lām, al-Jumhūriyya al-Yamaniyya, 1992.

21 *al-Shūrā*, March 6 1994, p. 9.

22 See, for instance *al-Mīthāq*, February 28 1994.

23 *Ṣawt al-'Ummāl*, July 1 1993, p. 1.

24 The article on which the suit is based appeared in *al-Taṣḥīḥ*, February 22 1993, pp. 1–2.

25 The offending article, *al-Jamāhīr*, August 13 1993; rebuttal, *al-Jamāhīr*, October 11 1993.

26 See a long report on the trial and the verdict, *al-Ṣaḥwa*, October 28 1993, pp. 1, 4, 7.

27 Ra'ūfa Ḥasan al-Sharqī, *al-Tanẓīmāt al-ahliyya: taqrīr li-Mu'tamar al-Tanẓīmāt al-Ahliyya al-'Arabiyya (CIVICUS)*, Jāmi'at Ṣana'ā', 1993, p. 9.

28 Chuck Schmitz, "Economic Reform in the Former PDR Yemen: A View from al-Hauta, Lahj," paper presented at the Middle East Studies Association annual conference, Washington, D.C., December 6–10 1995.

29 The new Yemeni Women's Union published two booklets describing its organization: Ittiḥād Nisā' al-Yaman, al-Maktab al-Tanfīdhī, *Mashrū' al-lā'iḥa al-tafsīriyya li-mashrū' al-niẓām al-dākhilī li-Ittiḥād Nisā' al-Yaman*, Dār al-'Arabī, 1991; and Ittiḥād Nisā' al-Yaman, al-Maktab al-Tanfīdhī, *Mashrū' al-niẓām al-asāsī li-Ittiḥād Nisā' al-Yaman*, Dār al-'Arabī, n.d.

30 *al-Mustaqbal*, August 1 1993, p. 11; *Ṣawt al-'Ummāl*, July 1 1993, p. 1; *YT*, September 2 1992, p. 2, December 23 1992, p. 2.

31 Sharon Beatty, Ahmed No'man al-Madhaji, and Renaud Detalle, *Yemeni NGOs and Quasi-NGOs, Analysis and Directory*, Sana'a: Royal Netherlands Embassy, May 1996. On the Gulf states, see Munira A. Fakhro, "Gender,

Politics and the State in the Gulf Region," paper presented to the American Political Science annual conference, San Franscisco, August 29–September 1 1996.

32 *YT*, January 15 1992, pp. 5, 15.

33 See, for instance, *al-Iṣlāḥ*, July 12 1993, p. 8, July 26 1993, pp. 2, 8; *al-Ṣaḥwa*, August 12 1993, p. 1.

34 Interview with Tariq Sinan Abu Luhum (head of ISWS), *YT*, April 22 1996, p. 3.

35 See *al-Ṣaḥwa*, July 29 1993, p. 2, August 12 1993, p. 1.

36 *YT*, January 8 1992, pp. 3, 14.

37 Aḥmad Jābir 'Afīf et al. (eds.), *al-Mawsū'a al-Yamaniyya* (*Encyclopedia of Yemen*, *EY*), Sana'a: Mu'assasat al-'Afīf al-Thaqāfiyya, 1992.

38 Account of founding in *al-Mustaqbal*, October 10 1993, p. 5.

39 al-Munaẓẓama al-Yamaniyya li-l-Difā' 'an Ḥuqūq al-Insān wa-l-Ḥurriyāt al-Dīmuqrāṭiyya (ODDRL), *al-Munaẓẓama al-Yamaniyya li-l-Difā' 'an Ḥuqūq al-Insān wa-l-Ḥurriyāt al-Dīmuqrāṭiyya: al-Niẓām al-asāsī*, Sana'a, 1992.

40 *Ṣawt al-'Ummāl*, February 13, February 20, February 27, and March 26 1992 covered the story on p. 1.

41 *al-Thawra*, October 9 1993, pp. 1, 2, October 10 1992, p. 1, October 13 1992, p. 1; interview with Judge Hamood al-Hitar, *YT*, January 27 1993, pp. 7, 9; al-Munaẓẓama al-Yamaniyya li-Ḥuqūq al-Insān (YOHR), *Mashrū' al-Niẓām al-asāsī li-al-Munaẓẓama al-Yamaniyya li- Ḥuqūq al-Insān*, Sana'a, n.d. (photocopy).

42 *Ra'y*, September 14 1993, pp. 1, 6; *al-Waḥda*, September 15–21 1993, pp. 1–2.

43 *al-Thawra*, March 2 1994, p. 2; *al-Waḥda*, March 3 1994, p. 1.

44 See for instance the account of YOHR's report on abuses in Aden prison published in *26 September*, March 24 1994, p. 1.

45 "Introduction to NCFE," Sana'a, n.d. (1993) (photocopy); *YT*, February 17 1993, p. 6, March 24 1993, p.1.

46 National Democratic Institute for International Affairs (NDI), *Promoting Participation in Yemen's 1993 Elections*, Washington, D.C.: National Democratic Institute for International Affairs, 1994, p. 22.

47 Ibid., pp. 22–25. See also pp. 122–24.

48 Ibid., p. 27.

49 "Yemeni Committee for Free and Democratic Elections: Constituent Charter," Sana'a, n.d.

50 For accounts of two major YAR conferences of the 1960s, see Aḥmad Qā'id Barakāt, "Mu'tamar 'Amrān," *EY*, pp. 933–34; and his "Mu'tamar Khamir," *EY*, pp. 930–31.

51 Paul Dresch, *Tribes, Government, and History in Yemen*, Oxford: Clarendon Press, 1989, pp. 361–79.

52 Renaud Detalle, "Yémen. Les élections législatives du 27 Avril 1993," *Monde Arabe Maghreb-Mashrek*, 141, July–September 1993, 3–26.

53 *Ra'y*, July 13 1993, pp. 2–3.

54 Anna Wuerth, "The Legal Status of Women in Yemen," report submitted to CID/WID project, Bureau of Applied Research in Anthropology, Tucson,

Ariz.: University of Arizona, March 1994; "Woman [sic] Status in the Legislation of the Republic of Yemen," proposal for a conference, Sana'a, November 12–16 1993. For a scholarly analysis of the subject, see Anna Wuerth, "A Sana'a Court: The Family and the Ability to Negotiate," *Islamic Law and Society*, 2, 3, 1993, 320–38.

55 Sheila Carapico, "Women and Participation in Yemen," *Middle East Report*, 173, November/December 1991, 15.

56 See also Sheila Carapico, "Yemen between Civility and Civil War," in Norton (ed.), *Civil Society in the Middle East*, vol. II, pp. 287–316.

57 Eng Seng Ho, personal communication to the author, February 1997.

58 See the two-page spread in *al-Mustaqbal*, December 22 1991, pp. 6–7; *YT*, December 25 1991, pp. 3, 6.

59 "Waqā'i' mu'tamar Saba' li-l-qabā'il al-Yamaniyyīn fī Wādī Saba'," *al-Taḍāmun*, October 25 1992, 5; see also pp. 3, 4. For other accounts see *YT*, December 6 1992, p. 11; *Ṣawt al-'Ummāl*, December 24 1992, p. 2; interview with Shaykh 'Ali al-Qibli Nimran, *YT*, January 13 1993, pp. 16, 15.

60 *al-Tashīḥ*, February 22 1993, pp. 1–2.

61 See also Paul Dresch, "The Tribal Factor in the Yemeni Crisis," in Jamal S. al-Suwaidi (ed.), *The Yemeni War of 1994: Causes and Consequences*, London: Saqi Books, 1995, pp. 33–55.

62 "The Code of Political Conduct," from the National Conference, Sana'a, September 12–15 1992, in *YT*, September 23 1992, p. 10; "National Conference's Political Communique," *YT*, November 25 1992, p. 8. See also *YT*, August 12 1992, p. 16, August 19 1992, p. 4.

63 *YT*, September 23 1992.

64 *YT*, September 16 1992, p. 10; October 21 1992, p. 10.

65 *YT*, December 2 1992, p. 4.

66 *YT*, December 9 1992, p. 15; interview with Sheikh Abdul-Rahman Ahmed Sabir, *YT* December 2 1992, p. 3 .

67 *YT*, November 18 1992, p. 16.

68 *al-Iṣlāḥ*, January 4 1993, pp. 4–5.

69 *YT*, December 30 1992, p. 4.

70 Mu'tamar al-Waḥda wa-l-Salām, *The Working Papers of the Unity and Peace Conference*, Sana'a, December 27–30 1993 (photocopies of working papers).

71 "Resolutions of the 'Unity and Peace Conference,'" *YT*, 6 January 1993, pp. 7, 11.

72 Hamoud Abdulhameed al-Hitar, "Primary Report on the Yemeni Elections Issued by EPC of the Unity and Peace Conference," Unity and Peace Conference (UPC) Election Protection Committee (EPC), March 5 1993 (English translation: sic).

7 CIVIC RESPONSES TO POLITICAL CRISIS

1 Thomas B. Stevenson, "Yemeni Workers Come Home: Absorbing One Million Migrants," *Middle East Report*, 181, March–April 1993, 15–20; Jeffrey Ian Ross, "Policing Change in the Gulf States: The Effect of the Gulf Conflict," in Otwin Marenin (ed.), *Policing Change, Changing Police*, New York: Garland Publishing, 1996, pp. 79–105; Eric Watkins, "Yemen's Riots

Prompt Talk of Reform,"*Middle East International*, 444, February 19 1993, 18.

2 Names and posts of the initial assignments are in *al-Thawra*, May 31 1993, p. 1.

3 *al-Iṣlāḥ*, July 26 1993, pp. 4–5.

4 *22 Māyū*, August 11 1993, p. 1.

5 *22 Māyū*, August 18 1993, p. 1; *Al-Hayat*, August 19 1993, p. 1.

6 This and the other documents cited below are usefully combined by Iris Glosemeyer, in *Liberalisierung und Demokratisierung in der Republik Jemen, 1990–1994*, Hamburg: Deutsches Orient-Institut, 1995.

7 Ittiḥād al-Quwā al-Waṭaniyya, "Bayān ṣādir 'an Ittiḥād al-Quwā al-Waṭaniyya," n.p., November 14 1993 (photocopy); see also Ittiḥād al-Quwā al-Waṭaniyya "Taqrīr muqaddam min al-lajna al-taḥḍīriyya ilā al-mu'tamar al-ta'sīsī al-awwal li-Ittiḥād al-Quwā al-Waṭaniyya," n.d.

8 *YT*, October 31 1993, pp. 1, 18.

9 *Ṣawt al-'Ummāl*, November 4 1993, p. 1.

10 *al-Waḥda*, November 10 1993, pp. 1, 2, 3, 18.

11 *al-Thawra*, November 4 1993, p. 1.

12 *al-Hayat*, November 28 1993, pp. 1, 4.

13 See Robert D. Burrowes, "The Yemeni Civil War of 1994: Impact on the Arab Gulf States," in al-Suwaidi (ed.), *The Yemeni War of* 1994, pp. 71–80, and Mark N. Katz, "External Powers and the Yemeni Civil War," in ibid., pp. 81–93.

14 For Gulf responses to the Yemeni crisis, see Joseph Kostiner, *Yemen: The Tortuous Quest for Unity, 1990–1994*, London: Chattam House, 1996, pp. 95–105.

15 See, for instance, interviews with 'Alī Nāṣir Muḥammad in *al-Tashīḥ*, October 11 1993, p. 3 and *Ṣawt al-'Ummāl*, October 14 1993. 'Abd Allāh 'Abd al-Majīd al-Aṣnaj of the old FLOSY movement and defeated NDF commander 'Abd Allāh 'Abd al-'Ālim also issued statements on the necessity of dialogue to resolve the political crisis.

16 See *YT*, October 31 1993, pp. 1, 18; *al-Hayat*, November 23 1993, pp. 1, 4.

17 *al-Hayat*, November 24 1993, pp. 1, 4.

18 *al-Hayat*, January 1, 3, 5, 6 1994, pp.1, 4; *al-Sharq al-Awsaṭ*, January 2 1994, pp. 1, 4.

19 For further analysis, see Renaud Detalle, "Pacte d'Amman: L'espoir déçu des yéménites," *Monde Arabe Maghreb-Mashrek*, 145, July–September 1994, 113–22.

20 *al-Thawra*, February 26 1994, p. 1.

21 'Abd al-Wahhab al-Mu'ayyad,column in *al-Wasaṭ*, 115, April 11 1994, pp. 20–23.

22 For an interview in English with Ṭāriq al-Faḍli, see Katherine Roth, "Afghanistan and the Yemeni Jihad: A Surprising visit to Post-war Aden," letter to Peter Bird Martin, Institute of Current World Affairs, Hanover, N.H., November 17 1994.

23 *Ra'y*, August 3 1993, p. 8; *al-Waḥda*, March 6 1994, p. 16.

24 For coverage of this event, see *al-Hayat*, December 24 1993, pp. 1, 4; *YT*, December 26 1993, p. 1; *al-Sharq al-Awsaṭ*, December 24 1993, p. 5, January

8 1994, pp. 1, 4; *al-Waḥda*, January 12 1994, pp. 1, 6; *'Adan*, January 18 1994; *Ṣawt al-'Ummāl*, January 20 1994, p. 3.

25 *al-Sharq al-Awsaṭ*, December 15 1993, pp. 1, 4.

26 *al-Ayyām*, March 16 1994, p. 2; *Ḥaḍramawt*, March 20 1994, pp. 1, 3.

27 *Al-Hayat*, December 23 and 24, 1993, pp. 1, 4; *al-Sharq al-Awsaṭ*, December 24 1993, pp. 1, 4; *YT*, December 26 1993, pp. 1, 5.

28 *al-Mustaqbal*, January 12 1994, p. 5; *al-Shūrā*, February 6 1994, pp. 1, 2; *Ṣawt al-Jabha*, March 1 1994, pp. 1, 2.

29 *al-Mustaqbal*, January 9 1994, p. 1.

30 *Ṣawt al-Jabha*, March 1 1994, p. 2.

31 *Ṣawt al-'Ummāl*, February 3 1994, p. 5.

32 *al-Thawrī*, January 13 1994, pp. 1, 14; *al-Mustaqbal*, January 16 1994, p. 5; *al-Waḥdawī*,' January 18 1994, pp. 1, 5.

33 *Ṣawt al-'Ummāl*, February 3 1994, p. 1; *al-Thawrī*, February 17 1994, pp. 1, 14; *al-Mustaqbal*, February 20 1994, pp. 1, 5; *al-Ayyām*, February 23 1994, pp. 1, 3, March 9 1994, pp. 1, 2; *al-Ḥaqq*, March 5 1994, pp. 1, 4.

34 *al-Thawra*, March 16 1994, p. 2; see also *al-Mustaqbal*, January 9 1994.

35 al-Mu'tamar al-jamāhīrī li-abnā' muḥāfaẓat Ibb, "al-Bayān al-ṣādir 'an al-mu'tamar al-jamāhīrī li-abnā' muḥāfaẓat Ibb," February 5 1994 (photocopy).

36 For instance, the resolutions of the tribes of Banī Jabr and Khawlān al-Ṭiyāl, "Mu'tamar qabā'il Banī Jabr Khawlān al-Ṭiyāl fī suṭūr," *al-Taḍāmun*, January 16 1994 (photocopy).

37 *al-Shūrā*, March 6 1994, pp. 1, 2.

38 *YT*, April 3 1994, p. 20.

39 *Ḥaḍramawt*, March 20 1994, p. 1.

40 *al-Mustaqbal*, March 20 1994, p. 2.

41 For instance, *al-Shūrā*, March 6 1994, pp. 1, 2, March 27 1994, p. 5; *al-Ayyām*, March 9 1994, pp. 1, 2; *al-Waḥda*, March 9 1994, pp. 1, 2; *al-Thawra*, March 11 1994, p. 1; *14 October*, March 23 1994, p. 2; *Ṣawt al-'Ummāl*, March 24 1994, p. 7.

42 Majlis Bakīl al-Muwaḥḥad, "Bayān ṣādir 'an Majlis Bakīl al-Muwaḥḥad," Sana'a, October 14 1993 (photocopy); Mu'tamar Bakīl, "al-Qarārrāt wa-l-tawṣiyāt (li-mu'tamar Bakīl fī Ānis)," n.d. (photocopy); Mu'tamar Bakīl, *Wathā'iq wa-adabiyyāt Mu'tamar Bakīl (Ānis) fī al-fatra 12–13 Yanāyir 1994*, n.p., 1994.

43 Warburton, "The Conventional War in Yemen."

44 Chuck Schmitz, "Civil War in Yemen: The Price of Unity?" *Current History*, January 1995, 33–36.

45 Sheila Carapico, "From Ballotbox to Battlefield: The War of the Two 'Alis," *Middle East Report*, 25, 4, 190, September–October 1994, 27.

46 "Yemeni Reform Grouping Political Platform," FBIS-NES-95-141-S, July 24 1975.

47 *26 September*, July 28 1994, pp. 1, 7.

48 "Memorandum to All Interested Parties from the Union of Yemeni Popular Forces (UYPF)," August 28 1995 (photocopy, issued in English in Washington, D.C. and Arabic in Sana'a).

49 Amnesty International Urgent Action Appeal, UA194/95: Yemen, August 9 1995.

50 "Memoranda to the President of the Yemeni Republic and the President [prime minister] and Members of the Council of Ministers from the Opposition Parties," Sana'a, July 19 1995 (in Arabic).

51 *YT*, April 22 1996, pp. 1, 5.

52 *YT*, June 17 1996, pp. 1, 5.

53 ODDRL, *al-Taqrīr al-sanawī li-'āmm 1994*, Aden: al-Munaẓẓama al-Yamaniyya li-l-Difā' 'an Ḥuqūq al-Insān wa-l-Ḥurriyāt al-Dīmuqrāṭiyya, March 1995; ODDRL, *al-Taqrīr al-sanawī li-'āmm 1995*, Aden: al-Munaẓẓama al-Yamaniyya li-l-Difā' 'an Ḥuqūq al-Insān wa-l-Ḥurriyāt al-Dīmuqrāṭiyya, 1996 (draft).

54 *The Constitution of the Republic of Yemen and Yemen Human Rights Organization the Basic Statute*, Yemen Human Rights Organization Publication No. 1, Sana'a, January 1995.

55 Rone and Carapico, "Human Rights in Yemen."

56 Yemeni Committee on Human Rights, *Yemen Human Rights Report*, 1, 2, Washington, D.C., July 1996.

8 POLITICAL MOVEMENTS, CULTURAL TRENDS, AND CIVIC POTENTIAL

1 *al-Thawra*, January 9 1995; *al-Hayat*, January 9 1995.

Glossary

ahl al-sūq	market people
ahlī	local, private, primordial
'āmil	governor, administrator
amn	security
'aqīl	"trusted one," trustee, supervisor
awqāf	endowments, endowments authority
baladiyya	municipality
bayān	resolutions, declarations
bayyā'	peddler
dīwān	sitting-room, reception room
fawḍā	chaos
fiqh	jurisprudence
al-ḥaraka al-ta'āwuniyya	cooperative movement, self-help movement
ḥaram, *hijra*, or *ḥawṭa*	sanctuary; protected space
Ḥāshid, Bakīl	major tribal confederations of Northern highlands
hay'at al-ta'āwun al-ahlī li-l-taṭwīr	local cooperative development association; LDA
hay'at al-taṭwīr	development board, development association
ḥiwār	dialogue, negotiations
ḥuqūq al-insān	human rights
i'āna	aid, mutual aid
iltizām	literally "obligation," system of tax and levy assessment
iqṭā'ī	feudal, tribute-collecting
i'tiṣām	demonstration, sit-in
ittiḥād	federation, confederation, union
jam'iyya khayriyya	welfare association
jayyish	collective labor, conscription, work-team
kuttāb	traditional grammar school
ma'had	institute, academy

majlis	council
Majlis al-Nuwwāb	Chamber of Deputies
Majlis al-Shūrā	Consultative Council, Senate
maqyal	discussion, salon, qāt session
masākīn	the poor, commoners
al-Mīthāq al-Waṭanī	National Pact
musā'ada	assistance
muzayyin	crier, entertainer
nādī	club
nāḥiya	district
niẓām	order
qabyala	tribal spirit, ideology
qaḍā'	sub-province
qāḍī	Islamic scholar
ra'iyya	peasant, tax-payer
ṣadaqa	charity, philanthropy
salafī	puritan, puritanical
sayyid	(also Hashemite or *sharīf*) lineage of the Prophet
shabāb	youth
Shāfi'ī	Yemeni Sunnī sect of Islam
shaykh	tribal or local leader; scholar
shūrā	consultation
sūq	market
ta'addudiyya	pluralism
ta'āwun	cooperation, cooperative
al-ta'āwun al-ahlī	local cooperation, comunity cooperative
tabarru'āt	donations, contributions
'ulamā'	scholars, students of Islamic law
'urf	(or *ḥukm 'urfī*) customary or tribal law
'uzla	sub-district
wādī	valley, river-bed
waqf	pious endowment
waqfiyya	endowment document
waqf khayrī	welfare endowment
zakat	tithe
Zaydī	Yemeni Shī'a sect of Islam

Bibliography

ARABIC SOURCES

'Abd al-Dā'im, Ḍarrār, "Hay'at taṭwīr minṭaqat al-Mukhā bayn al-qadīm wa-l-jadīd," *al-Ghad*, 3, 1977, 98–102.

'Abd Rabbih, Sālim 'Abd Allāh wa-Mund'ī Dayān, *Jabhat al-Iṣlāḥ al-Yāfi'iyya 13 Abrīl 1963–31 Yūlyū 1967 (wa-naẓra fi-al-niẓām al-qabalī al-ladhī sād qadīman fi-al-minṭaqa*, Aden: Mu'assasat 14 Uktūbir, 1992.

'Afīf, Aḥmad Jābir et al. (eds.), *al-Mawsū'a al-Yamaniyya*, Sana'a: Mu'assasat al-'Afīf al-Thaqāfiyya, 1992 (*Encyclopedia of Yemen*, *EY*).

'Afīf, 'Alī Ḥamūd, *Mu'jiza 'alā jibāl Ḥajja*, al-Sharika al-Yamaniyya li-l-Ṭabā'a wa-l-Nashr, 1974.

al-'Alīmī, Aḥmad Muḥammad, "al-Ta'āwun qadr wa-maṣīr: dirāsa ḥawl ẓāhirat al-ta'āwun al-ahlī li-l-taṭwīr," *al-Ghad*, 11, 1978, 7–31.

al-'Alīmī, Rashād Muḥammad and Aḥmad 'Alī al-Bishārī, *al-Barāmij al-intikhābiyya li-l-aḥzāb wa-l-tanẓīmāt al-siyāsiyya fi-al-Jumhūriyya al-Yamaniyya: dirāsa muqārana*, Silsilat Kitāb al-Thawābit, al-Mu'tamar al-Sha'bī al-'Āmm, 1993.

'Aqlān, 'Alī Qāsim, "al-Jabha al-Waṭaniyya al-Mutaḥḥida," *EY*, pp. 317–18.

"al-Jam'iyyā al-'Adaniyya," *EY*, pp. 324–25.

al-Aswadī, Muḥammad 'Alī, *Ḥarakat al-aḥrār al-Yamaniyyīn wa-l-baḥth 'an al-ḥaqīqa*, n.p., 1987.

Aṭrāf ḥiwār al-quwā al-siyāsiyya li-binā' al-dawla al-Yamaniyya al-ḥadītha, *Wathīqat al-'ahd wa-l-ittifāq*, Manshūrāt al-Thawrī, 1994.

al-'Awdī, Ḥamūd, *'An al-dīmuqrāṭiyya wa-l-dīmuqrāṭiyya al-ta'āwuniyya fi-al-Yaman*, Kitāb al-Ghad (4), al-Ghad, n.d.

al-Jadīd fi-al-tanmiya wa-'alāqathā bi-l-turāth: dirāsa 'an al-Yaman wa-l-buldān al-nāmiya, n.p., 1976.

al-Tanmiya wa-tajribat al-'amal al-ta'āwunī fi-al-Yaman, Kitāb al-Ghad (2), al-Ghad, n.d.

Bā Salīm, Ḥusayn 'Umar, *Dalīl al-Ṣiḥāfa al-Yamaniyya*, Wizārat al-I'lām, al-Jumhūriyya al-Yamaniyya, 1992.

Bā Ṣurra, Ṣāliḥ 'Alī, "Intifāḍat talāmīdh wa-ṭullāb madāris madīnat Ghayl Bā Wazīr fī Ḥaḍramawt 1958," *Saba'*, 4, October 1988, 142–53.

Baḥrān, 'Abd al-Ḥāfiẓ, *Wathīqat al-'amal al-ta'āwunī* , Kitāb al-Ghad (3), Sana'a: CYDA, n.d.

Barakāt, Aḥmad Qā'id, "Mu'tamar 'Amrān," *EY*, pp. 933–34.

"Mu'tamar Ḥaraḍ," *EY*, pp. 929–30.

"Mu'tamar Khamir," *EY*, pp. 930–31.

Barqa, Muḥammad Sālmīn Aḥmad, "al-Mu'tamar al-'Ummālī," *EY*, pp. 932–33.

"al-Niqābāt," *EY*, pp. 962–63.

"al-Niqābāt al-Sitt (ta'rīf)," *EY*, pp. 962–63.

al-Bayḍānī, 'Abd al-Raḥmān, *Asrār al-Yaman*, Sana'a: Kitāb al-Qawmiyya, n.d.

Bilfaqīh, 'Abdillāh Ḥasan, *Tadhkirat al-bāḥith al-muḥtāṭ fī shu'ūn wa-ta'rīkh al-Ribāṭ*, Maṭba'at al-Fajjāla al-Jadīda, n.d.

al-Ḥabshī, Muḥammad 'Umar, *al-Yaman al-Janūbī siyāsiyyan wa-iqtiṣādiyyan wa-ijtimā'iyyan*, Beirut: Dār al-Ṭalī'a, 1968.

al-Ḥarbī, Aḥmad Muḥammad, "Ẓāhirat al-Ta'āwun Al-ahlī li-l-Taṭwīr wa-atharhā fi-al-tanmiya al-iqtiṣādiyya wa-l-ijtimā'iyya," *al-Ghad*, 10, 1978, 6–31.

"al-Ḥaraka al-ta'āwuniyya wa-marāḥil taṭawwurhā," *Ittiḥad al-Ta'āwun al-Yamanī*, 3, 4, 1980, 17–32.

"al-Ḥaraka al-ta'āwuniyya wa-muqāwamāt al-dīmuqrāṭiyya al-ta'āwuniyya," *al-Ta'āwun*, 194, 1985, 4–12.

"25 'āman min al-'aṭā' al-ta'āwunī fī ẓill Thawrat 26 Sabtambar 1962–1987," al-Ittiḥād al-'Āmm li-l-Majālis al-Maḥaliyya li-l-Taṭwīr al-Ta'āwunī, n.d.

Hay'at Taṭwīr al-Ḥujariyya, *Hay'at Taṭwīr al-Ḥujariyya: Thalāth sanawāt min al-binā'*, n.p., 1976.

al-Ḥizb al-Ishtirākī al-Yamanī (YSP), *al-Barnāmaj al-intikhābī li-l-Ḥizb al-Ishtirākī al-Yamanī*, n.p., n.d.

al-Ḥizb al-Ishtirākī al-Yamanī (YSP), Sikritāriyyat al-Lajna al-Markaziyya, *Mashrū' al-barnāmaj al-siyāsī li-l-Ḥizb al-Ishtirākī al-Yamanī*, Mu'assasat 14 Uktūbir, 1991.

Ḥizb Rābiṭat Abnā' al-Yaman (RAY), *al-Khuṭūṭ al-'Arī ḍa li-manhaj wa-barnāmaj Ḥizb Rābiṭat Abnā' al-Yaman*, Dār al-Muhājir, 1992.

Ibrāhīm, Sa'ad al-Dīn, "al-Mujtama' al-madanī wa-l-taḥawwul al-dīmuqrāṭī fī-al-waṭan al-'Arabī," *al-Dī muqrāṭīyya*, 1, December 1991, 8–17.

al-Ittiḥād al-'Āmm li-Hay'āt al-Ta'āwun al-Ahlī li-l-Taṭwīr, *Kitāb al-ta'āwun: Tashrī'āt wa-manjazāt wa-ṭumūḥāt al-'amal al-ta'āwunī fi-l-Jumhūriyya al-'Arabiyya al-Yamaniyya*, al-Ittiḥād al-'Āmm li-Hay'āt al-Ta'āwun al-Ahlī li-l-Taṭwīr, 1977.

al-Ta'āwun: Wathā'iq al-mawsim al-thānī li-l-intikhābāt al-ta'āwuniyya wa-l-mu'tamar al-'āmm al-rābi', Silsila ta'kis nashāṭ Hay'āt al-Ta'āwun al-Ahlī li-l-Taṭwīr al-Yamaniyya (7), al-Ittiḥād al-'Āmm li-Hay'āt al-Ta'āwun al-Ahlī li-l-Taṭwīr, 1979.

al-Ta'āwun: al-Tashrī'āt al-ta'āwuniyya, al-juz' al-awwal, al-Ittiḥād al-'Āmm li-Hay'āt al-Ta'āwun al-Ahlī li-l-Taṭwīr, *c.* 1981.

Taqrīr al-amāna al-'āmma li-l-Ittiḥād al-'Āmm 'an a'māl wa-anshiṭat al-Ittiḥād al-'Āmm wa-l-Hay'āt al-Ta'āwuniyya wa-l-jam'iyyāt al-naw'iyya khilāl al-fatra al-intikhābiyya min Yanāyir 1982 ḥattā Yūnyū 1985, al-Ittiḥād al-'Āmm li-Hay'āt al-Ta'āwun al-Ahlī li-l-Taṭwīr, 1986.

al-Ittiḥād al-'Āmm li-Hay'āt al-Ta'āwun al-Ahlī li-l-Taṭwīr al-Yamaniyya, Idārat al-Thaqāfa wa-l-Shu'ūn al-I'lāmiyya, *Hay'āt al-Ta'āwun al-Ahlī li-l-Taṭwīr fi-al-Jumhūriyya al-Yamaniyya*, Silsila ta'kis nashāṭ Hay'āt al-Ta'āwun al-Ahlī li-l-Taṭwīr al-Yamaniyya (2), al-Ittiḥād al-'Āmm li-Hay'āt al-Ta'āwun al-Ahlī li-l-Taṭwīr al-Yamaniyya, 1975.

al-Ittiḥād al-'Āmm li-Hay'āt al-Ta'āwun al-Ahlī li-l-Taṭwīr, Lajnat al-Thaqāfa wa-l-I'lām, *Wathā'iq al-Waḥda al-Yamaniyya*, al-Ittiḥād al-'Āmm li-Hay'āt al-Ta'āwun al-Ahlī li-l-Taṭwīr, 1979.

Ittiḥād al-Ḥuqūqiyyīn al-Yamaniyyīn, "al-Bayān al-khitāmī li-l-mu'tamar al-ta'sīsī li-Ittiḥād al-Ḥuqūqiyyīn al-Yamaniyyīn," *al-Ta'āwun*, 194, 1985, 151–55.

Ittiḥād Nisā' al-Yaman, al-Maktab al-Tanfīdhī, *Mashrū' al-niẓām al-asāsī li-Ittiḥād Nisā' al-Yaman*, Dār al-'Arabī, n.d.

Mashrū' al-lā'iḥa al-tafsīriyya li-mashrū' al-niẓām al-dākhilī li-Ittiḥād Nisā' al-Yaman, Dār al-'Arabī, 1991.

Ittiḥād al-Quwā al-Waṭaniyya, "Taqrīr muqaddam min al-lajna al-taḥḍīriyya ilā al-mu'tamar al-ta'sīsī al-awwal li-Ittiḥād al-Quwā al-Waṭaniyya," n.d.

"Bayān ṣādir 'an Ittiḥād al-Quwā al-Waṭaniyya," November 14 1993.

Ittiḥād al-Ta'āwun al-Yamanī, "Ānis," *Ittiḥād al-Ta'āwun al-Yamanī*, 1, 1, June 1979, 31–38.

"al-Niẓām al-asāsī li-majālis al-tansīq al-ta'āwuniyya," *Ittiḥād al-Ta'āwun al-Yamanī*, 5 and 6, 1981, 132–35.

"Taḥlīl Iḥṣā'ī li-munjazāt hay'āt al-Ta'āwun al-Ahlī li-l-Taṭwīr khilāl al-a'wām 1973–1982," *al-Ta'āwun*, 194, 1985, 156–72.

Ittiḥād al-Ta'āwun al-Yamanī, al-Idāra al-'Āmma li-l-Raqāba al-Māliyya, "al-Taqrīr al-mālī li-l-ḥisābāt al-khitāmiyya li-Hay'āt al-Ta'āwun al-Ahlī li-l-Taṭwīr li-l-'ām al-mālī 1978–1979," *Ittiḥād al-Ta'āwun al-Yamanī*, 5 and 6, 1981, 98-1107.

Ittiḥād al-Ta'āwun al-Yamanī, al-Lajna al-Dā'ima, "al-Bayān al-khitāmī al-ṣādir 'an al-dawra al-i'tiyādiyya al-thāmina li-l-Lajna al-Dā'ima," *al-Ta'āwun*, 194, 1985, 30–32.

"al-Tagrīr al-mālī li-Hay'at al-Ta'awun li-l-'am al-mālī 1977–78" (CYDA mimeo).

al-'Izāzī, Muḥammad, "al-Maṣādir al-māliyya li-Hay'āt al-Ta'āwun al-Ahlī," *al-Ghad*, 4, 1977, 45–52.

"Aqd al-tanmiya al-thālith 1980–1990 wa-taqrīr lajnat al-shamāl wa-l-janūb," *Ittiḥad al-Ta'āwun al-Yamanī*, 3 and 4, 1980, 33–40.

al-Janāḥ al-Dīmuqrāṭī li-l-Mu'tamar al-Sha'bī, *Taṣawwurāt ḥawl taf'īl al-Mu'tamar al-Sha'bī*, Abū Ayman, 1992.

al-Jāwī, 'Umar, *al-Ṣiḥāfa al-niqābiyya fī 'Adan, 1958–1967*, Aden: Mu'assasat 14 Uktūbir, n.d.

al-Jihāz al-Markazī li-l-Takhṭīṭ, Ri'āsat al-Wuzarā', al-Jumhūriyya al-'Arabiyya al-Yamaniyya, *al-Khiṭṭa al-Khamsiyya al-Thāniyya 1982–1986*, al-Jihāz al-Markazī li-l-Takhṭīṭ, n.d.

al-Lajna al-'Ulyā li-l-Intikhābāt, al-Lajna al-I'lāmiyya, *Qānūn raqam (66) li-sanat 1991 bi-sha'n al-aḥzāb wa-l-tanẓīmāt al-siyāsiyya*, Mu'assasat al-Thawra li-l-Ṣiḥāfa, 1991) (English title, *Law No. (66) of 1991: Governing Parties and Political Organizations*, issued by the Information Committee of the Elections Supreme Committee).

Majallat al-Ghad, "Tajribat al-'amal al-ta'āwunī: munjazāthā wa-ṭumūḥāthā," *al-Ghad*, 2, 1977, 18–33.

Majlis Bakīl al-Muwaḥḥad, "Bayān ṣādir 'an Majlis Bakīl al-Muwahḥḥad," Sana'a, October 14 1993 (photocopies of typescript).

Māni‘, Ilhām Muḥammad, *al-Aḥzāb wa-l-tanẓīmāt al-siyāsiyya fī-al-Yaman (1948–1993): dirāsa taḥlīliyya*, Silsilat Kitāb al-Thawābit, al-Thawābit, 1994.

al-Miqdād, ‘Alī, “al-‘Amal al-ta‘āwunī bayn mā huwa kā’in wa-mā yajib an yakūn,” *al-Ghad*, 10, 1978, 102–07.

al-Mu’ayyad, ‘Abd al-Wahhāb, in *al-Ta‘awon: Cooperative Movement in Yemen: Its Beginnings and Development*, Kitāb al-Ta‘āwun (6), Sana’a: CYDA, n.d. (English and Arabic).

al-Ta‘awon: Cooperative Work and Its Role in General Education, Kitāb al-Ta‘āwun (8), Sana’a: CYDA, n.d. (English and Arabic).

al-Ta‘āwun: al-ḥaraka al-ta‘āwuniyya al-Yamaniyya: nash’athā wa-taṭawwurhā, Silsila ta‘kis nashāṭ Hay’āt al-Ta‘āwun al-Ahlī li-l-Taṭwīr al-Yamaniyya (6), Ittiḥād ‘Āmm Hay’āt al-Ta‘āwun al-Ahlī li-l-Taṭwīr, 1978. (inside cover in English: *Al Ta‘awon: Cooperative Movement in Yemen: Its Beginning and Development*, by Abdelwahab el Muayyad).

“Fī al-dhikra al-sādisa li-ta’sīs al-Ittiḥād,” *Ittiḥād al-Ta‘āwun al-Yamanī* , 2, year 1, July 1979.

al-Ta‘āwun: al-‘amal al-ta‘āwunī wa-dawrhu fī-al-ta‘līm al-‘āmm, Silsila ta‘kis nashāṭ Hay’āt al-Ta‘āwun al-Ahlī li-l-Taṭwīr al-Yamaniyya (8), Ittiḥād ‘Āmm Hay’āt al-Ta‘āwun al-Ahlī li-l-Taṭwīr, 1979.

“Alā ‘atabāt al-mawsim al-intikhābī al-ta‘āwunī al-rābi,” *al-Ta‘āwun*, 194, 1985, 13–16.

al-Mujāhid, ‘Abd Allāh Muḥammad, *al-Ta‘āwun wa-l-tanmiyya fī-al-Yaman: dirāsa taḥlīliyya li-l-mu’ashshirāt al-iqtiṣādiyya wa-l-ijtimā‘iyya li-munjazāt al-‘amal al-ta‘āwunī, al-juz’ al-thānī*, Silsilat Ittiḥād al-Ta‘āwun al-Yamanī(2), al-Ittiḥād al-‘Āmm li-l-Ta‘āwun al-Ahlī li-l-Taṭwīr, 1983.

al-Multaqā al-jamāhīrī al-awwal li-abnā’ muḥāfaẓat Ḥajja, “al-Multaqā al-jamāhīrī al-awwal li-abnā’ muḥāfaẓat Ḥajja al-mun‘aqad fī maḍinat Ḥajja,” January 1994.

al-Munaẓẓama al-Yamaniyya li-l-Difā‘ ‘an Ḥuqūq al-Insān wa-l-Ḥurriyāt al-Ḍīmuqrāṭiyya (ODDRL), *al-Munaẓẓama al-Yamaniyya li-l-Difā‘ ‘an Ḥuqūq al-Insān wa-l-Ḥurriyāt al-Ḍīmuqrāṭiyya: al-Niẓām al-asāsī*, Sana’a, 1992.

al-Taqrīr al-sanawī li-‘āmm 1995, al-Munaẓẓama al-Yamaniyya li-l-Difā‘ ‘an Huqūq al-Insān wa-l-Ḥurriyāt al-Dīmuqrāṭiyya, 1995.

al-Munaẓẓama al-Yamaniyya li-Ḥuqūq al-Insān (YOHR), *Mashrū‘ al-Niẓām al-asāsī al-Munaẓẓama al-Yamaniyya li-Ḥuqūq al-Insān*, Sana’a, n.d. (photocopy).

Mu’tamar Bakīl, “al-Qarrarāt wa-l-tawṣiyāt (li-mu’tamar Bakīl fī Ānis),”. n.d. (photocopy).

Wathā’iq wa-adabiyyāt Mu’tamar Bakīl (Ānis) fī-al-fatra 12–13 Yanāyir 1994, n.p., 1994.

al-Mu’tamar al-jamāhīrī li-abnā’ muḥāfaẓat Ibb, “al-Bayān al-ṣādir ‘an al-mu’tamar al-jamāhīrī li-abnā’ muḥāfaẓat Ibb,” February 5 1994 (photocopy of typescript).

“Mu’tamar qabā’il Banī Jabr Khawlān al-Ṭiyāl fī suṭūr,” *al-Taḍāmun*, January 16 1994 (photocopy).

Mu’tamar Saba’ li-l-Qabā’il al-Yamaniyya, “Bayān ṣāḍir ‘an al-amāna al-‘āmma li-Mu’tamar Saba’ li-l-Qabā’il al-Yamaniyya,” n.d.

al-Mu'tamar al-Sha'bī al-'Āmm (GPC), *Taqārīr al-Amīn al-'Āmm li-l-Mu'tamar al-Sha'bī al-'Āmm ilā al-Lajna al-Dā'ima, al-juz' al-thānī*, n.p., 1986.

al-Barnāmaj al-intikhābī li-l-Mu'tamar al-Sha'bī al-'Āmm, al-Mu'tamar al-Sha'bī al-'Āmm, n.d. (*c.* 1991).

Mu'tamar al-Waḥda wa-l-Salām, *The Working Papers of the Unity and Peace Conference*. From the Preparatory Committee, Mu'tamar al-Waḥda wa-l-Salām, Sana'a, December 27–30 1993: Collection of Working Papers for the Unity and Peace Conference, Sana'a, December 27–30 1993 (all in Arabic).

Mutawakkil, Muḥammad 'Abd al-Malik, "al-Ṣiḥāfa," *EY*, pp. 560–65.

Nājī, Sulṭān, "Dawr al-jam'iyyāt al-iṣlāḥiyya wa-l-nawādī fī-al-mujābaha al-siyāsiyya al-ta'līmiyya fī 'Adan khilāl fatrat tab'iyyathā li-l-Hind (1939–1937), *al-Tarbiya al-jadīda*, September/December 1982, 3–15.

Niqābat al-Ṣuḥufiyyīn al-Yamaniyyīn, "al-Bayān al-khitāmī li-l-mu'tamar al-'āmm al-khāmis li-Niqābat al-Ṣuḥufiyyīn al-Yamaniyyīn," *al-Ta'āwun*, 194, 1985, 149–50.

ODDRL, *Ḥuqūq al-insān wa-l-ḥuriyyāt al-dīmuqrāṭiyya fi-al-Yaman*, the ODDRL report on the condition of human rights in Yemen, 1994: Aden, March 1995 (in Arabic).

al-Taqrīr al-sanawī li-'āmm 1994, Aden: al-Munaẓẓama al-Yamaniyya li-l-Difā' 'an Ḥuqūq al-Insān wa-l-Ḥuriyyāt al-Dīmuqrāṭiyya, March 1995.

al-Taqrīr al-sanawī li-'āmm 1995, Aden: al-Munaẓẓama al-Yamaniyya li-l-Difā' 'an Ḥuqūq al-Insān wa-l-Ḥuriyyāt al-Dīmuqrāṭiyya, 1996 (draft).

Qāḍī, 'Abd Allāh, "al-Waṭan wa-l-ta'āwun," *al-Waṭan*, 3, 4, June 1980, 46–47.

Qānūn al-idāra al-maḥaliyya, *al-Jarīda al-rasmiyya*, 8, April 30 1991.

Qindīl, Amānī, "al-Jam'iyyāt al-ahliyya wa-l-mujtama' al-madanī," in *al-Dīmuqrāṭiyya*, 2, February 1992, 51–55.

al-Ṣā'idī, Aḥmad Qā'id, "al-Ittiḥād al-Sha'bī al-Dīmuqrāṭī," *EY*, p. 45.

"al-Jam'iyya al-Islāmiyya al-Kubrā," *EY*, p. 324.

"Jam'iyyat al-Iṣlāḥ," *EY*, p. 324.

Shahīr, Khālid 'Abd al-Jalīl, "al-Ittiḥād al-Yamanī," *EY*, pp. 45–46.

"al-Jam'iyyāt al-Yamaniyya al-kubrā," *EY*, p. 325.

"al-Jam'iyyāt al-Yamaniyya al-Kubrā (al-Jadīda)," *EY*, p. 326.

Sha'rāwī, Ḥilmī, "Mulāḥaẓāt ḥawl ḥuqūq al-insān al-jamā'iyya wa-l-ijtimā'iyya," *Ḥuqūq al-insān wa-ta'khīr Miṣr*, Cairo: Legal Research and Resources Center for Human Rights, n.d.

al-Sharqī, Ra'ūfa Ḥasan, *al-Tanẓīmāt al-ahliyya: taqrīr li-Mu'tamar al-Tanẓīmāt al-Ahliyya al-'Arabiyya (CIVICUS)*, Jāmi'at Ṣana'ā', 1993.

al-Shayba, 'Abd Allāh, "al-Taṭawwur al-tashrī'ī li-ḥarakatnā al-ta'āwuniyya," *al-Ghad*, 12, 1978, 77–86.

Tāhir, 'Alwī 'Abd Allāh, "al-Nawādī wa-l-jam'iyyāt fī 'Adan," *EY*, pp. 970–973.

"Wagā'i' mu'tamar Saba' li-l-qabā'il al-Yamaniyyīn fi wādī Saba'," *al-Tadāmun*, October 25 1992, 5.

Ṭarbūsh, Qā'id Muḥammad, *Taṭawwur al-niẓām al-intikhābī fi-al-Jumhūriyya al-Yamaniyya 1948–1992*, Manshūrāt 26 Sabtambar, 1992.

"Tawḍīḥ ḥawl ilghā' al-lijān al-ta'āwunī," *al-Ta'āwun*, 174–75, May–June 1982, 19.

ʻUbayd, Munā Makram "Kayf yuʼaddī al-mujtamaʻ al-madanī dawran fī-l-tanmiya." *al-Mujtamaʻ al-madanī*, May 1992, 12–13.
ʻUmar, Jār Allāh, "Fī jadaliyyat al-waḥda wa-l-dīmuqrāṭiyya," Aden, n.d. (mimeo).
"Ahamiyyat wa-mawqiʻ al-taʻaddudiyya al-siyāsiyya fī īṭār al-iṣlāḥ al-siyāsī," April 1 1989 (mimeo).
ʻUthmān, ʻAbduh ʻAlī, and Ḥamūd al-ʻAwdī, "al-Ḥaraka al-taʻāwuniyya al-Yamaniyya wa-l-tanmiya: musāhamat Hayʼat al-Taʻāwun al-Ahlī li-l-Taṭwīr fī mashārīʻ al-Khiṭṭa al-Khamsiyya al-Ūlā li-l-Tanmiya," paper presented to CPO, Sana'a, January 1980.
ʻUthmān, ʻAbduh ʻAlī, Ismāʻīl Muḥammad al-Faḍlī, and ʻAbd Allāh al-Wasamī, "al-Ḥaraka al-taʻāwuniyya al-Yamaniyya wa-mashākilhā," study presented to the Sixth Conference of Arab Co-operative Specialists, Sana'a, 1975 (mimeo).
ʻUthmān, Muḥammad ʻAbduh, "al-Tajriba al-taʻāwuniyya al-Yamaniyya wa-atharhā fī-al-tanmiya al-iqtiṣādiyya wa-l-ijtimāʻiyya," *al-Ghad*, 3, 1977, 40–58.
al-Wādiʻī, Aḥmad ʻAlī, *Ḥuqūq al-mar'a al-Yamaniyya bayn al-fiqh wa-l-tashrīʻ*, Silsilat al-Kitāb al-Thaqāfī(6), Mu'assasat al-ʻAfīf al-Thaqāfiyya, n.d.
Wathā'iq al-dawra al-intikhābiyya al-thāniya li-l-hay'a al-idāriyya li-l-majālis al-maḥaliyya li-l-taṭwīr al-taʻāwunī, Sana'a: al-Amāna al-ʻāmma li-l-majālis al-maḥaliyya li-l-taṭwīr al-taʻāwunī, 1989.
al-Wazīr, Ibrāhīm Muḥammad, *al-Waḥda al-Yamaniyya bayn al-fikr wa-l-mumārasa,* Dār al-Ḥikma al-Yamaniyya, n.d.
al-Yūsufī, ʻAbd al-Raḥmān, "al-Taʻāwun fī minṭaqat al-Ḥujariyya," *al-Ghad*, 1, year 2, September 1976, 78–86.

NEWSPAPERS

14 Uktūbir (14 October)
22 Māyū (22 May)
26 Sabtambar (26 September)
al-Ayyām
Ḥaḍramawt
al-Ḥaqq
al-Ḥayā (Al-Hayat)
al-Iṣlāḥ
al-Jamāhīr
al-Mīthāq
al-Mustaqbal
al-Quds
Ra'y
al-Ra'y al-ʻĀmm
Ṣawt al-Jabha
Ṣawt al-ʻUmmāl
al-Sharq al-Awsaṭ

al-Shūrā
al-Taḍāmun
al-Taṣḥīḥ
al-Thawrī
al-Thawra
al-Waḥda
al-Waḥdawī
al-Wasaṭ
Yemen Times

SOURCES IN ENGLISH AND OTHER EUROPEAN LANGUAGES

al-Abdin, Al-Tayib Zein, "The Role of Islam in the State, Yemen Arab Republic (1940–1972)," PhD dissertation, Cambridge University, 1975.

Abdulaim, Dirar, "The Cooperative Movement in North Yemen: Beginnings and Development," in al-Saidi (ed.), *The Cooperative Movement in Yemen*, pp. 22–39.

Abu-Amr, Zaid Mahmoud, "The People's Democratic Republic of Yemen: The Transformation of Society," PhD dissertation, Georgetown University, 1986.

Abu-Lughod, Janet L., "The Islamic City – Historic Myth, Islamic Essence, and Contemporary Relevance," *IJMES*, 19, 2, May 1987, 155–76.

Aden: Report for the Years 1957 and 1958, London: Her Majesty's Stationery Office, 1961.

Adra, Najwa, "Qabyallah: The Tribal Concept in the Central Highlands of the Yemen Arab Republic," PhD dissertation, Temple University, 1982.

Alkhader, Mohamed A., "Low Enrolment of Students at the Faculty of Education and its Effects on the Second Five-Year Plan," in Pridham (ed.), *Economy, Society, and Culture*, pp. 190–99.

Almadhagi, Ahmed Noman, "Yemeni–Saudi Relations in an Era of Democratization," paper presented at the Middle East Studies Association, Washington, D.C., December 6–10 1995.

Yemen and the United States: A Study of a Small Power and Super-State Relationship, 1962–1994, London: I. B. Tauris, 1996.

Amnesty International, "Yemen: Unlawful Detention and Unfair Trials of Members of the Former National Democratic Front," August 26 1993.

Amnesty International Urgent Action Appeal, UA194/95: Yemen, August 9 1995.

Ansell, Christine, "The Benefits of Rural Water Projects: An Impact Survey of 5 Villages," Sana'a, report to Transcentury Corporation, October 1981.

Arab–British Chamber of Commerce, *Focus on Yemen Arab Republic*, conference proceedings, London, November 4 1982.

el-Ashmawy, Mohamed Said, "Islamic Government and Civil Society," *al-Ahram Weekly*, October 29–November 4 1992, Cairo.

al-Attar, Mohammed Said, *Le sou-développement économique et social du Yémen: perspectives de la révolution yéménite*, Algiers, Editions Tiers-Monde, 1964.

Ayubi, Nazih N., "Withered Socialism or Whither Socialism? The Radical Arab

States as Populist–Corporatist Regimes," *Third World Quarterly*, 13, 1, 1992, 89–105.

Baldry, John, "The Anglo-Italian Rivalry in Yemen and 'Asir, 1900–1934," *Die Weld des Islams*, 17, 1-4, 1977, 155–93.

Banks, Arthur S., "People's Democratic Republic of Yemen," *Economic Handbook of the World 1981*, New York: McGraw Hill, 1981.

Barbarossa, Nicholas K., Kean K. Fuhriman, and A. M. A. Maktari, *Report on Water Resources Sector Study in the YAR*, Sana'a: US Agency for International Development, August 1977.

Bayart, Jean François, "Civil Society in Africa," in Chabal (ed.), *Political Domination in Africa*, pp. 109–25.

Beatty, Sharon, Ahmed No'man al-Madhaji, and Renaud Detalle, *Yemeni NGOs and Quasi-NGOs, Analysis and Directory*, Sana'a: Royal Netherlands Embassy, May 1996.

Berger, Suzanne, *Peasants against Politics: Rural Organizations in Brittany, 1911–1967*, Cambridge, Mass.: Harvard University Press, 1972.

Bianchi, Robert, *Unruly Corporatism: Associational Life in Twentieth-Century Egypt*, New York: Oxford University Press, 1989.

Bidwell, Robin, *The Two Yemens*, Boulder: Longman, Westview Press, 1983.

Bidwell, Robin (ed.), *Arabian Personalities of the Early Twentieth Century*, Cambridge: Oleander Press, 1986.

Birks, J. S., C. H. Sinclair, and D. A. Socknat, *Arab Manpower*, New York: St. Martin's Press, 1980.

"Aspects of Labor Migration from North Yemen," *Middle Eastern Studies*, 17, 1, 1981.

Blackmore, R. A., "Report on the Establishment of an Agricultural Distribution Cooperative in Sanhan, Sana'a Governorate, YAR," report to CYDA and Irish Concern, Sana'a, November 1976.

Bujra, A. S., "Political Conflict and Stratification in Hadramaut," *Middle Eastern Studies*, 4, 3, July 1967, 355–75.

"Political Conflict and Stratification in Hadramaut II – Nationalism and the Yemeni Revolution: Their Effects on the Hadramaut," *Middle Eastern Studies*, 4, 4, October 1967, 1–28.

"Urban Elites and Colonialism: The Nationalist Elites of Aden and South Arabia," *Middle Eastern Studies*, 6, 2, May 1970, 189–210.

Bukair, Salem Omar, "The PDRY: Three Designs for Independence," in Pridham (ed.), *Contemporary Yemen*, pp. 63–75.

Burrowes, Robert D., *The YAR: The Politics of Development 1962–1986*, Boulder: Westview, 1987.

"Oil Strike and Leadership Struggle in South Yemen: 1986 and Beyond," *Middle East Journal*, 43, 3, Summer 1989, 437–53.

"The Other Side of the Red Sea and a Little More: The Horn of Africa and the TwoYemens," paper presented to the Conference on the Horn of Africa, sponsored by the Middle East Institute and the Defense Intelligence College, US Central Command, MacDill AFB, Tampa, Fla., January 16–17 1990.

"Prelude to Unification: The Yemen Arab Republic, 1962–1990," *IJMES*, 23, 1991, 483–506.

"The Yemeni Civil War of 1994: Impact on the Arab Gulf States," in al-Suwaidi (ed.), *The Yemeni War of 1994*, pp. 71–80.

Carapico, Sheila, "The Political Economy of Self-help: Development Cooperatives in the Yemen Arab Republic," PhD dissertation, State University of New York at Binghamton, 1984.

"Yemeni Agriculture in Transition," in Keith McLachlan and Peter Beaumont (eds.), *The Agricultural Development of the Middle East*, London: Wiley Press, 1986, pp. 241–54.

"Autonomy and Secondhand Oil Dependency of the Yemen Arab Republic," *Arab Studies Quarterly*, 10, 2, Spring 1988, 193–213.

"Women and Participation in Yemen," *Middle East Report*, 173, November/December 1991, 15.

"The Economic Dimension of Yemen Unity," *Middle East Report*, 184, September/October 1993, 9–14.

"From Ballotbox to Battlefield: The War of the Two 'Alis," *Middle East Report*, 190, 25, 1, September/October 1994, 27.

"Gender and Status Inequalities in Yemen: Honor, Economics, and Politics," in Valentine Moghadam (ed.), *Trajectories of Patriarchy and Development*, Oxford: Clarendon Press, 1996, pp. 80–98.

"Yemen between Civility and Civil War," in Norton (ed.), *Civil Society in the Middle East*, vol. II, pp. 287–316.

Carapico, Sheila and Cynthia Myntti, "A Tale of Two Families: Change in North Yemen 1977–1989," *Middle East Report*, 170, 21, 3, May/June 1991, 24–29.

Carapico, Sheila and Richard Tutwiler, *Yemeni Agriculture and Economic Change*, Milwaukee: American Institute for Yemeni Studies, 1981.

Caton, Steven C., *"Peaks of Yemen I Summon": Poetry as Cultural Practice in a North Yemeni Tribe*, Berkeley: University of California Press, 1990.

Central Planning Organization, "Evaluation of the Second Five-Year Plan, April 1987," Sana'a: CPO, 1987.

Statistical Yearbook 1987, Sana'a: CPO, 1987.

Chabal, Patrick (ed.), *Political Domination in Africa: Reflections on the Units of Power*, trans. P. Chabal, Cambridge: Cambridge University Press, 1986.

Chaudhry, Kiren, "The Price of Wealth: Business and State in Labor Remittance and Oil Economies," *International Organization*, 43, 1, Winter 1989, 101–45.

The Price of Wealth: Oil and Labor Exporters in the International Economy, Ithaca: Cornell University Press, forthcoming.

Chaudhry, Shahid A., Abdallah Bouhabib, Michel Cretin, and Elco Greenshields, "People's Democratic Republic of Yemen: A Review of Economic and Social Development," Washington, D.C., World Bank (based on a field trip, February/March 1978).

Chazan, Naomi, "Africa's Democratic Challenge: Strengthening Civil Society and the State," *World Policy Journal*, 9, 2, 1992, 279–310.

Chelhod, Joseph (ed.), *L'Arabie du Sud, histoire et civilisation*: vol. II, *La société yéménite de l'hégire aux idéologies modernes*, Paris: Maisonneuve & Larose, 1984; vol. III, *Culture et institutions du Yémen*, Paris: Maisonneuve & Larose, 1984.

"L'Islam en Arabie du Sud," in Chelhod (ed.), *L'Arabie du Sud*, vol. II, pp. 13–55.

"Le système juridique traditionnel," in Chelhod (ed.), *L'Arabie du Sud*, vol. III, pp. 127–81.

Cigar, Norman, "Soviet–South Yemeni Relations: The Gorbachev Years," *Journal of South Asian and Middle Eastern Studies*, 12, 4, Summer 1989, 3–38.

Clark, Peter, "Aspects of Education in the Yemen Arab Republic," in Pridham (ed.), *Economy, Society, and Culture*, pp. 172–77.

Cohen, John M. and David B. Lewis, "Capital Surplus, Labor Short Economies: Yemen as a Challenge to Rural Development Strategies," *American Journal of Agricultural Economics*, 61, 3, August 1979, 523–28.

Final Report, Yemen Research Program, Ithaca: Cornell University Center for International Studies, Yemen Research Program, February 1981.

Cohen, John M., David B. Lewis, Mary Hebert, and Jon C. Swanson, "Development from Below: Local Development Associations in the Yemen Arab Republic," *World Development*, 11–12, 9, 1981, 1039–61.

Cole, Juan R. I., "Rival Empires of Trade and Imami Shi'ism in Eastern Arabia, 1300–1800," *IJMES*, 19, 2, May 1987, 177–204.

The Constitution of the Republic of Yemen and Yemen Human Rights Organization the Basic Statute, Yemen Human Rights Organization Publication No. 1, Sana'a, January 1995.

Cordesman, Anthony, *The Gulf and the Search for Strategic Stability: Saudi Arabia, the Military Balance in the Gulf, and Trends in the Arab–Israeli Military Balance*, Boulder: Westview, 1984.

Crouch, Michael, *An Element of Luck: To South Arabia and Beyond*, London: Radcliffe Press, 1993.

Daum, Werner (ed.), *Yemen: 300 Years of Art and Civilization in Arabia Felix*, Innsbruck: Penguin, 1988.

DeQuin, Horst, *Arabische Republic Jemen: Wirtschaftsgeographie eins Entwicklungs Landes*, Riyadh: n.p., 1976.

Detalle, Renaud, "Pacte d'Amman: L'espoir déçu des yéménites," *Monde Arabe Maghreb-Mashrek*, 145, July–September 1994, 113–22.

"Yémen. Les élections législatives du 27 Avril 1993," *Monde Arabe Maghreb-Mashrek*, 145, July–September 1994.

Diamond, Larry and Marc F. Plattner (eds.), *The Global Resurgence of Democracy*, Baltimore: Johns Hopkins University Press, 1993.

Di Palma, Giuseppe, "Why Democracy Can Work in Eastern Europe," in Diamond and Plattner (eds.), *The Global Resurgence of Democracy*, pp. 257–67.

Dostal, Walter, "Traditional Economy and Society," in Daum (ed.), *Yemen*, pp. 336–66.

Douglas, J. Leigh, *The Free Yemeni Movement 1935–1962*, Beirut: American University in Beirut, 1987.

Dresch, Paul, "The Northern Tribes of Yemen," PhD dissertation, Oxford University, 1981.

"The Significance of the Course Events Take in Segmentary Systems," *American Ethnologist*, 13, 2, 1986, 309–24.

Tribes, Government, and History in Yemen, Oxford: Clarendon Press, 1989.
"The Tribal Factor in the Yemeni Crisis," in al-Suwaidi (ed.), *The Yemeni War of 1994*, pp. 33–55.
Dresch, Paul and Bernard Haykel, "Stereotypes and Political Styles: Islamists and Tribesfolk in Yemen," *IJMES*, 27, 4, November 1995, 405–31.
Dunbar, Charles, "The Unification of Yemen: Process, Politics, and Prospects," *Middle East Journal*, 46, 3, Summer 1992, 456–76.
Entelis, John P., "Civil Society and the Authoritarian Impulse in Algerian Politics: Islamic Democracy vs. the Centralized State," in Norton (ed.), *Civil Society in the Middle East*, vol. II, pp. 45–86.
Fakhro, Munira A., "Gender, Politics and the State in the Gulf Region," paper presented to the American Political Science annual conference, San Francisco, August 29–September 1 1996.
Fayein, Claudie, *Une française médecin au Yémen*, Paris: Rene Julliard, 1955.
Gause, F. Gregory III, "The Idea of Yemeni Unity," *Journal of Arab Affairs*, 6, 1, Spring 1987, 55–81.
"Yemeni Unity: Past and Future," *Middle East Journal*, 42, 1, Winter 1988, 33–47.
Yemeni–Saudi Relations: Domestic Structures and Foreign Influences New York: Columbia University Press, 1990.
Gavin, R. J., *Aden under British Rule, 1839–1967*, London: C. Hurst, 1975.
Gellner, Ernest, "From the Ruins of the Great Contest: Civil Society, Nationalism, and Islam," *Times Literary Supplement*, March 13 1992; repr. in *Civil Society*, 7, July 1992, 12–16.
Gerholm, Tomas, *Mosque, Market, and Mufraj: Social Inequality in a Yemeni Town*, Stockholm: University of Stockholm Press, 1977.
Ghanem, Isam, *Yemen: Political History, Social Structure and Legal System*, London: Arthur Brobsthain, 1981.
Arbitration in the Yemen Arab Republic, Braunton: Merlin Books, 1988.
Glosemeyer, Iris, "The First Yemeni Parliamentary Elections in 1993: Practicing Democracy," *Orient*, 34 3, 1995, 439–51.
Liberalisierung und Demokratisierung in der Republik Jemen, 1990–1994, Hamburg: Deutsches Orient-Institut, 1995.
Goitein, Shelomo Dov, "Portrait of a Yemenite Weavers' Village," *Jewish Social Studies*, 17, 1, 1955, 1–16.
Gow, David et al., *Local Organizations and Rural Development: A Comparative Reappraisal*, Washington, D.C.: Development Alternatives Inc., 1979.
Green, James Wyche, "Local Initiative in Yemen: Exploratory Studies of Four Local Development Associations," report to the US Agency for International Development, Washington, D.C., October 1975.
Gueyras, Jean, "The Last Days of 'Ali Nasir," *Middle East Report*, 16, 4, July–August 1986, 37–40.
Halliday, Fred, *Arabia without Sultans*, London: Penguin, 1974.
"Yemen's Unfinished Revolution: Socialism in the South," *MERIP*, 181, October 1979, 3–20.
"Catastrophe in South Yemen: A Preliminary Assessment," *Middle East Report*, 16, 2, March–April 1986, 37–39.

"Moscow's Crisis Management: The Case of South Yemen," *Middle East Report*, 151, 18, 2, March–April 1988, 18–22.

Revolution and Foreign Policy: The Case of South Yemen 1967–1987, Cambridge: Cambridge University Press, 1990.

Arabs in Exile: Yemeni Migrants in Urban Britain, London: I. B. Tauris, 1992.

Haykel, Bernard, "Al-Shawkani and the Jurisprudential Unity of Yemen," *Revue du monde musulman et de la mediterranée*, 67, 1994, 53–65.

"Hizb al-Haqq and the Doctrine of the Imamate," paper presented to the Middle East Studies Association annual meeting, Washington, D.C., November 1996.

Herbert, Mary, "Interim Field Report: Local Organization and Development in Maghlaf, Hodeidah Governorate," Working Note No. 10, Ithaca: Cornell University Center for International Studies, Yemen Research Program, June 1981.

al-Hitar, Hamud, "Primary Report on the Yemeni Elections Issued by EPC of the Unity and Peace Conference," Unity and Peace Conference (UPC) Election Protection Committee (EPC), March 5 1993.

Hitchel, Brigittal, Herman Escher, and Martha Mundy, "Survey of the Ta'iz–Truba Road Influence Area," report to the IBRD, Sana'a, 1978.

Hudson, Michael C., *Arab Politics: The Search for Legitimacy*, New Haven: Yale University Press, 1977.

Huntington, Samuel P., "The Clash of Civilizations," *Foreign Affairs*, 72, 3, Summer 1993, 22–49.

Hyden, Goran, *Beyond Ujamaa in Tanzania: Underdevelopment and an Uncaptured Peasantry*, Berkeley: University of California Press, 1980.

Ibrahim, Saad Eddin, "Civil Society and Prospects of Democratization in the Arab World,"in Norton (ed.), *Civil Society in the Middle East*, vol. I, pp. 27–54.

Ingrams, Harold, *Arabia and the Isles*, London: John Murray, 1966.

International Fund for Agricultural Development, *Report of the Special Programming Mission to People's Democratic Republic of Yemen*, Rome: IFAD, June 1985.

International Labor Organization, Economic Commission for Western Asia, *Employment Problems and Policies in the Least Developed Countries (PDRY, Oman, ARY)*, Report 75-389, May 12–24 1975.

International Monetary Fund, *Republic of Yemen 1993 Article IV Consultation*, Sana'a, September 18 1993.

"Introduction to NCFE," Sana'a, n.d. (1993) (photocopy).

al-Iryani, Hamid, "School and Education – Formation and Development," in Daum (ed.), *Yemen*, pp. 375–88.

al-Iryani, Horia Mohammad, "The Development of Primary Education and its Problems in the Yemen Arab Republic," in Pridham (ed.), *Economy, Society, and Culture*, pp. 178–89.

Ismael, Tareq Y. and Jacqueline S. Ismail, *PDR Yemen: Politics, Economics and Society*, London: Frances Pinter, 1986.

Joseph, Richard, "Africa: The Rebirth of Political Freedom," in Diamond and Plattner (eds.), *The Global Resurgence of Democracy*, pp. 307–20.

al-Kasir, Ahmad, "The Impact of Emigration on Social Structure in the Yemen Arab Republic," in Pridham (ed.), *Economy, Society, and Culture*, pp. 122–36.

Katz, Mark N., "Yemeni Unity and Saudi Security," *Middle East Policy*, 1, 1, 1992, 117–35.

"External Powers and the Yemeni Civil War," in al-Suwaidi (ed.), *The Yemeni War of 1994*, pp. 81–93.

Khan, Muhammad Muhsin, *Translation of the Meanings of Sahih al-Bukari*, Gujranwala: Sethi Straw Mills (Conversion), Ltd., n.d., vol. II.

Kostiner, Joseph, *The Struggle for South Yemen*, London: Croom Helm, 1984.

Yemen: The Tortuous Quest for Unity, 1990–1994, London: Chattam House, 1996.

Kour, Z. H., *The History of Aden 1839–1872*, London: Frank Cass, 1981.

Liliane Kuczynski, "Les juifs du Yémen: approche éthnologique," in Chelhod (ed.), *L'Arabie du Sud*, vol. III, pp. 277–302.

Lackner, Helen, "The Rise of the National Liberation Front as a Political Organization," in Pridham (ed.), *Contemporary Yemen*, pp. 46–62.

PDR Yemen: Outpost of Socialist Development in Arabia, London: Ithaca Press, 1985.

Laws of Aden, 1955, vol. I.

Lewis, David B., "Local Development Associations in the Yemen Arab Republic," *Rural Development Participation Review*, 1, 2, 1980, 1–2.

Little, Tom, *South Arabia: Arena of Conflict*, New York and London: Praeger, 1968.

Lucet, Marc, "Les rapatriés de la crise du Golfe au Yémen: Hodeida quatre ans après," *Monde Arabe Maghreb-Mashrek*, 148, April–June 1995, 28–42.

Luqman, 'Ali Mohammad, "Education and the Press in South Arabia," in Derik Hopwood (ed.), *The Arabian Peninsula: Society and Politics*, London: George Allen & Unwin Ltd., 1972, pp. 255–68.

Mamdani, Mahmood, "Africa: Democratic theory and Democratic Struggles – Class between Ideas and Realities" *Dissent*, Summer 1992, 312–18.

"Memorandum to All Interested Parties from the Union of Yemeni Popular Forces (UYPF)," August 28 1995 (photocopy, issued in English in Washington, D.C. and Arabic in Sana'a).

"Memorandum to the President of the Yemeni Republic and the President [prime minister] and Members of the Council of Ministers from the Opposition Parties," Sana'a, July 19 1995 (in Arabic).

Merabet, Zohra, "A Survey on Development and Management of Water Resources in the Yemen Arab Republic," report to USAID, Sana'a, May 1980.

"A Survey of Water Activities under Foreign Assistance in the Yemen Arab Republic," report to USAID, Sana'a, October 1980.

Messick, Brinkley, "Transactions in Ibb: Society and Economy in a Yemeni Highlands Town," PhD dissertation, Princeton University, 1978.

"Prosecution in Yemen: the Introduction of the *Niyaba*," *IJMES*, 15, 1983, 507–18.

The Calligraphic State: Textual Domination and History in a Muslim Society, Berkeley: University of California Press, 1993.

Molyneux, Maxine, "Legal Reform and Socialist Revolution in Democratic Yemen: Women and the Family," *International Journal of the Sociology of Law*, 13, 1985, 147–72.

"The Law, the State and Socialist Policies with Regard to Women: The Case of the People's Democratic Republic of Yemen, 1967–1990," in Deniz Kandiyoti (ed.), *Women, Islam, and the State*, Philadelphia: Temple University Press, 1991, pp. 237–71.

Morris, Timothy Christopher John, "Adapting to Wealth: Social Change in a Yemeni Highland Community," PhD dissertation, University of London, 1985.

The Despairing Developer: Diary of an Aid Worker in the Middle East, London: I. B. Tauris, 1991.

al-Msaodi, Abdulaziz Kaid, "The Yemeni Opposition Movement, 1918–1948," PhD dissertation, Georgetown University, 1987.

Muller, Edward N. and Mitchell A. Seligson, "Civic Culture and Democracy: The Question of Casual Relationships," *American Political Science Review*, 88, 3, September 1994, 635–52.

Mundy, Martha, *Yemen Arab Republic Feeder Road Study: Report on Phase II (Wadi Mawr)*, report to the IBRD, Washington, D.C., January 1975.

Domestic Government: Kinship, Community, and Polity in North Yemen, London: I. B. Tauris, 1995.

Myntti, Cynthia, *Women and Development in Yemen Arab Republic*, Eschborn: German Agency for Technical Cooperation (GTZ), 1979.

Naji, Sultan, "The Genesis of the Call for Yemeni Unity," in Pridham (ed.), *Contemporary Yemen*, pp. 240–60.

National Democratic Institute for International Affairs (NDI), *Promoting Participation in Yemen's 1993 Elections*, Washington, D.C.: National Democratic Institute for International Affairs, 1994.

Nini, Yehuda, *The Jews of the Yemen, 1800–1914*, Chur: Harwood, 1991.

al-Noban, Saeed Abdul Khair, "Education for Nation-Building – Experience of the People's Democratic Republic of Yemen," in Pridham (ed.), *Contemporary Yemen*, pp. 102–23.

Nonneman, Gerd, *Development, Administration, and Aid in the Middle East*, New York: Routledge, 1988.

"North, South Yemen Sign Oil Exploration Deal with 5 Foreign Companies," *Gulf News*, March 15 1990.

Norton, Augustus Richard (ed.), *Civil Society in the Middle East*, vols. I and II, Leiden and New York: E. J. Brill, 1995–96.

O'Brien, Donal B. Cruise, "Wails and Whispers: The People's Voice in West African Muslim Politics," in Chabal (ed.), *Political Domination in Africa*, pp. 71–83.

Peipenberg, Fritz, "The Cooperative Movement of Yemen: Developments after 1985," in al-Saidi (ed.), *The Cooperative Movement in Yemen*, pp. 55–66.

Peterson, J. E., *Yemen: The Search for a Modern State*, Baltimore: Johns Hopkins University Press, 1982.

Petroleum Finance Market Intelligence Service, *Yemen: Border Disputes and Relations with Saudi Arabia*, Washington, D.C.: The Petroleum Finance Company, May 1992.

Pieragostini, Karl, *Britain, Aden, and South Arabia: Abandoning Empire*, New York: St. Martin's Press, 1991.

Pridham, B. R. (ed.), *Contemporary Yemen: Politics and Historical Background*, London: Croom Helm, 1984.

Economy, Society, and Culture in Contemporary Yemen, London: Croom Helm, 1985.

al-Rashid, Ibrahim, *Yemen Enters the Modern World*, Chapel Hill: Documentary Publications, 1984.

Yemen under the Rule of Imam Ahmad, Chapel Hill: Documentary Publications, 1985.

Renaud, Etienne, "Histoire de la pensée religieuse au Yémen," in Chelhod (ed.), *L'Arabie du Sud*, vol. II, pp. 57–68.

Rone, Jemera and Sheila Carapico for Human Rights Watch, "Yemen: Human Rights in Yemen During and After the 1994 War," New York, October 1994, vol. 6, no. 1.

Ross, Jeffrey Ian, "Policing Change in the Gulf States: The Effect of the Gulf Conflict," in Otwin Marenin (ed.), *Policing Change, Changing Police*, New York: Garland Publishing, 1996, pp. 79–105.

Roth, Katherine, "Afghanistan and the Yemeni Jihad: A Surprising Visit to Post-war Aden," letter to Peter Bird Martin, Institute of Current World Affairs, Hanover, N.H., November 17 1994.

Rugh, William A., *The Arab Press*, Syracuse: Syracuse University Press, 1979.

Sadowski, Yahya, "The New Orientalism and the Democracy Debate," in Joel Beinin and Joe Stork (eds.), *Political Islam*, Berkeley: University of California Press, 1977, pp. 33–50; also in *Middle East Report*, 183, July–August 1993, 14–21.

al-Saidi, Muhammad Ahmad (ed.), *The Cooperative Movement in Yemen and Issues of Regional Development*, New York: Professors World Peace Academy – Middle East, 1992.

Safran, Nadav, *Saudi Arabia: The Ceaseless Quest for Security*, Ithaca: Cornell University Press, 1988.

Al-Sayyid, Mustapha K., "A Civil Society in Egypt" *The Middle East Journal*, 47, 2, Spring 1993, 228–42.

"Non-Governmental Organizations, Political Development and the State with a Special Reference to Egypt," paper presented to the Conference on the Role of Arab and Middle East Non-Governmental Organizations in National Development Strategy, Cairo, April 1–3 1993.

Schmitz, Chuck, "Civil War in Yemen: The Price of Unity" *Current History*, January 1995, 33–36.

"Economic Reform in the former PDR Yemen: a view from al-Hauta, Lahj," paper presented at the Middle East Studies Association annual conference, Washington, D.C., December 6-10 1995.

Scott, Hugh, *In the High Yemen*, London: Macmillan, 1942.

SEC Information Committee, "Parliamentary Elections 27th April, 1993," pamphlet, Sana'a, n.d. (in English).

Semple, Jim, Sheila Carapico, Horst DeQuin, Paul Litjens, Ali Maziq, Peter Wass, and H. L. Van Loo, *Report of IFAD's Special Programming Mission to Yemen Arab Republic*, Report No. 1016-YA, Rome: July 1988.

Serjeant, R. B., "Historians and Historiography of Hadramawt," *BSOAS*, 25, 1962, 239–61.

"Some Irrigation Systems in Hadramawt," *BSOAS*, 27, 1964, 33–76.

"The Yemeni Poet al-Zubayri and his Polemic against the Zaydi Imams," in Sergeant and Bidwell (eds.), *Arabian Studies*, vol. V, 1979, pp. 87–130.

Serjeant, R. B. and Bidwell, R. C. (eds.), *Arabian Studies*, London: C. Hurst (ongoing).

Serjeant, R. B. and Ronald Lewcock, *Sana'a: An Arabian Islamic City*, London: The World of Islam Festival Trust, 1983.

al-Shami, Ahmad Muhammad, "Yemeni Literature in Hajjah Prisons 1367/1948–1374/1955," in Serjeant and Bidwell (eds.), *Arabian Studies*, vol. II, 1975, pp. 43-59.

Shamiry, Naguib A. R., "The Judicial System in Democratic Yemen," in Pridham (ed.), *Contemporary Yemen*, pp. 175–94.

al-Sharif, Abdu, "Yemen and Arabian Peninsula Security: Quest for Inclusion, Consequences of Exclusion," paper presented at the 1994 annual meeting of the American Political Science Association, New York, September 1–4 1994.

el-Sherbini, A. A., "An Analysis of Public Sector Management Development in the People's Democratic Republic of Yemen," desk study for UNDP, December 1989.

Smith, William and Associates, Neighborhood Urban Services Project, *A Summary Profile of Private Voluntary Organizations and their Services in Cairo*, Alexandria, Urban Giza, and Shubra Al-Kheima, prepared for USAID/Cairo, October 1984.

Springborg, Patricia, "Politics, Primordialism, and Orientalism: Marx, Aristotle, and the Myth of Gemeinschaft," *American Political Science Review*, 80, March 1986, 204.

Stanford Research Institute, *Area Handbook for the Peripheral States of the Arabian Peninsula*, Washington, D.C.: US Government Printing Office, 1971.

Steffen, Hans et al., *Final Report of the Airphoto Interpretation Team of the Swiss Technical Cooperation Service*, Zurich, 1978, I/109-I-110.

Stevenson, Thomas B., *Social Change in a Yemeni Highlands Town*, Salt Lake City: University of Utah Press, 1985.

"Yemeni Workers Come Home: Absorbing One Million Migrants," *Middle East Report*, 181, March–April, 1993, 15–20.

Stookey, Robert W., *South Yemen: A Marxist Republic in Arabia*, Boulder: Westview, 1982.

Stork, Joe, "Socialist Revolution in Arabia: A Report from the People's Democratic Republic of Yemen," *MERIP*, 15, March 1973, 1–25.

al-Suwaidi, Jamal S. (ed.), *The Yemeni War of 1994: Causes and Consequences*, London: Saqi Books, 1995.

Swagman, Charles, "Tribal Organization, Corporate Groups and Development: Contrasting Examples from the Yemen Arab Republic," paper presented at the Middle East Studies Association Meeting, New Orleans, 1985.

Development and Change in Highland Yemen, Salt Lake City: University of Utah Press, 1988.

Swanson, Jon C., "Some Consequences of Migration for Rural Economic

Development in the Yemen Arab Republic," *Middle East Journal*, 33, 1, 1979, 34–43.

"Bani Awwam, Hajjah Governorate: Economy, Organization, and Development," in Swanson and Hebert, *Rural Society and Participatory Development*, pp. 23–121

"Emigrant Remittances and Local Development: Co-operatives in the Yemen Arab Republic," in Pridham (ed.), *Economy, Society, and Culture*, pp. 132–46.

Swanson, Jon C. and Mary Hebert, *Rural Society and Participatory Development: Case Studies of Two Villages in the Yemen Arab Republic*, Ithaca: Cornell University Rural Development Committee, Yemen Research Program, September 1981, USAID/Y Project 220-0045.

Tobi, Yosef, "Histoire de la communauté juive du Yémen aux XIX et XX siècles," in Chelhod (ed.), *L'Arabie du Sud*, vol. II, pp. 119–40.

Tutwiler, Richard, "A Report on Small Water Projects in Yemen: Aspects of Social Impact and Recommendations for Future Actions," report for USAID, Sana'a, March 1978.

"Ta'awun Mahwit: A Case Study of a Local Development Association in Highland Yemen," in Louis J. Cantori and Iliya Harik (eds.), *Local Politics and Development in the Middle East*, Boulder: Westview, 1984, pp. 166–92.

"Tribe, Tribute, and Trade: Social Class Formation in Highland Yemen," PhD dissertation, State University of New York at Binghamton, 1987.

UN Economic and Social Council, ECOSOC/Beirut, "Tax Structure, Government Savings, and Tax Problems: A Case Study of Yemen," New York: United Nations Studies on Development Problems in Selected Countries of the Middle East, 1974.

Van Der Meulen, D., *Faces in Shem*, London: John Murray, 1961.

Van Hear, Nicholas, "The Socio-economic Impact of the Involuntary Mass Return to Yemen in 1990," *Journal of Refugee Studies*, 7, 1, 1994, 18–38.

Varisco, Daniel Martin, "The Adaptive Dynamics of Water Allocation in al-Ahjur, Yemen Arab Republic," PhD dissertation, University of Pennsylvania, 1982.

Varisco, Daniel Martin and Najwa Adra, "Affluence and the Concept of the Tribe in the Central Highlands of the Yemen Arab Republic," in F. Salisbury and E. Tooker (eds.), *Affluence and Cultural Survival*, Washington, D.C.: American Ethnological Society, 1984.

Verdery, Richard, "Local Development Association Finances and their Borrowing Potential," Washington, D.C.: Institutional Report No. 2, Chemonics, Inc. June 1982.

von Weisel, Wolfgang, "Theocracy in the Yaman: Mussolini's Arab Ally," repr. from *The Near East and India*, March 31 1927, in Reginald Sinclair (ed.), *Documents on the History of Southwest Arabia*, Salisbury, N.C.: Documentary Publications, 1976.

Walker, S. Tjip, Sheila Carapico, and John Cohen, "Emerging Rural Patterns in the Yemen Arab Republic: Results of a 21-Community Cross Sectional Study," Ithaca: Cornell University Center for International Studies, Yemen Research Program, March 1983.

Warburton, David, "The Conventional War in Yemen," *Arab Studies Journal*, 3, 1, 1995, 20–44.

Wass, Peter G. L., "The Role of Local Development Associations and the Confederation of Yemeni Development Associations, Yemen Arab Republic," Amman: Middle East Development Division, Ministry of Overseas Development, August 1976.

Watkins, Eric, "Yemen's Riots Prompt Talk of Reform,"*Middle East International*, 444, February 19 1993, 18.

Weir, Shelagh, *Qat in Yemen: Consumption and Social Change*, London: British Museum Publications, 1985.

"Tribe, Hijrah and Madinah in North-West Yemen," in Kenneth Brown, Michele Jole, Peter Sluglett, and Sami Zubaida (eds.), *Middle Eastern Cities in Comparative Perspective*, London: Ithaca Press, 1986, pp. 225–39.

"Trade and Tribal Structures in North West Yemen," *Arabie du Sud: Cahiers du Gremano*, 10, 1991, 87–101.

"Religious Conflict in the Yemeni Highlands," paper presented to the Middle East Studies Association annual meeting, Washington, D.C., December 1995.

Wenner, Manfred W., *Modern Yemen 1918–1966*, Baltimore: Johns Hopkins Press, 1967.

"Woman [sic] Status in the Legislation of the Republic of Yemen," proposal for a conference, Sana'a, November 12–16 1993.

World Bank, *People's Democratic Republic of Yemen. A Review of Economic and Social Development*, Washington, D.C.: World Bank, 1979.

Yemen Arab Republic Local Development Associations: A New Approach to Rural Development, Washington, D.C., March 1981.

People's Democratic Republic of Yemen, Special Economic Report: Mid-Term Review of the Second Five-Year Plan, 1981–85, Washington, D.C.: Report No. 4726-YDR, June 4 1984.

Yemen Arab Republic, Current Position and Prospects, Washington, D.C.: Country Economic Memorandum, Report No. 5621-YAR, 1984.

World Debt Tables 1986–87 Edition, Washington, D.C., 1987.

Wuerth, Anna, "The Legal Status of Women in Yemen," report submitted to CID/WID project, Bureau of Applied Research in Anthropology, Tucson, Ariz.: University of Arizona, March 1994.

"A Sana'a Court: The Family and the Ability to Negotiate," *Islamic Law and Society*, 2, 3, 1995, 320–40.

"Yemeni Committee for Free and Democratic Elections: Constituent Charter," Sana'a, n.d.

Yemeni Committee on Human Rights, *Yemen Human Rights Report*, 1, 2, Washington, D.C., July 1996.

"Yemeni Reform Grouping Political Platform," FBIS-NES-95-141-S, July 24 1975.

Zabarah, Muhammad Ahmad, *Yemen: Tradition vs. Modernity*, New York: Praeger, 1982.

Zubaida, Sami, "Islam, the State and Democracy: Contrasting Conceptions of Society in Egypt," *Middle East Report*, 179, November–December 1992, 2–10.

Index

Abyan, 23, 26, 28, 39, 44, 57, 79, *150*, 180, 186
Aden, *150*
  colonial rule of, 26–6, 88–93
  city of, 23–6, 30–1, 49, 57, 61, 75, 81, 90, 156, 161, 178, 181, 188
agriculture, 22, 26, 28–9, 34, *40*, 44, *45*, *47*, 63–4, 74, 75, 79,
agricultural cooperatives, 44, 54, 105, 109, 118, 131, 155
assassinations, 28, 36, *37*, 39, 56, 67, 126, 172, 174, 176, 204

B'ath, 62, 85, 100, 102, 119, *141*, 144, *149*, *150*, 151, 152, 172–5, 175, 186, *190*, 192

civil wars, 14, *16*, 19, *20*, 23, *37*
  1994, 54, 56–9, 178, 184–8
  North Yemeni, 30, 36, 57
  South Yemeni, 30, 36, 39, 57, 100, 158
constitutions & constitutional proposals
  colonial, 25
  PDRY, 31–2
  Republic of Yemen, 53, 137–8
    amendments, 57–8, 174, 189
    National Dialogue Committee & Document, 57, 176–80, 184, 186
  theocratic, 27, 30, 67, 98, 146
  YAR, 33, 38, 117–8, 126

East Africa, 23, 24, 25, 27, 30–1, 35, 87
education, 21
  community, 71–2, 79, 81, 98, *111*, 123–4, *128*, 129–31
  parochial, 27, 29, 42, 70, 76, 90, *111*, 123–4
  public, 23–4, 27, 29, 41, 90, *111*
  university, 41, 42, 159, 162, 208
Egypt
  influence in Yemen, 14, 30, 34, 96–7, 102, 114, 118
  relations with, 50
  see also Nasirite groups
elections, *20*
  colonial era, *16*, 24, 85–7, 90–1, 99
  PDRY, 31–2, 155
  Republic of Yemen, 139, *149*, *150*
    1993, 53–4, 59, 136, 142, 148–51, 160–1, 172–4
    1997, 191, 194, 196
  YAR, 38, 115–7, 122
electrification, 23, 27, 29, 45–6, *47*, 79, 80, 107–10, 113, 130

fishing, 31, 44, 45, 47, 75
foreign aid, 21–4, *40*
  and community development, 27, 127–9
  and democratization, 160–1, 194–5
  donors, 29, 40–5, 58, 127, 188
  economic development projects, 29, 108–9, 197
foreign companies, 24, 44–5, 48–8, 208

General People's Congress (GPC)
  founding of, 33, 38, 51–2, 116–8, *141*
  in Republic of Yemen, 53, 136, 140–2, 148, *149*, *150*, 151–2, 160, 167, *190*, 194, 203
Gulf War, *16*, *20*, 21, 171

Ḥaḍramawt, 23, 55, 61, 67
  external linkages of, 26–7, 50, 79, 96
  persons from, 39, 50, 157, 162
  politics in, 71–2, 95, *150*, 182, 193, 197
  society, 74, 79, 164
Ḥajja, 77, 110, 121–2, 127, *150*, 183
al-Haqq, *141*, 145, *149*, *150*, 151, 152, 157, 175, 186, *190*, 194, 204
health & health care, 23, 27, 29, 40–2, 55, 82, 89, 109, 113, 116, 119, 127, *128*, 129, 157, 196
Hodeida city, 31, 35, 40, 61, 66, 81–2, 112, 120, 130, 157, 183, 198
households, 28, 55–6, 64
human rights, 14, 51, 53, 56, 135, 139, 165
  abuses of, 25, 39–40, 59, 92, 188, 191–3
  defense of, 103, 157, 178, 197, 199, 210
  organizations, 104, 159–61, 192, 193, 198
  see also law; prisons; police; press

Iṣlāḥ (Yemeni Reform Grouping)
founding of, *14*, 38, 50, 124, 143
in Republic of Yemen, 57, 143–4, *149*, *150*, 151, 157, 160, 168, 172–6, 187, *190*, 191
Ibb
city of, 69, 98, 126, 182
region of, 28, 46, 67–8, 77, 142, *150*
imams, imamate, 13, 28–30, 33, 34, 66, 67, 69, 71, 77, 98–9, 121, 137, 204
India, Indians, 21, 24, 25, 27, 28, 68, 86, 87, 103
Indonesia, 27, 80, 101
intellectuals, 89, 104, 154, 193, 196
clubs, 81, 88, 90, 94, 97–8, 157–9, 161–3
faculty, 32, 39, 72, 184, 194, 196
'ulamā', 65–6, 71–2, 98–9, 181
International Monetary Fund (IMF), 22, 41, 54, 58
Islam, politics of
Irshādī, 52, 79–0, 95–6, 100
Muslim Brotherhood, 15, 98
Muslim modernists, 89, 95, 97, 106, 159
neo-Islamist movements, 11, 29, 62, 90, 133, 156–7, 162, 199, 203–5
see also law; education; intellectuals; waqf; jihad; imams; Shāfi'ī; Zaydī; Wahhabi

Jawf, 46, 55, 126, *150*
Jews, Jewish community, 61, 65, 75–6, 101
jihad, Afghan, 38, 42, 124, 194
Jordan, 50, 177, 180

Kuwait, 23, 27, 36, 41, 43, 106, 109, 121

labor force, 24, 35, 40, 45, 92, 172
labor unions, 25, 26, 88, 91–3
see also migration
land ownership
commercial, 29, 41, 46, 49
nationalized/privatized, 23–4, 31, 33, 34, 41, 44, 104, 155, 208
pre-capitalist, 28, 34, 61, 63, 67–9, 74–5
Laḥj 23, 26, 28, 61, 67, 79, 99, 147, *150*, 184, 186
law, 19
civil, 25, 32, 51, 153, 178, 194, 196–7
Islamic, 29–30, 59, 65–7, 95, 138, 165, 168, 204
lawlessness, 55, 126, 171, 176, 203
martial, 25, 29, 57, 86–7, 103, 1878
rule of, 14, 21, 26, 31, 52, 55, 59, 118, 178
tribal, 28, 64, 204
League of Sons of Yemen/ South Arabia (SAL, RAY), 91, 92, 99, 101, 103, *141*, 146, *150*, 152, 167, 175, 187, 194,
local administration, 31–2, 110–1, 114–8, 121–2, 126–7, 132–4, 182

Ma'rib, 13, 46, 48–9, 49, 52, 55, 126, *150*
al-Maḥwīt, 111, 113, 127, 129, 131, *150*
merchants & traders, 26, 31, 34, 45, 48–9, 66, 74, 88, 112, 130, 131, 206, 208
migration & remittances, *16*, 21
colonial era, 24, 25, 30, 91, 99
effects of Gulf War on, 54–6, 157, 165, 172
republican era, 34, 40, 48, 113–4, 119
military
coups d'etat, 33, 36, 115
interests of, 38, 48, 55, 57, 188, 205
recruitment, 62, 68, 78, 202
see also civil wars; assassinations; police and security forces
money & banking, 22, 24, 28, 34, 46–7, 47, 55–6, 116, 205

Nasirite groups, 15, 30, 62, 100, 103, *141*, 146–8, *149*, *150*, 151, 152, 167, 172–3, 175, 185
National Liberation Front (NLF), 28, 30, 31, 40, 64, 93, 100, *141*
National Democratic Front (NDF), 36, 57, 64, 185
Netherlands, 41, 43, 58, 127, 162, 210

Oman, *20*, 35, 105, 177, 180
opposition parties, opposition coalition, 145–8, 166–8, 173, 175, 187, 193
Ottomans, 14, 29, 67, 71

petroleum and oil, 21
domestic price of, 52, 58, 186
Yemeni production of, 13, 38, 48–9, 54–5, 96, 208
police & security forces
colonial, 25, 97, 103
Yemeni, 39, 59, 132, 139–40, 159, 177, 191–4, 197, 207
press & publications
newspapers, 97–8, 100–2, 119, *141*, 152–4, 176, 185
books & pamphlets, 71–2, 120–1, 123–4, 193
broadcast media, 87–8, 102, 151
censorship, 39, 51, 138–9, 153, 158, 191–2
prisons & prisoners, 39–40, 98–9, 101, 103, 137
professional class, 56, 196
syndicates, 88, 155–6, 182, 184

protests & demonstrations, 37, 51
sit-ins, 158, 184–5
street demonstrations, 55, 58, 86, 97, 163, 172, 197
strikes, 87, 92–3, 155, 167
tax resistance, 68–9, 74–7, 121, 125
see also labor unions
public sector, 30, 151, 206
foreign aid to, 24, 40–5
proportional share of economy, 22, 44–48, *45*, *47*, 49, 55, 57, 208
see also land ownership

roads
construction of, 27, 41, 62, 77, 79, 108–9, *111*, 112, 113, 121, *128*, 185
effects of, 119, 126, 129–31

Ṣaʿda, 69, 112, 126, 145, *150*
Sanaʾa city, 29, 31, 35, 41, 56, 69, 74, 75, 112, 118, 124, 130, *150*, 156, 161, 198
Saudi Arabia
aid from, 40, 42–3, 171
influence on domestic politics, 30, 36–8, 52, 152, 165, 187
relations with, 14, 50, 194
sayyid, 28–30, 61–2, 65, 69, 72, 79, 82, 95, 97, 99, 143, 145–6, 204
Shabwa, 49, 55, 146, *150*, 181, 184, 193
Shāfiʾī, 28, 29, 61–2, 66, 68, 70, 71, 89, 98, 102
Singapore, 27, 70, 71, 80
Soviet Union, 13, 14, 41, 43, 45, 49, 50, 51

Taiz
city of, 31, 35, 45, 61, 66, 69, 112, 119, 130, 156–7, 184, 198
region of, 28, 46, 67–8, 77, 80, 98, 120, 125, 131, 142, 143, 148, *150*, 157
taxation
modern, 34, 48, 119, 121, 124–5, *128*
tributary, 29, 34, 63, 66–7, 74–5, 77
Tihama, 23, 46, 61, 68, 69, 75, 77, 108, 112, 119, 120, 127, 131
tribes, tribalism, 26, 58, 62, 105
confederations, 38, 61, 68, 112, 122, 164, 204
Bakl, 52, 68, 134, 147, 165–6, 177, 181, 185–6, 177, 203
Ḥāshid, 33, 38, 68, 109, 111, 122, 143–4, 186, 203
conferences, 163–66, 183–4
economics of, 63–4, 68, 111–2
law, 28, 64, 203–4

Union of Popular Forces, *141*, 145–6, *150*, 192, 203
United Kingdom, 127
as colonial power, 14, 16, 23–8, 30, 42, 62, 68
United States, 36, 38, 48, 51, 127, 176, 177, 210

village associations, 73, 75–6, 80–2, 85, 91, 94, 97, 99, 109, 110, 125

Wahhabi, 62, 124, 145, 204
waqf & endowments, 63, 66, 69–72, 76, 78, 166, 189, 195, 205
water supply systems
modern, 23, 27, 29, 40, 45, 79, 80, *111*, 120–1, *128*
traditional, 29, 63, 70, 76
welfare associations, 70, 72, 75, 77, 79, 89, 93, 125, 133, 156–8,
World Bank, 41, 43–6, 50, 58, 108
women, 14, 52, 65, 143, 157, 199, 200, 202
economic activities, 64, 70, 73, 131, 127
in public life, 42, 70, 105, 148–9, 155, 157, 163, 173, 196–8
legal status, 32, 34, 58, 70, 95, 142, 162, 168, 197

Yāfiʿ, 68, 80, 94–5, 100
Yemeni Socialist Party (YSP)
as ruling party in PDRY, 31, 51, 165
in Republic of Yemen, 53, 136, 142–3, *149*, *150*, 151–2, 166, 168, 172–6, 187, *190*, 191

Zaydī, 13, 28, 29, 61–2, 66, 68, 70, 71, 89, 98, 145, 194

Printed in the United States
116997LV00003B/7/A

9 780521 590983